Critical Dialogues in Southeast Asian Studies

CHARLES KEYES, VICENTE RAFAEL, AND LAURIE J. SEARS,
SERIES EDITORS

Critical Dialogues in Southeast Asian Studies

These new perspectives in Southeast Asian Studies reconsider traditional relationships among scholars, texts, archives, field sites, and subject matter. Volumes in the series feature inquiries into historiography, critical ethnography, colonialism and post colonialism, nationalism and ethnicity, gender and sexuality, science and technology, politics and society, and literature, drama, and film. This scholarship sheds light on shifting contexts and contests over forms of knowing and modes of action that inform cultural politics and shape histories of modernity.

Imagined Ancestries of Vietnamese Communism:
Ton Duc Thang and the Politics of History and Memory
by Christoph Giebel

Beginning to Remember: The Past in the Indonesian Present
Edited by Mary S. Zurbuchen

Beginning
To Remember

THE PAST IN THE
INDONESIAN PRESENT

Edited by MARY S. ZURBUCHEN

SINGAPORE UNIVERSITY PRESS

in association with

UNIVERSITY OF WASHINGTON PRESS

Seattle

Published simultaneously in Singapore and the United States.

Singapore University Press, NUS Publishing
AS3-01-02. 3, Arts Link
Singapore 117569
www.nus.edu.sg/npu

ISBN 9971-69-303-8 (Paper)

University of Washington Press
PO Box 50096
Seattle, WA 98145-5096, U.S.A.
www.washington.edu/uwpress

Library of Congress Cataloging-in-Publication Data

Beginning to remember: the past in the Indonesian present/edited by
Mary S. Zurbuchen. – 1st ed.
    p. cm. – (Critical dialogues in Southeast Asian studies)
    Revised papers originally presented at a conference on history and
memory in Indonesia held at the University of California, Los Angeles in
April 2001.
    Includes bibliographical references and index.
    ISBN 0-295-98469-4 (pbk.)
    1. Indonesia—History—1945—Historiography. 2. Memory—Political
aspects—Indonesia. I. Zurbuchen, Mary Sabina. II. Series.
DS644.B43   2005
959.803'072'0598—dc22   2004021648

*Cover photograph of "Patung Dirgantara" in Jakarta by Rully Kesuma.
Used with permission.*

Contents

List of Illustrations

Notes on Contributors

Andi F. Bakti is a Research Fellow at KITLV (Royal Netherlands Institute of Southeast Asian and Caribbean Studies), and a Fellow at the International Institute for Asian Studies (IIAS), both at Leiden University (Netherlands). He was formerly Assistant Professor at the Department of Pacific and Asian Studies, University of Victoria (Canada), and held a Postdoctoral Fellowship at McGill University. His doctoral dissertation in International Communication and Development Studies was titled "Communication, Islam, and Development in Indonesia". In Indonesia, he is Assistant Professor at the State Islamic University (UIN), Jakarta. He is actively involved in security issues with the Canadian Consortium on Asia Pacific Security (CANCAPS), as well as with issues of governance, civil society, religious networks, and decentralization in Southeast Asia.

Daniel S. Lev is an Emeritus Professor of Political Science at the University of Washington in Seattle. A specialist in comparative politics with an area emphasis on Southeast Asia, his research has focused largely on politics, ideology, and legal systems particularly in Indonesia and Malaysia. His publications include *The Transition to Guided Democracy: Indonesian Politics 1957–1959* (Cornell Modern Indonesia Project, 1966); *Islamic Courts in Indonesia: A Study in the Political Bases of Legal Institutions* (University of California Press, 1972); *Legal Evolution and Political Authority in Indonesia: Selected Essays* (Kluwer Law International, 2000).

Hendrik M.J. Maier is Professor of Comparative Literature and Director of the Program in Southeast Asian Text, Ritual and Performance (SEATRiP) at the University of California, Riverside. He has published extensively on Malay literature, cultural transitions from colonialism to modernity, and has translated a number of Indonesian novels.

Katharine McGregor is a Lecturer in Southeast Asian History in the History Department at the University of Melbourne, Australia. She completed her Ph.D. titled "Claiming History: Military Representations of the Indonesian Past in Museums, Monuments and Other Sources of Official History" at Melbourne University in July 2002. Her most recent research compares efforts to re-examine the 1984 Tanjung Priok killings and the 1965 anti-communist killings. She is also a board member of the widely read magazine, *Inside Indonesia*.

Goenawan Mohamad is a poet and essayist based in Jakarta. Among his publications are five volumes of the well-known short literary and philosophical pieces *Catatan Pinggir*, which were selected and translated for two English titles, *Sidelines* and *Conversations with Difference*. Besides *Kali*, he has written another libretto, *The King's Witch*, a new interpretation of an old Javanese and Balinese story (*Calonarang*), which was performed with Tony Prabowo's music by the Juilliard School of Music at Lincoln Center, New York in 2000. After stepping down as editor-in-chief of the weekly *TEMPO* news magazine, he founded the Utan Kayu Center for Free Expression. He was the Regents Professor at the University of California, Los Angeles in 2001, and a Fellow at the Institute for the Humanities at the University of Michigan in 2002.

Ki Tristuti Rachmadi was born in 1939 in Central Java, where his parents were deeply involved in the artistic world of the Javanese *wayang kulit*, the shadow theatre. Ki Tristuti began to perform as a shadow master, or *dalang*, at the age of 15, and became widely acclaimed as a performer before he was arrested as part of the anti-communist purges of 1965–6 in Indonesia. From 1965 until 1979 Ki Tristuti was a political prisoner in jails on Java and in the detention camp on the island of Buru. Following his release in 1979 he began to write stories for shadow theatre performers, and in the late 1990s he finally returned to the stage. His first trip outside Indonesia took place in 2001, when Ki Tristuti was invited by several universities to perform in the United States. He lives with his wife, Maria Sri Lestari, in Solo, Central Java.

Anthony Reid is a Southeast Asian historian with particular interests in Indonesia and Malaysia. After studying in New Zealand and Cambridge, he taught and researched at the University of Malaya (Kuala Lumpur, 1965–70), the Australian National University (Canberra, 1970–99), and the University of California, Los Angeles (1999–2002). At UCLA he was founding Director of the Center for Southeast Asian Studies, which sponsored the conference that gave rise to this book. Since 2002 he has been founding Director of the Asia Research Institute at the National University of Singapore. His books include: *The Contest for North Sumatra: Atjeh, the Netherlands and Britain, 1858–1898* (1969); *The Indonesian National Revolution, 1945–1950* (1974); *The Blood of the People: Revolution and the End of Traditional Rule in Northern Sumatra* (1979); *Southeast Asia in the Age of Commerce, 1450–1680*, 2 Vols. (1988–93); *Charting the Shape of Early Modern Southeast Asia* (1999); and *Acehnese and Other Histories of Sumatra* (2004).

Degung Santikarma is an Indonesian anthropologist, journalist, and political activist. He has been the recipient of grants from the John D. and Catherine T. MacArthur Foundation and the H.F. Guggenheim Foundation for research on the massacres of 1965–6 and their cultural and political implications. In 2001 he founded *Latitudes*, a monthly magazine on Indonesian culture and politics. He is currently completing a book entitled *When the World Turned to Chaos: Violence and its Aftermath in Bali* in collaboration with Leslie Dwyer.

Klaus H. Schreiner presently heads the European Liaison Office of the International NGO Forum on Indonesian Development (INFID) based in Brussels (Belgium). He previously was a Lecturer at the Department of Southeast Asian Studies at the J.W. Goethe University in Frankfurt (Germany), and received a PhD in Modern History from the University of Hamburg in 1993. His main interests are Indonesia's modern history and political culture, and he has published books and articles on topics related to the use of history in the Suharto era, the role of Islam in Indonesian politics, and on regional conflicts and decentralization in Indonesia.

Laurie J. Sears is Professor of History and teaches history, theory, and literature at the University of Washington in Seattle. Her publications include *Shadows of Empire* (Duke, 1996), and the edited volumes *Fantasizing the Feminine in Indonesia* (Duke, 1996) and *Autonomous Histories, Particular Truths* (University of Wisconsin Center for Southeast Asian Studies, 1993). Her forthcoming edited volume is *Subject, Knowledge, Discipline: Southeast Asian Studies in 21st Century America*.

Karen Strassler is Hardy Postdoctoral Fellow in Visual Anthropology at the Peabody Museum of Archaeology and Ethnology at Harvard University. She is currently writing a book to be published by Duke University Press based on her dissertation (Michigan, 2003) on popular photographic practices in postcolonial Java. Her recent research addresses questions of historical memory, media and mediation, and the politics of visuality in post-Suharto Indonesia.

Fadjar I. Thufail is Rockefeller Fellow at the Simpson Center for the Humanities at the University of Washington, Seattle. He is also a PhD candidate in the Department of Anthropology at the University of Wisconsin, Madison, and Research Associate at the Indonesian Institute of Sciences (LIPI). He is currently completing a dissertation on the politics of representation and narratives of the May 1998 riots in Jakarta and Solo. He is a member of the Indonesian Transitional Justice Task Force, and has written several essays published in Indonesian media about the proposed Indonesian Truth and Reconciliation Commission.

Gerry van Klinken is Research Fellow with the KITLV (Royal Netherlands Institute of Southeast Asian and Caribbean Studies) at Leiden University. Earlier in professional life he was a physicist, teaching at universities in Malaysia and Indonesia for ten years. Since earning his PhD in Indonesian History (1996) he has taught and conducted research at universities in Australia, Indonesia, and the Netherlands. He began editing *Inside Indonesia* magazine in 1996 and remains on its board. In 2002–4 he was Research Consultant to the East Timor Commission for Reception, Truth and Reconciliation. His ongoing research on Indonesia emphasizes human rights, ethnicity, post-authoritarian transition, and historical memory.

Paul van Zyl is Director for Country Programs at the International Center for Transitional Justice in New York. He has acted as an adviser and consultant to human rights organizations, governments, international organizations, and foundations on transitional justice issues in many countries, including Colombia, Indonesia, East Timor, and Bosnia-Herzegovina. From 1995 to 1998, he served as Executive Secretary of the Truth and Reconciliation Commission in South Africa. He has also worked as a researcher for the Goldstone Commission, as a department head at the Centre for the Study of Violence and Reconciliation in Johannesburg, and as an associate at Davis Polk and Wardwell in New York. Mr van Zyl teaches law at both Columbia and New York University Law Schools. He obtained a BA and an LLB from the University of the Witwatersrand in Johannesburg and an LLM in International Law from the University of Leiden in the Netherlands.

Mary S. Zurbuchen is currently Director for Asia and Russia Programs with the Ford Foundation International Fellowships Program. She spent 15 years working in Asia with the Ford Foundation, first as Program Officer for Culture in field offices in Jakarta and New Delhi, and later as Representative for Southeast Asia with responsibilities in Indonesia, Thailand, Vietnam, and the Philippines. She received the MA in Southeast Asian Studies and the PhD in Linguistics from the University of Michigan, and from 2000–3 was Visiting Professor with the Center for Southeast Asian Studies at the International Institute of the University of California, Los Angeles. She has conducted research on language, literature, and performance in Indonesia, and wrote *The Language of Balinese Shadow Theater* (Princeton, 1987) as well as recent articles on historical memory in Indonesia.

Foreword

Any collaborative project owes its genesis and outcomes to multiple sources and energies. This is especially true for an edited book, and thus there must be space for acknowledging the contributions of the institutions as well as the many individuals who have together made this volume possible.

Over many years of living and working in Indonesia I was always intrigued by the ways in which the past has been recorded, remembered, obscured and recovered. Particularly salient were memories of 1965–6, which hovered below the surface of public life in a way that suggested eventual re-emergence when conditions would permit. When I completed my term as Representative in the Ford Foundation's office in Jakarta in August 2000, I had the opportunity to affiliate with the newly-established Center for Southeast Asian Studies (CSEAS) at the University of California, Los Angeles, and to pursue research interests in how the past is being revisited and re-interpreted in the Indonesian present. I am grateful to the Foundation and its staff, especially Alison Bernstein, Barry Gaberman, and Anthony Romero for their encouragement and support of these efforts.

I am enormously grateful to Professor Anthony Reid, then CSEAS Director, for his enthusiasm in welcoming me to UCLA and for his commitment to the conference "History and Memory in Contemporary Indonesia", which took place at UCLA on 6–7 April 2001 and from which the chapters in this book evolved. Reid and other UCLA colleagues provided intellectual encouragement and institutional backstopping of many kinds; many thanks to the UCLA International Institute, the Department of Asian Languages and Cultures, the Fowler Museum of Culture History, and the Department of Ethnomusicology in this regard. At CSEAS, Assistant Director Barbara Gaerlan's support was unflagging, and I thank her profusely. Graduate students affiliated with CSEAS contributed much to the conference and its aftermath, especially Juliana Wijaya.

To all the authors who presented their papers at the original conference, and later revised and reflected on their work in preparing the
chapters published here, I feel a deep gratitude for their willingness to
contribute their thinking and creativity on a subject that crosses the
lines and deviates from the conventions of many disciplines. There were
several people whose roles at the conference are not fully reflected in
this volume, and I would like to acknowledge Nancy Lee Peluso, Lies
Marcoes, Elizabeth Drexler, Mochtar Pabottingi, and Geoffrey Robinson
as provocative writers and thoughtful discussants. Jarrad Powell and
Kent Devereaux were very helpful in providing us with materials on the
Seattle production of *Kali*, and Eko Supriyanto contributed memorable
choreography as a preface to Ki Tristuti Rachmadi's shadow play. That
performance could not have taken place without the combined efforts of
Ki Tristuti and his troupe; Robert Brown of the University of California,
San Diego; and, senior artists Nyoman Wenten and DjokoWaluyo, along
with student gamelan players of the California Institute of the Arts, all
of whom volunteered their services for the performance at UCLA. I would
further like to thank colleagues at the University of California at Berkeley,
especially Ben Brinner, who worked to facilitate Ki Tristuti's travel to the
United States, and Nancy Lee Peluso, who collaborated on the conference
and other aspects of the University of California Consortium on Southeast Asia.

The origin of my interest in issues of history and memory is embedded in many hours of conversation and reflection with Indonesian friends
and colleagues who shared their understanding of the dimensions and
depths of the subject. Special mention goes to Hersri Setiawan, who first
opened my mind to the legacies of Indonesia's silenced voices; and to
Pramoedya Ananta Toer, Joesoef Isak, Putu Oka Sukanta, Hardoyo,
Asvi Warman Adam, Karlina Leksono, Onghokham, Ariel Heryanto,
H.D. Haryo Sasongko, Melani Budianta, Toenggoel Siagian, Taufik
Abdullah, Todong Mulya Lubis, Romo Sandyawan Sumardi, Degung
Santikarma, and Juliana Wijaya. Others both within and outside South-
east Asia who helped stimulate this work through the example of their
own include Sumit Mandal, Diana Wong, Leslie Dwyer, Sidney Jones, and
Thongchai Winichakul. John McGlynn of the Lontar Foundation, and
Priscilla Hayner and Paul van Zyl of the International Center for Tran-
sitional Justice, and Maureen Aung-Thwin of the Open Society Institute

all knew why the theme of "how we begin to remember" is so important, and were encouraging throughout this project.

I am fortunate to enjoy the friendship of Sharon Siddique in Singapore, Dea Sudarman in Jakarta, and Rhoda Grauer and Rachel Cooper in New York; their creative thinking, generosity and hospitality are gratefully acknowledged. Suzanne Siskel has been helpful in countless ways as a Ford Foundation colleague and a stalwart friend. Judy Mitoma is the source of wonderful companionship and moral clarity; I will always be deeply grateful for the opportunity to share her home and learn from her wisdom while working on this project. In addition, Nani Supolo provided dedicated support and research assistance in Jakarta.

From conference program to manuscript prospectus to finished book has been a long journey, and I have travelled in the fellowship of kind colleagues. Goenawan Mohamad gave permission to bring out the first published edition of *Kali*, and was generous in discussing the poetry and sharing his thoughts about Indonesia in transition. Laurie Sears was ever ready to help me in refining and shaping the presentation of these papers, contributing clarity and coherence. Henk Maier and Geoff Robinson both helped edit early paper drafts, and I thank them both.

The amazing editorial talents and organizational skills of Jennifer Winther have brought the text into its present much-improved form; her dedication in seeing the work to completion was exemplary.

I would like to thank Peter Schoppert and Paul Kratoska of NUS Publishing and Michael Duckworth of the University of Washington Press for agreeing to work together on bringing this title to the public, and for supervising the production process.

To all those not mentioned by name who made it possible to live, work, study, and become wiser through the years in Bali and Jakarta, I offer profound thanks. Finally, to my sons Toby and Nathan, I give what additional understanding I can of Indonesia, cherished as birthplace and home and desired point of return.

Cartoon by Nicholson from *The Australian* <http://www.nicholsoncartoons.com.au>.
Reprinted with permission.

INTRODUCTION

Historical Memory in Contemporary Indonesia

MARY S. ZURBUCHEN

This volume began with a conference in April 2001 at the University of California, Los Angeles on the subject of "history and memory" in Indonesia today. The critical event stimulating our thinking was, of course, the abrupt end of the 32-year rule of Suharto in May 1998, which had opened new spaces for addressing national crises and, in the hopes of many Indonesians, for improving troubled social and economic conditions. When former President Suharto stepped down, a flood of relief and euphoria inundated the landscape of public awareness. For a time it felt as though the New Order would simply dissolve, and a consensus called *reformasi* would effortlessly flow over the land, righting past wrongs and dispelling conflict.

It wasn't long before sober realities reappeared, however, and the weight of its history once again burdened Indonesia's future. Corruption, official secrecy and denial, religious and ethnic violence, and wrongheaded security policies leading to tragedy in East Timor, Aceh and other regions were realized to be persistent phenomena that the removal of Suharto could not dispel. The archipelago looked to be submerged in a sea of troubles including growing unemployment and decline in public services following severe economic contraction and soaring government debt; violent crime and upheavals in major cities; the military-linked sacking and international outcry around the independence referendum in East Timor; unprecedented exposure of corrupt and abusive practices of state security and justice systems; mounting Islamist militancy; episodes of deadly terrorist attack; and intense and bloody communal and intergroup conflicts in several regions. The unified coherence of Suharto's New Order was thoroughly discredited, as economic stagnation and growing discord undermined its core themes of stability and state-managed development.

3

This departure of the strong leader, who appeared to have deliberately fostered a kind of collective inability to imagine a post-Suharto future, did have the effect of opening up new possibilities for seeing the past. In the wake of Suharto's resignation, a surge of reflexive discourse on the New Order enlivened mass media and publishing, public policy debate, arts and culture, popular mobilization, and political activism. Some of this discourse harked back nostalgically to the pre-New Order period of passionate nation-building under charismatic founding President Soekarno[1]; some of it exhorted moral reform in focusing on the "corruption-collusion-nepotism" (KKN, *korupsi, kolusi, nepotisme*) of the Suharto regime. At the same time, alternative versions of national history were vaunted in memoirs and academic conferences, while local narratives increasingly contradicted or competed with state claims. Calls were issued from activist groups and victims' associations to "uncover" (*mengungkapkan*) events that had formerly been suppressed or highly controversial, most significantly the record of legal and human rights abuses of the New Order state and security apparatus.[2] Expectations grew that government would use its powers — through judicial channels,[3] the forging of new legislation,[4] or the public accounts of fact-finding commissions[5] — to open up hidden parts of the past for public scrutiny as part of Indonesia's new commitment to democratic practices.

There would seem to be a great deal of unattractive past to bring under scrutiny. A comprehensive Suharto-period roster of extrajudicial killings, illegal detentions, disappearances, kidnappings, forced removals, suppression of legitimate protest, gender violence and other injustices that various groups of Indonesians now would like to see addressed or redressed would exceed the bounds of discussion here. So would description of the systems of political imprisonment, civic disenfranchisement, stigmatization, censorship, secrecy, banning, and official harassment that long were visited upon critics and victims of the authoritarian New Order and that nurtured fear, silence and self-censorship in the world's fourth largest country for more than three decades. Yet the New Order's military-backed monopoly over the production and interpretation of the nation's history clearly served as a key tool in legitimizing the institutions of the "security state". Normative and ideological spheres were sharply inscribed through control over textbooks, media and publishing, arts institutes, museums, monuments, public ceremonies, and national symbols. Divergent perspectives, controversial events, and critical voices were not allowed to compete alongside the official record. Thus, after Suharto was gone, the pressure of what needed to be recalled, revisited, and reviewed could be intense, noted historian Taufik Abdullah: "Don't be surprised if now — after the main pillar of the 'all-consuming state' called the New Order has been felled — things that were 'forgotten' start to come forth and the validity of what was 'remembered' is interrogated" (*TEMPO*, 22 February 1999, "Yang Terlupakan" [my translation]).

These essays, then, represent an exploration of certain expressions, narratives, and interpretations of the past in Indonesia today. We hope to offer some understanding of what concerns Indonesians about their own history and what use they are making of it at present. We seek to examine how and why particular narratives, whether local or national, group or individual, have come to be written or represented. Through these writings we aim to chart some pathways toward deeper insight regarding the various contests over national cohesion, definitions of citizenship or power or identity, and ethnic or religious or regional memory that we witness in Indonesia at present, all of which are sites where the past is articulated or constructed in some way.

The Framework of Historical Memory

> ... I think how little we can hold in mind, how everything is constantly lapsing into oblivion with every extinguished life, how the world is, as it were, draining itself, in that the history of countless places and objects which themselves have no power of memory is never heard, never described or passed on.   (Sebald 2001: 24)

The terms "history" and "memory" are linked in a creative tension in much recent scholarly work,[6] as they are in the chapters of this book. The human sciences have, over the last decades, been heavily inflected by postmodern (and post-colonial, post-structuralist, etc.) paradigms of scholarship reflecting "suspicions about truth and the celebration of ambiguity" (Roth and Salas 2001: 3). The discipline of the historian is no longer a positivist exercise in which facts about the past are secured and ordered, and eyewitness narrative is well understood to conceal as well as to reveal. What can be obscured ranges from marginalized perspectives — the subaltern, as they have come to be called — to horror and crisis.

In the West, the challenge of representing the unrepresentable as disinterested "truth" emerged particularly forcefully through studies of the Holocaust. In the wake of World War II, "history" as a discursive practice could not easily encompass the magnitude of either the Nazi persecution or the full impacts on its survivors. Much more recently, German writer W.G. Sebald tried to understand how collective German memory failed to register the traumatic bombing destruction of 31 cities that killed 600,000 civilians in the later part of the war to "cast some light on the way in which memory (individual, collective and cultural) deals with experiences exceeding what is tolerable" (2003: 79).

In his critique of epistemology, moving in a somewhat different direction, Foucault drew on studies of how language represents truth from Nietzsche, Wittgenstein, and Barthes. In *The Order of Things* and *The Archaeology of Knowledge*, Foucault outlined not a science of history but a history of consciousness, and his claims that knowledge is made up of different systems of discursive practices have had wide-ranging impact on the human sciences.

The combination of these intellectual transitions — the latter a theorizing of knowledge as systems of language practice, the former a growing emphasis on awareness and engagement — has led historian Edith Wyschogrod (1998) to an "ethics of memory" that acknowledges the impossibility of recovering or representing the past completely. What are the responsibilities of researching or bringing forward questions of the past, such as mass killing, if we can never really be certain of knowing what actually happened? Whose memories are being represented, through which media, and to what purpose? A decade after the Cold War subsided, Vaclav Havel (1999) reflected that the most essential historical lesson for formerly communist societies is that "the only kind of politics that truly makes sense is one that is guided by conscience". A sense of the need for ethical perspectives in dealing with the problems of the past is thus a key theme emerging from 20th-century experiences, a viewpoint expressed by Stephen Lewis of the International Panel of Eminent Personalities reviewing the 1994 Rwanda killings, when he pointed to the international community's failure to intervene to prevent genocide, and the "tattered moral core" that still prevented adequate retrospective assessment (Lewis 2000).[7]

The concept of collective or social memory has clearly become central to understanding "how groups retain a sense of the past, and ... how a sense of the past can inform a group's politics, religion, art, and social life in general" (Roth and Salas 2001: 1). The role of personal memory is also important in shaping and transforming past experience, and its functioning equally problematic. People who have survived traumatic experiences may be unable or unwilling to express themselves; in post-war Germany, says Sebald (2003: 23), "the need to know was at odds with a desire to close down the senses". American politician and war veteran Bob Kerrey found, to his public discomfort, that his own memories of how Vietnamese civilians were killed at Thanh Phong in 1969 conflicted with accounts of other members of his Navy Seals unit. Sympathizing with Kerrey, novelist Tobias Wolff found in writing his experiences of the American war in Vietnam that he had forgotten certain forceful memories that "didn't fit my idea of myself". "Memory is a storyteller," says Wolff, "and like all storytellers it imposes form on the raw mass of experience. It creates shape and meaning by emphasizing some things and leaving others out" (Wolff 2001). Personal narrative brought into the public sphere also transforms others, with sometimes terrible result; "the social production of hate" between Sikhs and Hindus through rumour and unattributed personal accounts shattered a multi-ethnic community and led to the deaths of thousands of Sikhs in New Delhi following the assassination of Prime Minister Indira Gandhi in 1984 (see Das 2001).

What I refer to here as the emerging genre of "historical memory" thus acknowledges the intertwined yet discontinuous aspects of individual and social processing in shaping representations of the past in the present. Also referenced is the declining authority of written narrative as the source of historical understanding; today, the public garners "history" from television news, theme parks, and blockbuster movies as well as from textbooks or libraries. Amid the global flow of information and images, particular versions of history or personal memories are unstable, and can be revisited, reframed and recycled for new purposes. The controversy over the "Enola Gay" exhibition at the Smithsonian Institution in Washington, DC — in which documentation of Japanese suffering at Hiroshima and Nagasaki was excised, and senior staff resigned following divisive public debate and Congressional hearings — demonstrates clearly the contentiousness of "questions about for whom, for what objectives, and for whose community" history is presented (see Yoneyama 2001). And written history itself can still bring enormous repercussions, as with the representation of Japan's role in World War II in its national textbooks, which for decades has strained relations between

Japan and its Asian neighbours, for whom memory presents very different truths.[8]

The scope of historical memory embraces not only fixed texts or other emerging "sites of memory", but also processes of configuring memory, moments when the past can be reshaped and outcomes remain unresolved. Social memory can be wholly engineered at such moments: the first official act of the newly appointed Iraqi Governing Council in 2003 was to rewrite Iraq's national history through the declaration of a new national holiday and cancellation of others. In a more nuanced manner, scholars, museologists and others in South Africa are spearheading vigorous debate over how the indigenous, colonial, and apartheid histories of the country should be remembered and represented (Walker 2004).

At moments when societies change direction — whether sudden or prolonged, through violent upheaval or more peaceful rebalancing of power — representations of the past may disappear, be transformed, and acquire or lose authoritativeness. The collapse of communist states in eastern Europe gave the rubble of the Berlin Wall a new patina as important relics; when a German artist tried to claim copyright of a piece of the Wall that he had painted, and which had been donated to the United Nations, he was told that "you can't copyright history". Moments of configuring can involve ruptures in the process of recording the past, and rejection of certain kinds of memory when linked to concerns for security. In a chaotic East Timor in September 1999, invaluable archives of painstakingly collected, hand-written testimony from victims of violence were destroyed by the United Nations Mission in East Timor (UNAMET). During the violence following the popular referendum that decisively chose independence from Indonesia, the agency determined it would be dangerous to leave such records intact.[9] At such moments of transition competition between official and unofficial histories is intense, and the production or erasure of "memory" can take on a singular urgency.

Transitions and "Truth-seeking"

> I know you are asking today "How long will it take?" ... I come to say to you this afternoon, however difficult the moment, however frustrating the hour, it will not be long, because truth pressed to earth will rise again. How long? ... Not long, because the arm of the moral universe is long, but it bends toward justice.[10]

The 50th anniversary of the end of World War II in the mid-1990s provided a reflective moment for assessing mass violence and globalized conflict as themes of the 20th century. Looking at the scope of dramatic changes presently reconfiguring the world, we can point to the end of the "fearful symmetries" of the Cold War (Geertz 2000). This loosening of a once-familiar bipolar rigidity in world affairs into a shifting and dynamic set of unbalanced, emergent, reshaped, globalizing social and political exchanges and identities — what Clifford Geertz called the "world in pieces" — now requires us to look back at where we were to try and make sense of fundamental changes witnessed at once and everywhere.

In this context, Indonesia represents one of what have been called the "transitional" societies — places that are transforming systems determined by older geopolitical patterns into a post-Cold War configuration of markets, information, and new democracies. The study of these transitional processes in a country's economy, governance, applications of law and human rights, or cultural dynamics has become a large and fascinating field. We can look at Indonesia as one locus of these interlinked world-historical processes.

Beyond this, however, and moving more deeply into the theme of this book, Indonesia, as it struggles to emerge from habits of the New Order, also belongs to the group of countries coming to terms with legacies of violence or authoritarianism. Such societies are similar in finding it necessary or desirable to overcome portions of their histories in order to shape new futures. In the face of Geertz's "disassembly" of stable identities and affiliations, which seemingly defies any effort toward integrative understanding of how the world now works, the proliferation, urgency and parallel manner in which societies are revisiting and reassessing the past stands out as one dramatic example of new principles of affinity and intersection.

A few of the more recent examples from the legion of those available will suffice. Beginning with Europe, Belgium has begun to examine the violence and exploitation of resources which, under King Leopold II between 1885 and 1908, led to millions of deaths in the Congo, and has also officially acknowledged its direct role in the 1961 assassination of Patrice Lumumba, independent Congo's first Prime Minister (*New York Times*, 21 September 2002, "Belgium"). Other countries are beginning to confront episodes long ignored, even after transitions to new forms of government. Thus Croatians are acknowledging the slaying of ethnic Serbs as the territory became an independent state in 1991 (*International Herald Tribune*, 20–21 May 2000, "Croatians"). And in recognition of Polish complicity in the murder of Jews, a monument blaming the Nazis was removed from a site where 1,600 Jews were burned to death, when the killers were shown to be non-Jewish Poles (*New York Times*, 8 April 2001, "Poland"). In Spain, meanwhile, the violence of the Franco period is now the subject of exhibitions, a television series, and efforts to exhume mass graves.

In Latin America, where widespread shifts away from military rule spurred intensive transitional justice work, the new president of Argentina has retracted provisions that gave impunity to those implicated in the 30,000 "disappearances" during the 1976–83 dictatorship (*New York Times*, 18 June 2003, "Now the Dirtiest"), and the Chilean government is seeking to revoke prosecutorial immunity from former president and military strongman Augusto Pinochet. In Mexico, the mass killing of student protestors by soldiers just before the 1968 Olympic games is a subject newly under public scrutiny (*New York Times*, 7 February 2003, "Mexico"). And in El Salvador, remains were finally laid to rest of 800 people killed by the Salvadoran military in 1981, a massacre details of which were suppressed by the United States as well as the regime (*New York Times*, 11 December 2000, "In El Salvador").

Countries that have experienced repression and violence on a large scale seem to find it especially difficult to consolidate new national arrangements unless they are able in some measure to come to terms with the past. From Chile and Poland to Sierra Leone or Cambodia, approaches vary considerably. The war crimes tribunal on the former Yugoslavia is one of the most prominent examples of judicial action taken against those accused of violating human rights; nongovernmental organizations and human rights campaigners have also worked to have formal charges brought against notorious figures like Chile's Pinochet and former president of Chad, Hissene Habre.[11] Other processes have involved saying "never again" by making state atrocities public, as with the documentation of secret torture and detention in the renowned report "Brazil: *Nunca Mas*".[12] In the former East Germany, secret police files were opened for public scrutiny, while in Czechoslovakia strict lustration policies were applied to identify and eliminate communist collaborators from positions of power (see Rosenberg 1996).

Any such attempts to deal with the past are painful, full of risk, and not always successful. Transcendence over the worst kinds of atrocities may not be entirely achievable; in Russia, successful efforts by rights groups to document the graves of Stalin's Mass Terror have been given an ambivalent reception (*New York Times*, 11 November 2002, "Spaniards" and 20 October 2002, "As Its Past"). It is difficult to imagine how "justice" will be rendered to the tens of thousands of Rwandan Hutus currently charged with genocide of the Tutsi community and awaiting trial.

It may be easier not to remember, but impossible to forget, as Priscilla Hayner (2001) has written in her powerful book surveying the ways that more than 20 countries around the world have used official "truth commissions" to reveal secret abuses and seek acknowledgement of a wide variety of legacies of violence. While admitting the challenges of revealing and defining something called "truth", transitional justice advocates report that a public reckoning can, nonetheless, bring a variety of benefits. These include clarification and acknowledgement of "what happened", through lifting veils of denial and secrecy; responding to the needs and interests of victims, through enabling them to tell their stories and have their suffering recognized; contributing to justice and accountability through gathering information that may be used in formal legal proceedings; outlining institutional responsibility and recommending reforms; and promoting resolution of conflicts and reduction of tensions.[13]

The growing body of experience with truth-seeking endeavours has given rise to optimism as well as critiques and a certain skepticism. Many legal scholars and human rights organizations question whether truth-seeking really leads to either justice or resolution, and how impunity can be limited unless there is prosecution of offenders.[14] The sensitivity of approaches such as granting amnesty to perpetrators who confess their crimes — the most controversial aspect of the renowned South African Truth and Reconciliation Commission — has been used to argue that truth commissions could undermine the foundations of future justice in transitional societies. Still, many point to truth commissions to argue that in societies where the law is weak or corrupt, alternative strategies for making space for victims' truth outside the courtroom must be given priority.

Especially for traumas in the distant past, much can be achieved through shaping a public record in non-judicial ways sometimes termed "historical clarification". Through investigating the Tulsa Race Riots of 1921, where as many as 300 members of a thriving black community were shot, burned, lynched or otherwise abused, a recent Oklahoma state commission's report spurred public awareness of how government institutions abetted the violence (*New York Times*, 16 March 2003, "Coming to Grips"). While recognizing that "historical truth" is unattainable, the historian can nonetheless accept the responsibility for "historical truthfulness", through heightened awareness of the relationships between authors and subjects, and the limitations of observer perspective (Morris-Suzuki 2001).

The lessons from various truth-seeking practices — whether local or national, official or community-based — are still evolving across the panoply of societies examining troubled pasts. In one journalist's account of the day-by-day struggles, mistakes, conflicts, risks and triumphs of South Africa's commission, Antjie Krog (1998: 21–2) provides a troubled yet memorable reflection on what it meant to articulate both the desire for "truth" and the need for "justice" following apartheid: "If [the commission] sees truth as the widest possible compilation of people's perceptions, stories, myths, and experiences, it will have chosen to restore memory and foster a new humanity, and perhaps that is justice in its deepest sense."

Krog, like many others, doubts whether "reconciliation" can ever be assured as one of the outcomes of truth-seeking. Forgiveness is not among the obligations victims of violence can readily undertake. Yet the kind of resolution she suggests, the fostering of a new sense of shared humanity, would seem to lie behind the truth-seeking enterprise that currently is closest to Indonesia in both geographic and historical memory terms: that of Timor Leste, the newly independent East Timor. A Commission for Reception, Truth and Reconciliation (see van Zyl, this volume) is now working to facilitate community-based processes where perpetrators of a defined subset of crimes — many of them members of militias who fled the territory in 1999, and now wish to return — can acknowledge their actions and receive some measure of re-acceptance. The spirit of this effort is expressed in Tetum as:

Ho rekonsiliasaun ita hametan unidade iha ita rain Timor Loro-sae. Liu-liu iha ita nia komunidade.

By reconciliation we strengthen our unity in Timor Loro-Sae. Thus we have community.[15]

Forgetting and Remembering in Indonesia

> Certain matters require the generosity of forgetfulness, and others demand the honesty of remembrance.   (Barenboim 2001)

What does it mean to be Indonesian now, situated in the aftermath of the New Order and enduring economic downturn, political uncertainty, intergroup conflict, separatism, and religious extremism? In answering this question, Goenawan Mohamad (2001) recalls the moment of the 1928 Youth Pledge, when people from the many regions and ethnic groups of the archipelago agreed to "forget" their disparate origins to make themselves part of the new "imagined community" of Indonesia. Building on Renan's proposition that "forgetting is a crucial factor in the creation of a nation", Goenawan reflects on what he calls the "ethical moment" of the Pledge, which generated "a myth and a power", both of which are now in grave danger. He wonders whether the affirmation of universal values within a uniquely Indonesian "process of plurality" can be sustained at present, when "the forgotten, as it were, are coming back with a vengeance".

We might posit that questions of how to remember, or invitations for certain kinds of forgetfulness in the representation of the past would, now that the Suharto government's tight grip on the body of history has loosened, stretch their limbs and occupy a larger space in public life. As the authors in this volume eloquently demonstrate, such questions can be posed from many disciplinary perspectives, evoking a breathtaking range of lived experience and analytic stances. Why is it, then, that we have seen in Indonesia since 1998 so few thorough investigations, commissions,[16] trials, textbook overhauls, rehabilitation, or other examples of "getting to the bottom of" any one of the host of dimly understood incidents (*peristiwa*) that so many believe to have taken place? What is it that constrains and renders hesitant the work of historical memory, so that in Indonesia, as in post-war Germany, "when we turn to take a retrospective view … we are always looking and looking away at the same time" (Sebald 2003: ix)?

It would be unfair, of course, to expect Indonesian society to deal

with a diverse legacy of wrongs quickly and neatly.[17] When countries
like Spain and Japan need many decades to confront the record of the
Spanish Civil War and World War II, respectively, and Australia's Prime
Minister cannot bring himself to apologize for aboriginal sufferings as
part of national "Sorry Day", Indonesia can be understood to require
time to generate the social consensus, astute leadership, and robust
institutions needed to come to terms with grievances linked to very
different causes and constituencies. Systematic killings such as the
"politicide" of the left in 1965 or the "mysterious shootings" of the
1980s, episodic violence such as the shooting of Muslim demonstrators
in Tanjung Priok in 1984 or the killing of four Trisakti University students
in May 1998, abuses targeting individuals such as the murders of East
Java labour organizer Marsinah or Papuan leader Theys Eluay, detentions
and torture under military commands, and brutal acts, relocations and
impoverishment linked to resource exploitation — there are simply too
many sorts of "victims" to make a single narrative of "historical
clarification" possible. And there is no single tragic event, criminal category
or oppressive system that can serve as a rubric for mobilizing a broad
national effort among Indonesians — the way that "the disappeared" in
Argentina or "apartheid" in South Africa have done.

If Indonesians were to be asked which elements of the past most
needed to be aired or explained, some, but by no means all, would point
to the events of 1965–6, which led to perhaps a million deaths and
massive detentions of communist party members and "sympathizers"
around the country.[18] This is a view with which most foreign observers
would agree. "1965" certainly counts as one of the most deadly upheavals
of the 20th century; it put into place obsessive internal security systems
that eliminated political freedoms nationally and continue to constrain
many thousands of Indonesians through suspicion of communist
"contamination"; and the "30th September Movement of the Indonesian
Communist Party", which gave way to the counter-movement responsible
for these horrors and for Suharto's rise to power, has never been fully
explained. Because we have never fully acknowledged the truth of "the
1965 incident", the argument goes, we will not be able either to end
impunity or fully recover our common humanity.

However, much of the Indonesian body politic still finds "1965"
fairly indigestible, as the failure of former President Wahid's efforts to
provide national leadership on the issue indicates (Zurbuchen 2002:

571–3).[19] This is partly due to the persistence of the "discursive phantom of the Communist threat", in Ariel Heryanto's (1999) terms, a demon whose reproductions have penetrated historical awareness and popular culture and continue to be invoked to distract attention from one's own misdeeds or throw the political opposition off guard.[20] Many Indonesians, conditioned by the dominance of New Order official history and training in the regime's version of *Pancasila* ideology, believe that "1965" was a climactic and desperate moment of national treachery and crisis when the only option was "kill or be killed", and have little incentive to reconsider this received wisdom. Further, and especially pervasively in Java, the events of "1965" evoke the difficult business of defining and declaring "religiosity" in Indonesia — a problem that has renewed salience at present.[21]

There are other reasons why assessing the past seems such a hesitant business, of course. The country can be said to have begun a transition from authoritarianism, yet Suharto's resignation in 1998, dramatic as it was, turned out to be neither unambiguous nor decisive in terms of the "reform agenda". More than five years later, the military is not strictly under civilian control and government for the most part still serves the interests of the same elite that prospered under the New Order.[22] Corruption thrives, transparency and accountability are limited, and the justice system is still rife with influence-peddling. There has been limited impact at grass-roots levels from new policies that could foster truth-seeking aims,[23] and institutions such as the National Commission for Human Rights (*Komnasham*) must rely on fragile moral authority rather than large-scale operational resources or legal heft in order to have much influence. Despite the talents and energies of nongovernmental groups and advocates of accountability and truth-seeking, their ability to affect institutional and official mechanisms remains limited.[24]

Yet we need to dig deeper still, I think, to uncover another layer of ambivalence or diffidence regarding the past for many Indonesians. In the personal realm, it is clear that victims and survivors of violence must overcome considerable risk and fear to tell their stories. For example, 1965 was particularly disruptive within families and communities, and a great deal of memory remains below the surface. There has been little research on the dynamics of trauma in Indonesia, and few experts who know how to facilitate testimony from victims of violence. Witness protection is a fledgling endeavour being taken up primarily by religious groups and the National Women's Commission. Making private memory public is fraught with the dangers and possible repercussions of naming names, accusations and counterclaims, secrets revealed, and vengeance.

In addition, speaking to issues of the past from the locus of the personal may not be comfortable because national history (*sejarah nasional*) has been the monopoly of government, and ordinary people have not been seen as authoritative sources. Subaltern awareness in Indonesia often means reluctance to counter the hierarchy directly, and avoidance of declaration by the "I" in the act of asserting truth. In a revealing study of how colonial experience is remembered, Stoler and Strassler (2000) interviewed Javanese who had worked for Dutch families in the Netherlands East Indies. They found that their subjects were reticent about personal feelings, and would often "speak past, not back to, the colonial archive", perhaps under the shadow of New Order authorized history. Most public personal narrative in Indonesia fits the script of the "eyewitness to history" genre, as found in official oral history projects to record the memories of revolutionary "heroes".

One of the features of the recent past has been the emergence of personal memory as a touchstone for new histories. Whether among the rape victims of the Jakarta riots of 1998, the million or more Indonesians recently displaced from their towns and villages by violent conflict, ostracized former military and political leaders, or the families of political prisoners stigmatized under the New Order, there are wellsprings of remembrance that are starting to flow. Of course, individual memoirs and autobiographies have long been appearing in Indonesia, and they give us important windows on the imagination and experience of national identity and nation-building. But enabling victims of disruption and repression to speak and to be heard is an important and extremely difficult task.[25]

As Dwyer and Santikarma's research in Bali shows, language itself may be incommensurate to the articulation of memory; in 1965, all it took was a word to label someone a communist and ensure his or her death (Dwyer and Santikarma, unpublished). The issue of "giving voice" to ordinary Indonesians' experiences of the past means a powerful shift in the way agency and authority are generally articulated. Public life in Indonesia, wrote Clifford Geertz (2001) in a reflection on his experiences of the Soekarno period, is characterized by a "play of disjunctive discourses, separated registers of political expression". On the one hand are "emphatic

doings by emphatic personalities playing grandly to grand audiences",
while at the same time "furtive, allusive exchanges" take place behind
the scenes; "[i]t was as though the country was caught between grandi-
loquence and equivocation, stranded between speech styles without a
practicable system of civic discourse" (Geertz 2001).

Shapes of Record and Remembrance

The essays in this volume, taken together, suggest various ways that
histories in Indonesia are becoming elements of evolving civic discourse,
and how discursive strategies are shaping representations of memory.
Chapters are grouped in four sections, each reflecting a different set of
questions or methodological point of departure. Each section further
shines a different spectrum of light on the central questions of the volume
through juxtaposition of analysis, commentary, memoir, and reflection.

The chapters in Part One are anchored within the humanities, and
convey some of the potency of arts and literature in embodying historical
memory for their audiences. The implicit framework for this section is
the vitality and richness of oral traditions as "sites of memory" in the
Indonesian/Malay cultural sphere, and the ways that verbal art is spoken,
heard, shared, and interpreted in always-new contexts. Far from the
central monoliths of official historiography, singers, musicians, dancers,
and storytellers all over the archipelago render the shared past in ways
locally embedded and singularly powerful, as their performances can
never be fully captured by the printed page nor completely understood
outside the moment and place of utterance. The potential of oral
performance to provide counter-narrative and evoke solidarities is most
famously exemplified by Javanese and Balinese *wayang*, the shadow
theatre, revered and enjoyed as a many-layered art that interprets the past
— an inheritance of language, tales, power relations, and spiritual beliefs
— in terms of the present.[26]

The first section of this book is significant in bringing to publication
two performance texts drawing from the wayang heritage in distinctive
ways. The voice of the "true *dalang*", the shadow master, comes through
the memory of Ki Tristuti Rachmadi, a respected Javanese dalang
imprisoned without trial for 14 years and banned from public performance
for another 20 years under the New Order.[27] Little is known of many
of the artists and intellectuals killed or imprisoned in the wake of 1965,[28]

and this text represents more than a chronology of one person's experiences. Ki Tristuti closes his presentation by evoking historical memory in an important Javanese way. He uses the name "Suryosaputro", first given to him by former President Soekarno when he performed at the state palace, in this way affirming both the honour bestowed and a particular identity as part of the history of independent Indonesia.

What Ki Tristuti offered in the context of our academic conference at UCLA, shortly after first setting foot outside Indonesia and finding himself on the campus of a large metropolitan university, echoes the dalang's art, with its apologia, an episodic structure marked by rhetorical pauses ("esteemed audience"), as well as its alternation between new and old information, between revelations and referencing what is already known. While he captivates us with vivid language and knowing asides, he also lets his hearers understand that his talk is "just a small part of all that actually happened". In so doing he suggests the way a dalang structures his play, the *lakon,* as one dramatically expanded moment from within two vast universes of interwoven tales, inherited and transformed from their Indic origins, the epics *Mahabharata* and *Ramayana.*

Part of the dalang's art is to portray lessons about the human world within a larger order of things, and it is key that by the end of the night's performance the cosmic balance of conflicting powers has been restored. Ki Tristuti summons for his audience the shadows of actions linked to 1965 too dangerous to be spoken about from a conference room podium; as Laurie Sears reminds us, the climactic battle of the *Mahabharata* is regarded as "heavy and inauspicious" in Java and is not commonly performed. For Ki Tristuti, signalling that "calm will not be restored" in Indonesia until the wrongs of the past are settled, the final resolution of the lakon of 1965 has still to be played.

Goenawan Mohamad has long drawn upon the *Mahabharata* in his writings in order to illustrate moral ambiguities and conflicting perspectives. His libretto for the opera *Kali,* which premiered as a work of Jarrad Powell and Gamelan Pacifica, appears here in print for the first time, edited as a dramatic poem. The libretto also draws on the *Mahabharata,* which through its imagery of family ties and culturally resonant characterization supports Goenawan's exploration of how violence is a rupture that resists resolution. He depicts a world struggling with the "enigma of unfinished things", admitting that the dark events of 1965 and the record of New Order violence still colour Indonesian reality. The figures of blind Destarastra and blindfolded Gandari represent those who cannot see, and those who will not see. Just as the epic embodies clan conflict, fraternal killing, intergenerational guilt, and refusal to acknowledge the truth, so the legacy of 1965 brutality carries grave dangers for Indonesia's imagination of its destiny as a united people. Yet if Ki Tristuti suggests that 1965 will engender a kind of karmic outcome ("you reap what you sow"), Goenawan suggests that truth and justice are ultimately unreachable, swept up in a different kind of logic: "Gods create their own texts, / Long ones, like yards of cemetery plots."

Laurie J. Sears' penetrating essay on Goenawan's poetry also positions the *Mahabharata* as a site of memory, linking mythic and human time. Sears shines light on how the poet has rendered the "problems, doubts, blasphemies" of the epic tradition in a portrait of the dilemmas of truth and justice that has deep relevance for Indonesia. She weaves together the skeins of Goenawan's poetry, the background of violence and disruption at the end of the Suharto era, and both colonial literature and philosophical reflections on the melding of history and memory. In an echo of the best studies of shadow theatre, she shows how Goenawan's drama represents the inherited "history" of the *Mahabharata* — as with the poignancy of Karna's true identity and the choice between brotherhood and loyalty forced upon him — and also presents new elements and extrapolations from that tradition. In one of the richest of these innovations, Goenawan portrays Draupadi's humiliation, after she is wagered in the infamous game of dice, as a physical rape, with consciousness of horrific consequences: "And I knew that there would be a war, / For the gods always wanted it." In Sears' analysis, Draupadi's testimony of her humiliation represents the difficulties of bearing witness to the 1998 rapes in Jakarta and other episodes of sexual violence in Indonesia; such violence is also a particularly Indonesian site of memory, "a footprint / on buried stairs / of yesterday".

Kali takes us on a linguistic and symbolic journey along "myriad semantic rivers", in Sears' words. Goenawan's deep knowledge of the *Mahabharata*, and his renderings of its figures in his poetry and essays over many years, have enabled him to shape a new dramatic moment drawing on the polyvocality and symbolism of Javanese verbal art. A wayang story, which has no script, is played across many temporal, physical, and social contexts, and is not the "same" play each time. And like a wayang performance, the verbal shape of "Kali" reproduced here may live in other forms, moving from its origin as a libretto into other settings of dance, music, and theatre.

Both Ki Tristuti's evocation of the dalang's role and Goenawan's contemporizing of Javanese epic embody an essential linguistic and cultural feature which I see as the process of transmuting utterances of the past in the present moment. This intertextuality of oral performance and literature in Indonesia is, in practical terms, one of the most elusive aspects of teaching about Indonesian poetry and prose, and of assigning Indonesian literature a place in the great world "canon" of *belles lettres*. The dilemma of locating "memory" in texts, and the ways in which a language can or cannot be said to embody temporal reality, is expertly portrayed in Hendrik Maier's reflections on Malay stories. In the Malay (and by extension, Indonesian) universe of discourse, stories — and the sentences of which they are made — do not necessarily represent things that occurred as a sequence of past actions. Whereas narrative coherence in English is embedded in systems of tense, it is hard to pin down a "distinct temporal hierarchy" in Malay. There are other principles at work, changing how we must perceive the writer's art and challenging our notions of temporal localization and thus memory itself.

In his work on the articulation of contemporaneity in China, the anthropologist Xin Liu (2000) argues that "different ways of telling stories about oneself and others, which form different modes of memory as different ways of being in history, embed different conceptions of time". As an English speaker judging matters of historical memory in Indonesian texts, we are well advised to note the "constraints and particularities" of two distinct ways of rendering temporality. In Maier's compelling image, our efforts at translation are like "[l]eaning on our ordered collection of memories and looking through the window of English on Malay sentences and tales". Our notions of what is conclusive in the Indonesian experience, of what is definite, of agency, and of authority are all affected by grammatical disjunctures between two language worlds. Further, the representation of "history" and "truth" are also shaped by this kind of "temporal heterogeneity"; for Maier, chronicles as well as fiction reveal concern for performance, for oral recital that "forces us to search for memories" in the act of reading or listening. The characteristic "fragmentariness" of stories in which temporal and causal relations cannot easily be understood means that audiences create memories ("an experiential context") that are always unstable. New performance entails different shaping of memory.

Even in Indonesian literature on the Revolution, Maier argues, there is an incompleteness, shown by the remoteness or absence of the white soldiers who were the enemy. The Revolution appears as a process of seeking fulfillment through the spirit of nationalism, through experiences of heroism, betrayal or sacrifice that seem to be "taking place among us, in front of us — and perhaps even in us". A sense of identity and national belonging is forged through this textually-grounded search for "relevant memories to live by". In Part Two of this volume, writers portray multiple vantage points for discerning such relevant memories. Anthony Reid queries the salience of war and revolution as markers of national identity, first through comparison of how the 50th anniversary of the Allied victory in World War II was commemorated in Australia and Indonesia, and then by looking at how a half century of national independence was marked in the Karo Batak area of North Sumatra.

Along with neighbouring countries in Southeast Asia, Indonesia has used narratives of occupation, struggle, and victory over foreign enemies as a component of the nation-building enterprise.[29] Yet the Japanese era in Indonesia has received little in the way of public commemoration, and Reid notes the relative lack of interest of Indonesians in the anniversary of the transfer from Dutch colonial to Japanese occupation rule in 1942. Despite their acknowledged brutality, there is an ambivalence regarding the Japanese in Indonesian collective memory, in part because of the ways in which the occupation served to build and strengthen the independence leadership. Yet the memory of occupation is embodied at the most fundamental levels of social organization, states Reid, citing the late Mangunwijaya's critique of Japan's influence with "its atmosphere of uniforms, marching, inspection ceremonies, ... paramilitary language, attitude and behavior, security surveillance, and a whole set of commands and chains of instructions ...."

By contrast to the nation's scant memorialization of the Pacific War, Reid shows the citizens of Kebanjahe marking Indonesia's declaration of independence on 17 August 1945 through well-rehearsed rituals illustrating integralist history, the "progression from the contested turbulence of the past to an orderly society being instructed by paternalistic government". Certainly one of the most notable changes in Indonesia's recent historical discourse is the dissolution of, if not that paternalistic state itself, its singular monopoly on national history, which now appears polyvocal, dispersed, and regional in ways previously unnoticed. Andi F. Bakti's research on the legacy of the South Sulawesi rebel movement once led by the charismatic Qahhar Muzakkar shows an array of discursive forms in which this counter-narrative to national history is cast. Followers of Qahhar imagine their rebellion through legend, personal anecdote, belief in reincarnation, magical transformation, and the messianic tradition of the "just ruler". Memory of Qahhar is dispersed among isolated individuals, in clandestine cells and modern civic associations, each of which fosters its own aspirations — to counter Javanese domination, advance human rights, implement Islamic law, or promote regional autonomy or federalism. Styles of speech evoking the mysterious death and physical absence of Qahhar, or asserting his reappearance in the contested identity of Syamsuri, are memories that create a new life for the Qahhar movement in the present, much as the remembrance of Soekarno has done in popular culture elsewhere in Indonesia.

If the intentional "forgetting" of ethnic origins was once the condition for forging a unified independence movement, we are now witnessing renewed negotiation of just what regional remembrance entails. The passage of major national legislation in 2000 mandating both fiscal and administrative decentralization from Jakarta to the country's 3,000 district governments is arguably the most important and far-reaching change in the unitary state since independence itself. The emergence and assertion of local claims on history is expressed not only through dissent from the centralization paradigm and demands for local autonomy; it is also played out in the upsurge of ethnic chauvinism, local intergroup rivalries, and communal violence. For instance, a particularly brutal ethnic war between Dayaks and Madurese immigrants took place in West Kalimantan during 1996–7. Anthropologist Nancy Lee Peluso (2003) found that the image of the "Borneo Headhunter", and specific rituals formerly associated with headhunting wars, were reactivated through drawing upon cultural memory and methods used by the military to mobilize Dayaks in expelling rural Chinese in the "cold war" context of the 1960s.

Turning to Fadjar Thufail's analysis of the murders of "black magic" practitioners (*dukun santet*) and religious figures in East Java in 1998, we find a similarly highly contextualized pattern utilizing established memory (suspicion of dukun santet as threatening and powerful figures in rural Muslim society) within new scripts of power rivalry. According to Fadjar, each kind of narrative "explaining" the ninja killings emanates from a distinct interpretive realm. The ninjas are state-sponsored thugs for hire, they are disguised assassins of the Special Forces, they are agents of the dwindling Suharto regime, or they are surrogates for political rivals to then-President Wahid. In an evocation of the traumatic "collective animosity" that bloodied East Java in 1965, they further embody an older hostility between Muslim clerics and communists. The black-clad killers are linked to magic, shape-shifting, and the appearance of strangers in the village; personal anecdote and rumor activate mob violence. One of the most troubling aspects of what Fadjar observes is the lack of resolution of these competing memories or representations; once the ninja killings were no longer in the daily headlines, the public lost interest in who was behind the violence. Recalling Geertz's observation on indecisive endings in public affairs, the social memory giving life to the stories of ninja killings could, one imagines, be easily reincarnated.

The figure of reincarnation, which she sees as a series of "ruptures and continuities", was elaborated by Peluso during the UCLA conference in her comments on the chapters by Bakti and Fadjar. The analogy of rebirth can be a framework for perpetuating memory of local heroes like Qahhar, or for Indonesia's national awakening; indeed, the imagined genealogy linking the Majapahit empire and modern Indonesia has been enshrined in the nation's historical memory. Religion and ethnicity are potent zones where constructed identities are reborn through stereotypes: this group is "fanatic", that one "hot-tempered", in the cycle of violence recurring in particular regions.

Peluso's comments parallel interesting observations of cultural historian Ariel Heryanto (2001), who sees a great present danger to Indonesia stemming from the inability to overcome legacies from the past that he calls "identity markers". Heryanto claims that only the intelligentsia accepts the abstraction that ethnicity is socially constructed; in everyday life for most Indonesians ethnicity is deeply internalized — "something fixed for life, naturally endowed, inherent in the blood, and inherited via descent." Thus among Indonesia's Chinese minority, now asserting a newly invigorated ethnic and "native" status, Ariel notes a lack of critical perspective on the New Order's role in actively creating that "Chineseness". He also problematizes the "nation", which Indonesians tend to define as an inheritance of the past rather than as a relatively recent common project still underway, to use Benedict Anderson's formulation. This leads Indonesians to disregard the national aspirations of others — such as the East Timorese, with tragic consequences for the notion of "being Indonesian". The chapters found in Part Three provide a range of possible responses to Reid's question: "Will Indonesian collective memory be reconstructed for a more democratic era ... ?" These essays are grounded in the realization that the end of the Suharto period represents a pivotal point from which to view how national arrangements are being organized and historical memories articulated in the political arena.

Daniel Lev focuses on the absence of experiential assessment of the past among Indonesia's elite. He does not hesitate to define historical memory in pragmatic terms — "the ability to call up political knowledge and to put it to use in thinking about change," arguing that significant knowledge from the years before Soekarno's Guided Democracy "has been either lost, badly distorted, misremembered, or surrounded by a mythology that renders it inaccessible". Dominant historical memory establishes a rupture between Soekarno's Guided Democracy and the New Order, in part because the military controls historical discourse, and prefers not to acknowledge the extent to which it determined political outcomes well before the "September 30th movement" took place. For Lev, reform-minded Indonesians lack a historical memory of the capacities and useful institutions generated during the parliamentary years, which would provide "access to reasonably clear principles and standards once tried on Indonesian ground".

The realization that history has been an arena of manipulation and misrepresentation in the interests of power necessitates admission of new voices and sources of authority by the privileged academic sphere and the state. "Where memory fails or is subverted," says Lev, "knowledge has to be cultivated." The capacity for academic historiography to inscribe memory is explored by Katharine McGregor through the ubiquitous figure of Nugroho Notosusanto, senior New Order historian and major intellectual force whose architecture of national identity enshrined the interests of the military-dominated regime. Is there more to Nugroho's historical projects than a hegemonic devotion that silenced voices of leaders who were out of favour, such as the towering Soekarno, and valorized selected regime-friendly memories? He did perceive a wide-ranging locus situating historical memory in films, museum dioramas, and scripts for school plays (depicting the murder of the generals in 1965). Yet he was also devoted to writing fiction, into which he poured abiding nostalgia for the military career he did not have. It is in his stories that doubts and enigmas appear, the admission that official history may be countered through personal truth. Explaining why he wrote stories,

Nugroho confessed that "I can't use history to express my sympathy for the ordinary people in the viciousness of big events they can't control."

What becomes of history-writing in the wake of Suharto is, clearly, a question dogging many Indonesians. Following the work of Kuntowijoyo, historian Asvi Warman Adam posits a new wave of historiography, after the "decolonization" histories of the early years of independence, and the hegemony of official history under Suharto. The third wave, says Asvi, will bring proliferation of views, as those who were silent begin to make themselves heard and — as McGregor indicates — alternative interpretations counter Nugroho's legacy. The broadening and deepening of these challenges to representation is addressed by Gerry van Klinken, who sees hesitancy among the "custodians of national history" to transform their subject. Outside the discourse under state control, as Diana Wong (2001) has shown in her study of history and public culture in Singapore, lies a realm of memories marginalized in the official politics of forget-fulness. Van Klinken sees new energies emerging in the shape of alternative national histories, populist interpretations, ethno-nationalist accounts from various regions, and local histories that juxtapose specific identities of place alongside national stories. Instead of rigid hierarchies of static "national heroes", he hopes that fluid and competing portraits of a wide variety of actors and forces will play out the Indonesian past on the historical stage.

These trends in current "history-making" are enticing, and also invite some concerns and caveats about recasting the past in the light of major social or political transformation. For instance, one too often hears demands to *meluruskan sejarah,* to straighten out the historical record, so that the truth stands unambiguously for all to see. But, others say, this claim for the existence of a single "truth" or one version of the past leads inevitably back toward the kind of hegemony the New Order long imposed on the discourse of history (Farid 2002). Instead of straightening out history, says author and former political prisoner Hersri Setiawan (2000), we need to democratize it, allowing diverse voices and perspectives to be heard, and enabling personal truth to rest alongside collective remembrance.

There is no doubt that powerful new claims on Indonesian historical memory will bring important challenges in the spirit of *demokratisasi sejarah.* This is evident, for example, in the complex ways that women's history and gender roles are being configured at present. Muslim women are increasingly engaged with the textual inheritance of *fiqih* as a kind of historical discourse. As Lies Marcoes (2001) explained in her presentation at the UCLA seminar, the issue in 1998 of whether or not Megawati, as a woman, should be permitted to become head of state stimulated new women-centred arguments regarding leadership and political participation. Also within the Muslim community, recent declarations of some religious parties that *syariah* law must be applied for all Indonesian Muslims have spurred contestation over piety and pluralism. The alleged spiritual leader of the Jemaah Islamiyah terrorist network in Southeast Asia is an Indonesian, Abu Bakar Basyir, who was once imprisoned under Suharto as a religious extremist. It is not hard to imagine his authority among his followers as a victim silenced by New Order repression. The danger for alternative historiography, therefore, in writing "against" Suharto [and the painful legacies of the New Order] as a project of perceived victims is that this could lead to new kinds of unbalanced memories. Can national histories be written for a new generation of students that will situate, not eliminate, the cross-cutting categories of *pelaku* (perpetrator) as well as *korban* (victim)?

The national dilemmas of addressing history's absences and silences are nowhere more evident than in Aceh. There, the immortalizing of a centre-dominated "Indonesia" in national memory is inflicting serious harm, violating the local memory of an autonomous sultanate that is itself part of Aceh's contribution to that national project. And memory can be bathed in the shifting current of geopolitics; Indonesia's President Megawati and the military can now define their latest hardening actions in Aceh with diminished scrutiny from a United States caught in the narrow logic of its "war on terror".

The fourth and final group of essays in this volume brings together a set of reflections linked by the concept of "sites of memory", showing how narratives of identity and involvement are constructed through the non-verbal physical and symbolic spaces of public monuments and historical photographs; within landscapes of terrorism and tourism; or, as part of official public processes of acknowledgement and validation of personal trauma and suffering. Elaborating on theories of French historian Pierre Nora, Klaus Schreiner shows how the commemoration of the generals killed on 30 September 1965 at Lubang Buaya, the well in Jakarta where their bodies were found, enshrines the New Order's sacred mandate to save the nation from communism. Yet part of the meaning of Lubang Buaya is also history suppressed, says Schreiner — the mass killings that, though unacknowledged at the site, continue to magnetize historical consciousness through the pull of concealed trauma. In arguing that the monument can generate new meanings now that "experiential conditions of interpretation have changed" in Indonesia, Schreiner posits a role for Lubang Buaya in stimulating reconfiguration of public memory and private trauma.

If sites of memory can invoke remembrance, as Schreiner tells us, we actively engage with such sites through "witnessing" both embodied memory and its transformation under new interpretive conditions. We are also engaged with sites of memory through the discourse of media images, with photographs providing immediate framing of both local and global witnessing. In her recent book on photography of war atrocities, Susan Sontag (2003) writes that:

> Photographs that everyone recognizes are now a constituent part of what a society chooses to think about, or declares that it has chosen to think about. It calls these ideas 'memories', and that is, over the long run, a fiction … .What is called collective memory is not a remembering but a stipulating: that *this* is important, and this is the story about how it happened, with the pictures that lock the story in our minds.

In Karen Strassler's chapter, photographic images of *reformasi* recording the key role of student protests in the events of 1998 are sites of personal witnessing, as students at reformasi exhibitions celebrate the open display of tumultuous events in 1998 as validating their own recent memories. Both students and the photographs themselves are *saksi sejarah*, "witnesses to history". Strassler goes on to show how a process of memorializing became an act of forgetting as well, as reformasi images were "incorporated into a mythic history of 'youth struggle'", and thus passed into the narrative largely controlled by state institutions guarding national memory. "As students at reformasi exhibitions fetishized the photographic document as the locus of historical truth, they bypassed important questions about the contexts of image production and consumption and about the extent to which images of 'their own' struggle might be framed within historical narratives not of their own making." Strassler shows how the students' enthusiasm over what they saw as permanent historical documents was a nostalgic engagement that eventually became an "erasure" of their memories of the broader scope of reformasi's original aims.

The production and consumption of images is also a key theme for Degung Santikarma, writing on the representation of mass violence in Bali. He wonders why the experience of the horrific Kuta bombing of October 2002 — images of which were instantly globalized within the international discourse on terrorism — did not also provide the Balinese with a "site of memory", as it were, through which to witness and better understand the violence of the island's 1965 upheaval, when as many as 100,000 people were killed in a purge of "the left" that involved large-scale brutality within villages and families. In Bali, memories of 1965 have long been silenced amid the buildup of a huge tourism industry that situates Bali as a centre of peace "protected" by its own religion and culture, "free from the effects of encounter with historical complexity or conflict". Santikarma argues that local, national, and international interests have inscribed an image of Bali that resists certain memories while extolling others, a proposition that the Sari Club bombing itself seemed to validate: "Bali could be victimized by violence, but its essence remains stable. Bali had become a terrorist target, but terror itself was alien to Balinese."

Santikarma suggests that resolving the legacy of Bali's violent past is not a matter of creating monuments as sites of memory: "What is needed is a space to speak and communicate freely and without fear, and a language that can encompass both those who speak and those who would listen for wisdom." In the final chapter of this section, the issue of remembrance returns to the question of how societies as well as individuals can forge common understanding through processes of acknowledgement and truth-seeking. Paul van Zyl presents existing paradigms for transitional justice as applied in Indonesia, East Timor, and South Africa, pointing out the strengths and weaknesses of a range of comparative experience. The analysis bears some important implications: first, that Indonesia, should it choose to acknowledge its troubled human rights history, will have to craft ways of doing so that fit its own diversity of cultures and legacies of violence, as well as its own discursive systems of expressing the past and assigning accountability. No ready-made model for national truth-seeking can be imported, and no government-scripted "reconciliation" ceremony can mandate a "forgetting" of past wrongs through official fiat. Van Zyl's comments on the ongoing truth-seeking work in independent East Timor further suggest that Indonesia may need to embrace community-based processes of shaping and retrieving historical memory in efforts to resolve numerous and diverse instances of violence. And finally, the lessons from truth-seeking endeavours in other transitional societies show that the past needs to be dealt with in a holistic combination of judicial, social, and commemorative processes.

* * *

In an afterword to Pipit Rochiyat's memoir about witnessing and participating in the 1965 killings in Java, Benedict Anderson (1985) recalls Cifford Geertz's observation regarding the impact on scholarship of troubled historical memory. Geertz had written:

> Since the last terrible months of 1965, all scholars of Indonesia ... are in the uncomfortable position of knowing that a vast internal trauma has shaken their subject, but not knowing, more than vaguely, what its effects have been ... Emotions surface extremely gradually, if extremely powerfully, in Indonesia: 'The crocodile is quick to sink,' they say, 'but slow to come up.' Both writings on Indonesian politics and those politics themselves are permeated right now with the inconfidence derived from waiting for that crocodile to come up.

Although much has changed since Geertz's 1972 characterization, the image is still apt, almost eerily so. The currents of change and contestation that swirl around the archipelago these days have, if anything, shown us that a number of crocodiles remain submerged in Indonesia's waters. There is a powerful interplay of revealing and obscuring what "actually happened" that makes the study of the past a complex challenge. Sometimes the acknowledgement of the past is coded for special audiences; a memorial for Chinese youths killed by the military in Banyuwangi, East Java is found in a quiet corner of a local cemetery. Often the past remains stubbornly negated, as in the historical dioramas found within the massive, ornate stone monument called "Museum Bajrasandi", in Renon, Bali. The monument is intended to show the development of Balinese civilization from Neolithic times to the present; the display illustrating the post-independence period depicts a trajectory of growing prosperity and harmony without a single image to suggest the massive tragedy of violence in 1965. Not infrequently, official commemoration seems to embody inauthentic memory: as this is written, a monument is being newly dedicated in Jakarta in memory of the dead of the May 1998 riots that brought down Suharto. The statue of two men (one ethnic Chinese) holding aloft the national symbol of the Garuda eagle is called *Monumen Persaudaraan* (Brotherhood Monument), and has been widely criticized for its "sad detachment" from the reality that no one has yet been held accountable for the murder, rapes, looting and arson that the government's fact-finding commission concluded were probably masterminded (*Jakarta Post*, 19 May 2004, "May Monument").

In this discussion I have argued that Indonesians are engaging with their various pasts in ways that are both congruent with and distinct from the approaches to historical memory found in other societies experiencing broad transitions. This volume joins a growing number of studies of historical memory, which itself is an emerging discursive genre that needs expansion, shaping, and refining. This is not a book about violence, or about Indonesia's human rights record. The essays collected here are commentaries on the ways that history and memory are conjoined and interacting across a range of fields and cultural expressions. Each author presents a picture of how the Indonesian past exists in the present moment, from his or her own vantage point. Many other images could be explored and captured, for the past is waiting in multitudes of sites of memory, in all its textual, performative, memorialized, and socially embedded richness. Regarding the play of historical memory in Indonesia is like viewing the photographic exhibitions so popular in the wake of Suharto's fall, at which we each gather evidence of our engagement, and we each perform a clarifying act of witness.

Notes

[1]   The 100th anniversary of Soekarno's birth in 2001 was celebrated with ceremonies, memorial conferences, books and extensive press coverage; see, for example, the special editions of *TEMPO* 4–10 June 2001, "Bung Karno"; and *Basis*, Mar.–Apr. 2001, "100 Tahun".

[2]   Two collections covering efforts to study and document New Order violence are *Asian Survey*'s special issue Jul./Aug. 2002, "Legacy of Violence", and Anderson (2001).

[3]   While a number of powerful politicians and officials have been investigated and charged with corruption, only Suharto's crony Muhammad (Bob) Hasan was imprisoned following conviction. Suharto's youngest son, Tommy, was convicted in a land fraud case, then absconded after sentencing; a long manhunt finally led to his arrest and further conviction in 2002 in connection with the murder of the presiding judge in the original trial. He is now in the same island prison of Nusakambangan as Hasan.

4   Parliament enacted a new Human Rights Law in 1999, which was followed by a Human Rights Court law passed in late 2000. Under the second act, police and military figures charged with crimes related to the 1999 violence in East Timor have been tried, but only lower-ranking officers were convicted.

5   Among numerous fact-finding commissions established by Suharto's successors, the Tim Gabungan Pencari Fakta (TGPF, Joint Fact-Finding Team) appointed to look into the violence of May 1998 is noteworthy; see Purdey (2002).

6   See, for instance, Nora (1989: 9): "Memory takes root in the concrete, in spaces, gestures, images and objects; history binds itself strictly to temporal continuities, to progression and to relations between things."

7   On the Rwanda killings, see Gourevitch (1998).

8   When textbooks appeared in 1982 that minimized Japanese atrocities at Nanjing as well as massive forced labour mobilization, demonstrations and protests broke out in Beijing, Taipei, Seoul, Pyongyang, Hong Kong, Hanoi, and Bangkok; Tokyo's governor Shintaro Ishihara and other voices in media, academic circles and politics continue to keep the "revisionist" viewpoint alive. See *International Herald Tribune*, 22–23 Jan. 2000.

9   Geoffrey Robinson, discussant's comments, conference on "History and Memory in Contemporary Indonesia," University of California, Los Angeles, Apr. 2001. I am grateful to Robinson for many thoughtful suggestions during this project.

10   Martin Luther King, Jr., speech to civil rights marchers at Montgomery, Alabama, 21 Mar. 1965.

11   For a chronicle of how war crimes in the 20th century were addressed by the international community, see Neier (1998).

12   See Weschler (1990) for a fascinating description of Brazil's experience.

13   See Hayner's (2001) analysis of the strengths and limitations of each of these elements in actual practice.

14   See discussions in Minow (1998), Columbia University School of International and Public Affairs (1999); and Roht-Arriaza (1995).

15   Communication from Helene van Klinken, 10 July 2003.

16   There has been a host of special commissions assigned to look at specific controversies including East Timor, Aceh, Tanjung Priok, May 1998, and also corruption and the personal wealth of civil servants. Critics point to flawed investigations, equivocation in reports, and a general lack of clear outcomes from these bodies; see Purdey (2002). After a lengthy drafting process over more than three years, a draft bill establishing a "Truth and Reconciliation Commission" (Komisi Kebenaran dan Rekonsiliasi) has now been forwarded to Parliament by President Megawati, and a Special Committee (Pansus) was established to review the legislation in July 2003.

17   As historian Hue-Tam Ho Tai (2001) has written in her introduction to a volume considering the "memory projects" of another Southeast Asian society, Vietnam, "deciding to remember a century's worth of historical change is a matter of grave difficulty for a society."

18   For an assessment of what is known about 1965, and recent efforts to re-examine the "incident", see Cribb (1990) and Zurbuchen (2002).

19   Wahid (or Gus Dur) won the parliamentary vote for President in late 1999, displacing the unpopular B.J. Habibie, who had been Suharto's Vice President. In a vote for impeachment in mid-2001, Wahid was forced out of office, and succeeded by his Vice President, Megawati Soekarnoputri, daughter of the nation's first President. As of this writing, Megawati must contest a presidential poll in mid-2004, following parliamentary elections in April from which her party (PDI-P, Democratic Party of Struggle) emerged significantly weakened.

20   In a recent op-ed commentary, Heryanto linked the persistence of assertions about communism's potential resurgence in Indonesia with the country's stagnant education system (*Kompas*, 7 March 2004, "Komunisme").

21   Budiawan Purwadi (2003) has done important new research on grass-roots reconciliation efforts between Muslims and survivors of the slaughter (in which organizations such as Nahdlatul Ulama's Ansor played a significant role).

22   As one Jakarta acquaintance told me, "It's the same 200 families still controlling everything."

23   The process of reversing regulations stigmatizing people with connections to 1965 events was begun by President Wahid, but administrative changes have been unevenly applied.

24   In a development that could affect many ex-political prisoners from the 1965 period, the State Administrative Court in Jakarta affirmed in July 2003 that normal identity cards valid for life (instead of the temporary or specially marked ones given to ex-prisoners) must be provided for citizens who have not been legally proven to have committed a crime.

25   Two recent publications in Indonesian seek to reach a broad public in presenting experiences of survivors of the 1965 violence and former political prisoners; see Sasongko and Budianta (2003) and Roosa *et al.* (2004).

26   A new collection of studies on wayang genres is found in Mrazek (2002).

27   This account of his professional life originated as an extemporaneous conference presentation in Indonesian, which he later recreated in writing for the translation presented here.

28   Hersri Setiawan (1985) has provided a valuable account.

29   See, for example, the essays in T. Fujitani *et al.* (2001), and in Huen and Wong (2000).

PART ONE

Translator's Note: *My Life as a Shadow Master under Suharto*

The account of Ki Tristuti Rachmadi's professional life given here is based on the author's oral presentation at an academic conference at the University of California, Los Angeles, in April 2001. Ki Tristuti subsequently produced a written version in Indonesian for the present volume, and in so doing has contributed a powerful memoir touching upon major themes of the decades of post-independence Indonesia.

There are many remarkable aspects of his account. Among these are the recollections of life in the detention system under which more than 1,000,000 Indonesians were imprisoned — almost entirely without trial — following the violent events of 1965–6, which had likely claimed between 500,000 and 1,000,000 lives. While personal memoirs of lives of political prisoners are starting to appear — the best known is Pramoedya Ananta Toer's *The Mute's Soliloquy* (1999) — few are available to non-Indonesian readers. The text is also important in its portrayal of experiences of one member of the enormous group of Indonesians who were, and to a varied extent continue to be, stigmatized because of links, direct or indirect, to the former Communist party (PKI) and affiliated organizations prior to 1965. Even after his release from exile and detention on Buru island, it was another 20 years before Ki Tristuti could perform in public without fear.

Most unique is Ki Tristuti's presentation of his career as a *dalang*, or shadow master, in the *wayang* theatre, perhaps the most widely revered of all the archipelago's hundreds of art forms. He wants his audience to understand that being a dalang has provided the arc of his lived experience, and throughout the text he continually relates events to his own artistic growth and consciousness.

In fact, Tristuti Rachmadi at an early age was emerging as one of the most popular and widely acclaimed dalangs in Java. In those times, being commissioned to perform in distant places such as West Java or Lombok was exceptional. He was still in his early 20s in the early 1960s when he was invited to perform for then-President Soekarno, a passionate lover of shadow theatre who liked to bring rising stars to play at the presidential palace in Jakarta and critique their performances. Ki Tristuti recalls having breakfast with Soekarno after the all-night performance and being told that yes, he probably had the makings of a satisfactory dalang. When Soekarno offered rich gifts as payment for the play, Tristuti replied that he only wished for Soekarno's blessing. He was rewarded with this in the form of a new name, Suryosaputro, "Son of the Sun God", which he still uses.

Soekarno was the charismatic anti-colonial leader whose populist, contradiction-filled vision for Indonesia combined nationalism, leftist rhetoric, and religion. Many young artists and intellectuals were inspired to create and write for the revolutionary cause, or for groups opposing Soekarno's increasing authoritarianism. The wayang world was suffused with ideology; the names of the plays, or *lakon*, Ki Tristuti mentions all suggest a political grouping: *Janaka Banteng*, "Janaka The Champion" refers to the Nationalist Party symbol of the buffalo or *banteng; Udawa Waris* could be translated as "Udawa Inherits" or "Udawa Divides the Land", suggesting the land-reform programmes of the Communist Party; and *Wahyu Lintang Rembulan* could refer to an Islamic theme when glossed as "Crescent Star Boon".

Ki Tristuti himself did perform under the rubric of the communist party-linked cultural organization *Lembaga Kebudayaan Rakyat* (Lekra), which was linked to the Communist party, the PKI. Following the attempted or preventive "coup" of the 30 September Movement 1965 — for which the party was blamed — Theodore Friend (2003: 114) has written, "Indonesia went through a political detoxification campaign of savage momentum and sweeping proportions", as leftist sectors in society were eliminated through widespread killings and detentions. During his arrest and imprisonment, Ki Tristuti was told that when Soekarno saw his name on a list of leading cultural figures who were to be "finished off", the President urged that he be spared.

Survival as a former "communist" in post-1965 Indonesia was humiliating and difficult, however, and the hardships Ki Tristuti experienced as he tried to re-establish his livelihood were severe. Not only had he lost his family during the long years in detention, but he was completely unable to perform. Official policy made it illegal for former political prisoners to work in education, the arts, the media, in the public sector, and many other roles. The deep satisfaction of being a dalang in relation to a public, which helped Ki Tristuti survive on Buru, was denied him; it is impossible to miss the irony in his description of being "freed" in 1979. His name remained well-known in artistic circles throughout the following two decades, but few would openly discuss his controversial background. As he describes in this text, and many performers have attested, Ki Tristuti's influence on wayang performance continued to be powerful as he provided story summaries, plot outlines, and descriptive or dialogue passages to many other artists.

In presenting major events of his own life, Ki Tristuti infuses his presentation with verbal art and rhetorical touches familiar from the wayang world. His sense of destiny as one bearing the "soul-stuff" of a dalang is strong, and provides the narrative coherence of the text. He uses humour, irony, and elliptical references so satisfying to wayang watchers, as when he talks of the end of "yellowing everything" that came when the Golkar party, which dominated all politics for more than 30 years with its yellow flags and regalia, suddenly looked powerless after President Suharto's downfall. As his audience, we are moved by his return to the stage, in faltering health, to confront the new performance styles and altered aesthetics that inform shadow theatre at the turn of the new century. His personal enjoyment of the moment of ultimate recognition is unmistakable, even as he warns that Indonesia itself has not fully resolved the deeply embedded conflict that removed him from the public arena for so long.

As this is written, Ki Tristuti continues to perform in Java, and has been commissioned for a number of high-profile appearances in Jakarta and elsewhere, including one performance for a "reunion" of former political prisoners.

My Life as a Shadow Master under Suharto

KI TRISTUTI RACHMADI

Honourable audience and conference participants:

I am Tristuti Rachmadi from Solo, Indonesia. Today is Saturday, 7 April 2001, and I am here at the invitation of the committee for the conference "History and Memory in Contemporary Indonesia", of the Center for Southeast Asian Studies at the University of California, Los Angeles.

I feel happy to have this wonderful opportunity, and wish to extend copious thanks to all who have kindly invited me here, to join in contributing to this conference on the history of Indonesia — on the basis, of course, of my own capacity and experiences.

Honoured listeners:

I was born in a small village called *Sugihmanik* in the area of *Grobogan* district, Central Java, Indonesia, on Wednesday, the 3rd of January 1939. It was no doubt divinely ordained that I be born into a family of shadow theatre artists. My father, the late Suryatman Yososudarso, was a *dalang* in the shadow theatre. My mother was the child of a dalang during the Dutch colonial era. Beginning in my mother's womb, the soul-stuff of a dalang was poured into me. For that reason, even though I did sample some formal education (elementary and secondary, and a two-year mathematics course), my life's journey eventually took me in the direction of the shadow master's world.

I began to perform all-night shows from the age of 15 (in my third year of middle school) in about 1953–4. My career progressed gradually in accord with the times. Essentially, as a professional dalang I have passed through three eras, namely the Old Order, the New Order, and finally the Reform (*Reformasi*) period from about 1998 until today.

As for the world of shadow theatre during the Old Order, I can still recall its simplicity. The dalang still functioned as the sole artist leading the entire eight-hour shadow play performance. At that time there was no influence from cassette recordings or television, not to mention VCDs. Shadow theatre still dominated the tastes of the public, especially on Java. And wayang performances had not yet sharpened into a medium for political propaganda, or religion, or anything else. If they were, it was done in a skillful and pleasing way.

Beginning in the 1960s, the influence of external ideologies started to appear noticeably in the shadow theatre — such as in the stories *Janaka Banteng, Udawa Waris, Wahyu Lintang Rembulan*, among others. This happened because the political climate in Indonesia was heating up. At the end of the Old Order was the 1965 incident, which led to the change to the New Order. I do not wish to talk about matters of politics, so I will just tell the story of my own life, particularly my career as a shadow master.

From 5 November 1965 (a Friday) until 10 October 1979 — 14 years — I lived from one prison to another: Beteng Ambarawa prison, Purwodadi prison, Nusakambangan, and finally discarded to Buru Island. I asked myself: what did I do wrong? What is my sin? It appears there is no other answer: I was a victim of Indonesia's political upheaval. It has always been true that whenever there's an uproar, the little people become the hapless victims. I was just a dalang in the shadow theatre, making a living by means of my skill with wayang stories. I was not a functionary in a political party, I was not a government official, or a big capitalist controlling the gears of the Indonesian economy. Again, Tristuti Rachmadi here is just one of the ordinary people, but at that time I too was caught up in the national tragedy that has wounded the heart for so many years, with never the due process of law and justice. Suddenly arrested, then driven into the pen for 14 years, and no right to ask about any of it, it had to be accepted, full stop.

Honoured listeners:

Yet beyond all of that, I eventually became aware that only through that long and dark journey was I empowered by God to become the one dalang in the world to perform in the midst of suffering, jailed, for many years. I was not hired to play in the ordinary way, but rather was part of the prison itself. Under the government of the Suharto regime I underwent more than enough physical and mental pressure. In prison I (along with thousands of companions who shared my fate) was treated in an extremely inhumane manner. We had only obligations, with no

rights at all. What was provided for food, health, shelter, and other basic
needs was entirely insufficient. We only had sufficient rules — don't do
this, don't do that, this is forbidden, that is forbidden ....

In the year 1968 my beloved wife could no longer stand the pressures
of her life, and I was abandoned to languish in suffering. She and the
children lived with another man, and later went far away out of the
country. Life's bitterness was complete; I had lost everything — wife and
children, possessions, respect, the right to life, and all, all, was forcibly
seized by the regime that ruled in the New Order era.

Honoured listeners:

Thousands of people suffered physically and spiritually inside that
iron cage for 14 years, including myself. Yet I recalled the long-ago advice
of my teacher — a good dalang is one who can bring pleasure to people
in hardship, even though that dalang himself also suffers. If a dalang
performs with fine gamelan instruments, puppets, and sound equipment,
accompanied by accomplished musicians and singers, with a large cash
payment, in a grand performance space, and the dalang plays with spirit
and has success, *there is no special achievement in all of that, it's simply
ordinary!!!* As we say in Javanese, it's *lumrah.*

But if there is a dalang who plays without a single *rupiah* in payment,
with simple instruments, accompanied by so-so musicians and singers,
and the play takes place in an atmosphere of sadness, yet the dalang
fulfills his duties as a performer energetically, responsibly, and is successful
such that those in hardship find joy, and the hopeless gain new spirit,
only then can he be called a TRUE DALANG. Such was the teaching
of my *guru* in the time before I went to prison. A dalang is a dalang.
You can make a living; go ahead and seek public acclaim, but the identity
of a dalang must be clear: namely, he is an artist who serves the public
around him.

Remembering that lesson from my teacher was enough to completely
change my way of thinking at the time. My vengefulness was transformed
into insight. Sad, heartsick and dejected, I changed to become positive and
optimistic. I altered my daydreams about "what if ..." to become a
flaming new energy, in accord with the qualities of my dalang's art. In
the first years, 1965 to 1970, I started to perform in the cells of the
political prisoners without any accompaniment whatsoever. I played in
the style of telling folktales, without *gamelan* or vocal music. This usually
took place after the evening meal, before sleeping, when my friends would

ask me to tell wayang tales. For about an hour I would tell of Bima, Arjuna, Gatotkaca, and so forth. It was just storytelling, and not yet a performance. Once in a while I would spice it up with important dialogue passages, or add humour to lighten the atmosphere, and sometimes I would sing short poems and verse fragments.

During those years my friends had the idea that this storytelling could be accompanied by basic instruments made from eating and bathing implements, such as tin plates, aluminum cups, bowls, pails, and scoops. All of these were tuned to resemble the scale of the gamelan. All of this could look very funny, but for me there was an indelible meaning. I felt proud that amidst such misery I could still entertain my fellow sufferers without any notion of self-interest. Do you suppose that in this world there is another dalang besides myself who has played to the accompaniment of dinner plates? No way!!!

How true are the words of the elders long ago, that if you want to be aided, first give help to others. If you want to be healed, treat your fellows. If you want to have pleasure, entertain your friends. I practiced this advice with positive effects. Despite the many stresses in prison, my heart was gladdened because I often brought joy to my friends. Occasionally the warden would allow me to tell stories using a "hand-speaker", a loudspeaker device, so my voice could be heard in the cells where other prisoners were held. Even the guards listened to my stories. Strange, isn't it, that free men could enjoy listening to the stories of someone oppressed? That is what took place in the years 1965–70.

Honoured listeners:

In August 1970, along with thousands of companions I was moved from Nusakambangan prison and taken on a ship of the Indonesian Navy to be discarded on Buru Island. It had a fancy name — "Buru Island Rehabilitation Installation" — but in practice it was nothing more than a place of exile. In the beginning, I was downhearted to set foot in that place of mangrove swamps and sago marshes. But later on, my optimism fired up again. I carried on with my noble duties as a dalang, entertaining my fellows.

On Buru prisoners could move around more freely because the place was a kind of agricultural project. During our free time, after clearing the brush, digging drainage ditches, and so forth, from about five until six in the evening, we made a sort of gamelan from metal salvaged from insecticide cans, asphalt containers, and so forth. So we had a gamelan ensemble with *slendro* and *pelog* tunings. In the woods there were many wild animals, including deer. We would eat the meat, and the skin was dried to make shadow puppets: those were the deer-hide puppets of Buru Island. Among the 12,500 or so political prisoners, there were some who had experience playing gamelan, and they became our musicians. Since there were no women on hand, the singers were chosen from among the men who had performed *ludruk* theatre in the East Java style, as they could emulate the voice of the *pesinden*. Thus we had a group, with a dalang, musicians, singers, a shadow theatre gamelan, uniquely found in exile on Buru. What about our costumes, then? Well, we made do. We borrowed from some buddies who had brought a piece or two of *batik* cloth, albeit faded, a *surjan* jacket, and a head-scarf. Hilarious, right? No!! It was touching.

And what about my spirit? It never faded!! I always performed with enthusiasm, and all the friends responded to my spirit. They watched, fascinated, from beginning to end, as scene by scene they enjoyed the show without moving from where they sat. Where were the commander and his guards? They were watching, too. And if the senior officer happened to be a Javanese, then I was commanded to perform even more often. Incredible, right? A man who is suffering is ordered to entertain a free man.

That is a quick overview of how I carried out professional obligations as a dalang while in exile under the New Order. I was there[1] from 1970 until October 1979; in the evenings I performed, and during the day I still had to labour — hoeing, harvesting, guarding the water, carrying building materials, etc. It was truly bitter, like swallowing a quinine pill, but whether I wanted or not I had to walk those dark paths until 1979.

Esteemed audience:

On October 10, 1979 I was expelled from the hell of Buru Island, and "freed". I decided to return to Semarang to be with family, because there was nothing left for me in my native place, Purwodadi. From Semarang I sought a livelihood in Yogyakarta, then in Pati, and finally in the city of Solo. Although the word used was "freed", that was merely a political expression. I still had no right to live like other citizens. I was not allowed to perform, and to get work anywhere one had to have a letter showing one was "clean", which was not possible for me to obtain. Meanwhile even my Identity Card (KTP) was given the symbol ET, meaning ex-prisoner. My life from 1979 to 1999, exactly

20 years, was like someone suffering from leprosy, a communicable disease for which there is no treatment, and from which all distance themselves. Suharto was amazing; officially he was full of humanitarian feeling, so that prisoners became "freed". But in practice this was no more than a slow kind of murder. Really extraordinary!! To whom could I complain about this injustice? Before being freed on Buru, I and all the other political prisoners were ordered to sign a DECLARATION stating our WILLINGNESS not to bring formal complaints or charges about any matter concerning our imprisonment. Thus I was like a speechless person who has eaten a jimson fruit — so very bitter its taste, making one unable to utter a single word. That's how it was for me and my companions at that time.

Esteemed audience:

To get back to the soul of the dalang: for 20 years I had to struggle to stay alive, seeking an income here and there amidst great difficulty. Yet in the midst of that shadowed journey, my dalang's soul still burned bright. It did not dull, but became sharper still. I didn't pine, but filled each moment with positive activity, and among other things, I wrote. I wrote Javanese literature, specifically texts for the shadow theatre. God blessed me in this. My writings were popular and were purchased by professional dalangs. I wrote short shadow plays, semi-complete ones, and elaborate ones. I also wrote *Janturan, Silsilah, Bantah, Tembang, Banyolan*[2], and so forth. These were of interest and were used and read by well-known dalangs such as Ki Anom Suroto, Ki Manteb Sudarsono, Ki Purbo Asmoro — in short, almost all the dalangs in the Solo region used my creations. The prices for the scripts varied; some sold for Rp. 25,000, others for Rp. 50,000, and for very complete scripts I was paid Rp. 500,000. Even though those prices were actually very cheap when compared with some of their performance fees in the millions of rupiah, for a person afflicted with misfortune such as myself, all that could be said was "thank you". I felt fortunate to be able to earn money for daily meals. Odd, isn't it?

In addition to writing, I would sometimes go along with the troupes of popular performers as the dalang's personal assistant (*penyimping*). For each performance I was paid Rp. 50,000 — not bad ... for buying a bit of kitchen salt. It's just unfortunate that none of my written works mentioned the name of the writer, and as time passed more dalangs copied from other dalangs without my knowledge, so that I was never paid even a cent. Well, it makes no difference, figure it as an investment in good deeds. Once in a while I happened to perform myself during that period, but the risks were great indeed. After performances, many anonymous letters arrived filled with threats and insults. I was also often summoned by the government and rewarded with groundless hostility. Funny, isn't it? They get angry with a person who brings enjoyment to the public. Such is their power!!

But the most important thing was that my dalang's spirit was not extinguished, it still burned. Both in practicing the dalang's art before the screen, and in my writing, I have always been a true dalang. Many students at the Advanced School of Indonesian Arts in Solo (STSI) drew their knowledge of shadow puppetry from me. Many of the advanced students from the shadow theatre department sought me out. This meant that from 1979 to 1999 my mind was always filled with the particulars of shadow theatre. Not too bad!!

Esteemed listeners:

In May 1998 came the moment the Suharto regime collapsed, to be followed by the Reform era. The period of "yellowing" everything ended, and the fangs of the New Order were pushed aside by the student movement progressing toward democracy. The hinges of daily life seemed to begin moving a little more freely, even though here and there the remnants of the New Order were still perceptible. With this new wind of Reform, I began to go out and appear on the shadow theatre stage, though I wasn't as popular as other dalangs right away. In the Solo area I performed without an "Artist's License" from the national education department, and there was no problem. But in Pati district, in Grobogan, and a few other districts I needed to have the license to complete the permit requirements for the police (this was actually an old regulation from the Suharto era). Only in December 2000 did I successfully obtain the Artist's License. I started performing from step one, hired by my relatives (without payment), later on in the venues of fellow dalangs (at Anom Suroto's on the day *Rebo Legen*[3], at Manteb's on *Selasa Wegen,* Warseno Slenk's on *Setu Legen,* etc.). Of course this involved a modest fee. Eventually I began performing in government venues, including the campus of STSI and the Central Java Cultural Center in Solo, for a reasonable honorarium.

It's regrettable that when I finally came back to the shadow theatre performance arena I was so old — 62 years — that my physical stamina was not up to par. I was short of breath, so that my voice was no longer melodious, with a slack body that could not manipulate the puppets well. In addition, times had changed: the world of shadow theatre has recently become quite different from what it was in my youth. The shadow theatre left by the New Order is far removed from its former venerable quality. Wayang performances now are brightened up with *campur sari,* meaning other kinds of music mixed with gamelan, with pop singers and comedians who are allowed to stand up, dancing on the stage. Wayang stories are overwhelmed by the audience request numbers, by comedy and dance, so that the plot line is obscured or disappears altogether. I don't have it in me to perform in that way, but what can one say if that's what has happened? I ask myself: Why is it only now that I have the chance to perform, and not yesterday, or 20 years ago? Well, that's over; it doesn't matter, as long as I hold fast to my identity as a true dalang.

Esteemed audience:

With a sincere heart I offer many thanks to the colleagues in the United States (specifically at UCLA, UC Berkeley, UC Santa Cruz, Wesleyan University, Brown University and also in New York) who have invited me to perform here during this month of April 2001. This is truly medicine for a heartache that has gone unhealed for the past 35 years. At the same time, this shows the world — especially the shadow theatre community — that a dried-up leaf considered useless can nonetheless be sought after here in the United States. And because I have the blood and soul of the dalang, it's no surprise that my train of thought is often shaped by wayang philosophy, which talks about the law of *karma*, or the results of past actions. As you sow, so shall you reap. For those who have sown the 35 years of my suffering, sooner or later even they will reap their own harvest of pain. Moreover, from planting a single corn kernel, you can reap a hundred seeds. That is why I believe that until that harvest is collected, calm will not be restored in Indonesia.

Honoured listeners:

This story of mine is just a small portion of all that actually happened. May it benefit efforts to establish truth and justice for all. For all my errors and deficiencies, I humbly beg your forgiveness. Thank you.

TRISTUTI RACHMADI SURYOSAPUTRO

Notes

[1]   In the detention camps on Buru island in Indonesia's Maluku Province.
[2]   Descriptive narration, genealogy, debate, sung poetry, clowning.
[3]   Days cited are named according to the five-day week of the Javanese market calendar, combined with the seven-day week.

Kali: A Libretto

GOENAWAN MOHAMAD

I was barely six years old when I learned that my father died with three bullets in his head. I did not see the body. My sisters prevented me, the youngest, from seeing the gruesome sight, but stories filtered in through the mouth of our terrified housemaid. That was my first encounter with the violence of Indonesian modern history.

In mid-1947, the Dutch troops who entered our town came to arrest Father, and about five days later Mother was told that they executed him. A firing squad took his life on a soccer field near the military barracks, after five days of interrogation.

Mother sent my eldest brother-in-law to bring the body home. Off he went, on a horse cart to a place I never knew; it could have been the Dutch garrison's post, or the town's hospital, or the soccer field. The rest of the family stayed at home, waiting.

Gloom and dread shrouded our house like a foul dusk; almost everyone was in tears, not quite believing that we would see Father come home dead, and wondering how he would look and how much pain he endured after the shooting.

At 5:00 p.m. my brother-in-law returned. It took four solid hours for him to collect the body and carry it in the hired horse cart back to the family house. In the evening, after a hurried funeral, I saw him still in a state of shock. Even as a child I understood his pain. He was the first to see the three open wounds in my father's head and touch the smelly half-dried blood on his face. I remember seeing Mother, weeping silently, embrace him.

Somehow she, a strong woman who joined Father during his exile in West Papua in the late 1920s, managed to preside over the mourning in a dignified manner. Years later she told me that she knew the killing would take place; a couple of nights before the arrest, she said, Father told her about his strange dream. In the dream an old man kindly offered him three *nangka* fruits, with the seeds that look like bullets, and he took them all, gladly. They tasted wonderful. "Your father knew

47

that his death was imminent," she told me. "Three bullets would send him to eternity."

Father was never a national hero; he was just one of those political activists who went to prison several times, was exiled in a distant detention camp, and believed in something that gradually became a kind of faith, with a tint of sentimentality: the readiness to give one's life to an idea they called "Indonesia". Almost every town in Indonesia has a solemnly built graveyard for men and women of similar zeal — people who believed that to kill or to be killed was part of the revolutionary rite towards freedom.

It was the time when violence was part of a greater design and justice made unpleasant but precise symmetry.

After 1965, the symmetry, with its hidden script of redemption, has become twisted. On the first day of October 1965, six Army generals and one young officer were kidnapped, shot, and thrown into a narrow well several kilometres away from Jakarta.

The remaining military top brass accused the communists of being behind the assassination. Since early 1960s, the political tension between the communists and other political groups was such that in no time a terrifying wave of blood and destruction followed. Thousands were massacred, jailed, tortured, and labelled as "godless communists" who perpetrated the 1965 "coup". Even President Soekarno, with all his charisma and influence, could not prevent the horror. Through a systematic media campaign, the victims were portrayed for eternity as the evil element of Indonesian history.

What historical or divine design can make such large-scale brutality legitimate? In my father's days, the executed, the exiled, and the jailed ones were parts of the Republic's narrative of rebirth. After 1965, the murdered and the prosecuted were thrown into the abyss. After 1965, memory is both the origin and the continuation of violence.

Growing up in Central Java, I learned that there is a variation of the theme in the Mahabharata stories: justice has a violent shape. As the *dalang* in the Javanese shadow puppet theatre masterfully describes it, the ferocious war between the Pandawas and the Kurawas, their kin, is more about remembering the loss of the Hastina kingdom than about a future happiness. At the end, the Pandawas, who believed they were wickedly tricked in a game of dice by the Kurawas and lost the throne to them, destroyed them 12 years later, in the great battle at Kurusetra. The tragic side of the story, however, is its subtext of futility: members of the Pandawas' second generation were all killed. Victory has its own melancholy, but in this case it has a gloomier face: the Mahabharata is ultimately a political history without promise.

And yet in the dalang's narration the violence is glorified endlessly — by banishing the Kurawas to the abyss. And when the morning comes, and the all night performance ends, the rest is silence. Despite my enthusiasm for wayang as a theatrical form, I found it was disappointing that no dalang would allow the Kurawas a return to a different story.

And this was precisely how the post-1965 regime under Suharto used the wayang story to explain the 1965 violence. It portrayed the communists as the vanquished Kurawas. No one asked how the communists would perceive the allusion, after seeing the murder of their leaders and their comrades, the destruction of their party, and the failed attempt to fight back, and later, the debacle of the ideals they stood for, often courageously.

It was their absence from the discourse that is disturbing. It inevitably led to further killings, imprisonment, torture, and kidnapping, which is the ugly side of the 30 years of Suharto's New Order. It became increasingly clear that in this history of atrocity, silence produces legitimacy. Unfortunately, when free and dissenting expression is muzzled, we can hardly hear the victim scream.

I had to deal with this problem when I was the editor of *TEMPO*, before the weekly was banned for the second time in 1994. One incident that kept haunting me was when three young men came to my office bringing the pictures of their dead father after he was tortured by a local military garrison in Senen Raya, Jakarta in the early 1980s. The wounds and the bruises on the poor old Chinese man's body were terrifying to look at, even in the pictures. The kids wanted me to write about the brutality, with an implied sense of protest. But I did not dare to do it. I feared my office would be physically attacked and the magazine banned. My sense of guilt stays with me until today.

It was around the time of this incident that I started to think about the way to confront seriously the problem of fear and forced silence. It happened that in 1995, Kent Deveraux, Jarrad Powell, and Tony Prabowo asked me to join them in a collaborative work to produce a contemporary opera. I felt honoured, and it was not difficult to agree since several of my poems had been put to music by Tony Prabowo, whose work impresses me. When I met Jarrad Powell in Seattle, where he taught at the Cornish School of Music, he gave me a short, beautiful Indian poem about the genesis of Kali, or Death, that began with the yawning of Brahma. We agreed to use the poem as the basis of the story.

Actually, I have never liked operas. I saw several performances in Sydney and New York, and each time I fell asleep. But I knew that it was about time I should write a kind of wayang play in a different form and from an entirely different angle — to recognize that even the Kurawas, in their destruction, speak.

Since I had neither skill nor desire to write a story, the result was a series of short and long poems, starting with the only dramatic scene I could imagine from the Mahabharata, when Destarasta, the old father of the Kurawas, the man who should have reigned over Hastina but was deprived of his throne because he was born blind, stands in his empty palace, waiting. Gandari, who blindfolds herself, sits next to him. No dead body of their sons and their kin is brought home from the carnage in Kurusetra, but reports of death and loss come one by one, almost every hour. The only companion they have is Sanjaya, the man who is endowed by the gods with the power to see the brutal battlefield miles away.

In this version, there is no real story line. There is not even a central figure — not even Kali, the reluctant goddess of death, who tries but fails to refute the eternal gaze of the gods that puts the singular and ephemeral human existence into the iron box of destiny. There is not even a consistent focal point: the poem or poems slip from the words of the blind king and the blindfolded queen into a different narrative of butchery. Words and images flow into the libretto from what people told me about 1965 in Java and Bali — or even from what I read about the Cultural Revolution in China and about the more recent incidents like the grisly images of the killings of "witches" in East Java and the clashes between the Dayaks and the Madurese in Kalimantan. There is a verbatim quote from reportage filed by Richard Lloyd Parry for *The Independent* of how the Dayaks treated the butchered Madurese; the power of the description is such that it resists being transformed into poetry or any other form. It occurred to me that myths, poems, and journalism had to lean on each other in dealing with hatred and cruelty of such intensity.

This is especially true because language shaped by Indonesia's painful experience has a quite untidy past. For this reason, I do not think I am capable of writing an explanatory piece about *Kali*. I am compelled to recognize the darker side of communication, which, to me, is inevitable when you are in a state of shock — like when my brother-in-law saw and touched the gaping wounds on my father's head.

* * *

KALI[1]

SCENE 1 – Prologue

CHARACTERS: CHORUS.

First, there is a hall, and inside the hall, a chessboard of alien knights, four-footed rooks. A blindfolded woman, the Queen on a wheelchair, listening to the slow-paced steps of pawns, of the groping King, blind, walking into the room, a silhouette on a shaking screen. First there is a hall, and no luster, and a pair of thrones.

CHORUS: The Queen loves the shape of imaginary beings, and a feel of dusk.
The King is thinking of twilight's birds.
You hear them all, gurgling calls of fowls, evening geckoes, dull-sounded lizards, gnats darting to the darker side of the yard.

Somewhere something must live and breathe, somewhere, something.

You hear herons gliding over the mix of the roar and moan of war, crows calling from the green, dogs' howls in a remote ravine.

***

SCENE 2 – Gandari & Destarasta

CHARACTERS: GANDARI, DESTARASTA.

DESTARASTA: I smell the stink of spleen, leftovers from last night's offering.

GANDARI: But I know of no offering last night.

DESTARASTA: You are right, Gandari, but I smell it.

He is 66, and she 53. It is the ninth day of their solitude. It is the tenth day. It is the eleventh day of their solitude. He remains seated next to her, rubbing the slate cover of the seat. The breeze, filtered by the door, soothes the room as they try to listen to the uncertainty of the open porch.

DESTARASTA: They say the war has dispersed the stars into the dark.

GANDARI: Like exiles, weightless.

DESTARASTA: Aimless.

GANDARI: Like exiles, but bright.

DESTARASTA: Because of the night, Gandari.

GANDARI: Because of the night, your Majesty.
Like exiles.

[JAVANESE][2]

Lir lintang binuwang	Like a star falling
Mring langit lir luweng	Deep into the sky
Panjer padhang	Toward light bright
Ing pusering peteng.	In the belly of night.

* * *

SCENE 3 – The Eleventh Day

CHARACTERS: GANDARI, DESTARASTA & MESSENGER.

CHORUS: The blind hear the drone of midges, the churning of the leaves and the daybreak.

The dawn sees a monsoon-stained sky, tense shrieks of swans, a man on a bloodstained horse.

You hear herons gliding over the mix of the roar and moan of war, crows calling from the green, dogs' howls in a remote ravine.

DESTARASTA: I hear the swan's shrieking.

A limping man walks through the gate.

MESSENGER: Destarasta, my lord.

DESTARASTA: Gandari, it's the messenger.

The Queen stands from her wheelchair, as if to honor something she knows in the space of her recurring dream, before she says ...

GANDARI: Please say no word, Destarasta.

The King's grief is invisible.

GANDARI:

[JAVANESE]

Sinamuna dukha sinamuna	Hidden sorrow hidden
Paduka, satrya	You, warrior
Jumenenga.	Enthroned.

The King shivers and they listen.

Jagad, dewa, bathara	World, god, deity
Nampik paduka,	Shunned you
Winalesa tinampik	Avenged, shunned
Ing lelimengan,	Into the darkness
Lir muksa.	The void, vanished.

Siluning socaning dilah,	Eye blinded bright
Suryaning surya	Sun within sun
Ajrih ing saktining sumpah	Trembling before the awesome oath
Taberining tapa.	Diligent in denial.

DESTARASTA: Be brief, young man.

MESSENGER: Your uncle, the great Bhisma …
He died slowly at dusk. They killed him.

*Now the light, shifting, casts different shades to the floor as the messenger
disappears and the blindfolded Queen points her finger to the soundless
door. Then the King touches her other hand and says …*

DESTARASTA:

Bhisma of seventy screams
Bhisma of a hundred wounds
Bhisma of a thousand dead
Bhisma

And he says no more.

* * *

SCENE 4 – The Twelfth Day

CHARACTERS: GANDARI, DESTARASTA, MESSENGER & KALI.

*It is morning. The dawn sees a monsoon-stained sky, tense shrieks of
swans, a man on a bloodstained horse, a shout.*

MESSENGER: This is the twelfth day, my Lord.
Last night they cut down Dursasana,
Your son fell and the earth was damp.
A man came to the fight and slashed him.
He ripped his belly open.
Snatched his heart out.
Sucked his gore.
I saw a woman washing her hair
In his blood.

GANDARI:

[JAVANESE]

Duh, paduka,	Oh, your majesty
Sidheming ndalu	Mysterious as night
Kinganingaya dewa,	Misery of the gods,
Kinganingaya.	Misery.

DESTARASTA: And they'll kill Durna.
And they'll kill Karna.
And they'll kill Salya.

GANDARI:

[JAVANESE]

Sinamuna dukha sinamuna	Hidden sorrow hidden
Paduka, satrya	You, warrior
Jumenenga.	Enthroned.

Somewhere, they say,
You can sense the earth plates twitching.
You can see no wound but pus purling like flowing lava.
Somewhere, they say, self-exiled hills burst
And spurts of black blacken all plumes and petals.
Nightjars flee.
They say the birds plunge themselves into a shattered cliff.
No one believes it.

But somewhere something must live and breathe.
Or it may be the thick, toneless rain.

Chorus: The room is like a mouth opening its jaws that speak no word.

The thrones, the blind King, the blindfolded Queen, and the two warriors who walk in like two signs cut from the gloom in a half-finished afternoon, two worn-out warriors who stare at lines of light slipping in through the clefts of the tiles.

DESTARASTA: Did they get Durna?

MESSENGER: Yes, my Lord.

DESTARASTA: Did they get Karna?

MESSENGER: Yes, my Lord.

DESTARASTA: Did they get Salya?

MESSENGER: Yes, my Lord.
Men fell like half-cut mantises,
And the lake shriveled.

After silence.

CHORUS: Listen. Someone had to let the light pour down on the lake. But the gods said no. They would never leave the demons defiled by the daybreak, even if they knew that someday the dark would be banished by their repeated words, and they would have nothing else. Nothing else ...

GANDARI: They murdered all my sons.

KALI: I am the mother of your sorrow.
I am the sister of your grief.

GANDARI: You murdered all my sons.

KALI: You want this to end
And I will give you a door that opens on an unsuspecting sea,
Blue as in a child's dream.
You want a sun remembered before dusk
And I will give you a city with angels and torches.
But Brahma created me from his yawn.
"Go and become Death," he said,
"For the earth needs a cycle."
Willows wane, streams spent, laughter silenced.

I know he wants the grace gone, just before the burst.
It is his story of boredom.

GANDARI: But they murdered my sons.

KALI: I am the mother of your sorrow.

GANDARI:

[JAVANESE]

Duh, Suyudhana, lesah langit	Oh, Suyudhana, flattened sky
Bawana alum	Withered earth
Ing rangkahing para dewa	Heavenly prison
Janma wasana.	Life's end.

The Kurawas are all gone.

KALI: You close your eyes.
You refuse to see it.
It is gods' madness.
Come here.
I like the sight of a bird on a pale tree
With an acrid crumb on its mouth.
I like the smell of half-burnt dung,
The enigma of unfinished things.

GANDARI: They murdered my sons.

* * *

SCENE 5 – Kali and Brahma

CHARACTERS: KALI, BRAHMA & GANDARI.

*Outside the hall of gods, Brahma created Death. Kali would wave her
purple hands, he said, and things would be all right. Inside the hall, the
assembly said nothing. Later someone saw Death hopping from a slow-
moving moon, dancing with a headless corpse. It was Kali's first dance.*

KALI: Willows wane, streams spent, laughter silenced.
The grace was gone.
On certain nights,
Gods create their own texts,
Long ones, like yards of cemetery plots.
And they invite Death,
And they make the day start
With no one repelling the rain.

BRAHMA: I remember you were in Dhenuka
Standing on one foot
For fifteen million years,
Surrounded by people
You should have slaughtered.

KALI: I was in Dhenuka.
And I cried.
I was in Mount Meru.
And I cried.

BRAHMA: But you are Death, my child, you are Mertyu.

KALI: So I am Death.
And you give me no mirror.
I look at myself on the bronze of the night,
On the silver of the dawn.
My eyes are wet with tears
That fall on the open wounds of the dying.
You said,
"Your tears will gouge ulcers in the bodies you must kill."

BRAHMA: But you are Death, my child, you are Mertyu.

KALI: So I am Death. I am Mertyu.
I like the sight of a bird on a pale tree,
With an acrid crumb on its mouth.
I like the smell of half-burnt dung,
The enigma of unfinished things.

I gave my breasts to the foul-skinned shepherd of the North.
I lost my home.
I lost my name.

They saw me lounging on the warm ash of a pyre,
Clutching the burnt skull of a woman, screaming.

I was in Dhenuka
And I cried.
I was in Mount Meru
And I cried.
My eyes are wet with tears
That fall on the open wounds of the dying.

GANDARI: [Javanese *suluk*: *sendhon tlutur*][3]

Surem-surem diwangkara kingkin,
lir manguswa kang layon, o
dennya ilang memanise,
wadananira layu
kumel kucem rahnya maratani, o!
e marang saliranipun,
meles dening ludira kawangwang,
nggana bang sumirat, o!

The sun is gloomy with sadness,
As if it were burying a corpse,
Its face is pale
And its pallid blood staining
The body all over,
It is sad at the sight of its blood,
The sky is alight with red.

* * *

SCENE 6 – Gara Gara

CHARACTERS: CHORUS.

The testimony begins with a noise of footsteps. You see a listless body of lights. Six men walk from the battlefield of Kurusetra, coming out from the fog, each holding a spiked head.

A dove-like bird flies in the sky. They say the sky is heavy. A huge pair of unidentified wings strains the clouds. A woman moves from an unlighted corner, in a silent swirl, her long, dirt-stained white cloth endlessly unfolding, as if somebody is stripping her, forever, futilely.

CHORUS: No thing existed, nor did nothing exist,
There was no air-filled space, no sky beyond.

Who held it all? And where? And who secured it?
Was water all there was, deep?

There was neither death nor immortality then.
There was no sign of night, nor of day.
Where no wind blew, one Being breathed
Other than it, no thing was there.

Darkness was hidden by darkness in the beginning
An endless ocean
Featureless, unlit.

But now the Sun extends his arms
The rose-colored dawn clouds
Imprison darkness.

Was there below? Was there above?
Who really knows? Who will here proclaim it?

[INDONESIAN]

Semula tak ada ada, juga tak ada
Semula tak ada ruang, juga langit lempang
Siapa menahan semua? Di mana pula? Siapa menguncinya?

Semula tak ada mati, tak ada abadi.
Semula tak ada tanda malam atau sianghari.
Di mana angin timpas, Wujud pun bernafas.
Selebihnya, tak ada apa-apa.

Kini matahari merentang tangan: awan fajar
Memenjarakan malam.

Adakah air di sana,
Sedalam alir?

Gelap sembunyi oleh gelap pada mulanya — laut semata
Tak bercorak, tak bercahaya.

Adakah bawah di sana, adakah atas di sana?
Siapa gerangan tahu? Siapa akan mengucapkan itu?

* * *

SCENE 7 – Balarama & Draupadi

CHARACTERS: BALARAMA & DRAUPADI.

BALARAMA: Who are you?

Somebody shouts: "They call her DRAUPADI."

DRAUPADI: My husband the King
He staked everything
To the Kurawas in a cruel game of dice.

BALARAMA: My queen —

DRAUPADI: My husband the King staked his lands and his wife but knew nothing of the way of cheats and gamblers. He lost everything.

BALARAMA: My queen,
Now I remember what happened to you, in the hall of the princes.

DRAUPADI: My husband the King did nothing.
Just before midnight Prince Dursasana came to fetch me, shouting,
"Come, woman, you have been won!"
And I refused.

BALARAMA: Yes, you refused.

DRAUPADI: But he grabbed my hair,
And dragged me into the hall of the dice, and undressed me.

BALARAMA: And the Kurawas watched.

DRAUPADI: He raped me.

BALARAMA: And the Kurawas watched.

DRAUPADI: All the old and dignified men in the assembly knew everything.
They spoke nothing.

BALARAMA: Nothing.

DRAUPADI: It was at dawn
when I smelled the stench of foul sperm all over my body.
And I knew that there would be a war,
There should be a war,
For the gods always wanted it.

BALARAMA: You know, they like the truth,
A violent kind of symmetry.

DRAUPADI: Yes, they like truth.

BALARAMA: They were the ones who brought in the flood
And praised the purge
And shouted, "locusts"
After a dream of purity,
And plagued the city
With flies and frogs,
And the death of the firstborn,
And the pain of dogs.

Yes, they like the truth.

CHORUS: There was neither death nor immortality then.
There was no sign of night, nor of day.

[INDONESIAN]

Semula tak ada mati, tak ada abadi.
Semula tak ada tanda malam atau sianghari.

DRAUPADI: Should I weep?
Should you weep?

BALARAMA: Maybe you won't. Tomorrow you'll stretch your hands
And sing, and you'll see the dust change.

* * *

SCENE 8 – Reports

CHARACTERS: BALARAMA, DRAUPADI, CHORUS & WITNESSES.

And they see the six men who walk to the center stage, coming from the battlefield of Kurusetra, stepping out of the fog, each holding a spiked head.

REPORT[4] : I saw a couple of blood-stained heads on Tuesday afternoon in a village an hour's drive from the town. They were visible from a few hundred yards away, standing on oil drums on either side of the road. The heads had been taken just a few hours before, and they looked ... they looked like all the other heads I had seen.

They were a middle-aged couple, a few years younger than my own parents. Their ears and lips had been shaved off with machetes, giving them a snarling, sub-human look. The wife's nose had also been removed, and a cigarette had been pressed into the cavity. Her eyes were clenched tight shut, and above them an atrocious wound had been cut deep into her forehead.

CHORUS:

[INDONESIAN]

Pada kutil daun-daun,
Pada atom putih embun
Pada buih laut pagi
Sesuatu lahir-kemudian kembali

Pada bata rumah tua
Pada genting kaca yang mengejutkan kita
Pada kusen-kusen yang luka
Aku tahu ia tak lagi di sana.

In blistered leaves,
Pale atoms of dew
In the ocean foam of dawn
Something born, then gone

In the bricks of an ancient house
In startling mirror-truth
In wounded window panes
I see they are no more.

BALARAMA: Someone will always do what the gods want us to do.
I remember rodents swarming all of a sudden
From unknown holes, just before the war.

DRAUPADI: I remember that too.

BALARAMA: I thought the war had erased everything.

DRAUPADI: No. The war hasn't.
I've seen the sun sitting, colorless,
On the edge of ponderous ruins
Mute, careless. I laughed. They say it's the end.
I don't know.

But who are you?

BALARAMA: I am Balarama.
I know the Pandawas.
I know the Kurawas.
But the gods do not know me.

DRAUPADI: The gods only celebrate the truth.

BALARAMA: I am afraid they do.
They like you.
You are one of the Pandawas.

DRAUPADI: The gods celebrate me and
My fury, my dark-crossed face,
My pallid shape.

The gods celebrate me
After a night of rape.

REPORT: On December 13, 1965, they arrested a man from Uluwatu. They cut his head, they cut his legs, they cut his hands and they hanged them on a tree next to the zoo. And people came to see, some loved to see, his dead eyes stayed open, the iris avoiding the sky, and the wounds darkened by the city's dust, by the city's flies. I saw a cloud of flies making black marks on the skull's dried blood, like black signs of sin, like black signs.

BALARAMA: I thought the war had erased everything.

DRAUPADI: No. The war hasn't.
Look. They carry Kurawa heads.
I washed my hair in the rapist's blood,
And the wave and the wind went down, behind me,
Like a surge of cheers.

BALARAMA: Maybe you are Memory.

DRAUPADI: Maybe I am just a footprint
on buried stairs
of yesterday.

REPORT: On May 13, 1998, they took somebody else and stabbed him.
They cut his liver into small pieces, and ate them in a party of revenge.

Come, come, come, they say.

On May 14th, they dragged his widow to the bush
And forced her to kneel under the tree,
To look at her husband's head, to weep.

They asked her, do you recognize him,
And she said, "yes,"
And they asked her, was he evil,
And she said, "yes."

* * *

SCENE 9 – Krishna

CHARACTERS: KRISHNA, KALI, BALARAMA, CHORUS, &
A VOICE.

*On a huge wheel in the sky, Krishna walks, and in the marketplace of
Bedahulu, people see him and kiss the ground.*

KRISHNA: In the beginning was light
Of a thumbnail moon
And the words became lines
And darkness began to drawl.

CHORUS:

[INDONESIAN]

Pada mulanya adalah cahaya
Sejak bulan sekuku kaki
Dan kata pun menjadi baris
Dan gelap gagap.

KRISHNA: Look.
This is a theatre of clarity
And the world resists no more.
Let the weight of our dream fall
Into the dawn.

A VOICE: Too much light.
Too much liquid light.

KRISHNA: But this is the morning of the gods
And of the obelisk.
This is the morning when we carve the first cipher,
Driven into a mass of stone, like an ancient blade,
And I say, "So the earth shivers, and the law is born."

A VOICE: I hear the sound.
Someone says it's like the voice of dying.

KRISHNA: Yes, it is.
But don't be afraid,
Don't grieve,
Don't hope.

A VOICE: I don't want to hope.
I have my tightened throat.
I listen to subterranean growls.
I walk. We weep. We believe in death.
I think of a damp kingdom, of sullen days of ash.

And yet we whistle.
And yet we grow, and fly like good-for-nothing birds, groping for the
road.

We find the trek of lost dogs, and we hate.
You always say to kill is to begin.
I think I know why.

KRISHNA: Don't be afraid,
Don't grieve,
Don't hope.

*The crowd surges to stop a woman, probably she is Kali, who comes from
the desert. Krishna disappears from the sky.*

KALI: Now you see the white color of truth
And of death.

BALARAMA: I see the purity of hate.

KALI: The authenticity of space.

BALARAMA: The blindness of time.

KALI: O, Lord, bring in the flood,
Praise the purge,
Shout, "locusts"
And plague the city
With flies and frogs,
And the death of the firstborn,
And the pain of dogs.

The crowd disperses. On the huge wheel in the sky, Krishna returns. Below, someone sits on a straw mat, reading, "Now the earth sits on its own stillness. The sky becomes strong. The landscape is as level as a flat roof."

***

SCENE 10 – The Funeral Pyre

CHARACTERS: KALI, DESTARASTA, GANDARI, & CHORUS.

CHORUS: Now and then the end begins with trees,
Shrouded line-ups of trees.

The blindfolded queen sits still,
Gathering the patience of the forest.

It is infinity.

Even the hermits who walk with the King
Into his shelter
Know that it's the rain
That grasps the distance.

The distance is green.
No one gives it a name.

DESTARASTA: This is the place.
I can even hear
The drone of insects
And the daybreak.

CHORUS: Yes, this is the place, the space,
To entomb the blind king's time.

And yet tree barks open their pores
And gas passes through:
Life's first cue.

GANDARI: This is the place.
The air grips you.
The sacred warns you
And tells you to endure.

CHORUS: But what if the gods said something untrue?

At dawn, even before the birds,
Some hurried gods insist on hearing words.
Send us words they say, make them your sacrifice.

But the forest hides the words.

The trees put them back to silence,
And they become a dream.
Up in the gods' sky there is a circle of haunted dark
Where violence gleams.

DESTARASTA: I dream of Kali.
I dream of a limestone cave.
Each night I escape
To the brink
And listen to the bats and the wind.

I hear the passing of pollen grains
As if life was here, then there, then here again;
While leeches suck a doe's shin
And lily leaves snare a careless fly,
A noiseless daily savagery.

I dream of Kali.
The gods keep sending their acidic signs
Through cracks and joints.

KALI: Go to the Gangga
And you'll hear me, dimly,
From the brackish water
Of the estuary.

You'll hear the flow taper
Under a vapid menace
Of unseen vapors.
Go to the Gangga.

CHORUS: And they walk to the Gangga, like two trembling cranes,
And the scent of the pines follows them.

GANDARI: I see a penumbra of fogs.
Pre-dawn ghosts swimming to the hills,
Fireflies flicking past a fisherman's door.

The sun hides its furtive imps
Under the fish bed,
And the river forgets.

DESTARASTA: But the sky is disappearing.
The sacred scares me.
The pure kills my body.
The sacred scares me. Gods scare me.
The place says a prophecy.

CHORUS: It is inevitable.
Gods create their own texts,
Long ones, like yards of cemetery plots.
They invite Death, and Death is here,
A salt-splattered face,
Standing below this flood-formed levee,
Where the flow stays drab and the stream heavy,
As the river moves away from a distant gorge
To an indifferent gray sea.

KALI: You'll find me between the delta and the sea.

GANDARI: So you are Kali.
I heard your anklets crashing,
A different wind rushing,
A different odour,
A gentle thunder
Before I die.

KALI: I am here to end a cycle.
I am here to enkindle
A thousand stems
Of desiccated leaves,

I am here to retrieve
Cut-off petals,
Withered anthers,
Torn down gossamers.

I am here to set the world anew.
I am here to burn you.

CHORUS: The foliage turns into a furore of flame.
The forest shoots burning bodies of birds into the dark
Like fireworks of heat,

Carcasses of dying doves darting off to the dark
And raining down, scorched, torn, grisly.

KALI: But there will be a rebirth of destroyed birds and lost seeds.
There will be a rebirth of scorched lice, dead centipedes.
There will be you, to die, to give.

The queen opens her blindfold. She sees the charred, headless body of the king. She hears the howls of hyenas in pain, the shrieks of smoke-blinded marmosets.

* * *

SCENE 11 – Prince Urinara

CHARACTERS: PRINCE URINARA, HAWK & DOVE.

The blindfolded Queen thinks of a terrified bird. The wounded warbler fled, a hawk chasing, she cried for help, and there was a young Prince who opened his window and put her on his lap. And he was not aware of Death. He nursed the gnawed part of her nape. He wiped the blood dripping from the wound. And he was not aware of Death. Then he saw the dark crown of a falcon.

The bird of prey said, "She is my food. And I am hungry," and the Prince refused the plea. "I am your quarry," he said. He cut his own biceps. He offered his bleeding flesh. The falcon liked it. But the cutting never ended. The bird, the hawk and the wound grew, merging into a convulsion of pain, and the room was all blood, the Prince fainting, falling...

* * *

SCENE 12 – Kali's Dance

CHARACTERS: KALI, DESTARASTA, & GANDARI.

GANDARI: Look, we are all slain.
Kali, the fire is devouring me.

KALI: I will dance
In a distant city of ashes
On gods' ominous hills.

My limbs are ruined fossils
Of the sediment of grief,

But I will dance.

END

Notes

1   An opera with music by Jarrad Powell & Tony Prabowo, libretto by Goenawan Mohamad, produced and directed by Kent Devereaux, with stage direction by Melissa Weaver. Originally staged in a workshop performance in Seattle, June 2000.
2   Translations from Javanese by Laurie J. Sears.
3   Translation of the Javanese sung poem (*suluk*) called *sendhon tlutur* is by Gary Lichtenstein, from Soestayo Darnawi, *A Brief Survey of Javanese Poetics* (Jakarta: PN Balai Pustaka, 1982).
4   Material for the "Reports" in Scene 8 was taken from reportage in *The Independent*.

The Persistence of Evil and the Impossibility of Truth in Goenawan Mohamad's *Kali*

LAURIE J. SEARS

The nature of the killing in 1965–66 — commonly dispersed, nocturnal and by small groups — was such that no one could possibly have had first or even second hand involvement in more than a tiny portion of the total number of deaths.   (Cribb 1997: 7)

This paper analyses Goenawan Mohamad's "dramatic poem"[1] *Kali* as it blends Indic and Javanese Mahabharata stories and past and recent violence in Indonesia since 1965–6. Goenawan, as he is known in Indonesia, has written a text that is a meditation on violence and the persistence of evil in the world. The text both personalizes the violence through a retelling of the last days of the Bharatayuddha War, and depersonalizes the violence through the testimonies of unnamed witnesses describing scenes of killings in Indonesia that took place in 1966 and 1998. Ultimately *Kali* is about the memory of violence and the ways in which those memories are inscribed and transmitted. I suggest that Goenawan uses the Mahabharata story as a *lieu de mémoire*, a "site of memory" in the words of French historian Pierre Nora (1989), on which to hang stories of violence and atrocity so that they might be shaped in memory and preserved. I suggest that one person's memory of violence witnessed is enough to keep that memory alive for a generation, long enough to make sure that it will not be forgotten.

Before turning to focus on many meanings that *Kali* weaves together into a narrative masterpiece, some words about the language of the text are necessary. *Kali* is written in three languages, and Goenawan is fluent in all three. Poetry in Javanese was written to be sung, as *suluk* or mood songs are sung in several genres of Javanese shadow theatre and human theatre. One such passage in Javanese attempts to capture the sorrow and misery of the protagonist's son who has lost everything — all his brothers, his kingdom, and soon his life.

Duh, Suyudhana, lesah langit	Oh, Suyudhana, flattened sky
Bawana alum	Withered earth
Ing rangkahing dewa	Heavenly prison
Janma wasana.	Life's end.

Other poems in Indonesian are also written for music although they work equally well as poems. Much of the dialogue of the dramatic poem is written in English, either to be sung or narrated. These passages have a haunting beauty; words are strung together in startling ways that suggest both visual and emotional imagery. The text of *Kali* was written in the process of collaboration with American and Indonesian musicians and singers and dancers. But the poem stands on its own as a piece of literature that could be performed as a dramatic play as well as an opera. In what follows in this interpretive essay, the words and phrases of the poem guide the interpretation. It is the power of Goenawan's poetry, quoted liberally in this essay, which makes the reader/audience think about violence, memory, ethics, and truth in vivid new ways.

* * *

In his brilliant and macabre turn-of-the-century novel *Old People and the Things that Pass*,[2] Louis Couperus, one of Holland's most celebrated novelists, took elements from his boyhood memories of the colonial Indies and wove them into a compelling novel. In what is known as the "Indies Letters" [Indische Letteren, the literature of the Dutch East Indies], colonial life was bathed in illicit love-affairs, precocious sexuality, frowned-upon inter-racial liaisons, and an often decadent atmosphere of gambling, drugs, and "native" irresponsibility. The "old people" in Couperus's 1906 novel are truly old — in their 90s — and the memories of their evil deeds as faithless murderers in the Indies are about to pass with them into the silence of death. There was an adulterous affair, its discovery, and the murder that accidentally ensued when an angry husband discovered his wife's philandering. There was also a doctor who had to sign the death warrant and say that the murder was a suicide. This he did in return for sexual favours from the beautiful adulteress. These crimes of passion, murder, blackmail, and deceit locked the woman and her two lovers into a secret complicity for 60 years. During these years, the three spent hours of each day together in the woman's home in The Hague, surrounded by their large extended family members. Now they are all old — so very old — and they are waiting to die and bury their illicit past with them.

But the past refuses to die. Harold Dercksz, the darling of his father — then a young boy of 13 — awoke that night in the immediate aftermath of his father's murder. He heard the muffled voices, the dragging of the corpse. He saw the blood-stained floor. And as he grew older, he realized he must carry the knowledge of the crime of that night with him through his life. When we meet him in Couperus's novel, he too is already old, and he too is waiting for the murderers to die. And the private hell of memories that haunt him is visible to him in a visceral way.

> He could not understand why he need grow so old, while the things passed so slowly, went silently by, but with such a trailing action, as though they, the things of the past, were ghosts trailing very long veils over very long paths and as though the veils rustled over the whirling leaves that fluttered upon the paths. All his long aftermath of life he had seen the things go past and he had often failed to understand how seeing them go past like that was not too much for a man's brain. But the things had dragged their veils and the leaves had just rustled: never had the threat been realized; no one had stepped from behind a tree; the path had remained desolate under his eyes; and the path wound on and on and the ghostly things went past … Sometimes they looked round, with ghostly eyes; sometimes they went on again, with dragging slowness: they were never brought to a standstill. (Couperus 1920: 88)

Here the memories become embodied in tangible images; they take on a life of their own. They follow Dercksz throughout his waking life. He calls these memories simply "the Thing".

> All the years of his life, he had seen the Thing rise up again, like a vision, the terrible thing begotten and born in that night when, being no doubt a little feverish, he had been unable to sleep under the heavy, leaden night, which still held up the rain in powerful sails that could not burst and allowed no air through for him to breathe. The vision? No, the Thing, the actual Thing …   (Couperus 1920: 88)

* * *

French historian Pierre Nora, building on ideas from Frances Yates, used the notion of a building, text, or monument as *aide mémoire* — something that can "codify, condense, anchor" memory — as the organizing concept for his extended collection of books on the construction of France's national memory (Nora 1989: 25 n.).[3] In his novel, Couperus presents his characters' memories as sites of haunting, secrecy, and repression. The memories become "Things" that slither in the corner of one's eye — "Things" that look back. The three characters who have committed murder, adultery, and blackmail have each other to keep them sane. They grimly share the guilt and horror of their deeds. But the murdered man's son Dercksz has no one with whom he can share the horror. The horror itself becomes the *aide mémoire*, his lifelong companion. Tied together in Couperus's novel are horror, memory, and silence. The characters cannot forget their horrors, but they maintain their silence for over 60 years. And yet Nora's interrogation of history and memory seems apt to explain the strategies of the characters in *Old People and the Things that Pass.*

> … [I]f history did not besiege memory, deforming it and transforming it, penetrating and petrifying it, there would be no *lieux de mémoire.* Indeed, it is this very push and pull that produces *lieux de mémoire* — moments of history torn away from the movement of history, then returned; no longer quite life, not yet death, like shells on the shore when the sea of living memory has receded.   (Nora 1989: 12)

The old people in Couperus' novel might call their affliction "no longer quite life, not yet death". But it is the silence that these people maintain for so long that arrests the movement of history that Nora describes. We must amend Nora's words to read: "If history *cannot* besiege memory, deforming it and transforming it … there will be no *lieux de mémoire.*" But what exactly is the history of which Nora speaks? Can one separate history and memory so easily? Historians must use recorded memories to write their histories. The most favoured of these memories are called "primary sources" or "eyewitness accounts". In the discipline of history, the eyewitness account is prized above the "secondary source" account, that which is put together from a collection of sources that may include eyewitness accounts. Since the "linguistic turn" in humanities and social science scholarship that began in Europe in the 1970s and then spread to the U.S., the boundaries between primary and secondary sources have been elided for some historians. The rise of trauma studies, and the realization that eyewitness accounts are often distorted by the traumatizing experience of witnessing, has combined with the decentring of the "subject" in scholarship informed by postcolonial and poststructural theories, thereby making room for new approaches to understanding constructions of both history and memory.[4] While these issues will be addressed tangentially in this paper, my foci are the ways in which story, myth, and poetry can be used to both record and structure memory and to unsettle notions of verifiable truth.

As noted above, Goenawan's text of *Kali* uses the ancient Indic and Javanese Bharatayuddha[5] story as a *lieu de mémoire*, a way of remembering the violence that has haunted Indonesian history since the rise to power of the New Order government in 1965–6 with a bloodbath of enormous proportions. Because of the brutality of the New Order regime, its censorship practices, and its whitewashing of its complicity in the deaths of over half a million supposed communists in several months between October of 1965 and April of 1966,[6] stories and memories of the violence, except for the one put forward by the New Order government itself, were repressed in most instances until the fall of the New Order in May of 1998. At this time, scholars — both Indonesian and non-Indonesian — and people who had been afraid to speak up for several decades, began to compile stories of the killings. In the heady and volatile days of May 1998 when the persistent intervention of students succeeded in ousting Suharto from power, change-of-regime violence once again appeared, allowing memories of the older violence to surface at the same time. The seemingly short-lived weakening of the Indonesian army in this period, and especially during the subsequent Habibie and Abdurrachman Wahid presidencies from 1998 to 2001, led to startling ethnic violence in many parts of Indonesia due to the army's reluctance to give up power, as most would argue, or to the lack of strong military control, as army apologists would claim.

* * *

The brutality set in motion by the New Order regime and its army continues from the mass slaughter associated with its rise to power, to the continuing massacres in East Timor from 1975 up through 1999, through the *petrus* [*penembakan misterius*, mysterious shootings] killings

of 1983, and the persistent civil war in Aceh. Although scholars note that
the level of violence increased greatly from the Old Order of President
Soekarno to the New Order of President Suharto, the period from 1950
to 1959 when President Soekarno officially instituted the Guided
Democracy period that prefigured the New Order, seems more the
aberration than the rule. Indeed, from the Javanese princely wars of the
17th to the mid-18th centuries, and the brutality of the VOC [the Dutch
Trading Company that was active in the Indies from roughly 1600 to
1800] through the 19th century that saw the last stand of the Javanese
nobility against the Dutch in the Java War from 1825–30, and the
continuing rebellions of the late 19th and 20th centuries against the
Dutch; and on into the years of the Japanese Occupation and the
Indonesian Revolution, Java has been a violent place for centuries. Perhaps
this accounts for the continuing popularity of the stories of a great war
between the two sides of one large family that has been recounted in the
Bharatayuddha stories in Java for at least 1,500 years.

Over the past few years in Indonesia and among scholars of Indonesia
both inside and outside the country, questions remain unanswered on
how to deal with ongoing legacies of violence. As political scientists
discuss the apparatuses of state power that give rise to violence and the
vertical and horizontal networks through which violence moves, poets
and artists document violence in different ways. One question that the
artists address is how to gain understanding of violence down to the
ground, at the human level. How to deconstruct and recount violence
without trivializing it? As anthropologist Val Daniel (1996: 4) asked in
his book on Tamil-Sri Lankan violence, how to write an ethnography of
violence without it turning into a pornography of violence? Poetry provides
one possible answer, and Goenawan Mohamad's dramatic poem *Kali*
illustrates the way.

* * *

Goenawan Mohamad was born in north central Java in 1941 as the
Japanese Occupation of Java was about to begin. He was four years old
when the war ended and six when Dutch soldiers came, arrested his
father, and killed him a week later. The family moved to Wonosobo, a
Republican area of revolutionary Java where Goenawan began his
schooling. Then Wonosobo was bombed by the Dutch, as nine military

planes dropped bombs on the small town. Goenawan's brother-in-law joined the guerrillas and, as a child, Goenawan saw the guerrillas return bloodied from their encounters with Dutch forces.[7]

In 1964 Goenawan and others signed the "Cultural Manifesto" [*Manikebu, Manifesto Kebudayaan*] proclaiming their right to artistic freedom. But those were the days when the politics of Lekra, the left-leaning arts organization, was in its heyday, calling for artists and writers to adhere to the aesthetics of socialist realism. Goenawan remembers that he became something of an outcast and soon left the country to study in Belgium. It was while Goenawan was in Belgium that the Soekarno government fell and the killings began. When Goenawan returned to Indonesia in 1967, he heard first-hand stories of the killings from friends and acquaintances. Many people he knew were in jail or dead. Others would be sent in 1969 to the prison island of Buru in eastern Indonesia, where Goenawan and other journalists were allowed to visit in the early 1970s. Goenawan knew that there were people there from his village but he recounted how he could not bear to meet with them.

When Goenawan was in his teens and early 20s, leftist politics were strong, and it seemed to many young intellectuals that socialism or communism was the ideology of Indonesia's future. Now communism has become a nostalgic term that belongs to the past. In his reflections on the fate of those who fought and died for communism, Goenawan feels a profound sadness. Not only did many fight and die, but they died for something that soon came to mean less than nothing. After directing the purges of those labelled as communists, the New Order regime became virulently anti-communist, and any connection with communism or those who had professed it was a serious liability that could lead to death or imprisonment throughout the 32 years that the regime was in power.

In his dramatic poem *Kali*, Goenawan chooses to tell the story of the Bharatayuddha War from the perspective of the losers. In the story of *Kali*, Goenawan reflects on what it means to lose both physically and ideologically, as the communists in Indonesia did in 1965–6, but still survive. Thus Destarasta, the blind father of the 100 Kurawa brothers, traditionally portrayed as the arch villains of the story, becomes the protagonist of the play. The play begins at the very end of the War, as the last of Destarasta's sons are killed in battle. The narrative action of the play focuses on the question of justice. After such horrific strife and loss, where is justice? The drama raises the issues of god, destiny, victims, and perpetrators. No one emerges from the Bharatayuddha War innocent.

All are implicated in the violence and the desire for revenge that follows each act of brutality and humiliation. Goenawan's play forces the audience/readers to question their faith or belief in god or gods. Among the many questions that surface, Goenawan stresses one: if god is just, how can god be powerful, and if god is powerful, how can s/he be just?

Goenawan started his well-known news magazine *TEMPO* in 1971, and served as its editor-in-chief until it was closed down by the New Order in 1994. In this capacity, Goenawan reported and reflected upon violence in a journalistic style. In his poetry and essays, Goenawan reflects upon violence in more palpable ways. One of the compelling voices in the dramatic poem of *Kali* is a journalistic one that inserts news reports — purporting to tell of events in Indonesia in 1966 and 1998 — into the last days of the Bharatayuddha War. In this intermingling of ancient story with contemporary events, Goenawan follows in the tradition of Java's shadow masters and other storytellers. The dramatic poem is not about history and memory *per se* but about the persistence of evil and the impossibility of truth. By using the Mahabharata cycle of stories as a *lieu de mémoire*, a site from which to remember stories of violence through linking them with stories of violence that go back hundreds of years, Goenawan's text links mythical and human time.

* * *

For those unfamiliar with the Indic and Javanese Mahabharata cycles of stories — tales still told in song, dance, text, and performance throughout South and Southeast Asia — a short synopsis will do. The tales tell the genealogy of the great Bharata clan, as the two sides of the family escalate their rivalry over who will rule the kingdom. A great amalgam of myth, religion, and didacticism, in the Mahabharata tales Indic gods incarnate on earth as kings who interact with the members of the Bharata family. The denouement of the story of the rivalry between the members and allies of this large family is a great war, the Bharatayuddha War. In the war, the five sons (the Pandawas) of the late king are arrayed against the 100 sons (the Kurawas) of the late king's blind brother, who inherited the throne when his brother died; the winner will rule the kingdom. All the brothers have been raised together and taught by the same teachers. All know one another well. The gods seem to be on the side of the Pandawas, since the incarnate god Krishna serves as the charioteer for Arjuna, middle-son of the five brothers and, in some tellings, the strongest of them

all. The story ends with the destruction of most of the male members of
the Bharata family and some of the women, too. The only ones left at
the very end are the Pandawas — whose sons have all been killed — and
the old blind king and his wife — whose sons, all 100 of them, have also
been killed. The blind king and his wife — she too is blind as she chooses
to bind her eyes to share her husband's affliction — are the hero and
heroine of Goenawan's dramatic poem.

The setting of the poem is the end of this great war as the last of the
blind king's sons and advisors are being killed off: Bhisma, Durna,
Dursasana, Karna, Salya. All these characters are great heroes — well
known to South and Southeast Asians from Pakistan to Bali — and their
deaths are viewed with awe, even in Islamic Java where Goenawan was
born and raised. Into this mix of ancient tales, Goenawan then adds a
character well known in India but hardly known at all today in Java —
the Hindu goddess of death — Kali. As Goenawan tells it, he took the
idea of writing about Kali from a poem about the goddess being born
from a yawn of the Indic creator god Brahma, in a moment of boredom.[8]
This idea of the goddess of death and destruction being born from
boredom intrigued Goenawan, and he wove Kali into the final days of
the Bharatayuddha War. "But Brahma created me from his yawn," Kali
explains to the grief-stricken Queen in scene 4.

"Go and become death," he said,
"For the earth needs a cycle."
Willows wane, streams spent, laughter silenced.
I know he wants the grace gone, just before the burst.
It is his story of boredom.

Kali is the character responsible for the deaths of so many great heroes
— thousands, millions — even as Kali consoles the mother of those
heroes, who blames Kali for her sons' deaths. Kali says to the Queen, "I
am the mother of your sorrow. I am the sister of your grief." Kali rants
against her own fate as the goddess of death. She too has been betrayed.
In Goenawan's text, the birth of Kali seems to symbolize the birth of evil,
beauty, death, joy, jouissance. Kali dances as corpses burn.

***

Maurice Merleau-Ponty (1958 [1945]: 174,175) calls the work of art a "nexus of living meanings". Goenawan's text has its own particular nexus of meanings, drawing its inspiration from many sources: the Indic and Javanese Mahabharata stories, the Old Testament, the Upanishads, Greek theatre, Javanese *suluk* (shadow theatre mood-songs), Dante, news reports, and postcolonial theory. But the language and imagery of the Old Testament — concern with the birth of "law" — is especially prominent. "So the earth shivers and the law is born," says the Indic god Krishna in scene 9 of *Kali*. According to Goenawan's text, the law is born from the carving of the first cipher into a mass of stone — a very Old Testament image. It is the birth of "law" that begets the cycle of good and evil, birth and death, atrocity and vengeance. Once the law is born, once good and evil are defined by the law, then a holocaust is inevitable, Goenawan seems to say. "Memory," Nora (1989: 8) reminds us, "remains in permanent evolution ... vulnerable to manipulation and appropriation ... " It is this permanent evolution and the malleability of memory that makes each act of violence open to interpretation as a "nexus of living meanings".

In the scene that follows the entry of Kali into the final days of the Bharatayuddha War, as the blind King and Queen lose their sons, one by one, Goenawan inserts a scene called the *gara-gara*, the name of the scene performed in the classic style of Javanese shadow plays at about one in the morning. It is a scene where politics often intrude into the world of the performance, where clowns usually appear, where advice is sought and given. But Goenawan's scene introduces another character from the Mahabharata, the fierce and conflicted Draupadi. In Indian Mahabharata tales, Draupadi is the common wife of the five Pandawa brothers, the "winners" of the Bharatayuddha War. In many Indian tellings of the tale, it is Draupadi who sets the action in motion through her laughter and derision of the eldest Kurawa brother Duryudhana at one point in the story. In Java, Draupadi is the wife of only the eldest of the Pandawas, Yudhistira, the would-be king. In both India and Java, the disrobing of Draupadi in the Assembly Hall of the Elders, after a game of dice wherein Duryudhana and his uncle try to cheat Yudhistira and their cousins out of their rights to the kingdom, makes the Bharatayuddha War a certainty. It is only through the divine intervention of the god-incarnate Krishna that Draupadi's garment becomes a never-ending cloth, thus halting her humiliation in the hall where all the men are assembled. The excess of cloth strengthens both Draupadi's faith in the need for the war to come

and her desire for vengeance. After the story of the cloth unfolds, all know
there is no turning back.

Goenawan was inspired by a modern re-telling of the story of Draupadi
written by Mahasweta Devi and translated by Gayatri Spivak.[9] Spivak
(1988: 183) calls the Mahabharata an "accretive epic, where the 'sacred'
geography of an ancient battle is slowly expanded by succeeding generations
of poets so that the secular geography of the expanding Aryan colony can
present itself as identical with it and thus justify itself". Thus in India,
the transmission of the Mahabharata in poetry, play, and song serves to
support and make sacred the Indian state. But in Islamic Java, the
Mahabharata stories are not coterminous with the Indonesian state. As
a poet, Goenawan uses Mahabharata stories to critique the state; he uses
the ancient characters to tell new stories of the postcolonial state and its
failures.

Mahasweta's short story "Draupadi" takes place in the 1970s in
India when the Indian government was cracking down on the Naxalites
who were allied, supposedly, with the freedom fighters of East Bengal.
Draupadi, the heroine of the story, is a tribal woman whose husband has
just been killed, and she is a guerrilla fighter. The story tells of her capture
by the Indian military, after which she is repeatedly raped by a gang of
soldiers. Her garments and body are torn, but rather than seeking to cover
herself with cloth when called before the Indian military commander
Senanayak, she walks unclothed up to him and laughs in his face. She
wants him to see exactly what he had ordered his men to do to her.

Draupadi shakes with an indomitable laughter that Senanayak simply
cannot understand. Her ravaged lips bleed as she begins laughing. Draupadi
wipes the blood on her palm and says in a voice that is as terrifying, sky
splitting, and sharp as her ululation, "What's the use of clothes? You can
strip me, but how can you clothe me again? Are you a man?" (Spivak
1988: 196). Here it is Draupadi's lack rather than her excess of cloth that
disturbs and frightens the powerful men, seeming to forecast their ruin.

Goenawan was impressed with Mahasweta Devi's story — with this
other Draupadi's rape and her willingness to proclaim it. In his text of
Kali, Draupadi narrates her story to Krishna's brother Balarama. She tells
how she was dragged by her hair into the hall of the dice, how she was
undressed there, and how she was raped while all the men watched. She
articulates her rage.

"All the old and dignified men in the assembly knew everything.
They spoke nothing ....

It was at dawn
when I smelled the stench of foul sperm all over my body.
And I knew that there would be a war, ...
For the gods always wanted it." (*Kali*, Scene 7)

Goenawan wrote this after the fall of the New Order government and
the rapes of the Chinese women in Jakarta, which may have been
orchestrated by elements within that government. When *TEMPO*, the
news magazine that Goenawan edited for decades until it was closed
down by the New Order in June 1994, reopened its publishing in
October 1998 with Goenawan as editor, the story of the Chinese women
and the atrocities they suffered, was on the cover (*TEMPO*, 6–12 Oktober
1998, "Investigasi" and "Pemerkosaan"). The headline reads: "Rape:
Story and Fact." Rape became an issue, a discourse, in Indonesia in a very
public way.

Naming the "disrobing" of Draupadi in the Assembly Hall of the
Elders a "rape" introduces a major new element into the story. In the
past, the story of Draupadi in India focused on the ability of her faith
in Krishna to keep her from being further humiliated. In Java, the story
does not focus on Krishna's power but rather on the episode as the
prelude to war. In Java, I have never seen this story performed in the
repertoire of the shadow theatre.[10] This is not surprising, as Javanese
shadow masters have usually avoided the heavy and inauspicious stories
of the Bharatayuddha War and the series of stories that lead up to it.[11]
In a review of the Seattle performance of *Kali* published in Indonesia,
Indonesian journalist Irfan Budiman commented on Goenawan's rendering
of the Draupadi episode:

> Another part [of Goenawan's text] that is unusual is the presentation
> of Draupadi, who in this composition is raped by Dursasana. Draupadi
> complains bitterly to Balarama how the Kurawa [Kaurava] only
> witnessed this humiliation; how the Pandawa sat dumbstruck and when
> the dawn came, she smelled the stench of sperm that covered her
> body .... Why raped? In the story [*pakem*] that we know Draupadi's
> shawl [*selendang*] cannot be torn off by Dursasana because of the
> protection of dharma [*pelindungan Darma*]. This is the accusation that
> Goenawan's libretto brings, with the unlimited power of gods, wickedness
> and evil happen in the world.   (Irfan Budiman 2000)

Goenawan's text and libretto have not yet been performed in Indonesia, although there are plans to bring a production of *Kali* to Europe. Even in the post-Suharto period, Goenawan's text would be seen as controversial, and the rape of Draupadi might be one of the most controversial innovations to the story.

In Goenawan's text, Draupadi and Balarama continue to discuss what was done to Draupadi. When Draupadi says that the gods wanted war, Balarama replies, rather cynically, that the gods like the truth — "A violent kind of symmetry" — and Draupadi agrees. Who are these gods who like the truth? For Goenawan, these gods are Old Testament ones. Balarama describes the gods.

> "They were the ones who brought in the flood
> And praised the purge
> And shouted, 'locusts'
> After a dream of purity,
> And plagued the city
> With flies and frogs,
> And the death of the firstborn,
> And the pain of dogs.
>
> Yes, they like the truth." (*Kali*, Scene 7)

The questions that Goenawan is addressing in this passage and continually throughout this dramatic poem have to do with truth, divinity, testimony, and violence. Mixing images from the Mahabharata with those from the Old Testament, and more recent images of violence from postcolonial Indonesian history, suggests that if there is anything universal about ideas of divinity, it must be that God or gods like violence, that violence is the language of divinity. In this equation, violence thus becomes a kind of truth.

While he was writing the text of *Kali*, Goenawan, like many other intellectuals in the 1990s, was reading the work of Emmanuel Levinas, one of the most influential postwar French philosophers.[12] Levinas, who fought in World War II and was a prisoner of war, was concerned with issues of truth, violence, ethics, and subjectivity. Goenawan's thinking about violence and truth were stimulated by this work, especially Levinas's attempt to separate truth from the Heideggerian "being". For Levinas (Peperzak *et al.* 1996: 99), the problem was clear: "Representation governs the notion of truth, and thereby every meaning is governed by ontology." Levinas set about, as Derrida would do in the same period, to recover knowledge from being. Levinas was eventually able to find a certain answer to the question of violence in his work through his focus on the ethical, and through his interest in Jewish ethics and teachings; Goenawan's vision is darker.

> "Gods create their own texts,
> Long ones, like yards of cemetery plots.
> They invite Death, and Death is here,
> A salt-splattered face,
> Standing below this flood-formed levee,
> Where the flow stays drab and the stream heavy,
> As the river moves away from a distant gorge
> To an indifferent gray sea." (*Kali*, Scene 10)[13]

The concern with "being" and its analysis, which Heidegger thought might displace the role of a transcendent spirit that saturated thought and philosophy, was recognized and replaced in Levinas's work by responsibility and the possibility of acting "for-the-other", even after his experience of the holocaust.

But the crush of the last half century, most of it chronicled by Goenawan in his journal *TEMPO*, the same visions of an overdetermined violence in Java and Bali in the 1960s, in East Timor and Kalimantan in the late 1990s, violence in India, Israel, Rwanda, Bosnia, has led Goenawan to seek something else out of these persistent stories and memories of inhumanity. If there is a *rasa* or mood to *Kali*, the French idea of jouissance might best express it — in the face of such wanton violence the only answer is gruesome celebration. Kali dances in relentless yet sober abandon, accepting her fate to be the destroyer of the world, yet demanding to know why she has had to suffer such a fate, as if an answer could be given. Goenawan's text questions the gods' control over the definition of truth. "But what if the gods said something untrue?" the chorus asks. Destarasta replies in fear: "But the sky is disappearing. The sacred scares me. The pure kills my body. The sacred scares me. Gods scare me." There is an apocalyptic sense in which the world can only be made anew by total destruction, and this is indeed the theme of the Indic Mahabharata stories that Goenawan has used as his template.

Silencing and Witnessing

Historian Michel Rolph-Trouillot (1995: 48) has discussed the practice of silencing in his book on Haitian history: "One engages in the practice of silencing. Mentions and silences are thus active, dialectical counterparts of which history is the synthesis." Certainly the New Order government of Indonesia was skillful in silencing its critics. The largest silence surrounded the killings of 1965–6, killings which may have taken the lives of up to a million people, most of whom died in Java and Bali (Cribb 1997: 12–3). The government silenced all stories of the killings except its own. New stories of the 1965–6 violence have appeared in Indonesia since the relaxing of press censorship that began at the end of the New Order and has been one of the most enduring benefits of the post-New Order period.[14] Goenawan's play, which uses the Bharatayuddha War of the Mahabharata stories as a *lieu de mémoire* for these stories of the killings of 1965–6 and the more recent violence of 1998, intersperses the testimonies of unnamed witnesses within the action of his dramatic poem.

Scene 8, after the story of Draupadi and her conversation with Balarama, is called simply "Reports". In his stage directions, Goenawan has six men walk to centre stage, each holding a spiked head. The first report tells a gruesome story from the recent violence in Kalimantan by an unnamed witness who saw blood-stained heads, and tries to describe them.[15] The most powerful phrase relates, "The heads had been taken just a few hours before, and they looked ... they looked like all the other heads I had seen." Here is Kali's weariness with killing, death, and disfigurement. As I read this particular story of the taking of heads, the images that come to mind mix older colonial stories of head-hunting in Kalimantan with similar stories of the taking of heads and other body parts in the killings of 1965–6 in Java, Bali, and north Sumatra. Conflating practices once condemned by missionaries and colonial officials alike were in the 1960s condoned by the Indonesian Army and government, as long as the heads were communist heads.

The next witness tells a story that Goenawan heard in Bali about the killings of 1965–6. It also involves killing and dismemberment, and here the witness tells how they hung the body in a tree for all to see, and how the people came and "loved to see" the victim. The third and last witness tells a story from the violence of May 1998 in Jakarta. Here a nameless victim is brutally murdered, and then his liver is cut out, and the killers eat it. More horrible yet, they drag his wife out to see her disfigured dead husband, and they ask her if he was evil and she replies, "yes". Very simply here, the degradation of humanity becomes transparent in that simple "yes". When threatened with such horror, the victims can only murmur whatever their oppressors want them to say, whatever may save them from a similar fate. Murder, brutality, betrayal: all are part of Kali's dance.

The poetic and dramatic strategies of Goenawan's interspersing of these testimonies within the larger narrative of the Bharatayuddha War are both affective and challenging. The testimonials are stories of nameless people told by nameless witnesses, yet we believe they are true. The juxtaposition of the realistic genre of testimony set against the mythic characters of the dramatic poem strengthens the realism of the reports. In the larger Mahabharata story into which these testimonies are folded, we have well known characters whose fates are similar. For those who have grown up surrounded by Mahabharata tales, the deaths of Bhisma, Durna, Karna, and Arjuna's son Abimanyu are profoundly personal and disturbing. And we know who the killers are: they are their students, their brothers, their cousins. And surrounding these brutal testimonies, we have Draupadi and Balarama continuing their conversation.

> Balarama: "I thought the war had erased everything."
>
> Draupadi: "No, The war hasn't.
> Look. They carry Kurawa [Kaurava] heads.
> I washed my hair in the rapist's blood,
> And the wave and the wind went down, behind me,
> Like a surge of cheers."
>
> Balarama: "Maybe you are Memory."
>
> Draupadi: "Maybe I am just a footprint
> on buried stairs
> of yesterday."

Here we see Goenawan's reflections on memory and its equation with violence itself. Like a footprint worn into a stairway from thousands of feet pressing down in similar yet individual ways, this is Goenawan's phrasing of Nora's *lieu de mémoire* for a nation familiar with violence. Draupadi's story is one among millions of now buried footprints telling stories of violence, humiliation, and resignation. And Draupadi knows that this war — any war — does not erase anything. Wars only add to the weight of memory, paving the way for new violence.

Goenawan's use of testimony in *Kali* highlights the inability to name the witnesses of the violence that we know has happened. Draupadi, as name and memory, must stand in for all the women who were raped in the violence of the New Order government. In *TEMPO*'s issue about the rapes of the Chinese women in May of 1998, the names of the witnesses and the victims were for the most part withheld or disguised.[16] One woman who had volunteered to go to the U.S. to testify about the rapes was mysteriously killed a few days before her scheduled trip. Rape was the ultimate punishment for poor women labour activists like Marsinah during the New Order period. Even telling Marsinah's story after her brutal rape, torture, and murder at the hands of Army people landed playwright Ratna Sarumpaet in jail, while Marsinah's murderers have still not been found or named. So Goenawan tells Draupadi's story and calls it a rape; he has Draupadi accuse the fathers and husbands of witnessing the rape and doing nothing to stop it. Everyone becomes implicated in the violence of the New Order regime — witnesses, bystanders, and victims alike.

Levinas sees the ubiquity of violence even in the most moderate of times. He says: "For me, the negative element, the element of violence in the State, in the hierarchy, appears even when the hierarchy functions perfectly, when everyone submits to universal ideas. There are cruelties which are terrible because they proceed from the necessity of the reasonable Order." And Levinas finds the answer to the problem of violence in the particularity of each individual human. "To remedy a certain disorder which proceeds from the Order of universal Reason, it is necessary to defend subjectivity."[17] It is through speaking with an/other in a situation where the ego's relation to alterity is both "noncomprehensive and nonsubsumptive" that Levinas finds the ethical and sees the "face" of the other.[18] The idea of the "face" is an important concept for Levinas; it is that which makes each person human, unique, and necessarily alienated.

It is the ethical potential of each unique face that leads toward the necessity for testimony in Levinas's thought and, I would suggest, in Goenawan's *Kali*. But Levinas is aware that testimony has often been mired in Heideggerian ontology and needs to be situated in particularity to liberate itself from "being".[19] Perhaps this can help us to reflect upon the facelessness of those who testify in *Kali* and the actual mutilation of the faces of the victims whose stories are related. The only particular "faces" and speech events in Goenawan's text are those of the Mahabharata characters. And what is unique in these depictions are the intimate conversations between characters who usually remain more character types than nuanced characters in many Mahabharata stories.[20] And in the harshest accusation levelled against the blind king Destarasta and his wife Gandari, Kali says to them in scene 5: "You close your eyes. You refuse to see it." Their sin is that they have closed their eyes to the evil that has unfolded from the avarice of their children. They are truly blind. They are not witnesses; they do not see the truth. Some might see here an indictment of the New Order ruler and his wife who also let the avarice of their children destroy their state.

Trouillot (1995: 151) reminds us: "But the historicity of the human condition also requires that practices of power and domination be renewed.... Only in the present can we be true or false to that past we choose to acknowledge." What he is saying is that domination and oppression must continue in order for people to remain silenced. He suggests that we are responsible in the present. People themselves in their own ways choose the pasts that they wish to remember, and this is an ongoing process. But memories are not without their price. People choose to remember at their own risk, and this seems also to be a message of Goenawan's text and of life under the New Order. In *Kali* scene 9, Krishna says to Kali, to his brother Balarama, and to the chorus of witnesses: "Don't be afraid. Don't grieve. Don't hope." But certainly this is an ironic voice. How can humans not be afraid? How can they not grieve? How can they not hope? This is how we go on living in the face of evil. Someone in the crowd, unnamed, replies to Krishna and concludes with the words: "You always say to kill is to begin. I think I know why." To kill is to begin the cycle of birth, death, destruction, and rebirth; and thus the violence always continues.

When Kali explains her creation from Brahma's yawn, she says that Brahma told her to become death because the earth needs a cycle. Without death, without the cycle of birth and death, there would be no life. The creation of death is always already coeval with joy, jouissance, violence, and evil.

> "Listen. Someone had to let the light pour down on the lake.
> But the gods said no. They would never leave the demons defiled by
> the daybreak ..." (*Kali*, Scene 4)

I asked Goenawan many times about these lines in his text, as I found the idea of demons defiled by daybreak particularly compelling. Would not the daylight be defiled by the demons? How can a demon be defiled? And who is "they" who would not let the demons be defiled? For me, these lines capture much about *Kali*. They indicate a blurring of the boundaries between good and evil, between gods and demons. Levinas says: "Each word meaning is at the confluence of innumerable semantic rivers" (Peperzak *et al*. 1996: 37). The idea of demons defiled by daybreak suggests that even demons have their limits, their order. And is there a god or gods who would allow the brutal deaths of thousands, yet would not let the demons be defiled by the daybreak, by light? What might happen in the world if a demon was defiled? Kali would continue her dance.

> Kali: "Now you see the white color of truth
> And of death."
> Balarama: "I see the purity of hate."
> Kali: "The authenticity of space."
> Balarama: "The blindness of time." (*Kali*, Scene 9)

Here again, the text of *Kali* takes us along myriad semantic rivers. Both truth and death are white, hate is pure, time is blind. But the authenticity of space is another line of the poem that intrigued me. To explain what he meant, Goenawan gave the line, the idea, a "face". In the Mahabharata tales, the five Pandawa brothers have an older brother whose true nature has been hidden from them. Their mother Kunthi had been given a magic power by the gods when she was quite young. She had been practising austerities and had attracted the notice of the sun god Surya, who gave her a boon: she would be able to call down a god to conceive his child whenever she wanted by saying a certain magic prayer. And Surya then left her pregnant with her eldest son Karna. But she was so young, and it would have been devastating to have a child out of wedlock. So she put the baby in the proverbial basket and let him sail down a river, hoping kind people would rescue him. Karna was indeed rescued and went on to become a major supporter of Duryudhana, the eldest of the Kurawa brothers and the Pandawas' mortal enemy.

Karna does not know who he is until just before the Bharatayuddha War begins. Both his mother and then Krishna come to talk to him, to beg him to join his brothers in the war. They tell him who he is. But the

Pandawas had always rejected Karna and made fun of him. It was Duryudhana who recognized Karna's power and took him as a friend and advisor. Karna is loyal to Duryudhana. He promises his mother one thing: he will only fight with Arjuna. Thus, whoever is killed in the battle between Karna and Arjuna, Kunthi will still have five sons.

Karna has no authenticity of space, Goenawan told me.[21] Cast aside by his mother, rejected by his brothers, Karna is a liminal man with no clear place. The authenticity of space is repressive, Goenawan said. In other words, it is the belief that there is an authentic space where a family, a people, a religion, a nation belongs that leads inevitably to war. A people's belief in their authenticity of space ultimately becomes repressive.

Conclusion

The Mahabharata has been called the epic of subversion in India.[22] Unlike the other great collection of stories that forms the Ramayana cycle, Mahabharata stories admit all kinds of inconsistencies, problems, doubts, blasphemies, and an uncontrollable excess of words into their midst. But the stories have been known in some form in India for at least 2,500 years and in Java for at least 1,500. They provide a language which offers diverse and conflicting views of the world. They give large ideas human faces. And the stories serve as *loci memoriae*, memory places, for Goenawan's text. Through these stories we remember Draupadi's outrage and humiliation, echoing the humiliation of all women dishonoured for the glory of heroes. Early in Goenawan's text, a messenger comes to tell the blind king of the death of another of his sons.

> "Last night they cut down Dursasana,
> Your son fell and the earth was damp.
> A man came to the fight and slashed him.
> He ripped his belly open.
> Snatched his heart out.
> Sucked his gore.
> I saw a woman washing her hair
> In his blood." (*Kali*, Scene 4)

This is the story of Draupadi's revenge for her humiliation. It is one of the most monstrous stories. One of Draupadi's husbands, the ruthless and powerful Bima, has vowed to kill Dursasana and drink his blood for what he did to Draupadi. Draupadi herself has vowed not to bind her hair until

she can wash it in Dursasana's blood. In this story we recognize the
testimonies Goenawan has woven into the text of *Kali*. And they easily
slide over and blend into the older stories.

In 1994, I wrote to Pipit Rochiyat, one of the few participants in the
killings of 1965–6 in east Java who has had the courage to write about
it, and asked him if the Bharatayuddha stories had circulated at that time.
In his ironic and bitter reply, he attributed the stories that he had heard
to the maidservants at his father's house.

> They told me, and I was still a kid, that the behavior of the Kurawa
> [Kaurava] was exactly like that of the Communists: they grabbed
> things, they were coarse, they didn't know the rules, etc. (Demonstrations,
> demands, uproar, boycotts, etc.). This was pretty much the perception
> among the people in the villages around the Sugar Factory of Ngadirejo,
> fourteen miles south of Kediri (east Java). You may know that at that
> time we Pandawa [Pandhava] were continually harassed by the
> Communist Kurawa. They liked to grab land, just like the Kurawa took
> the land of the Pandawa. Thus it was fitting or 'normal' to kill the
> Kurawa, even to slaughter them in brutal ways (remember the story of
> Sangkuni's mouth being ripped apart, Duryudana alias Suyudana's
> head being smashed or Dursasana's throat being slashed and his blood
> gulped down a wide-open mouth and then pissed out until it was all
> gone, just like Johnny Walker).[23]

According to Pipit, it was easy to kill the communists because they were
just like the villains from the Mahabharata stories. And it was fitting to
kill them in similar ways.

Benedict Anderson has recently written an insightful commentary on
Kolonel A. Latief's confessions from his involvement in the abortive coup/
counter-coup of 30 September 1965.[24] In Anderson's call for more
witnesses to step forward, he suggests that the New Order was ruled by
Petrus ("Mysterious Shootings" by mysterious killers and killings, the
way in which the New Order had worked). But Goenawan's text is
compelling because he uses the Mahabharata stories to remind us that
the killers were not mysterious at all. They were the victim's brothers,
uncles, cousins, wives, and neighbours.

To return to the quotation that served as the epigraph for this essay,
Robert Cribb describes the killings of 1965–6 as having taken place in
small groups such that each person would only have had knowledge of
a small number of deaths. Each person who took part in the killings

would have known their fellow killers and their victims — often very well
— but would not have known how many others knew of their killings
or how many others took part in other killings. This returns to the Dutch
novel by Couperus whose images began this essay. There were the old
people waiting to die and to take their memories of violence with them.
In waiting for the "Thing", the evil, to pass, finally the three perpetrators
of the crime are all dead, after 60 long years. And before they died, they
thought they had succeeded in hiding their crimes from their families and
society. They did not know that the child Harold had witnessed the crime.
They did not know of the love letters that remained as evidence. And so,
a child and a grandchild know, and one or two others, but each thinks
that the others do not.

> Yes, Steyn, in the confidence arising from their association, after first
> lunching together, had told him of the letter which he had read, in the
> act of tearing it up, with Adele Takma in the old gentleman's study; and
> Lot, in utter stupefaction, had heard everything: Lot now *knew* ... and
> thought that he alone knew, together with Steyn and Aunt Adele....
> How terrible, those passions of former days, of hatred, of love, of
> murder!
>   ... And, gazing wearily into the pearly evening distance, which
> began to turn pink and purple in the reflection of the setting sun, he
> felt — he, the grandchild of those two murderers — felt dread descending
> upon him, gigantic, as a still invisible but already palpable, wide-
> winged shadow: the dread of old age. O God, O God, to grow so old,
> to wait so patiently, to see things pass so slowly! (Couperus 1920: 382–
> 3; ellipses in original).

It has been over 37 years since the violence that inaugurated the New
Order. There are indications that the survivors and children of the victims
of that violence want to know more, want the stories to be told. But the
perpetrators of violence, they are much less eager to bring their stories
into the light.[25] Some scholars have suggested that many people who
identify with the perpetrators of the violence of the 1960s — in east Java,
for example — do not feel any guilt about the events and believe the
communists got what they deserved.[26] The need for some form of truth
for the atrocities committed in Indonesia during the 32 years of New
Order rule seems to be talked about more by Euroamerican or Australian
scholars and observers than by Indonesians themselves, although a number
of projects are ongoing in Indonesia and in Holland where Indonesian

researchers attempt to collect memories and stories of New Order repression.

With the present intention of the U.S. government to resume the training and funding of the Indonesian military, one wonders if the dangers of confessing one's sins of omission or commission might not be too great. It is in this light that a play like *Kali* can allow the testimonies of the past to seep through the silences. Perhaps it is on the stages and in the performance halls of Indonesia where the search for the truth must take place. Levinas has asked: "Can things take on a face? Is not art an activity that lends faces to things?" And then he replies, "We ask ourselves all the same if the impersonal but fascinating and magical march of rhythm does not, in art, substitute itself for sociality, for the face, for speech?" (Levinas 1989: 10). Goenawan's dramatic poem *Kali* answers this question by showing how art is not always a substitute for sociality, and how it can take on a face in a powerful and demanding way.

Notes

1   Goenawan Mohamad called the rendition of the text of *Kali* included in this book a libretto, the most accurate description of his text when he wrote it. When Goenawan agreed to publish *Kali* in this book, we intended to call it a "performance text" because it was written for a performance held in Seattle in June 2000. But the text of *Kali* has taken on a life of its own and now exists in newer and different forms. Goenawan has been collaborating with Kent Devereaux, Jarrad Powell, and Tony Prabowo in bringing the text to life on the stage. The Seattle performance was indeed an opera, but the text that was given to me in spring of 2000 was already superceded by the time of the performance. I originally wrote a draft of this paper based on the text I received and since then, Goenawan, Mary Zurbuchen, and I have gone over every line of the text to make sure that it is indeed a rendering of the text that Goenawan wants to see in print. But the text of *Kali* goes on, changing scenes, lines, poems, and words as it bends to the collaborative work of musicians, dramatists, and choreographers. As such, the poem remains very much in the tradition of Javanese poetry from which it takes some of its inspiration. Poems become dramas and dramas change the words of the poems. Current events are inserted into ancient stories. Characters from the past sit next to political figures in the present. For these reasons, and because the libretto originally produced by Goenawan no longer serves as "the" libretto for *Kali*, we are calling the text a dramatic poem. Goenawan wrote the text in three languages: most of the dialogue is in English; poetic passages and traditional songs are in Indonesian and Javanese.

2   The novel was published in Dutch under the difficult-to-translate title *Van oude menschen, de dingen, die voorbij gaan* in 1906, and translated and published in

English in 1920. The ellipses in this passage and the next one are in the original.

3   Nora took the inspiration for his work on sites of memory from Yates (1966). Yates is interested in the classical art of memory and traces this art from its origins in ancient Greece up through its use in the emerging scientific debates of the 17th century. Yates takes the Latin word *locus* [site or place] from the work of an unknown Latin teacher of rhetoric in Rome compiled in ca. 86–82 B.C.E. Memory, one of the five parts of rhetoric, can be enhanced through association with a place, often an architectural site (see pp. 6–7). What Nora added to this was the association of the *loci memoriae* with the modern nation.

4   The literature on history, trauma, and memory is too rich and plentiful to cite. Many studies have appeared on trauma and remembering in relation to holocaust memories, the Tuol Sleng archives of Cambodia, and the various truth commissions set up in places like South Africa, Haiti, Chile, or Guatemala. See, for example: Caruth (1995); Das *et al.* (2000); Hartman (1994), and various articles in the journal *History and Memory*.

5   The spellings of this ancient tale and its characters vary between India and Java. For example, texts in Java often use the spelling "Bratayuda" to refer to the war. Since Goenawan sometimes prefers Sanskrit-styled spellings, I will follow his usage throughout this essay.

6   The killings continued sporadically for the rest of 1966 and even into 1967, but the bulk of the killings were over by March of 1966 and thus took place in a very short period of time (Cribb 1997: 18).

7   Goenawan Mohamad told this brief story of his early life to my Indonesian history class at the University of Washington, Seattle on 15 Apr. 2002.

8   Goenawan obtained the poem from Jarrad Powell, his musical collaborator on the Seattle performance of *Kali*, and a musicologist and composer who teaches at Cornish College in Seattle.

9   See Bengali author Mahasweta Devi's short story "Draupadi", written in 1981, and Spivak's translation and commentary (Spivak 1988: 179–98).

10 It was reported to me by the Javanese-American performing artist Dylan Widjiono (Seattle, Washington, 25 June 2002) that a dance drama story of the disrobing of Draupadi was performed in Yogyakarta in the mid-1990s.

11 Recent innovative puppeteers often find this type of story appealing since the 1980s, when shadow theatre began to change in major ways. One story that is often performed from this series is "Krishna Duta" or Krishna as Messenger. Another is "Karna Tinandhing" or Karna Meets his Match, the story of the great battle between Arjuna and his — unbeknownst to him — eldest brother Karna, who fought with the Kurawas rather than his own brothers. For more on these newer performance styles, see Mrazek (1999, 2000) and Sears (1996: chapter 5).

12 Levinas was born in Lithuania, educated in Ukraine and in France, and studied briefly in Germany with Heidegger in 1928–9. He became a French citizen in 1930 and, after Heidegger joined the Nazi Party, Levinas became one of the major critics of Heideggerian ontology. He also moved beyond Husserlian phenomenology, the subject of one of his earliest studies (Peperzak *et al.* 1996: vii–xv).

13   Levinas has also clearly struggled with the question of the existence of God. Summarizing Levinas' thoughts on God, Peperzak notes: " ... God is referred to as having passed into an immemorial past, a passing that has left a trace from which the human Other rises up as primary command." It is this faith in responsibility to a human Other that gives Levinas hope (Peperzak *et al.* 1996: xi).

14   See, for example, Ryter (2002) for unheard and gruesome stories of the killings in Medan. For a discussion of censorship under the New Order, see Maier (1999).

15   Goenawan said that this was taken almost verbatim from article by Richard Lloyd Parry in the *Independent* about the ethnic and religious violence of 1998–9 in West Kalimantan, where local Dayak people and transmigrant Madurese engaged in bloody battles.

16   See *TEMPO* (12 Oct. 1998, "Rape") for the story about the eyewitness to a gang-rape of a young woman. The woman is given a fictitious name (Marthadinata) and so is the victim of the crime.

17   Levinas made these comments in conversation with Jean Wahl and others after a reading of his essay "Transcendence and Height" to the *Société Française de Philosophie* on 27 Jan. 1962 (Peperzak *et al.* 1996: 23).

18   This particular summary of these ideas comes from the editor's brief introduction to the first essay "Is Ontology Fundamental?" (Peperzak *et al.* 1996: 1–2). What follows is my own conclusions drawn from several of the essays in the book.

19   Levinas says: "The disclosure of being governs testimony" (Peperzak *et al.* 1996: 100).

20   From my own 25 years of familiarity with Javanese shadow theatre performances where Mahabharata characters regularly appear, I have come to believe that the ability of a puppeteer to make the characters human is the mark of a great shadow master.

21   Conversation with Goenawan Mohamad, Seattle, Washington, 16 Apr. 2002.

22   This was discussed at a conference on the Ramayana held at the University of British Columbia in June 2000. The comment was made, I believe, by Prof. Robert Goldman.

23   See Sears (1996: 228) for the full quote; see also Rochiyat's powerful essay translated by Benedict Anderson (Rochiyat 1985).

24   See *Indonesia* 70 (Oct. 2000, "Petrus") for Anderson's discussion of Latief and the Petrus killings carried out under the direction of the New Order government in 1983 in Java. For Latief's confessions, see *TEMPO* (6–12 Oct. 1998, "Kami") for the interview with Latief, who was imprisoned from 1966 until 2000.

25   For one story told by a perpetrator who then becomes a victim, see Rochiyat (1985). For stories of a survivor of the violence, see Pramoedya Ananta Toer's (1999) memoirs of his years as a political prisoner on the island of Buru. See also Part III of "Riding the Tiger", a documentary by Australian filmmaker Curtis Levy in which Indonesians discuss on film their memories of 1965–6.

26   This viewpoint was brought up by anthropological researcher Chris Brown at a lecture on the scope and possibilities for truth commissions in Indonesia given by Dr. Mary Zurbuchen at the University of Washington in Seattle in May of 2001. Some might observe that given the New Order's suppression of any but its own version of 1965–6, it is not surprising that most Indonesians have internalized official antipathy toward communist "traitors".

In Search of Memories —
How Malay Tales Try to
Shape History

HENDRIK M.J. MAIER

How does Malay, and in particular Indonesian, the language's most prominent 20th-century form, create and confirm memories in these days of modernity? Let us start with a fragment from the very beginning of H. Kommer's *Nji Paina*, a Malay tale that was published in 1900 in Batavia.

> *Sebermoela di tjeritaken adalah satoe roemah ketjil di desa Poerwa di tanah Djawa wetan, poenjanja seorang Djawa, bernama Niti Atmodjo, djoeroetoelis fabriek goela, dan roemah itoe ada terdiri di bawah itoe boekit iang adanja di pinggir kali, iang tiada dalem aernja. Di roemah itoe, Niti tinggal sama istri dan anak anaknja, laki laki dan prampoean. Semoea poetranja Niti Atmodjo ada pegang pekerjaan di fabriek goela.*

From these beginnings grows the tale of Niti Atmodjo, a clerk at a sugar factory who is forced to give his daughter Paina to the factory's manager, Mr. Briot, a big man who is driven by lust. Reluctantly, Paina moves in with the manager but before long she makes sure that she is infected by a contagious disease by willfully entering an area under quarantine; with that disease she has herself kissed (and probably more than that) by Mr. Briot.

> *... Kemoedian Nji Paina berangkat keroemah toean Briot, iang memang soedah toenggoe datengnja dengen tiada sabaran. Ketika ia liat Nji Paina dari djaoeh, ia segrah hampirken padanja, teroes pelok dan tjioem Nji Paina, iang amat tjantik dan elok itoe. Sagenap hari Nji Paina moesti doedoek di pangkoeannja toean Briot dan tiada brentinja ditjioemi oleh toean itoe.*

As a result, Briot is infected too. He dies a painful death, whereas Nji Paina survives — and the end is a happy one:

> *... Nji Paina kamoedian di nikahken dengan saorang Djawa hartawan, dan tinggal hidoep roekoen, dan beroentoeng sampei di hari toea.*

It reads like an allegory of the colonial situation, Nji Paina being the strong and inventive native who kills colonialism, personified in Mr. Briot, be it not without a sacrifice: her face is scarred for the rest of her life. The local population: suppressed but smart; the colonizer: rude and ignorant. A memorable tale indeed: in Jakarta *Nji Paina* is regarded as one of the trailblazers of "modern Malay literature".

* * *

When European writers compose a short story or a novel they usually choose the past tense. As if the tales they compose relate events that have already taken place and, more importantly, have already been concluded. As if writing about the world is necessarily following the world's time. It holds for "literature", and it also holds for journalism, the form of writing that deals with the present par excellence and yet prefers to present tales in the past, completed and over. Hence it is almost self-evident that we translate Kommer's tale in the past tense, the more so because the book cover tells us that "this very beautiful tale took place in Eastern Java not long ago". As if the world is speaking for itself, offering us problems as well as solutions from beginning to end.

If we focus on the words of action and pretend that the other words in the Malay paragraphs have an exact equivalent in English (which they do not, of course, and the following is only an effort to give a readable word-by-word translation), the above fragments of *Nji Paina* could be translated as follows:

> To begin, it is told, there was a small house in the village of Poerwa in the land of East Java; it was owned by a Javanese man, named Niti Atmodjo, a clerk at a sugar factory, and that house was standing at the bottom of the hill, on the bank of a river of which the water was not deep. In that house, Niti lived with his wife and his children, boys and girls. All the sons of Niti Atmodjo were working in the sugar factory.

...Then Nji Paina left for the house of Mr. Briot who, of course, was waiting for her arrival, impatiently. When he saw Nji Paina from afar, he immediately came to her, and he embraced and kissed Nji Paina, so beautiful and elegant. The whole day Nji Paina had to sit on Mr. Briot's lap and ceaselessly he kissed her.

...And then Nji Paina was married to a wealthy Javanese, and lived in peace and good fortune to the end of her days.

The translation makes the tale sound like every other tale in English: the past tense suggests that the tale is completed and over, the protagonists move from a beginning through a crisis towards a conclusive end. Perhaps it is too easy to say that the past tense only indicates a past in reality; in particular, Weinrich (1964), Hamburger (1968), and Benveniste (1966) have shown that the tense system that is used in narratives or tales is operating alongside the tense system that is used in non-narrative (let us say: everyday communicative) genres — and that the latter are more complex and confusing in terms of tense. Be that as it may, the effect remains the same: the events are located in history; conclusions can be drawn; and endings can be made into memories.

In reading English tales we are not accustomed to much variance of temporal possibilities — and by abiding by the distinct temporal hierarchy that is created in a speech act of a persona (not necessarily the writer him/herself), we turn tales into fiction: it may have happened in the past (cf. Fleischman 1990: 107). As if in narratives the past tense has an a-temporal dimension, leaving the possibility open that the narrated events could happen again — and that is what our concept of literature is all about: it teaches us about the many possibilities in our world, filled with life and love and death, at once shaped and propelled by our memories. Thus the reading of tales is pushed onto an ambivalent level that touches our lives in indirect ways. Tales are strings of words about events and people that have already passed away, but not really. They are allegories that have some memorable connection with reality and history, but not necessarily so. They give memories and they confirm memories. They do so in a distinct order and with a distinct ending.

Back to the act of translation: we tend to read *Nji Paina* as a tale of events that actually took place not so long ago. We could perhaps even read it as a fairy tale, did we have the courage to translate the first phrase with "once upon a time". Once the choice of the past tense has been

made, we steer *Nji Paina* into the genre of realistic fiction, a novel form
of telling tales that, experts tell us, emerged in the land of Java at the
beginning of the 20th century by way of print.

On the basis of Lukacs's ideas about the rise of the novel (Lukacs
1963) we could claim that, reminiscent of the emergence of the novel in
European languages, a creative memory emerged among Malay speakers
in Java at the beginning of the 20th century in which words did not only
point to the past but also to the future. Meaning was separated from life,
the essential from the temporal (cf. Benjamin 1968: 99) — and thus
experience was reshaped in a subjective way, no longer bound to
"tradition", anonymous and totalitarian, alone. Malay writers such as H.
Kommer, Marah Roesli, and Takdir Alisjahbana allegedly turned away
from the idea that they made part of the totality of life. By doing this they
distanced themselves from the tellers of tales who, trying to relate events
as they had been said to happen and operating within the so-called
"Malay tradition", worked on the assumption that their attempts to
retain meaning were embedded in a totality that did not need to be
questioned: reality would shine through the words on its own. A sense
of fragmentariness was substituted for the knowledge of totality, a desire
for conclusive tales for indifference to coherence, so to speak. Kommer,
Roesli, and Alisjahbana are modern writers.

It should not come as a surprise that not everyone who has reflected
on that substitution has been happy with it. Walter Benjamin, for one,
evoked the disappearance of the storyteller by way of a very moving and
ambivalent nostalgia. But then, such nostalgic ideas about a substitution
of a narrative consistency for a world's coherence may not apply to Malay
writers at all. Constrained by the lack of a clear and unambiguous system
of tense, Malay tellers of tales in the land of Java have not been able to
follow the example of European novelists, if only because the Malay
language and its lack of a distinct past tense did not allow them to create
tales that were completed, coherent, and rounded off.

Malay tellers remained bound to shaping mere sequences of words
and combining fragments, unable to endow them with a comprehensive
significance, incapable of creating rounded-off conclusions, and lasting
and definite memories of them.

***

In Malay, always in the process of emergence in the ever-moving network of negotiations among words and sentences, notions of tense do not play the prominent role they do in, say, English or Dutch. Of course, the language does have a number of lexical elements that can be used to evoke a sense of present and past whenever speakers and writers find that necessary. More often than not, however, the temporal framework in which sentences and phrases present actions, events, and progress remains vague or implicit.

We could wonder what effect this virtual absence of tense has on the Malay presentation of the world. We could also wonder if speakers and writers of Malay have a certain unwillingness to explore the possibilities of indicating time in their conversations and writings. To what extent are forms of active and preventive censorship involved, the result of a policy of language standardization, for instance, or the product of a totalitarian government of a state that wants to be a nation? Or is this absence primarily a matter of ignorance or indifference, of fear or a lack of desire? Or should a certain incapacity of the language itself — its systemic limitations and constraints — account for this frequent opacity?

When we talk about the virtual absence of tense in Malay, we talk about "tense" as the "grammaticalized expression of location in time" (Comrie 1985: 9)[1] and about "Malay" as a language, that is: a distinct set of structures that rules and reflects the combination and selection of an ever contracting and expanding group of words into sentences and beyond. But then, Malay words do not only follow a grammar and the world of structures that is reflected in that grammar; they also evoke a context, verbal as well as non-verbal. The term "Malay" refers not only to a language, but also to a discourse, that "experiential context of language" (e.g. Becker 1979: 244), or to languaging, the energy that "combines shaping, storing, retrieving and communicating knowledge into one open-ended process" (Becker 1995: 9) — and driven by that very energy, people have been spreading the Malay language over Southeast Asia, in spoken and written forms, in an ongoing diaspora.

Malay words appear to follow the rules that are laid out in grammar books and dictionaries, but they also make figures in a context, at the level of particularities — and the conflict between these two capacities could probably most effectively be expressed, following Becker, in the terms "language", based on memory, and "languaging", driven by experience, respectively.

Languaging as the "experiential context of language": the word "context" also occurs in the formulation that Sneddon constructed about tense in his recently published reference grammar of Indonesian (a recent form of Malay and a heavily constructed one at that):

> In Indonesian the form of the verb does not change to indicate tense or aspect. A sentence such as '*Dia pergi ke kantor*' carries no indication of whether the verb refers to a regular occurrence or to a single occurrence and, if the latter, when it happens in relation to the present. This is inferred by listeners from the context within which the utterance is made.   (Sneddon 1997: 197)

And then Sneddon offers a number of sentences that suggest how Malay speakers may (or should) use separate lexical elements to indicate past, present, and future time in case they feel obliged to neutralize the absence of tense in the words that express an action. Sneddon's formulations are loose, and necessarily so: the memory of Indonesian is not very strong among its users — and the grammar is not very strong either. *An Indonesian Reference Grammar* is an excellent example of the undecided conflict between prescription and description that characterizes every book of grammar: language and languaging tend to move in opposite directions, as a system struggles with an open-ended process.

Malay, in short, is a language that accounts for numerous sentences or utterances which, firstly, carry no indication of whether the action that is expressed refers to a regular occurrence or to a single occurrence and, secondly, do not tell when that action happens in relation to the present.

What does this lack of temporal localization mean in practice? A sensible way to show its implications is to undertake the act of translating a Malay sentence into a sentence in another language: in order to acquire some distinct sense of one language we should have an awareness of at least two languages. In order to have a sense of an identity, of being more or less safely embedded in a stable system, we need to develop the awareness that there is another identity that we could try to master by way of building yet another system of memories and remembrances. Knowing a language or pretending to know a language implies we have retained so many memories of particularities that we have constructed a framework that is able to account for many particularities to come.

Very often, Becker's words read like useful metaphors. "Mastering another language is like collecting memories of yet another series of particularities," he tells us — and in the case of Malay, our efforts to construct another solid framework from the memories of particularities are bound to perish in elegant deceit, if not despair. "Speaking a language is like looking through a window, a lookout post on the world, on our fellows, and on other languages;" this statement of a prominent 20th-century man of letters, Octavio Paz (1990: 40), sounds like yet another useful metaphor. The words of these two writers are useful in that they seem to catch some prominent notions of a language, a system we try to construct from particularities and then use to account for those very particularities and new ones. Reading texts in another language should make us realize that we are caged in a glass house. Gaining knowledge of another language should make us realize that we are in search of memories of particularities.

Such realizations should make us feel uneasy indeed. Who likes to be caged? Who wants to keep on searching? How do we collect memories and keep them ready for use? And do metaphors not often silence the nitty-gritty elements of reality?

Leaning on our ordered collection of memories and looking out through the window of English on Malay sentences and tales — let us call that a tentative definition of the act of translation — could only make us aware of the constraints and particularities of both languages. Sneddon's sentence "Dia pergi ke kantor" is a case in point. It could be translated as "he went to the office", "he goes to the office", "he will go to the office", "he was going to the office", "he is going to the office", and "he will be going to the office". In short, "Dia pergi ke kantor" evokes and refers to a wild heterogeneity of activities and contexts at once. Translating could be described as the effort to silence such heterogeneity, be it only to create a new one. Translation is a term for the attempt to make choices, be it only to open up novel ones: we are obliged to make a choice between the six possibilities this Malay sentence is offering us — and as a matter of fact, there are many more than six as "kantor" refers to definite and indefinite (to "the office" and "an office") as well as to singularity and plurality (to "office" and "offices"), and "dia" refers to "he" and "she" simultaneously. But then, how do we make a choice from altogether more than 30 possibilities?

The meaning of "Dia pergi ke kantor", Sneddon and Becker would tell us, is constrained by the context in which the sentence occurs. Firstly, it evokes modern and urban life, the life of bureaucracy and administration (of the nation-state, to use yet another metaphor) — and we could, at least, wonder why Sneddon gives a sentence that is so strictly time- and space-bound in a grammar that tries to step out of time, into a glass house. Does he perhaps want to suggest that Indonesian is a modern form of a language, a contemporary form of "classical Malay" in which neither the word "kantor" nor the concept occurred? Secondly, we could wonder why Sneddon makes a third person singular go to an office, with all the confusion that comes with that activity, rather than a first or a second person singular. Grammars, it seems, prefer examples in which a third person singular performs the actions — as if teaching and prescription are most convincing and effective when they create a distance so as to pretend a distinct objectivity and an abstract kind of scholarship beyond the constant dialogue between a "you" and a "me". "Dia pergi ke kantor" reads like a short-cut to fictional discourse, in short. Like the seed of a narrative. Sneddon's fictive conclusion could be reformulated in terms of Fleischman's admirable study of tense: actions that are expressed in Malay tend to "avoid or confuse a commitment to explicit temporality and completion" (Fleischman 1990: 265). No past, no present? Incomplete, unfinished?

Perhaps it should be emphasized once more that the fact that the Malay language does not have systemic and consistent marking of tense does not mean that speakers and listeners, writers and readers of Malay do not know how time can be expressed. The mere availability of auxiliary words that can be added to the verbs, such as *akan*, *belum* and *sudah*, usually translated as "will", "not yet", and "already", respectively, sufficiently shows that they (or we) are very well able to locate events and activities in times and places that are remote from the here and now of their (or our) acts of speaking and writing. But then, such lexical elements are often lacking, leaving the localization in time implicit or absent — and the most simple conclusion should be that the lines along which users of Malay refer to reality, history, and experience follow patterns that are different from the ones English speakers and writers make. Memorization seems to work in different ways.

From our English glass house, we can see that Malay sentences tend neither to create nor presuppose a distinct temporal order within or outside the text. As a consequence, every time listeners hear a sentence, every time readers read a tale, they are forced to make figures in a particular context and make sense of the series of words accordingly. We have to create rather than discover meaning; moving along the words, we shape rather than confirm a coherent and hence memorable awareness of their context. Memorization will constantly be subverted and thwarted in this open-ended process.

Speakers and writers of Malay, in reverse terms, have difficulties in providing the descriptions of events and actions that seem to be completed in the moment of telling with the consistent depth that is needed to call them "history" or "reality". In this context of talking about Malay it is hard, if not impossible, to stick to the English words "history" and "reality", embedded as these two are in English discourse and not in Malay. Running the risk of performing Heideggerian word-plays and etymologies, we could claim that the Malay words that dictionaries offer us as the closest equivalents of "history" and "reality" point at ways of accounting for the world that are different from the English ones. *Sejarah* — as the dictionary will tell us, "history" — still has a strong echo of "genealogy", a form of presenting the past in a pattern that is sequential and linear rather than completed and rounded off. *Kenyataan* — as the dictionary will tell us, "reality" — comprises "tangibility", "visibility", and "truth", three words of which the close relationship in English is questionable, to say the least. Perhaps *kenyataan* could be translated with "exteriority" — but such a choice would silence the heterogeneity of the Malay word and open up another heterogeneity in English.

The use of the past tense in English implies that the events that are narrated are finished and over, and that the speaker/teller is able to present them in a rounded-off picture. There is a closure, in short, which enables the speaker to give the events a moral meaning; every utterance, that is, steers us to an allegorical interpretation of sorts, endowing actions and events with a comprehensive significance that they do not have as long as they are shaping a mere sequence (White 1987: 14). That very past tense and the concurrent comprehensiveness remain implicit in Malay, and as a result its tales, no matter how short, tend to continue shaping a mere sequence of particularities, open-ended and confusing: they are not able to locate events in times and places that are different from the here and now of the act of speaking or writing itself. Lacking a consistent or distinct depth in time, tales leave it to readers and listeners to make figures, to make a string of figures out of them, in a never-fulfilling and open-ended process of reading or listening. In the Malay case, endings terminate a tale rather than conclude it (White 1987: 16); they give a tale a sense of fragmentariness in an indefinite (or infinite) sequence that escapes completion and coherence.

Termination rather than conclusion: Malay tales, it seems, lack the coherence we are looking for, both in terms of their communicative situations and in terms of "literature'". They appear to invent or evoke a world every time again, rather than being intent on concluding and reflecting it. The art of combination makes it almost impossible to acquire in-depth and well-organized memories. Obviously, this has far-reaching consequences for our understanding and interpretation of tales, series of words which, our own memories tell us, present us with the activities that one or more protagonists are undertaking in order to reach a final situation, which, different from its beginning, is somehow located in the real world of time and space.

* * *

Leaning on English, we are aware of the capacity of Malay to refer to various temporal contexts at once and its tendency to conflate past, present and future. We are confronted with the question of whether in a translation a distinct choice is fair and whether it is correct to read Kommer's tale as a first effort to write realistic fiction in Malay. Why not translate the verbs in the Malay tale in the present tense to begin with?

> To begin, it is told, there is a small house in the village of Poerwa in the land of East Java; it is owned by a man named Niti Atmodjo, a clerk at a sugar factory, and that house stands at the bottom of the hill, on the bank of a river of which the water is not deep. In that house, Niti lives with his wife and children, boys and girls. All the sons of Niti Atmodjo are working in the sugar factory.

> ...Then Nji Paina leaves for the house of Mr. Briot who, of course, is waiting for her arrival, impatiently. When he sees Nji Paina from afar, he immediately comes to her, and he embraces and kisses Nji Paina who is very beautiful and elegant. The whole day Nji Paina has to sit on Mr. Briot's lap and ceaselessly he kisses her.

> ...And after this Nji Paina is married to a wealthy Javanese, and is living in peace and good fortune to the end of her days.

The use of the present tense could give the tale a different "feel". It gives us an experience that is different from a tale that is narrated in the past tense. *Nji Paina* becomes more direct and immediate; it hits us head-on, so to speak, forcing us, for one, to be confused not only about its fictional character but also about its report-like character. Is this a tale of a forced "marriage" between a Javanese lady, beautiful but powerless, and one of those Europeans, always greedy and rude? Should *Nji Paina* perhaps be read as a general or comprehensive statement about the colonial situation, as an allegory? Maybe *Nji Paina* never existed. Maybe the tale is just pure fantasy. But then, is it not a tale about a particular woman who once lived in East Java, and is it not a realistic tale, driven by violence of the conventional kind that is the central theme in so many tales produced in the beginning of the 20th century, both in Dutch and Malay? Perhaps *Nji Paina* does not only signal the emergence of what is now usually regarded as a novel form of Malay writing, called realism.

How could this temporal heterogeneity, this inconclusiveness of Malay be retained in an English translation? A solution could be to switch between past and present, between unmarked and marked, and use them interchangeably, so as to preserve the constant doubleness, moving back and forth between the performative mode of visualization and the documentary mode of chronological reporting (cf. Fleischman 1990: 265–6). Thus the particularity of the Malay sentences is maintained — and we have to decide for ourselves, every time anew, how to read this particular sequence of sentences by slowly making figures out of the series of words.

> To begin, it is told, there was a small house in the village of Poerwa in the land of East Java. It is owned by a Javanese man, named Niti Atmodjo, a clerk at a sugar factory, and that house was standing at the foot of the hill, on the bank of a river of which the water is very deep. In that house, Niti lives with his wife and children, boys and girls. All his sons worked in the sugar factory.

> ...Then Nji Paina left for the house of Mr. Briot who, of course, is waiting for her arrival, impatiently. When he sees Nji Paina from afar, he immediately came to her, and he embraced and he kisses Nji Paina, who was very beautiful and elegant. The whole day Nji Paina has to sit on Mr. Briot's lap and ceaselessly he kissed her.

> ...And then Nji Paina was married to a wealthy Javanese, and is living in peace and good fortune to the end of her days.

Linguists will tell us that the switching of tense in a tale is virtually always a mark of orally performed narratives; it evokes the theatre and its characteristic features, such as direct speech, asides, repetitions, expressive sounds, and gestures. Fleischman (1990) takes medieval texts in French as her example, but it seems permissible to take Malay tales as another one: the experiences of *Nji Paina* are meant to be read aloud, or to be played out — as if *Nji Paina* should be read as a script for a play.

A Malay tale always carries the traces of a performance. It evokes recitals. It forces us to search for memories — and we will never find them once and for all.

***

Telling a tale as a performance, shaping meaning and memory in the act of reading: this brings us to the second example. They are fragments from one of the tales that, published by Balai Poestaka in the 1920s and 1930s, were made the canon of late-colonial Malay literature in the 1950s, the result of the always intriguing dynamics of cultural authority. Allegedly modelled on Dutch examples, the Balai Poestaka tales are usually interpreted as good examples of realism; context-bound narratives, they seem to offer comprehensive pictures of the situation in the Indies in the first decades of the 20th century, in the same way realistic novels in Dutch and English are assumed to give comprehensive pictures of the 19th century world of "Europe". Reliable sources for historians, they read like reports of information, like referential texts — as if facts and experiences in the Indies were speaking for themselves, shining through the words.

***

Soekreni Gadis Bali (Sukreni, Girl of Bali), written by I Gusti Njoman Pandji Tisna (later Anak Agung Panji Tisna), was first published by Balai Poestaka in 1936 and has gone through various reprints (and editions) since. It is a tale about Soekreni, in later editions: Sukreni, a sweet and caring young woman who falls victim to the schemes of her evil mother. It is a tale of greed and power situated on the island of Bali, ending in the death or ruin of the main protagonists. George Quinn made an admirable and careful English translation that was published in 1998 under the title of *The Rape of Sukreni* (an interesting translation of the Malay title, by the way). He opted for the past tense: the tale has a beginning, a middle, and an end, and it is a realistic tale about the bad effects the introduction of the money economy had on Bali. *The Rape of Sukreni* seems to tell us a lot about life in Bali in the 1920s, urging the reader to create a set of figures of things to come. The text on the back cover of the English translation reads like such a figure in itself: "*The Rape of Sukreni* offers a unique and dark view of the island's future."

* * *

The opening of "Sukreni" is as follows:

> *Di pinggir jalan kecil yang berkelok-kelok, di antara kebun-kebun kelapa menuju ke Bingin Banjah, desa yang belum dapat disebut desa benar, hanya sekumpulan rumah-rumah orang tani saja, adalah sebuah kedai. Orang yang mula-mula datang ke situ tidaklah akan menyangka bahwa rumah itu sebuah kedai, apa lagi letaknya tidak di pinggir jalan benar, melainkan dalam pekarangan yang berpagar. Yang akan masuk ke situ, mesti melalui sebuah pintu bambu dahulu* (Panji Tisna 1978: 1).

Quinn translated it in the past tense:

> Off to the side of the narrow road that twisted through coconut groves on the way to the village of Bingin Banjah was a hut. A newcomer to the village — if Bingin Banjah could be called a village, for it was little more than a cluster of peasants' homes — might be forgiven for not knowing that the hut was in fact a food stall. After all, the stall wasn't even directly on the side of the road, but at some distance and within a fenced-in piece of ground which had a bamboo gate to mark its entrance.

Not without reason, the translator returns to this very same paragraph in his "Afterword" in which he convinces us that many elements in Panji Tisna's tale should remind us of elements of Balinese theatre, such as the stage, the protagonists, and the actions. "In the ostensibly unremarkable opening passage (–) Panji Tisna recreates such a stage" — and if *Soekreni* could indeed be read and performed as a theatre play, it remains a question why the passage was not translated in the present tense:

Off to the side of the narrow road that twists through coconut groves on the way to the village of Bingin Banjah is a hut. A newcomer to the village — if Bingin Banjah can be called a village, for it is little more than a cluster of peasants' homes — may be forgiven for not knowing that the hut is in fact a food stall. After all, the stall isn't even directly on the side of the road, but at some distance and within a fenced-in piece of ground which has a bamboo gate to mark its entrance.

Here, too, both present and past tense are possible, and the English translator could have chosen to switch between the two so as to express this ambivalence. Once again, this is not to say that Malay tellers of tales do not (and did not) know how to refer to past and present, how to create the depth of a temporal hierarchy. Numerous Malay words can be translated with "in those days", "earlier", "before", "some time later", "months have passed", "already", "not yet", "suddenly", and "once upon a time"; and not seldom the teller steps into the tale to assure the public that this has really happened or that s/he has heard it from someone else, thus trying to push the tale's events into the past, before the moment of the act of telling. But then, such words of time are not very frequent, and whenever they are used it is usually not very clear whether they create a temporal distance between fragments in the tale itself or between such fragments and the world outside the tale — historical reality, that is. Moreover, such relatively rare indications of time are silenced by the embedding sentences prior and after, and this lack of time indications restores the heterogeneity of meaning — and then the reader or listener is once again forced to make figures rather than see a grammar confirmed. An open-ended process, in short, that does not allow for any depth.

A good example of this lack of temporal depth or absence of temporal hierarchy is given at the beginning of chapter 7:

Beberapa bulan telah lalu. Kehidupan orang di Bingin Banjah masih sebagai biasa, tiada berubah. Kedua kedai di situ tetap bersaingan juga, bahkan lebih keras lagi persaingannya. I Made Aseman tidak pernah lagi masuk ke kedai Men Negara, sejak terjadi perbuatan keji di situ, apalagi karena I Gusti Made Tusan sejak itu pun tidak menampakkan diri lagi. Entah apa yang terjadi atas diri I Gusti Made Tusan, maka ia tak datang-datang lagi ke kedai kecil itu. Ke desa Bingin Banjah pun sudah jarang benar ia datang, seolah-olah desa itu sudah aman benar.

In his English translation, Quinn gives us:

> Several months passed. Life in Bangin Banjah was as it always had been; nothing seemed to have changed, except perhaps that Men Negara and Pan Gara were competing even more fiercely than before. Following the incident at Men Negara's, I Made Aseman had not set foot in the coffee shop again. Nor for that matter had I Gusti Made Tusan who, for some unknown reason, seemed to have changed. Not only had he given up his habit of visiting the shop; he now rarely visited Bingin Banjah at all. Bingin Banjah, it appeared, was now free of crime.

The English, constructing a coherent paragraph of temporal hierarchy, tends to ignore the readers' constantly returning experience of heterogeneity while shaping a context. The Malay words resist such clarity:

> Several months pass (are passing, have passed). Life in Bangin Banjah is (was) as it always was (is, has been); nothing seems (seemed, had seemed) to change (have changed, be changing), except perhaps that Men Negara and Pan Gara are competing (were competing, compete, competed) even more fiercely than before. Following the incident at Men Negara's, I Made Aseman does not set foot (has not set foot) in the coffee shop again. Nor for that matter does (has) I Gusti Made Tusan who, for some unknown reason, seems to have changed (be changing). Not only is he giving up (did he give up) his habit of visiting the shop; he now rarely visits (is visiting) Bingin Banjah at all. Bingin Banjah, it appears (appeared), is (was) now free of crime.

Malay tales, so it seems, constantly slide away into temporal ambiguities, and the resulting heterogeneity and inconclusion give them a certain dramatic if not theatrical quality of "presentness". Tales are ready to be presented, to be performed. Tales such as *Nji Paina* and *Soekreni Gadis Bali* — could we call them "literary", "fictional", "realistic", or should we stick to the Malay word *sastra* and claim that this Malay word does not have an equivalent in English? — have the power to enwrap their public in an immediate way, as if their sentences are not above or beyond us but around us, direct, threatening, confusing; they impose themselves upon us as if we have to re-enact them in the present, forcing us to make sense of them at the very moment they confront us. Malay sentences are forcing us to make figures with no end. They make it impossible to create stable memories.

* * *

This power to carry us along holds even for tales that are emphatically located in days gone by. For so-called historical novels such as Pramoedya Ananta Toer's *Buru Quartet*, for instance, in which the years around 1900 are necessarily pictured by way of verbs that situate the protagonists' actions as much in the present as in the past. It holds for tales about the Revolution of 1945 too.

Take *Dari Hari ke Hari* ("From Day to Day"), for example, written by H. Mahbub Djunaidi and published in 1975. It is a "novel" that, situated in the years 1946–8, describes the experiences of a Jakarta family in Central Java through the eyes of a young man. "With careful observations, the tale moves along (*berjalan*) in a smooth and lyrical style, and here and there it is full of humor so that it creates pleasure," the back cover tells us in Malay.

Once again it may be best to take the first paragraph, as we expect it to set the tone for the rest of the tale:

> *Sore yang jatuh membuat kereta api, si Jerman tua bangka itu, menjadi anggun dan muda. Sekarang dia memekik-mekik, waktunya mengambil kepastian: inilah daerah republik yang betul-betul republik. Sungai Bekasi yang malas sudah terlewat, terlempar jauh ke deretan gerbong belakang. Bau batu bara dan jerami menampar dari hampir semua jurusan.*
>
> > *Ayahku menjenguk ke luar jendela.*
> >
> > *"Nah, sekarang kita semua jadi pengungsi. Pengungsi sama sekali berbeda dengan pelarian, karena kita bukan pencuri atau garong(–)"*
> >
> > *Kuloloskan badan ke luar jendela. Terima kasih kepada kereta api yang tak kuasa lari keras dan tak berkaca, leluasa aku melambai-lambai, menangkap angin dengan jari-jariku, dan percikan abu yang tak tampak oleh mata.*
> >
> > *Tapi pasukan republik itu tampak dengan jelas, rebah di pinggir rel.*

The falling evening makes the train, that old tough German guy, become handsome and young. Now it shrieks and shrieks, time to make the decision: this is the area of the Republic which is really truly republican. The lazy river Bekasi has already been crossed, it has been thrown far away behind the line of carriages. The smell of coal and straw is hitting hard from almost all directions.

My father looks out of the window.

"Well, now we all are refugees. Refugees are quite different from fugitives because we are not thieves or bandits(–)"

I wriggle my body out of the window. Grateful to the windowless train that is not strong enough to go fast, I wave and wave as I please, with my fingers catching the wind, and the sparkles of ash that are invisible to the eye.

But the troops of the Republic are clearly visible, they collapse along the rails.

The Malay is as heterogeneous as ever, and once again we could decide to make switches of tense, trying to make a figure of every sentence separately:

The falling evening made the train, that old tough German guy, become handsome and young. Now it is shrieking and shrieking, it was time to make the decision: this is the area of the Republic which was really truly republican. The lazy river Bekasi was already crossed, it is thrown far away behind the line of carriages. The smell of coal and straw is hitting hard from almost all directions.

My father looked out of the window.

"Well, now we all are refugees. Refugees are quite different from fugitives because we were not thieves or bandits (–)"

I wriggle my body out of the window. Grateful to the windowless train that was not strong enough to go fast, I wave and waved as I pleased, and with my fingers I catch the wind, and the sparkles of ash that were invisible to the eye.

But the troops of the republic are clearly visible, they collapsed along the rails.

This impossibility of deciding between repressing the experience of the present and ignoring knowledge of the past concurs with another feature of Malay tale-telling: tales consist of fragments between which the connections, causal and temporal, are not easy to fathom. Djunaidi's *Dari Hari ke Hari* is a good example of this: readers are forced to make the links between these fragments, and between these fragments and reality, while they are moving along the sentences — and they will never be able to decide in a conclusive manner and create deep memories. Time and again we have to make the figures, creating an experiential context in the process, constantly shifting and jumping. We should refrain from translating the Malay word *roman* on the cover-page with the English word "novel": the Malay *roman* seems to refer to a "sequence of short tales", always in a process, rather than to a coherent whole in which the constituent elements can be fitted together and made into an ordered set of memories.

Malay tales are necessarily fragmentary. To put it in negative and absolute terms: Malay tales are never self-contained, coherent and closed off. More often than not, the teller is forced to kill his protagonist in order to terminate the tale rather than conclude it by way of a closure: violence — illogical and unlawful, immediate and sudden — is the most self-evident way to make an end to the presence of words. It leaves Western readers — accustomed to reading a "novel" as if it were a well-designed and complete construction, with built-in patterns that can be discerned in a careful reading — puzzled if not unconvinced: life should not end in death but in the solution of a conflict among people who in the alternative world of fiction could easily stay alive, no matter how mortal they are.

Constantly switching in time. Heterogeneous. Immediate. Incomplete and inconclusive. The indifference of Malay toward making a consistent distinction between present and past, as well as the unwillingness of its speakers and writers to do, so has yet another effect: Malay literature has necessarily remained a literature of short stories, of fragments, that is. The calls for "the great national Indonesian novel" that, since the early 1950s, have been made by critics who were used to reading European novels in their original languages, have remained unanswered.

* * *

Early modern Malay literature — a cursory term for the artful writings in Malay which, published in the first half of the 20th century, were given a place in sastra Indonesia by critics in, subsequently, Batavia, Djakarta, and Jakarta — reads like a corpus of very realistic tales. *Nji Paina* and *Soekreni Gadis Bali*, *Karena Mentoea* and *Sitti Noerbaja* seem to present their public with pictures and sketches of a daily life world that, in terms of time and place, was very close to the act of writing. They provided their readers, so it seems at first sight, with sketchy pictures that were recognizable and plausible, reminding them of news in newspapers, equally fluid, sequential, and temporary. But do these tales really present complete and well-designed pictures? Did they shape new memories? Did they offer true stories or real stories, as opposed to false or imaginary stories? Do they reflect history? Were they not lacking certain features of reality? Are they not ignoring or silencing the most prominent elements of the late-colonial world?

Power structures, colonial hierarchies, and white people are lacking in Balai Poestaka tales. Instead, fragments of the world are evoked in which only local people are operating; the main protagonists, educated people with great anxieties, are struggling with "modernity" and "novelty" rather than with their annoyance, awe, and admiration of Europeans, and they are struggling with a language without memory rather than exploring their own memory. The protagonists are what readers themselves were told to be: struggling with tradition or *adat*, giving sense to the world around them in which old customs and habits appear no longer appropriate. Europeans are occasionally present but only as demons and policemen — and the absence of temporal depth and hierarchy keeps us from collecting memories and comprehension. Moving along in a sequence of fragments, Balai Poestaka tales have the effect of presenting us with far-reaching claims of immediacy: Asri and Sitti, Soekreni and Toeti are still among us, if not in us. *Karena Mentoea, Sitti Noerbaja, Soekreni Gadis Bali*, and *Lajar Terkembang*, fragmentary and loose constructions, read like very immediate and partial presentations of a misty world, indefinitely inviting us to shape new memories which are constantly questioned and subverted by confusion and silence.

Perhaps the Balai Poestaka tales, until recently considered of crucial significance in the Malay canon, are not realistic in the way we tend to read English or Dutch novels, after all — or maybe we are confronted here by the need not only to distinguish two languages, but also two kinds of realism: the form of writing that successfully tries to be memorable to its readers, and the form of writing that tries to present its readers with pictures of the world and constantly fails to do so.

Balai Poestaka novels do not offer pictures of the colonial situation but rather force their readers to make sense of instability and heterogeneity. A realism of sorts, perhaps. "Creative realism" may be a sensible term. It is like an effort to describe a memorable house by leaving out an emphatic mention of the walls and foundations that hold it together. Surrealism would be the wrong word for this creative realism of Balai Poestaka; if we are to make use of available terms, "nationalistic" would be another appropriate term, as these novels are trying to evoke a nation — as if *bangsa* is the equivalent of "nation", which it is not — in which the colonial structures of power are silenced, the European masters are absent, and natives are anxiously dealing with natives only in unsolved questions of love, life, and death. Equally fragmentary in terms of order and more heterogeneous in terms of time, the so-called "Medan novels" and the "Sino-Malay novels" are even stronger in playfully keeping the readers away from comprehension and hierarchy, order and memories. Somehow, the distinction between "fiction" and "referentiality" seems not very appropriate if we try to describe Malay writing in terms of literature and journalism. Perhaps Malay tales should be described in terms of a conflict between comprehension and relevance, or between depth and surface, for that matter.

* * *

The same fragmentariness and incompleteness can be found in the tales that deal with the Revolution. They, too, create but a partial picture of the world: the heroics and antics of the local people, anxious, nervous, are pictured at length while the enemies remain in the distance, almost out of sight. Tales about the Revolution tend to present us with pictures of a war without an enemy; the native fighters do not confront the white soldiers on the other side, but each other and themselves, in search of courage and treason, in search of relevant memories to live by. Never is the Revolution presented in a comprehensive or realistic picture — unless we assume that a Revolution is like clapping with one hand.

The lack of tense, the lack of lexical elements of time on a sentence-to-sentence level remains the same in the tales that were told by the generation that succeeded the Balai Poestaka generation in Djakarta: figures are made, first by the writers, then by the readers — and the Revolution imposes itself on us in an eerie immediacy. It is as if the acts of heroism, the pictures of nationalism, the process of growing up are taking place among us, in front of us — and perhaps even in us. The Revolution may be over but its spirit was to keep inspiring Indonesians for a long time to come. It is still in and around us.

Malay writers in Indonesia have had difficulties in emerging from this mould of the Revolution: the clapping with one hand was to remain the major subject in the "national literature of Indonesia" that emerged after 1949. Perhaps this creative obsession confirms the basic meaning of sejarah as genealogy rather than history: around a single figure in the genealogy of Malay writing, called the "Generation of '45" (*Angkatan '45*), tales are woven that tend to shape indefinite figures of courage and sacrifice in the name of the "nation", just like the generation of Balai

Poestaka is evoking experiences around the conflict between tradition and modernity, and the Poedjangga Baroe around subjectivity and inspiration, *soekma*. Time and reality are controlled and very loosely memorialized by way of some catch phrases in horizontal strings rather than by a chronological and vertical hierarchy. History never acquires any depth.

"Realism" in the sense of the effort to describe historical events and adventures, summarized in more or less exemplary protagonists, remained of a partial and puzzling character, to be created and performed in every particular context anew: as if memories do not know where to go and, therefore, evaporate as soon as they have been worded. As if the colonial days are being re-enacted in every tale, again, as something present. As if the Revolution is hanging in the air, ready to grab us — and then takes a certain distance again, constantly shifting between past and present, as Djunaidi's tales so clearly show.

The past is brought to the present by way of the figures readers and listeners have to make from the sentences. In order to make sense of the series of fragments that constitute a tale, we have to participate in the telling or performance, try to construct new fragments of memory — and as soon as the tale is finished, we feel like failing and falling. Some kind of collaboration is required, but there is no closure. We should be willing to explore the constant shifts between the present tense, verbalizing unconfigured particulars of visualized spectacles, and the past tense, used for events and actions that are informed by a retrospective intelligibility (cf. Fleischman 1990: 11) — and if that willingness is absent, the tale does not have a meaning at all. And the search for memories remains incomplete, if not unfulfilled.

This voice of creative realism has continued to drive the tales that have been produced since the bloody events after the military coup of October 1965 — the communists were to play the role that, successively, the Dutch soldiers, the colonial situation, and the Dutch colonial masters played before: they hardly are given an existence in words, and insofar as their presence is acknowledged at all, they are described and pictured like violent demons, from a distance. No memories should be evoked. No efforts should be made to come to terms with the reality of murders and slaughters and their shadows. History does not speak, but words do. Of course there was a certain unwillingness involved, and distinct forms of censorship — the massacres and their aftermath should not be made a part of the collective memory of the nation. More important, however, is the incapacity of the language to shape a coherent, consistent, and comprehensive world.

In retrospect, it should not come as a surprise that writers have continued to turn away from "history" and "reality". Was it intentional or by chance that the work of Iwan Simatupang, Putu Wijaya, and Danarto, tales that avoided tense in very intense ways, became the new standard of excellence in the so-called modern Indonesian literature, *sastra Indonesia modern*? No nationalist tales any longer, but tales of impossibility — in which, once again, surface prevails over depth, fragmentariness over conclusion and comprehension. Reality is pushed aside, and memories are made impossible.

More than ever before, Malay literature is now a sequence of short stories with a strongly performative character in which, every time anew, history is evoked rather than recalled, created rather than discovered. In this open-ended process of languaging, in this switching and shifting in time, memories are beyond us, ahead of us. And so is their complement, hope.

Note

1   "locating a situation on the time line, relative to some already established time point, or being simultaneous with, prior to, or subsequent to the already established time point".

PART TWO

Collective Memories of the Qahhar Movement

ANDI F. BAKTI

W hat we might now term "regional autonomy" or "decentralization" was also an important and divisive issue in the first decade of Indonesian independence. In the 1950s, resistance to the centralizing policies of the political elite in Jakarta generated rebellions and separatist movements in South, Southeast, and North Sulawesi, West Sumatra, West Java, Aceh, South Kalimantan, and the South Moluccas. The central government responded to this unrest with military force, crushing one rebellion after the other. Memories of the movements — both of the hope with which they began and the violence with which they ended — were not so easily crushed, and they began to resurface at the end of the 20th century.

In South Sulawesi, as in most other regions, underground separatist strategies merge with regional educational, socio-cultural and economic improvement programs (Aceh is exceptional in that it has never ceased to challenge the central government). Based on field work conducted in late 2000 in South Sulawesi, the present chapter demonstrates how myths and memories of Qahhar Mudzakkar, the charismatic separatist leader, play a role in contemporary regional movements. Qahhar's legacy varies among contemporary movement members and non-members, and is recalled differently to serve different interests of regional politics or movement vitality. Leaders and former members of Qahhar's separatist movement have largely operated underground, and in hiding, in the years since his death. Current leaders still coordinate their operations through staff and cells so that many members do not know each other. In this context, remembering Qahhar and focusing on his person as the movement embodied, serve as a point of identification for many of the individual members. This theme is examined below through interviews with current members and contrasted with the kinds of memories of Qahhar held by non-members. A movement's lineage is not the only frame in which a past leader can be remembered, however, and my data also show that remembering Qahhar can take shape as a set of issues and key terminology.

Rebellion and Leadership in Sulawesi: Historical Summary of the Qahhar Movement

Although many dispute his death, the histories of Qahhar's life and career are generally consistent. He was first involved in the Indonesian Independence struggle against the Dutch in Java (1945–50), and despite his accomplishments, was passed over for leadership by then President Soekarno and other high-ranking officials. With the support of loyal followers, however, Qahhar established his own command and proclaimed a guerrilla war against the Republic in 1950.

Eight months later, he joined the *Darul Islam* (DI) or *Negara Islam Indonesia* (NII, Islamic State of Indonesia) founded by S.M. Kartosuwiryo in West Java. After three years, on 7 August 1953, he formally announced the integration of Sulawesi into this Islamic state, and was subsequently named National Deputy Minister of Defense of NII or *Darul Islam/ Tentara Islam Indonesia* (DI/TII), the Islamic State/Indonesian Islamic Armed Forces). Ultimately, Qahhar declared the outright independence of Sulawesi in 1957, as the Darul Islam weakened in other regions (West Java, Aceh, and South Kalimantan).

Communications among regions continued to break down over the next few years, and on 14 May 1962, Qahhar proclaimed the independent East Indonesia *Republik Persatuan Islam Indonesia* (RPII, Islamic Federated Republic of Indonesia), with its centre in Sulawesi and himself as "caliph" (cf. Gonggong 1992: 202, Tihami 1984: 58). On 15 December 1963, 14 months before his alleged death (3 February 1965), acting on the advice of his foreign minister, Kaso Abdul Ghani, he decided to sever all political links with Javanese Indonesia as the only means of saving Sulawesi from Javanese domination, using the motto, *Selamatkan Sulawesi!* ("Save Sulawesi!"). Qahhar and Ghani agreed to form the *Republik Persatuan Sulawesi* (RPS, Federal Republic of Sulawesi), with Ghani as acting President or *Pemegang Kuasa Organisasi* (PKO).

After Qahhar's death, Ghani consolidated his organization and the separatist movement during an 11-year term as RPS president. He came to rely in particular on the help of Dr Hasan Muhammad Di Tiro, who served as the ambassador and foreign minister for the renamed *Republik Persatuan Sulawesi* (Federal Republic of Sulawesi), and also as the representative (*wali*) of *Negara Aceh Merdeka* (Free Aceh State) in exile.[1] Ghani also worked with the RPS Prime Minister, Sanusi Daris, who, despite making the jungle his refuge, served as Ghani's successor when the latter passed away on 13 July 1976.

On becoming president of the RPS, Sanusi faced serious challenges in coordinating the organization from his hiding place in the South Sulawesi forest. Aside from a courier and a cook, he had no assistants; his staff were scattered in various towns in Kalimantan, Sumatra, South and Southeast Sulawesi. To thwart the government's intelligence networks and lingering suspicion of former leaders of the 1950–65 movement, they left no administrative evidence of their activities.

Despite their careful management, however, military intelligence captured the alleged head of a gun smuggling operation in 1982, but failed to uncover the link between the smuggler, the independence movement, and Sanusi. This incident has resonated in the creation and perpetuation of myths about the movement since that time. During the interview in which the gun-smuggling event was retold to me, a member of the movement whispered that the smuggling had continued until recently, and that many of the guns used in the 1950–60s remained buried in the Sulawesi jungle. To what extent this information is true remains to be seen, particularly in light of the fact that the Indonesian military has worked with determination to crush the movement since the 1982 incident. Although such myths have a potential of reaching beyond the members of the movement into the general population, no one has ever seen these weapons.

Despite all precautions, Sanusi was arrested on 5 October 1982, and along with other senior leaders was brutally interrogated and tortured during a two-year-long detention and trial held in Makassar, South Sulawesi. Sanusi won his release when the prosecution failed to prove his active involvement in subversion.[2] According to some sources, however, Sanusi's release was the result of intervention by South Sulawesi "favourite son" Muhammad Jusuf, then the Minister of Defense and Chief of the Armed Forces.

Following his release Sanusi went abroad, apparently to look for Qahhar, who, some followers maintain, is still alive in exile.[3] Although he failed to locate Qahhar, Sanusi did succeed in organizing meetings with supporters in Malaysia. Results of discussions were made known to active leaders and members in Indonesia and overseas through personal messengers.

After Sanusi's death, a meeting was held in Malaysia for representative RPS leaders from Sarawak, Sabah, Kuala Lumpur, Riau, and Sulawesi. Syamsul Bachri, also known as Sjamri Fattah, was elected as the new president. A native of South Sulawesi, he has lived in exile in Malaysia and Singapore, but still manages to travel to Riau and quite often as far as Sulawesi. At the same time in Indonesia, the *Dewan Pengemban Amanah Rakyat Republik Persatuan Sulawesi* (DPA-RPS, People's Trusteeship Legislative Council of the Federal Republic of Sulawesi) was founded under the leadership of Muhammad Ishaque in his capacity as Vice President of the *Front Pembebasan Rakyat Sulawesi* (FPRS, Sulawesi People's Liberation Front).

Apart from working closely together on human rights issues, the DPA-RPS and FPRS aim at the consolidation of old members and the recruitment of new members, particularly the children of veterans and martyrs of the 1950–65 movement. They work within universities, socio-religious organizations, research centres, and NGOs. The Council and Front are cell-based organizations, and only their leaders (Abdul Fattah and Muhammad Ishaque, President and Vice President of the FPRS respectively) know the individuals who periodically organize meetings.[4] Each cell includes district and sub-district leaders as well as divisions or sub-divisions assigned to specific groups, tasks and sectors, such as youth, intelligence, economic, political, security, and legal sectors, among others. Branches of the Council and Front allegedly exist in Southeast Asia, South Asia, the Middle East, Europe, the United States, and Australia.

While the international spread of the movement may be exaggerated among followers, claims are made that it is supported by at least 17 countries and by the United Nations, as a result of lobbying by its representatives living abroad. The belief that the movement is well known abroad contributes to the increasing support given to the movement within Indonesia. However, supporters abroad, mainly those living in East Malaysia, Kalimantan, and some in Sumatra, place most of their hope in the actions of their colleagues in nearby Sulawesi rather than others more distant, sustaining the centrality of the original movement.

A few comments on methodology are appropriate here. Given their practice of working underground and members' fears of being identified, knowledge of the activities of the Council and the Front is hard to obtain. I was, however, given the opportunity to attend several meetings, had the chance to get to know some members, a number of whom I had personally met before, and was able to request information on the provision that no questions be asked of a respondent's current tasks. This measure was taken, of course, to ensure secrecy and prevent a wider than necessary awareness of the organization's activities. Often my questions were answered with "sorry, I do not know that". I suspect that in these situations the respondent was trying to preserve secrecy, or simply thought that only the leader knew the answer to my questions. When I repeated my questions to the leader, he would answer the question vaguely or simply change the subject. These situations repeated themselves when I attended formal meetings, during which the discussions tended to be vague. Eventually, however, by asking fewer questions and letting participants simply talk anonymously, I managed to understand some of these discussions, especially with relation to the organization's branches and activities. Drawing upon everyday conversational communications between the members of specific organizations or identifiable groupings relating to the past revolution, my approach can be characterized as ethnographic and ethnomethodological (cf. Van Maanen 1988; Garfinkel 1967).

Remembering Qahhar the Person

My analysis begins by describing how the original movement is sustained within a "core group" of contemporary Qahhar loyalists, most of whom believe that he is still alive. Rumours of his death are refuted by witness accounts of him in exile and explanations of him as a *tomanurung* (one who descends from heaven).

The core group includes a number of members of NGOs who are involved in a varied field of activities ranging from cooperatives, legal practice and farming, to youth training, and professionals employed in Sulawesi as teachers, lecturers, lawyers, consultants, and engineers. Members treat the issue of Qahhar's alleged death as closed for discussion because Qahhar, in a speech he purportedly made shortly before he left, declared: "I'll go away from you all for some time, don't ever try to look for me, because you simply can't. But, if I want to, I can easily find you." Many members believe that the Front leader, Abdul Fattah, managed in the past to meet with Qahhar regularly. However, when I asked him directly about the particulars, his answer was vague:

> It is exactly like when Prophet Ishmael was about to be slaughtered by his father, Prophet Abraham. Ishmael lived because he was replaced with a sheep. Or it is like the story of Jesus, who [according to Muslim belief] was replaced before his crucifixion by a man who had betrayed him and whose face and body were suddenly made to look like those of Jesus. Jesus himself was saved by God and brought to Heaven. Just as Jesus will come back again to continue his mission as a Muslim prophet, Qahhar will soon come back to continue his mission. I received messages from him from time to time, through a spiritual link, while I lived in the jungle in South and Southeast Sulawesi.

As this and the following quotations demonstrate, memories of Qahhar framed by quasi-spiritual contact shape the movement's collective memory and are central to how the movement sustains its cohesiveness long after the alleged death of its leader. One of the Front leader's assistants, also a member of the core staff, told me:

> One day, I accompanied the leader on a visit to his mother who was apparently sick. We went to her house in Lanipa, Palopo. The leader entered the bedroom, but I was reluctant to follow him and stayed in the living room. I heard a man's voice besides the leader's talking, laughing, and coughing sometimes. Then I went downstairs, into the yard. A few minutes later, I went back up to the house verandah. There I saw Qahhar's mother standing, looking healthy. Then I said to myself, this lady is not sick at all. The leader was still talking on friendly terms with another man whom I believed to be Qahhar.

Ampang, one of the members of the staff said: "a man I met in the Grand Mosque of Palopo told me that he had grown up with Qahhar. They both had taken care of buffalos when they were little." Ampang then told me to go and meet this man, which I did. He shared his experience with me:

> When I was a boy of about six, I went to see my uncle. There I saw a boy standing up, leaning against a pillar of the house. I then went into the bedroom, where I saw another boy sleeping on the bed. Then I asked, "Who is this boy?" My uncle said, "He is Ladomeng, your cousin." Then I said, "Who is outside in the living room, who also looks like Ladomeng?" Then the whole family looked at the boy standing outside. They were all in shock thinking him to be a supernatural being.

The two boys were brought together and found to be identical, including their clothes. A week later, one of the boys passed away. Nobody knew which boy was really Ladomeng and which was not. It is widely believed that the one who passed away was Ladomeng and the one who was alive was the supernatural being. This boy was still called Ladomeng when I was with him, until much later. When he went to school in Java, his name was changed to Abdul Qahhar Mudzakkar.

Another version that claims to refute Qahhar's death draws on the Sulawesi tradition of a tomanurung[5] who comes to earth to serve the ruler by protecting the general population from corrupt, authoritarian, and abusive leaders. According to the myth constructed and believed by his followers, Qahhar is a tomanurung. A tomanurung never dies, but ascends temporarily to heaven, awaiting the time when it is necessary to come back. Suggestions that Qahhar is a tomanurung, however, are usually buttressed by accounts of him living in exile (cf. Tihami 1984) where he is both engaged in strategic work and at the same time practicing Sufi meditation.

According to the information collected by Anhar Gonggong (1992: 174), however, Qahhar was killed in 1965 by Corporal Sadeli of the Indonesian army. Astray in the forest near the Lasolo River area, Sadeli reportedly heard a radio playing, and he approached the source of the sound, knowing that Qahhar always carried with him a transistor radio. Initially, Sadeli wanted to capture the man alive, but when he saw him holding a grenade, he shot to kill. He then compared a photo of Qahhar he had with him to the dead body and concluded that the man he had shot was truly Qahhar. The body was photographed, and this is the photo that later circulated among Qahhar's followers, who did not believe the face of the body to be that of their leader. The body was retrieved from the jungle by helicopter and flown to Makassar, where it was received at Palemonia Hospital by Jusuf (a member of the Indonesian military given the task of stamping out the rebellion). Jusuf simply announced that the body was that of Qahhar, but only one of Qahhar's wives, two children, and an uncle were authorized to see the body. Corry van Stenus, another wife of Qahhar, was on her way to visit her husband's body in Pakue when she was informed by Jusuf that "there is no point in her trying to see him, since Qahhar has already gone and been brought to Makassar". Abdullah, a son, came from Java along with his sister and an uncle, and was invited by Jusuf to directly identify the corpse of his father. He recognized his father from the eczema on his foot and his dentures.

Doubts remain lingering over Abdullah's claim, however, for it is alleged that Jusuf merely faked the death on the basis of an earlier face-to-face meeting with Qahhar. Many believe that when they met in Bonepute, first on 21 October 1961, and then on 12 November of the same year (later on called the "Bonepute Agreement"), Jusuf suggested to Qahhar that he go into hiding. And then, it is said among the followers, they embraced tearfully. According to this version, Qahhar agreed to be picked up by helicopter to make his escape, while another retrieved someone else's body in his place. According to the sources collected by Tihami (1984: 102), the body was dropped in the sea between Makassar and Jakarta so that no one would be able to claim that it was not Qahhar's. Of course the government's version of these events is that Qahhar is truly dead, a position sustained by both Harvey (1974) and van Dijk (1981).

Yet another version was related to me by Ishaque, whose source was Mansur, a close assistant of Qahhar.

'Qahhar and I were laughing,' said Mansur, when Qahhar's death was announced on the radio. Qahhar then said, 'Right, that's me who got killed,' and with a laugh he asked, 'How could this be?' A few days after the radio announcement, Mansur was suddenly left alone by Qahhar, while he was taking a bath in the river. Qahhar disappeared, and Mansur never saw him again.

Referring to Mudzakkar (1962), Ishaque told me the following:

Look at one of Qahhar's books in which he already mentions a few years before the armed conflict near the Lasolo river that "I will return all my supporters and military and police into the lap of the Republic of Indonesia, except the MOMOC (Moment Mobile Commando), Qahhar's core military division, on the condition that Javanese Communism will be banished for ever from the soil of Indonesia. But, if one day the Communists ever come back, I will also come along with the MOMOC to confront them, until they disappear completely.

Thus, when President Wahid proposed rescinding the parliamentary act banning Communism (TAP MPRS XXV/MPRS/1966) from Indonesia,

Ishaque commented, "That's probably what Qahhar meant as the time for him to come back."

His followers, meanwhile, reject the claim that he was killed at all. One of them told me:

> It is impossible that he was killed by Soekarno's military. During that last armed contact near the Lasolo River, in the village of Pakue, Qahhar was quite a distance (a three-day walk) away from the place where the fighting took place. Moreover, Qahhar was always surrounded by at least two platoons of armed bodyguards. He was never alone; he always carried a rifle, not a grenade, as was mentioned on the radio news and in the newspapers about his alleged death. Government news stories were pure propaganda.

Another staff member told me:

> I was in that platoon, and I was with Qahhar while the battle in Lasolo was taking place. When a courier told Qahhar that our manpower was weakening and more support was needed in Lasolo, a platoon was sent. But I was still with him, until my platoon was eventually asked to join our forces in Lasolo. Then we left Qahhar alone. On the way to the battle, I met someone who told me that the war was over, and I returned to see Qahhar. Qahhar was not there anymore, but I saw a helicopter close by, just taking-off, leaving the area where he was. I believe that Qahhar left with that helicopter for safety reasons. He was not dead; there was no trace of bloodshed.

In short, the contemporary movement can capitalize on the mystery and controversy of Qahhar's death. Although Abdullah identified the corpse as his father's, others doubted his capacity to do so. In fact, he had spent most of his childhood in Java with his mother. He rarely saw his father, and had only spent three days with him three years before, although they shared a bed. "The problem is that no one else saw the corpse. I did, however," said Abdullah.[6] Although Ishaque's third-hand account of Qahhar's escape seems to be less reliable than Abdullah's first-hand account, it is Ishaque's version that has galvanized the movement's followers. Social mythologization has been at work on transforming Ishaque's vision, while Jusuf's silence, wittingly or not, has conspired in expanding the myth. Ultimately, what these tales show is that Qahhar's ideology and aspirations remain alive in the memories of his followers. It seems as if they need to believe that their leader is or was alive.

Remembering Qahhar's Ideas

In addition to evoking stories of his escape or his tomanurung status, staff members also institutionalize their stance on Qahhar's death through the use of slogans attributed to the leader himself. At meetings, I heard regularly such slogans as "Javanese colonialism", "Majapahitism", and "Javanese syncretism and communism" (cf. Mudzakkar 1960, 1961; Gonggong 1992: 204). The thrust of these slogans is to construct memories and ties between the original movement and the contemporary situation: members of the movement identify themselves as having been colonized by the Javanese, who are literally depicted as foreigners. The movement therefore sees itself as anti-colonialist, directing their attacks at the Javanese in particular. In the words of Laica Marzuki, a professor at Hasanuddin University, "The trauma of Javanese hegemony is seen as the syndrome of Majapahit authority." Among core staff members of the contemporary movement, I was also told that "It is not the Javanese that we do not like, but their exploitative domination, their colonialization, and their openness to communism," and "Some of us, including Qahhar, are married to Javanese because we love them, but we do not like their corrupted values."

The movement's members also reject the national transmigration policy that is seen as simply a means to spread Javanese domination over the outer islands and infuse all the nation's peoples with Javanese values. Further, they view the national family planning scheme as a means to control the growth of non-Javanese. As one staff member argued:

> In the presence of larger numbers of Javanese transmigrants and their allies from Madura and Bali in Jakarta, non-Javanese will, in the long-run, become minorities in their own homelands. Just like the Indians in America and the aborigines in Australia. In the outer islands, land taken by the government becomes that of the transmigrants and is thus lost, from the perspective of outer islanders.[7]

In terms of the economy, members believe that local natural resources and the proceeds derived from their sale have been taken away from them so as to feed and enrich the Javanese. Socially, they believe that Javanese values have become strong and predominant in the national framework, largely because of the constant support of the military and central bureaucracy, both of which are regarded as being Javanese dominated.

One staff member told me that Javanization is taking place everywhere, and politically, perhaps this claim is not inaccurate. The Javanese system of local government has been transferred en bloc, following exactly the familiar break-down in Java between *kabupaten* ("district"), *kecamatan* ("sub-district"), and *desa* ("village"). Until recently, this system was largely unknown beyond Java: the outer islands had their own systems of rule, different from the multiple palace-centred Javanese system, not only in names and titles but also in essence. The same staff member continues:

> Look at all the offices — they are always full of Javanese. They occupy most of the so-called 'wet' [lucrative] positions. If you go to a bank, you will notice that there are many Javanese names associated with positions of director or manager. In military and police offices, most officers are Javanese. Their names are quite obvious, for example, full of 'su/soe sounds' like Suharto, Soewarno, Soebroto. When they talk, you will immediately know, because of their Javanese accent. Our system of government has been Javanized. Our system of akkarungeng/ akkarungang ('government') has disappeared. We have to do something.

Thus understanding the hostility faced by transmigrants requires not only attention to the contemporary situation but also understanding of the way that the rhetoric of contemporary followers in Sulawesi draws upon slogans that perpetuate Qahhar's separatist movement.

Similar links can be made in the realm of culture. People believe that the local cultures of Sulawesi, like those in the other outer islands, have been destroyed by the Javanese. As one staff member told me:

> The school system and curriculum, TV and radio programs, and mass media in general, they are all Javanese products which represent the Javanese culture. Remember the Pancasila indoctrination workshops — we were forced to memorize this Javanese philosophy since 1978. Qahhar had correctly predicted 16 years earlier [1961] in his book that this was to be the future ideology of Indonesia. Our languages are basically disappearing. Bahasa Indonesia is strongly influenced by Javanese vocabulary, since many national leaders are Javanese. That is why Malaysians find it difficult to understand the Indonesian language, even though the two come from the same root. Many children in Sulawesi, particularly in the cities and towns, are now strangers to their own local languages. They are embarrassed to speak their mother tongue, and some of them are trying to speak a Javanese dialect. Some

non-Javanese children are even given a Javanese name. People don't even realize what they are doing!

The Javanese and their culture are portrayed as destroying local Sulawesi culture, but interestingly enough there is no complaint about the spread of Bahasa Indonesia, basically a foreign language derived from Malay, at the cost of local languages. Obviously it is not the foreignness that people in Sulawesi object to, but rather the cultural imperialism of the central government dominated by Javanese. Invoking memories of Qahhar by using his language thus creates continuity of the movement in 1950 to the present. Core members thus evoke Qahhar and his ideas to create a collective memory within the movement itself that allows for some flexibility in dealing with both historical and contemporary events.

Perspectives of Non-members

Beyond the opinions of those who are committed to the movement (as described above), how do other publics remember Qahhar and his movement? The data presented below was collected from people representing four different groups: (1) those who have never been members but who are very aware of the movement; (2) those who used to be part · of the movement during Qahhar's lifetime but left it before Qahhar's alleged defeat; (3) those who used to be members of the movement during and after Qahhar's leadership, but have since stopped; and (4) young people who have only learned of Qahhar and the movement recently.

One person from the first category, those who were not members but who were aware of the movement, told me:

> When I was young, I knew that Qahhar was very influential and involved in the struggle to liberate Sulawesi. I had relatives who had joined his cause, and we read about the movement in the media and [heard about it] on the radio. I myself decided however to remain in Makassar and study. Thank God, I did not join this movement. Had I been involved, I would not have finished my studies. I eventually worked in an office and had a good income. A cousin of mine, however [who had joined the movement], is now working as a farmer, cultivating cocoa in the countryside. He seems to have a hard life. In order to help him, I took his son to stay with me, thus allowing him to study in university.

Another representative of this category told me:

> I did not join Qahhar because I knew that he could not win. His
> movement cost us a lot. How many people were killed at the time?
> Almost every family in South Sulawesi had a member involved in this
> movement and it only brought them suffering. Thus, even if the move-
> ment were to be revived today, I would never join.

Another individual said:

> I was told by my father that had he joined the Indonesian military after
> 1965, he would have been a second lieutenant, only one rank lower
> than he was under Qahhar. My father regretted that Qahhar did not
> advise him to make this move. Why did he not do it on his own accord,
> though? Probably because he expected Qahhar to return. My father
> passed away without any of this happening. I feel sorry for him. He
> waited for so long.

Overall, non-members who were knowledgeable about Qahhar's movement
were, for varying reasons, not enthusiastic about supporting it. Rather,
they recollect that they did not support Qahhar or his movement at the
time, that they would not do so now and that Qahhar and the movement
brought suffering to the people of Sulawesi. Questioning the ability of the
movement to succeed then and now was also a theme of an informant
in the second category, one who had been a member of the original
movement but who had since left:

> I used to be part of the movement in the 1950s. However, I left after
> a while, because our suffering was too great. There was not much food,
> our inheritance was just used up. We used to have buffaloes and cows,
> but they were gone. Our house had been burnt by the Indonesian
> military (TNI). We had a piece of land but we could not cultivate it
> during the war. So I fled to Sumatra. I only came back recently to visit
> my relatives in Makassar. If the movement emerges once again, I will
> support it but not join, until its goal is clear to me.

One informant from the third category had been a member of the
original movement even beyond the time that Qahhar was allegedly
killed. Although he remained a faithful member for a time, he eventually
withdrew and would only support a revived movement if a leader to
replace Qahhar could be found:

After the 'departure' of Qahhar in 1965, I decided to establish a rattan and wood retail business. For a couple of years in the 1970s, I remained active in meetings. Since 1984, however, I have been questioning the strength of this movement. There is no clear leader to follow. Some former leaders have fought against each other for power. If Qahhar is alive today, he is quite old, and the situation of the country is quite different from what it was 35 years ago. It is impossible for him to lead a country now. I once went to Malaysia, believing that the leader [Qahhar] was still active there. When I arrived, I was told that people there expect people in Sulawesi to be more active. I then concluded that the movement is weak. It cannot be relied upon. The Javanese are stronger and stronger. There is no way for us to defeat them. Why don't we just work with them? However, if the movement becomes strong again, of course I will join, provided the strategy is changed and the leader is reliable.

Representatives of the last category, youths who have only recently learned about Qahhar and the movement, offer interesting contrasts within the group itself. The first quote below is from an active boy scout who has learned of the movement through its contemporary activities, and who has a relatively positive impression of it:

I did not know anything about Qahhar's movement until I was told about it by my friends and read in the newspapers about his return. I was curious to know more, and I continued reading about him and his movement, and I even attended the public speech of Syamsuri [believed by some to be Qahhar, see below]. I am interested to know more about Qahhar, since I believe in the need for a democratic federal state.

The second quote, by contrast, is taken from interaction with a group of students, two of whom answered my question about knowing Qahhar. The first knew nothing of him, but the second offered an interesting (and largely inaccurate) explanation of who Qahhar was:

Asked if they had heard about Qahhar and his movement, one of them, a science student, answered, 'I have never heard of him. I know Professor Abdul Kahar Mudzakkir, a member of the Jakarta Charter, who prepared the national constitution of Indonesia, but I know nothing about Qahhar. Or is he the man you mean?' Another student interrupted and said: 'Yes, we know about him. He betrayed the country and declared a rebellion against Soekarno. But isn't he Javanese? He was a bad guy, apparently — I am not sure though — I don't really remember what I learned in the Pancasila workshop' [a compulsory ideology course taught in schools throughout the country].

These data suggest that the memories of Qahhar and his movement are quite varied, ranging from support (among youths) either directly for Qahhar or for the contemporary movement, to bitter memories of the original movement and negative feelings towards Qahhar. The difference between younger and older respondents' attitudes needs to be explored further, but my preliminary findings suggest that both mass media and the school curriculum may be influential in shaping contemporary opinions among young Indonesians. Although the present research does not address the impact of media directly, the following section highlights two prominent organizations that have developed from the Qahhar movement and that are active in contemporary politics. Given their active roles, these organizations, their staffs and activities, appear frequently in mass media and are thus important for understanding perceptions of the contemporary Qahhar movement in Indonesia.

Organizational Contentions

In the post-Suharto period, the tacit ideological perpetuation of the Qahhar movement by core members through myth and personal recollection emphasized above has taken a more institutionalized form. I discuss two prominent branch organizations in the present section. The first, *Komite Persiapan Pelaksanaan Syariat Islam* (KPPSI — Organizing Committee for the Preparation for the Application of Islamic Law) is a Sulawesi-based organization founded by Qahhar's son, Abdul Aziz, and others in October of 2000. The main purpose of KPPSI is to promote the implementation of Islamic law in South Sulawesi. The second organization is *Pusat Amanat Referendum Rakyat Sulawesi* (PARAS, Center for Trusteeship of the Sulawesi People's Referendum). PARAS was also established in 2000, and it focuses on gaining popular support for a referendum (asking either to remain within the unitary state of Indonesia or to work towards independence) in Sulawesi. Contrasting these two organizations illuminates how contemporary branch organizations built from the original Qahhar movement develop their focus and organizational strategies using varied sources.

KPPSI: Islamic Law, Leadership, and Regional Politics

Abdul Aziz, the leader of KPPSI, is a science graduate from Hasanuddin University in Makassar, and although he lacked a strong background in Islamic studies, his expertise gained him enough credibility to be named director of a *pesantren* (religious boarding school) branch of Hidayatullah in Makassar. Abdul was initially supported by K.H. Syamsuri Abdul Madjid, whom he had first met while he was the director of the Pesantren Hidayatullah in Jakarta. Syamsuri had been appointed as a temporary teacher and eventually became the pesantren's *kyai* or religious teacher on a part time basis.

The main strategy of KPPSI committee leaders for implementing Islamic law in South Sulawesi is to rely on interpersonal communication with regional opinion leaders. Specifically, KPPSI maintains communication with the *Tri Pimpinan Daerah* (TRIPIDA, Three Regional Leaders of Local Government) which refers to the district chief, police chief, and military chief. The KPPSI committee seeks approval from these authorities to address the public on a specific issue of Islamic law, and then produces mass gatherings and public forums. K.H. Syamsuri in particular was usually called upon to deliver religious speeches at these meetings, in which he duplicates many of the themes central to Qahhar's presentations. In fact, many loyal followers believe that Syamsuri is in fact Qahhar himself, pointing out that even his signature is remarkably similar to the founding leader's. When asked, however, Syamsuri states: "I am not Qahhar, I am Syamsuri." The ambiguity of Syamsuri's identity is, in fact, tied to the ambiguity of the organization's mandate. Despite Syamsuri's claims, many audiences have nonetheless misspelled his name as "Kamsuri" and concluded that the name Kamsuri is basically the abbreviation of Kam = Kahar Mudzakkar; Su = Sulawesi; and Ri = Republik Islam Indonesia. This explanation supports one follower's claim that Syamsuri (and the movement) are "basically struggling for RPII". Indeed many of the members of the KPPSI Committee believe that the organization's goal is to realize the RPII proclaimed by Qahhar in 1962.

According to members of KPPSI, for Islamic law to be implemented, they must, above all, encourage Muslims to be pious and to avoid deeds prohibited by Islam. As for non-Muslims, I was informed that their religions would be respected as long as they respected Islam. "Muslim brothers and sisters would pay *zakat*," I was told, "and non-Muslims would pay a tax … all the while treating non-Muslims fairly and negotiating with them as equals." I was assured that "This [practice] would thwart religious aggression and exclusivity." Respondents told me that these are the reasons why the government has given its approval to their Committee. Members of the Committee did acknowledge that some individuals belonged to the so-called Jundullah, the "militias" or "soldiers of God". These militias are more aggressive, and are known to attack bars where alcohol and drugs are sold and where they believe prostitution is practiced, demanding that the institutions be closed. Despite the fact that some members of Jundullah claim affiliation with KPPSI, Abdul Aziz Qahhar has denied this. He has also denied that KPPSI supports Jundullah at all. M'din, a close assistant of Aziz, assured me that "We do not tolerate the aggressive actions of Jundullah. We need to use a persuasive approach to our people rather than a coercive one."

In addition to ambiguity about KPPSI links to Jundullah, there is contention among KPPSI members about the claims stating that Syamsuri is in fact Qahhar. One member claims that "He is probably a Javanese military intelligence officer trying to identify potential leaders and supporters of Qahhar. But he is not Qahhar, for sure." The issue is potentially divisive, however, because it suggests that the Islamic movement as a whole is not cohesive, as is stated in one media report [*Sabili*, no. 15 (8), 5 January 2001: 76: "this is a strategy used by the enemies of Islam to divide Qahhar's relatives and followers, in order to move people's attention away from Qahhar's initial goal"]. Arguments against the claims that Syamsuri is Qahhar emphasize that "Syamsuri is not very good in reciting the Qur'an", which is basic knowledge for a kyai — a post that Qahhar held. "He was a graduate of the Muhammadiyah High School (Muallimin) in Solo, Java," one member recalled, emphasizing that Qahhar was very fluent in his Qur'anic recitations and even spoke Arabic fluently. Ultimately, the claim that Syamsuri is Qahhar is not accepted because the former lacks his predecessor's charisma, articulateness, and attention to contemporary issues. One member told me that "The subject of his [Syamsuri's] speeches remains the same as they were in the 1950s, meaning he does not follow the issues of the contemporary situation. I believe if he really were Qahhar, Syamsuri would change his rhetoric ...." Marlia, another member, told me:

> One of Qahhar's wives (Sitti Hamie) saw Syamsuri, but Syamsuri did not recognize her. She says that Syamsuri is not Qahhar. 'I know Qahhar very well, intimately. Syamsuri does not seem to know either

[sic] Buginese, Makassarese, or Torajanese. He does know some words of these languages, but his pronunciation sounds awkward and he definitely has an accent. Qahhar had no accent at all when he spoke these languages, because he was born and grew up here. He was native. Moreover, Syamsuri did not recognize me at all, meaning he is not Qahhar. I have lived with Qahhar for years. He would have recognized me right away.

Even with multiple pieces of evidence suggesting that Syamsuri is not Qahhar, the question of his identity is contested. One KPPSI member went to Sarawak to check the validity of the claim that Syamsuri really is Qahhar, and on his return to Sulawesi, he spread the news that Syamsuri is not Qahhar. Another member, who believes that Qahhar is still alive, told me a story about Qahhar's face-to-face meeting with Jusuf when the latter served as Chief of Military Command XIV/Hasanuddin and "Lightning Operation" Commander (*Komandan Operasi Kilat*).

> In Longi, in the village of Awo, on 30 November 1964, Qahhar addressed his followers and said their struggle would observe a cease-fire so as to develop a new strategy. He then asked who among the members of the audience would become a martyr to replace him. Most members of the audience were reportedly ready to assume this burden, but Qahhar asserted one condition — 'that the martyr has to look a bit like me.' Then four members of the audience were selected: one from Southeast Sulawesi, one from Enrekang, one from Banjarmasin, and the last one from Ambon. Each of them was given a forgery of one of Qahhar's official papers and Qahhar's initials were printed on their underwear. Apparently, the one who was killed was from Southeast Sulawesi. According to Ishaque, the son of this man, named Beddu, has testified that this story is true and that his father was the one who was killed, not Qahhar. The photo that was circulated was [his] father's, not Qahhar's.

Another member of KPPSI added that "it is possible that Syamsuri was the one from Banjarmasin. He was younger than Qahhar that day. Thus Syamsuri is not Qahhar."

On the other end of the spectrum, firmly believing that Syamsuri is Qahhar, are some former leaders of the old Islamist rebellion (DI/TII) in Sulawesi, including Ali A.T., Kyai Djunaid Sulaiman, and Djufrie Tambora of Southeast Sulawesi. "When Djufrie was just about to die, Syamsuri was present until the funeral, confirming that he was really Qahhar," says one member of KPPSI. Other signs were interpreted as proofs of Syamsuri being Qahhar. When Marzuki Hasan, Qahhar's former Minister of Information, was sick, Syamsuri was seen whispering in Hasan's ear, and Hasan answered by nodding. It was speculated that Hasan had, in doing so, confirmed that Syamsuri was Qahhar. According to Djunaid Sulaiman, Qahhar's former Minister of Justice, in an interview in *Sabili* (29 November 2000), "Syamsuri is truly Qahhar. I knew Qahhar quite well since we were in Java together and then in Sulawesi together. Cut my neck off if he is not Qahhar."

Mansyur Suryanegara, a historian at Padjadjaran University, Bandung, also believes that Syamsuri is Qahhar. "Djunaid Sulaiman was a close friend of Qahhar," Mansyur argues, "and he is a respected religious leader (kyai); if he tells us that he recognized his own friend, we should believe him." For Mansyur, "the efforts of the Indonesian military were not successful: although Qahhar was said to have been captured, it was not the case. This is exactly what happened with Tan Malaka [another Indonesian hero]. Tan Malaka had escaped while the authorities detained someone who resembled him." For Mansyur, many leaders have "look-alikes", much as Saddam Hussein of Iraq does, in order to protect their own life. "Furthermore," Mansyur says, "whether Syamsuri is believed to be Qahhar or not, this is not Syamsuri's goal. He has already changed his life, replacing the old strategy with a new one. His goal is to create a community which is based on God's teaching, filled with peace and solidarity."

Despite the strength that these claims might have among some followers, on 17 August 2000, a group of 37 family members and close friends of Qahhar signed a declaration stating that Syamsuri is not Qahhar, holding that Qahhar died a martyr on 3 February 1965. They ask that people keep this in mind and reject the authority claimed by Syamsuri's followers, who misuse the name of Qahhar. The declaration asks Syamsuri to cease those activities that resemble Qahhar's past practices; he and his followers are encouraged to realize that they are misleading the public and they should therefore apologize, not least to Qahhar's surviving family members. The declaration goes as far as threatening legal measures if Syamsuri refuses to heed it, and according to Abdullah Ashal, a lawyer and notary, Syamsuri can be accused of committing a crime.

Even the family's views are not clear and consistent, however, and some family members who signed the declaration used to believe that

Syamsuri was Qahhar. Abdul Aziz told me over the telephone that his father, Qahhar, was there with him in the pesantren (when it was Syamsuri who was there). I asked "Are you sure Syamsuri is truly your father? It's hard to believe; you've got to be careful!" to which he replied, "That's relative, you are right. But, we now have the leader we need." I also asked other children of Qahhar about Syamsuri. Zainab and Muslimin maintained that Syamsuri is not Qahhar and that Qahhar is a martyr. However, while the names of all his children are listed in that declaration, some did not sign the declaration. It is possible that those who initially believed in Syamsuri came to realize either that he is an impostor or that including their names in the declaration would help them avoid government suspicion of involvement in separatist politics.

Since the family's declaration, however, the belief that Syamsuri is Qahhar has in fact diminished, but during the same period, the activities of the KPPSI have expanded and received growing support from the masses. By generating media coverage and exposure, the controversy may in fact have contributed to this growing support. On a flight to Makassar, one of the movement's members, M'din, told me:

> Even if Syamsuri is not Qahhar, we can see that the response of the people to Qahhar's struggle and ideology remains strong in the heart and memory of the South Sulawesi community. He remains popular and remembered. Thus the appearance of Syamsuri can have a positive side effect in that he has been successful in socializing and popularizing, once again, the ideas of Qahhar, particularly in promoting Islamic teachings among the Muslims, not in an aggressive way, but through persuasion.

Thus the KPPSI, while embroiled in debates about Qahhar's death and Syamsuri's identity, has begun to forge a popular base in support of implementing Islamic law in the region. In fact, Syamsuri and the ambiguity of his identity can be seen as a tool by which the movement is able to link itself to the past and the original movement, while at the same time inserting itself into contemporary politics of Islamic revival. This revival in Indonesian national politics and culture is well known, and the KPPSI appears to draw upon that broader movement while remaining focused on the immediate region. The KPPSI's goals are articulated in regional terms, and the myths of its historical founder and links to the original Qahhar movement strengthen the regional flavour of the organization. Organizational strategy and structure are shaped by regional and local histories, while the message articulates a more nationally salient purpose. I now turn to a discussion of PARAS to highlight how, despite its similar base in the Qahhar movement, its organizational strategies and position in national politics differ markedly from KPPSI.

PARAS: Discourses of Separatism

In contrast to the KPPSI, PARAS draws its organizational strategy from other regional movements throughout Indonesia, particularly from East Timor and Aceh. At the same time, however, it claims a shared history with the Qahhar movement, and in this way is true to its particular location in Sulawesi. Its strongest tie to the Qahhar movement is through promoting regional separatism.

PARAS was established in 2000 during the month of Ramadan. Its main purpose is to popularize the idea of conducting a referendum in Sulawesi that would establish it as a separate, autonomous region. The name of PARAS was chosen for the new organization because of its literal meaning, "face". Tasreng, one of the founding members, told me that, "Figuratively, it means to show the face of the Sulawesi movement after decades of hiding underground." Organizationally, PARAS is modelled on the *Sentral Informasi Referendum Rakyat Aceh* (SIRA, Center for Information on Referendum of Acehnese People), with branches in all provinces, and sub-branches in all districts, across Sulawesi. Tasreng emphasized the importance of regional exposure, stating, "we will do our best for this project, and in so doing we are planning to establish agents to reach our supporters in all sub-districts and villages in the remotest areas of Sulawesi. We already have massive numbers of followers in the countryside." Saladin, another leader in PARAS, reinforced this emphasis, directly linking the regional exposure to Qahhar:

> Since Qahhar fought mainly in the rural areas, where the majority of the population lives, his supporters remain strong there. They have strength not only within Sulawesi, but beyond. The Bugis-Makassarese have spread diasporically in Southeast Asia, and since the defeat of Qahhar in 1965, the number of Sulawesi emigrants has increased. These emigrants have established strong overseas networks. The so-called KKSS (*Kerukunan Keluarga Sulawesi Selatan*, South Sulawesi Family Association) can be found in every Indonesian province, where they foster closely-knit community relationships.

PARAS' plans include encouraging research and training for extra-curricular or off-campus activities, such as organizations for self-defence and boy scouts, seminars on leadership and management, and courses to improve the knowledge of Islam. PARAS wants to become affiliated with all research centres in Sulawesi, and it seeks to contact the so-called "disappointed but rich people of Sulawesi" who were kept out of the circles of power during the presidencies of Suharto and Wahid. Among these people are such influential professional, political and business figures as Ryaas Rasyid, Arnold Baramuli, Beddu Amang, Tanri Abeng, Yusuf Kalla, Basri Hasanuddin, Muhammad Ghalib, and even B.J. Habibie. According to one of its leaders, "although these people probably have no link with the movement, it is important for PARAS to approach them on the basis of their displeasure with the central government, parti-cularly during Wahid's presidency. We have a common goal. However, in approaching them, we need to use extra care." For PARAS, it is felt that the influence and financial support of the above people could be critical in furthering PARAS' programs.

PARAS members are typically active in the universities as lecturers, researchers, and students, as well as in secondary schools as teachers, or as NGO activists. Many of them are the children of former soldiers and veterans of the DI/TII. Not surprisingly, their parents constantly im-pressed upon them the importance of carrying on their struggle for independence. The pictures and books of Qahhar (Mudzakkar, 1380 H [1960], 1381 H [1961], 1382 H [1962]) are regularly xeroxed and distributed in mosques, in particular in Palopo, Qahhar's hometown. Some PARAS members have opened businesses and cooperatives in order to financially support their mission. One of its members told me: "Now is a good time to go into business, since the monopoly of Suharto's family and its cronies has been reduced. This new context allows us to enter various economic sectors, such as inter-island and international trade and the export of commodities from Sulawesi." One of the leaders of PARAS, Saladin, told me that he would negotiate with the central government so that the proceeds of all state companies in Sulawesi, trading in natural gas, steel, nickel, gold, sugar, and cement, be kept within the region. "This could be a strategy ultimately leading to full independence. Indeed, should autonomy be obtained, it will pave the way to liberation. If this attempt fails, it will make our movement even stronger. Thus we win either way," says one member.

Other goals of PARAS, according to its secretary, Marlia, are: establishing a vision for the new state which is conducive to modern society; recruiting trusted and committed persons; and the gradual socialization of the idea of the referendum itself. In order to pursue these objectives, various strategies will be followed, among them: creating new economic and political partnerships within parties and with other population groups; strengthening the research centres in all provinces and universities; selecting new board members, and training them in organization, leadership, management skills; writing for the mass media and research; and creating a database of martyrs, veterans, and followers. In fact, according to Marlia, PARAS published two open declarations, in early April 2001 in *Fajar*, a daily newspaper in Makassar. Flyers were also circulated among students, professors, and scholars that raised the issue of the destiny of the Sulawesi population presently suffering as a result of Javanese colonization. These flyers have been circulated throughout the five provinces of Sulawesi.

Interpretive Reflections

Qahhar's followers have persistently constructed their memories of him, and subsequently moulded organizational ideas according to their own — to use Thayer's (1968, 1987) words in his communication theory — "situations", "needs", "susceptibilities", "intentions", "purposes", or "internal relationships". These dynamics hold true beyond the organizations and networks of members to relationships with the central government. In their memories and rhetoric, their leader remains active, physically or psychologically. They remember Qahhar, and some of them await him, as a tomanurung, or messianic leader.

In remembering him and invoking his mission, contemporary followers also anticipate the possible political consequences (such as being identified, captured, detained, tortured, and killed). It is this anticipation that links the original movement to the present. The revolution of the 1950s and, in particular, the movement of Qahhar, remain strongly embedded within the collective and personal memories of many people in South Sulawesi. These memories are reflected more concretely in underground activities closely related to the ideas and struggle of Qahhar, including anti-Javanese statements against Jakarta's alleged role as colonizer ("Majapahitism"), and in enthusiasm for democratic government based on notions of a federal government of Sulawesi. The aim of democratic government goes beyond the original movement and the region, however, recognizing a trend towards government that respects the existence of other authorities within a globalizing world.

The transfer of leadership during the Suharto era seems to have been a strategy to maintain the legitimacy of the movement, although it was relatively inactive compared to its role during the post-Suharto years. The movement is being revived now, particularly after the creation of the two prominent organizations KPPSI and PARAS. In contrast to the public presence of these contemporary branch organizations, however, the core of the movement purposely retains a low profile and cultivates its aura of secrecy, allegedly to avoid the violence that surrounded its efforts in the past. Thus the legacy of Qahhar, and memories of the past, remain an important part of how groups in Sulawesi organize themselves and strategize their political agendas at the local and national levels.

The emergence of B.J. Habibie along with his cabinet branded as "SDM" (*Semua Dari Makassar* — All From Makassar) proved to some that Sulawesi natives can play a role in national as opposed to regional politics. But although Sulawesi is now visible on the national level, Qahhar is only viewed as a powerful spokesperson on the local or regional level. Few who follow Habibie's role in national politics are aware of the regional rebellion and this charismatic person. Thus only at the local and regional level is the mystery of Qahhar's death or escape a salient issue. Access to his body was denied at the time he was allegedly killed, and Qahhar has no gravesite. The mystery persists partly because those who were directly involved, such as M. Jusuf, have yet to make definitive public statements.

As for Syamsuri and the controversy over his true identity, a polarization seems to be developing among Qahhar's followers, but again, only on the local and regional level. If Syamsuri continues to act as if he were Qahhar, but fails to adapt his performance and rhetoric to the current social situation of the Sulawesi people, his present followers may eventually lose faith in him and reject him. People in contemporary Sulawesi need more than a committed leader; they are looking for a skillful guide who understands what his people need and knows how to plan, apply, and evaluate strategic development programs. A messianic leader cannot prevail if he/she fails to fulfill the most basic demands of his or her contemporary citizens. Until now it has been the myths that have appealed to the popular imagination. In a society where oral tradition remains very much alive, such myths combine a sense of historical pride with a fondness for the mysterious. Also at play here is the belief within that society in the emergence of a just king.

In line with the strong local belief in the existence of just kings, it is interesting to note how even today, memories of a charismatic leader such as Qahhar can influence socio-political circumstances . This could also be the case for Indonesia in general. Soekarno, for example, despite all the flaws of his presidency, is still revered sufficiently that his daughter became a populist heroine and served as President. In fact, it would seem that it is very hard for Indonesians to replace a charismatic leader, even an authoritarian or deceased one. The commitment to the charismatic leader is inconsistent, however, even at the regional level. Different branch groups emphasize the leader's role differently, sometimes only figuratively, as is the case for PARAS, and sometimes as a central concern of the organization, as is the case with KPPSI.

Conclusion

Qahhar's ideas are alive today and I have identified how these are perpetuated and broadened locally and abroad through cell-based organizations. Gone underground after Qahhar's alleged death, the movement generated myths, which strengthened past memories shared well beyond its initial members. Indeed, the controversies perpetuated around Qahhar's death, especially the notion that Syamsuri is Qahhar himself, help socialize and popularize the movement. Qahhar's death and its mythicization through images of leadership such as the tomanurung or "Just King", effectively feed and cement today's national sentiment in the region. Anti-Javanese and anti-cultural imperialism slogans are now integrated into a discourse focused on human rights and local identity.

Research shows that in all three branches of the continuation of the Qahhar movement — the contemporary loyalist organization, KPPSI and PARAS — there is frequent divergence between the leaders and members about short-term goals. Indeed, when members have wanted to take public action, the movement's leaders have held them back saying: "wait, there is no guidance on this yet". This was seen soon after the fall of Suharto in 1998, when some members of the movement's staff hoisted the RPS flag in front of the Mandala monument in Makassar — only to be asked ten minutes later by their leader (Abdul Fattah) to lower it. The movement's leaders, so it seems, do not want to take any action which might outstrip the intentions of the "ultimate awaited" leader. Here again, an ambiguity is created: most followers feel that the awaited guidance is from Qahhar, while others assume this guidance is to come from God, who will indicate the best timing for their actions. A blurred reference to Qahhar, a "just king", and God is thus made, making action difficult. For the leaders, this ambiguous reference to Qahhar or God could be a way to stress the uninterrupted leadership of the movement as well as a way to avoid responsibility for the actions of the membership. Recalling or perpetuating the "myth" surrounding Qahhar, or claiming that the "ultimate" leader is still alive, enables these leaders to legitimize their own power.

These memories of Qahhar are firmly shaping the current local political landscape in South Sulawesi. However, the various branches and organizations stemming from Qahhar's ideas have not coalesced, although all make strong reference to Qahhar in different ways. But, unlike Qahhar, they choose to avoid armed conflict. Qahhar's message has great resonance for the younger generation, among university students in particular. Books by Qahhar and cassettes and photos of Syamsuri are sold everywhere. Seminars on Qahhar draw large audiences. Qahhar is indeed the symbol of independence from the Javanese centre, with a message that is well-grounded and resonant for many people in South Sulawesi, especially at a time when social, political and economic factors surrounding the tensions in Indonesia between the once-dominant centre and the periphery are in transition.

Notes

1   From the perspective of foreign affairs, the Aceh and Sulawesi sovereignist groups can be said to remain a two-in-one movement to this very day.
2   As evidence of his alleged crime the police had produced only some inoperative guns, a broken typewriter, and plain pieces of paper and carbon paper. Sanusi asserted that the latter were being used to write a Duri-Indonesian language dictionary, the draft of which was seized by the police.
3   In 1997, Sanusi died of a heart attack in Sarawak, Malaysia while planning a journey to Southern Philippines, Pakistan, Afghanistan, Libya, the Middle East, Europe (to meet with Hasan Di Tiro), and the United States.
4   "For security reasons, we must always consider others as our enemies," Fattah told me.

5   According to Bugis-Makassarese belief, tomanurung were the ancestors of the kings
    of South Sulawesi.
6   Abdullah's identification was confirmed, however, by Hasan La Kalloe, a former
    member of the movement, and is a first-hand account, while Ishaque's information
    is a third-hand version based on Mansur's account. Both Mansur and Ishaque have
    passed away, while Abdullah and his sister (Faridah), brother in-law (Andi Sumange)
    and uncle (Adam) are living witnesses with whom we could pursue the issue further.
7   However, this comparison seems to be based on an excessive fear of Javanese
    hegemony. Indeed, the process of transmigration to Sulawesi has been quite different
    from the European migrations to America and Australia, for while the former is being
    imposed, the latter was achieved (mostly) by free will. In addition, it took much
    longer for the European population to become the majority in these two continents.
    The same rhetoric was used by the East Timorese when they freed themselves from
    the Javanese yoke. Aceh and Papua are experimenting with a similar discourse. In
    essence, members of the movement resist the centralizing policies carried out by the
    government in the economic, social, cultural, and, of course, political spheres.

Ninjas in Narratives of Local and National Violence in Post-Suharto Indonesia

,FADJAR I. THUFAIL

Our Japanese friends may be surprised to see that the word *ninja* has entered the vocabulary of contemporary Indonesian politics. The ninja — a mythical figure, his head covered with a black mask, a samurai sword in his hand — emerged in Indonesia during the intense struggle over political power after Suharto was forced to resign in 1998. In August of that year, a few months after the transfer of power from Suharto to Habibie, newspapers began to publish reports about the appearance of ninja troops in East Java. The ninjas, it was said, sought out *dukun santet* (black magic practitioners) who lived in the rural areas around Banyuwangi, Pasuruan, and Situbondo — and killed them.

Had the ninjas only killed dukun santet, it would probably not have made the national news.[1] In 1998, however, it turned out that most of the victims were rural Islamic preachers and teachers (*kyai*) who were closely affiliated with the Nahdlatul Ulama (NU), an Islamic mass organization whose membership includes some 35 million Indonesians. Between August and December 1998, at least 253 people were assassinated, allegedly by ninjas. The NU claimed that most of the victims were their affiliates and established a fact-finding team to investigate the massacre, eventually concluding that the killings reflected the political struggle on the national level (*Jakarta Post*, 22 January 1999). In fact, national media picked up the ninja murder spree and cited it as yet more proof that the New Order regime had not yet disappeared.

Connecting the killings in East Java with the national political struggle presented the public with a narrative that the military were the perpetrators of the terror. Some analyses suggested that the ninja troops were actually units of Kopassus (*Komando Pasukan Khusus*), the elite troops of the Indonesian Armed Forces trained in guerrilla strategies and counter-terrorism (Aditjondro 2000; Cribb 2000). Their involvement, it was suggested, showed that the Army was seeking to recapture political power by spreading terror and creating chaos in society: once society plunged into chaos, the military could vindicate an intervention in order to restore "order". In public discussions and concurrent rumours, the killings in East Java have often been interpreted as part of a grand strategy of the military, trying to convince the Indonesian people that the army is the only force able to restore social order in these post-Suharto days.

Since the fall of Suharto, the nature of a new political culture and public sphere are contested at many levels, and the multiple narratives of ninja killings shed light on the complexity of this process. In this essay, I am thus less interested in uncovering the true story about the so-called ninja affair; others have discussed whether or not the military was involved. Instead, I want to explore the question of how Indonesians are coping with uncertainty and violence in the post-Suharto era. In doing this I will try not to fall into a discourse of victimization in which local people are portrayed as victims without voices and agency. In other words, I seek not to reconstruct a single narrative of ninja violence in East Java during the final months of 1998, but to explore the contesting ninja stories in order to shed light on the discourse and the imagination that people have used to resolve their anxieties about post-Suharto political life.

Public accounts of the ninja murder spree have served as evidence of state-sponsored violence: the ninjas allegedly extended the power of the state by inflicting terror and violence upon its citizens. Aditjondro (2000) has studied the links between the ninja troops and the military and paramilitary death squads, special units usually deployed by a fascist state to suppress resistance and pro-democratic movements. He has shown an interesting correspondence between the guerrilla tactics used by the Indonesian military in East Timor and the ninjas' clandestine killing strategy as reported by eyewitnesses in East Java villages, and concludes that the military may have been involved in spreading the terror and masterminding the killings. It may be true, yet we should remember that the evidence of the military's involvement remains scant:

the security apparatus has provided only very limited access to the investigative reports it has produced.

Many other accounts and interpretations are available, however, and are discussed at length in this essay. Shortly after the first ninja attacks, narratives in the form of rumours, gossip, statements, and newspaper accounts abounded as people began to find maimed victims in public places. Scholarly essays on the ninja affair, however, do not incorporate or acknowledge these narratives (Aditjondro 2000; Cribb 2000), despite the important role they play for villagers trying to make sense of the killings. Moreover, the perpetrators of the attacks — whoever they are — seem to have also dwelled on the same narratives to rationalize their choice of victims, their strategies, and their modes of killing. These narratives provide important insights into how violence is connected to the on-going political struggle as well as to the memory of past political experiences (Ricoeur 1984). The ninja killings in East Java took place at a time when expectations of democratization were reaching a climax — and as chaos broke out following the dismantling of the strongly centralized political regime. The narratives of the ninja affair thus convey a sense of anxiety: Indonesians were caught in the tensions between what they perceived as "order" and as "disorder". Moreover, the narratives are like stories that are "hanging without a rope" (Steedly 1993): they seek to revisit the past in order to make sense of present experience that remains clouded in ambiguity and uncertainty. The narratives themselves remain ambiguous, caught between the certainty of order and the confusion of disorder, between the hope of the present and the contested memory of the past — in an effort to resolve the legacy of New Order's culture of violence. Narrative practices — statements, rumours, gossip, and reports — as well as acts of violence, engage us in the process of constructing a public sphere. The narratives discussed below illuminate how the nature of that public sphere is highly contested in post-Suharto Indonesia.

Narratives at the Local Level and in the National Media

It all began a few months before the end of 1998 while Indonesians were still caught up in the euphoria over Suharto's resignation. In an atmosphere of hope that the country was moving toward becoming a democratic society, news of ethnic and religious conflicts began to appear in the media. Sporadic incidents of arson and destruction of religious buildings surfaced in several parts of Java, recalling a sense of fear from the aftermath of the bloody riots in May 1998. This was the time when public confidence in the transitional government of B.J. Habibie (Suharto's successor and protégé) deteriorated rapidly. Only a few people believed that Habibie's government, perceived as nothing but an extension of the Suharto regime, was able to resolve the economic and political crises the country was facing. Chaos and confusion captured the popular mood, especially in the locations where riots had recently taken place.

When news of the ninja killings first surfaced in East Java in July 1998, it received little public attention. I remember only fragmentary stories of how a dukun santet had been killed by a mob, and such stories are far from unusual in places where sorcerers are believed to be able to cause mysterious illness and death; retaliations, often through mob lynching, are not uncommon in East Javanese villages. Collective violence has been a frequent reaction to black magic, and the police rarely arrest those taking part in it. When news and rumours of dukun santet killings emerged, people therefore assumed these were cases of mass violence against people who were suspected of practicing black magic.

In August 1998, slightly different stories were spreading. The killings continued, but by this time the victims were identified as local kyai (Islamic preachers and teachers), and local chapters of Nahdlatul Ulama (NU) immediately claimed the murdered kyai as their affiliates. Within a month, killings by masked "ninja" figures had spread from Situbondo, Banyuwangi and the surrounding areas, to Malang, Madura, and other parts of East Java. Bodies of kyai, slain and tortured, were found in many places: hanging from a tree, left on the street, or dumped in a river.

Up to December 1998, reports of the exact number of murdered kyai remained confusing, but local and national media were soon conducting their own investigations. The police launched an investigation soon after the NU reported the cases, but were unable to provide the exact number of victims. Nor were they able to arrest or identify the perpetrators or others accused of terrorizing other kyai. Dissatisfied with police performance, the NU had established its own fact-finding team to collect testimonies from local people who had witnessed the killings and had recovered mutilated bodies. Choirul Anam of the East Java NU chapter, who led the investigation team, claimed that ninjas had killed 253 people in Banyuwangi, Jember, Situbondo, Bondowoso, Sampang, Pamekasan,

and Pasuruan when they concluded their investigation in December 1998.²
Anam further said that the perpetrators used "special daggers inscribed
with the likeness of a dragon" and planned to kill five hundred people
altogether (*The Jakarta Post*, 12 January 1998). Given that most victims
were members of NU, the team concluded that the killings were not
merely criminal acts, but attacks on one of the key groups of the Muslim
community.

As a matter of fact, kyai murders were only part of the stories and
rumors circulating at the time about unidentified troops going after
Islamic leaders. Many kyai reported that they had been threatened by
strangers suddenly appearing in front of their houses, or approached by
strangers when they were alone. These narratives named the strangers
"ninja", and travelled quickly over the East Java countryside. Anxious
villagers formed night-watch patrols to confront the mysterious figures.
Far from protecting the village from ninja attacks, however, these patrols
cultivated a different sense of terror. Reports appeared that the village
patrols were lynching those whom they alleged were ninja, although in
some cases the victim turned out to be someone unable to produce an
identification card.

Village patrols attacking strangers were not limited to East Java.
Two men on their way to visit relatives were reportedly murdered in Pati,
a town in the northern part of Central Java more than 500 kilometres
from Situbondo. In Pemalang, another town in Central Java, three
Jakarta-based Astra Credit Company employees were killed when they
took a rest on their way back from Surabaya to Jakarta (*The Jakarta
Post*, 9 November 1998). Apparently, the patrols did not pay attention
to the actual identity of the individuals they attacked: when strangers
were unable to identify themselves, they were assaulted. In some cases
the victims could be properly identified after they were killed, but in
other cases the police reported that the victims had been mentally ill
persons who had been left on their own so that they could be killed.
Their conclusions were based on the reports of captured victims from
Semarang and Temanggung in Central Java, who uttered meaningless
words and were unable to answer patrol or police questions (*The Jakarta
Post*, 12 November 1998).

In the last few months of 1998, the word ninja thus became quickly
associated with "terror" and the "killing of strangers". In Bangkalan on
the island of Madura, three police detectives were murdered by a mob

when they tried to capture a suspected criminal and the suspect began to shout "ninja!" (*The Jakarta Post*, 11 February 1999). Such incidents suggest that the word ninja became associated with public anxieties about invisible danger, or could be used to incite mob violence.

The ninja affair has never been solved, nor has anyone been able to elicit detailed testimonies or information from ninjas who were captured and interrogated by village patrols. Asked who instructed him to come to the neighbourhood, one captured ninja only replied, "I am instructed by nobody but money." This kind of answer enraged the masses and prompted them to torture their victim. Mob violence, however, did not uncover any information about the suspected ninja's identities. Rather, it prolonged the mystery of their identity and contributed to the popular conviction that the ninjas were somehow part of a political conspiracy.

Ultimately, local initiative to organize night patrols led to increased anxiety and did not provide a heightened sense of security among the villagers as was originally intended. Violence committed by the patrols mediated the sense of anxiety deriving from the fact that neither the patrols nor the police could offer explanation why there had been "strangers" found in and around the villages in the first place. Even bodily torture of these strangers failed to resolve the uncertainty that the local people felt when encountering and trying to elicit information from them. The police's inability or unwillingness to investigate the presence of unidentified persons thoroughly supports an interpretation that links the local situation to national politics. In other words, the local people's anxiety is in part a manifestation of the larger political transition.

So far, NU has been the only mass organization interested in investigating the ninjas. On completing its investigation, the NU fact-finding team submitted its report to its headquarters in Jakarta. Commenting on the report, Abdurrachman Wahid, then NU chairman, remarked that "the influence of Jakarta was also felt," accusing some Cabinet ministers of masterminding the sordid affair (*The Straits Times*, 30 October 1998). Wahid was not the only one who assumed that the assassination of NU kyai was linked to national politics. Amien Rais, the chairman of Indonesian Mandate Party (PAN) and a leader of the competing Muslim organization, Muhammadiyah, as well as other critics of Suharto, alleged that the former President was behind the killings, although they acknowledged that there was no concrete evidence to support their accusations (*Tempo Online*, <http://www.tempo.co.id> [11 June 1998]).

While no one has yet been able to demonstrate convincingly how and why national political actors might have cultivated an interest in the ninja affair, it can be argued that the ninja killings required some organizational capacity. Furthermore, the fact that the killings occurred in various places and that most of the victims were NU kyai suggests that these actions were coordinated. Munir, of the Commission for Missing Person and Victims of Violence (*Kontras*), an NGO actively involved in investigating the New Order's practices of violence, aired his suspicion that there were indications of "a pattern of slaughter" and of "planned operations" (*Tempo Online*, <http://www.tempo.co.id> [10 October 1998]).

In a recent article on the New Order's violent practices, Cribb (2000) has suggested a link between the "policy" of *petrus* (*penembakan misterius* — mysterious shooting [see Siegel 1998]) and the ninja killings. Given the culture of violence that the New Order cultivated, evidenced in Suharto's 1983–4 instructions for the military and police to kill criminals and former convicts and leave their bodies in public places as a "shock therapy" for other criminals, Cribb (2000) asserts that the parallels in ninja killings suggest that Kopassus is the most likely perpetrator of the killings. He further argues that the New Order security apparatus frequently used techniques of terror and torture to suppress criminality and resistance movements.[3] The ninja affair merely continues this tradition of extra-judicial killings meant to spread terror and threaten political enemies of the New Order regime. Cribb points to the fact that NU leader Abdurrachman Wahid had been one of the most vocal critics of the Suharto regime, and this should serve as an explanation of why the NU had become the target of violence.

Despite the distinctive similarities between military practices and ninja killings, the true identity of the ninjas remains unclear. No one has been able to provide satisfying public evidence, let alone an answer to the question of who the ninjas really are, although eyewitnesses have testified to seeing individuals of a muscular, military-type physique. The undisclosed identity of the ninjas allows different interpretations, one being that they were military people.

Narratives from within the National Political Sphere

Perhaps we should say that no interpretation or explanation is better than any other; rather, each emerges from an interpretative realm within the political public sphere. In post-Suharto Indonesia, this political public sphere remains highly contested, and the fact that one particular interpretative practice becomes more popular than others is the result of power negotiations among a variety of political groups struggling for power.[4] I suggest that the discussions about the figure of the ninja, and the interpretative practices that accompany it, could be read as reflections of the contest for political power in post-Suharto Indonesia: the narratives of the ninja shed light on the construction or re-enactment of particular political, public practices.

NU has been deeply affected by the ninja terror. Most of the victims have been identified as kyai; moreover, NU's involvement should be seen as a manifestation of its fear of being involuntarily caught up in a state-sponsored political struggle, reminiscent of the events in 1965–6 when the NU's youth wing, *Barisan Serba Guna Ansor*, took part in military-sponsored killings and hundreds of thousands of Communist Party (PKI) members and leftists lost their lives (Hefner 2000; Sulistyo 2000). From the start, NU leaders have been wary of a possible connection between the ninja killings and the events of 1965–6: former communists, some of them have argued, are taking revenge at last.

The memories of the massacres of 35 years ago are a substantial theme of the narratives of NU leaders whenever they try to explain why NU kyai have been murdered. For example, Kyai Yusuf Hasyim offered this explanation:

> [the event] is not merely a crime ... [it] shows a collective animosity and this is how they [the perpetrators] organize their revenge .... Those who have spread rumors about the dukun santet perhaps hate the institution of kyai — or they are Communists. For a long time, the Communists have been anti-religious. Wherever the Communists take power, first they will eliminate religious leaders.
>
> (*Forum Keadilan*, 2 November 1998)

Hasyim is one of the most respected NU kyai. He is the charismatic leader of Pesantren Tebu Ireng, the largest Islamic boarding school in East Java. Despite his high social status, he also received telephone threats

from someone who called and warned him that he "should not make
the third mistake". Asked what the mistake would be, the caller said,
"don't help the dukun santet". Kyai Hashim soon realized that the first
and the second mistakes were his involvement in previous anti-communist
activities: in 1948 he took part in fighting the communists in Madiun,
while in 1965 he was the leader of Barisan Serba Guna Ansor, responsible
for the killing of communists in East Java.

Hasyim was convinced that the killing of NU kyai had been "planned,
organized, driven by a collective sentiment, national in scale" (*Forum
Keadilan*, 2 November 1998). He concluded that the killings had been
the work of the communists or the relatives of those killed in 1965–6.
From Hasyim's point of view, the ninja affair has its origin in the unresolved conflict between communists and Muslims — and this conflict,
driven by memories, explains why the NU *ulama* (religious authorities)
have been killed and terrorized.

Kyai Hasyim's comments show one way that the ninja's work might
be related to national politics: the ninja affair is a manifestation of the
struggle against the communists, and that struggle is perceived to be
pursued on the national level. Amien Rais, the leader of Muhammadiyah,
nationalized the ninja affair in another way: he accused former President
Suharto of being the mastermind behind the killings in East Java and
creating an issue that could divert public attention from allegations of
corruption and human rights abuses in the past. Rais states, "Suharto's
cronies and loyalists still want to fight back. They don't want reform and
they want to distract public attention from any probe into his family's
wealth" (*The Straits Times*, 7 November 1998).

Daniel Sparringa, a political analyst at Airlangga University in
Surabaya, makes a direct link between events in East Java and the
national political struggle in Jakarta. Given the timing, strategy, and scale
of the killings, Sparingga has argued, events were obviously related to
"a power struggle within the elite that has made Banyuwangi and other
areas an ideological battlefield" (*The Straits Times*, 30 October 1998).
National politics in Indonesia has been shaped by a continuous rivalry
between the traditionalist NU, on the one hand, and the modernist
Muhammadiyah, on the other, and both parties have gained support from
cabinet ministers and Army generals, political actors who played a
significant role in provoking conflicts.[5] The possibility that cabinet
ministers were involved in the ninja affair has also been explored by

Abdurrachman Wahid and other senior NU leaders in East Java who publicly claimed that a cabinet minister with affiliations with the military and the modernist Muslims had supported the killings (*The Straits Times*, 30 October 1998).

Narratives that explain violence in Indonesia as the work of the state have permeated the discourse of violence during and after the New Order, a regime that has always been involved in violent events. However, this kind of explanation may be incomplete, as it reduces violence to an instrument in the hands of political groups within the state apparatus. Instead of holding narratives of state violence as the only explanation of how and why acts of violence have taken place, one could try to develop an eye and an ear for contesting forces voiced through other channels. Accounts in the media, eyewitness reports, testimonies, and life histories can be used to make the negotiations within the public sphere more visible.

Narratives about the ninja affair originate in various public spheres, and each mediates the production of what the anthropologist Michael Herzfeld (1997) has called "cultural intimacy". Cultural intimacy steers the production of meaning within a social group (from the smallest community of a village to the community of a nation-state); it is created through the use of shared metaphors, either verbal or pictorial. I argue here that narratives of the ninja affair mediate different constructions of cultural intimacy and that the various narrators evoke them in order to situate themselves in the realm of the national public.

The cumulative effect of various incidents suggests that the ninja affair was indeed linked to national level politics. For example, Kyai Hasyim, a member of the national Supreme Advisory Council (*Dewan Pertimbangan Agung*), received phone threats not in Jombang, his hometown in East Java, but in Jakarta, where he occasionally resides. Hasyim himself thus contended that this suggested the national scale of the affair. In content, Hasyim's narrative evoked national memories of the communist threat, embedded in his personal experiences as a national political actor. National memories of the 1965–6 killings provided a framework through which Kyai Hasyim attempted to make sense of the ninja killings and locate his own experience of being threatened (cf. White 1997). He connected his story of the killings with the story of the communist threat evoked by the New Order state apparatus whenever it had to deal with a political challenge from opposition groups.

During Suharto's regime, the story of the communist threat had become a symbol of a national state of danger: whenever the Suharto regime felt that a political crisis was near, its state apparatus made the communist plot resurface so as to re-integrate the national public in cultural intimacy. Kyai Hasyim's narrative shows, however, that the state is not the only agent interested in evoking the national public; a national political actor himself, Hasyim wanted to occupy a place in the negotiations over how the post-Suharto national public should look. In evoking the memory of 1965–6 massacres, he (and perhaps other political actors as well) drew distinct boundaries between secular and religious politics and ideologies; the tensions between these two have been a prominent trope in the narratives of violence ever since the 1965–6 killings.

While Kyai Hasyim referred to individual and national experiences in the 1965–6 killings, Amien Rais, another national political actor operating from a different Islamic political base, emphasized the role of the Suharto regime. His interpretation should be read in the context of the struggle for political reform (*reformasi*), however, rather than in the context of the cultural politics of national memories which inform Kyai Hasyim's narrative. Different from Hasyim and the NU, Amien Rais and the Muhammadiyah organization had been less involved in the 1965–6 killings. Rais established himself in the forefront of the political opposition against the Suharto regime, presenting himself as one of the leading figures in the reformasi movement. In his comments on the ninja affair Rais presented himself more as an actor within reformasi than as a representative of a particular religious organization with a long memory.[6] For Rais, the post-Suharto national public should evade every possible influence of the Suharto regime, since reformasi, in the vocabulary of its proponents, meant a total correction of the New Order abuses of power. Post-Suharto Indonesia should, according to Rais, become a transformed nation-state with a new political public. Rais' narrative stems from his political involvement in the contemporary struggle for reformasi, in contrast to Kyai Hasyim's that drew on memories and personal experiences.

The killings, while still mysterious, can be read as a summary of a nation in political crisis, and read in this way the historical, social, and temporal particularities of the events themselves are not very relevant: what counts are the tales about them. The narratives of Hasyim, Rais, and Abdurrachman Wahid show that various political figures operate from different places within the public sphere, providing contrasting interpretations of the ninja killings in terms of different groups within the nation-state. The cumulative result of these narratives can be described by what anthropologist Stanley A. Tambiah (1987) terms "focalization", or the process of focusing the narrative of a violent event on a particular theme and stripping it of local specificities. In the narrative of the ninja killings, this focus is nationalized in that the killings are given a national significance. Moreover, the nationalization of narratives about the ninja allows for the construction of a political public sphere in which discussions about the national significance of the event become a sign of intimacy between participants in the public sphere. National actors, such as Kyai Hasyim, Amien Rais, Munir, and Abdurrachman Wahid, feel the necessity to locate the violent events within the national public rather than confine it to the local public. The events, thus construed, signify a threat to the nation; the ninjas are communists, regime loyalists, or military agents in narratives that are further elaborated upon by the media. The focalization of the ninja narrative is thus one way that different actors can claim their place before the national public.

Encountering Ninjas in the Village

> Villagers surrounded Rokhmin, who had just witnessed a ninja killing Kyai Ilyas.
> 'After killing Kyai Ilyas, the ninja calmly left the scene,' Rokhmin said.
> 'Since we did not see him why did you not inform us?'
> 'I could not speak. I felt my mouth was gagged. It was when we met at …'
> 'So, he was there …?'
> 'Yes.'
> 'I was there too, but I saw nothing but a cat.'
> 'A cat? That one that walked calmly in front of Kang Sobari?'
> 'That cat? Damn it! You're not lying, are you?'
> 'I pointed at it, but suddenly I could not speak.'
> 'The people said the ninja had turned himself into a cat.'
> (*The Jakarta Post*, 29 October 2000)

This conversation about the ninja turning himself into a cat took place among villagers in East Java. Others testified that they saw a ninja "running on electric wires", "jumping from rooftop to rooftop", "arriving like the wind and disappearing like the breeze", and other uncommon manifestations such as a bird, dog, or another animal (*The Jakarta Post*,

29 October 2000). In the eyes of many villagers, a ninja is someone or something that possesses supernatural powers. People believe that only such a being can elude the watchful night patrols and murder kyai without being caught. The fact that the police have been unable, or reluctant, to arrest a single ninja has strengthened people's conviction that the ninjas are *sakti* (gifted with supernatural powers). The assumption that there was a tie (of what?) to Suharto has been suggested by religious leaders and those situated in the realm of national political sphere. For the locals (i.e. villagers), it was nothing other than that the ninja were sakti.[7]

Not only did the ninjas threaten important national figures such as Kyai Hasyim, they also spread terror among villagers, particularly in the areas where Islamic teachers or preachers are living. As the terror and killings continued in 1998, people became more cautious — and innocent victims fell by the hand of furious night patrols. In villages, potential victims were rarely given early warnings, unlike the national figures discussed above. Rather, the ninjas appeared suddenly at the door in the dead of night, killed, and disappeared.

The virtual invisibility of ninja's practices has reinforced popular beliefs that one should prepare oneself with magical powers in order to counteract possible assaults. A traditional strategy proven to be effective in countering supernatural powers is a collective attack on the perpetrator, reminiscent of the type of collective violence by which dukun santet have been murdered in East Java. I have not been able to confirm media reports that people perform rituals to challenge the ninja; however, collective attacks on people who were suspected of being ninja are not a uncommon practice.

One could argue that people's violent reaction to ninja terror simply reenacts a tradition or culture of violence, and that those committing the acts of violence are "running amuck" (from the Malay/Indonesian *amok* or *amuk*). These explanations are hard to accept for two reasons. First, the assumption that people re-enact a culture of spontaneous violence ignores the possibility that they have deliberations before an individual or a collectivity commits the deed. Second, the assumption that people become amok suggests that they are unconscious of their act or that their violent act serves as an outlet for psychological tensions. Both explanations fail to account for violence as a cultural act that mediates social anxiety, the result of fast-changing social and historical contexts.

Seen as a cultural act, violence serves as a commentary within the political public sphere, and in this sense it operates as part of a discourse on identities and citizenship.

The most apparent sign of national citizenship in Indonesia is an identity card, *Kartu Tanda Penduduk* (KTP).[8] When a crowd interrogates a stranger, it always asks for his card, which offers information on where the bearer resides so that those who check it are able to determine whether the person they are dealing with is a local or a visitor.[9] Showing an identity card, in other words, is a gesture to acknowledge one's place in a community — from the villager's point of view, the notion of "local" refers to the geographical space of a *kabupaten* (regency). Those who are coming from another regency or province are considered visitors (*pendatang*) and, therefore, they must be interrogated more cautiously. Reports of village patrols killing alleged ninjas usually mention that the victims were not local people and came from another regency or province.

Acts of mob violence were, in fact, usually preceded by an interrogation: the members of a patrol asked the unknown person to identify himself, and if he failed or refused to do so, people did not hesitate to resort to violence in order to elicit the requested information. Looking at violent conflicts between Sinhalese and Tamils in Sri Lanka, Appadurai (1998) has argued that violence sometimes serves to mediate the anxieties Sinhalese or Tamils feel about the uncertain identity of their opponents; the subsequent torture upon the body of a suspected enemy mediates the desire to "prove" the purity of the enemy's identity. Something parallel seems to take place in the case of ninjas, whose alleged killing practices have heightened the sense of anxiety among villagers. However, the ninja affair is not a commentary on the purity of ethnic identity — a situation that may exist in Sri Lanka — but a commentary on the certainty of a national citizenship and of participation in the national public sphere.

The New Order's sense of cultural and political order depended on the certainty that an individual or a group should be contained properly within the boundaries of an ethnic, geographic, or religious space. The discourse of culture that was promoted by the New Order regime demands a declaration of affiliation to an ethnic or religious group. Above, this ethnic and religious affiliation stands for the nation as an ideal construct comprising different ethnic groups. Citizenship within the Indonesian

nation is, therefore, both similar and different from the membership of
a particular ethnic group. Possession of an identity card implies the
subjection to the distinct norms, values, and practices that reflect the
"essence" of a certain religious and ethnic identity; the state requires that
its citizens claim membership in a distinct national entity. However,
during the months of ninja terror — a few months after the collapse of
Suharto's government — the state lost its authority as the major agent
for maintaining the integrity of cultural essence and of interrogating the
identity of individual citizens. It also failed to sustain the sense of order
that used to be embedded in the strictly policed realm of the national
public sphere. We have witnessed, then, how night patrols took on the
state's role and exercised the right to interrogate and shape the national
public sphere.

I would argue that the killing spree by alleged ninjas illustrates a
moment of crisis in which 'Indonesia' as a nation became problematic.
The act of violence against mysterious enemies seems to be a commentary
on the failure of "Indonesia" to serve as a sign for a nation or provide
a cohesive national citizenship. Unless the stranger could prove his
relationship with the local community, he ran the risk of being threatened
by the village patrol. To show that he is an Indonesian citizen is not
enough to avert suspicion from villagers, however, because identifying
oneself as a national citizen might invite even more suspicion, as
the public believed that strangers and ninjas might have been linked to
the state and to national politics. To demonstrate one's affiliation to the
state — a government employee or part of the security apparatus — can
in fact be dangerous. The act of violence committed by villagers is,
therefore a commentary on the politics of the state, a comment that
first appropriates the vocabulary of the state's cultural politics and then
deploys it to claim a space for citizenship in the fractured and disintegrating
space of the nation-state. In Indonesia, the nation-state still serves as a
discursive signifier on which any political talk, commentary, and even act,
can be anchored. It suggests that talk about significant events needs to
be resituated in the political public sphere.

Epilogue

As I write this essay (in 2001), no one seems interested in uncovering more
stories on ninja activities in East Java. Press articles have become fewer
and fewer. Perhaps the lack of published information has limited broader

efforts to address the issue. In my interpretation of media accounts, however, the talk about ninjas appears to illustrate the process that Tambiah (1987) has so eloquently described as the "focalization" of news and rumour about violence and social conflicts. In his comparative study of ethnic conflicts in South Asia, however, Tambiah has not given much emphasis to the agency responsible for the practice of "focalization" or "nationalization" of narratives; he seems less focused on exploring the question of why "focalization" becomes so indispensable in a certain historical or social context.

In this essay I have tried to illustrate how narratives as well as acts of violence can mediate social anxiety about the existence and the form of a nation-state. Discussions about the ninja affair proliferated soon after the first report came out, a few months after Suharto stepped down. Although the New Order government has collapsed, public anxieties about the nation-state remain. Comments by politicians, scholars, military officials, and bureaucrats echo similar concerns about the ninjas' linkage to national politics. It seems that for these actors the tragic killings in East Java can only be interpreted through the lens of national politics. I would argue that the process of "stripping out of the details of the event", that Tambiah has demonstrated with respect to ethnic riots in South Asia, is to be less concerned with the reality of the event itself. As White (1987) has argued, the imagery of historical reality is always embedded and shaped in the telling of the historical event. The fact that a ninja killing is a "national event" owes nothing to the involvement of the state apparatus. In other words, the involvement of the military does not necessarily render the event as having a national significance. Nationalization of the killing takes place through comments and narrative representations as recounted by political actors who have invested their narratives with an imagery of threat to the nation-state.

It is perhaps far from coincidental that the nationalization of narratives takes shape through comments by national politicians. However, further elaboration reveals that each politician deploys different cultural resources to evoke the national significance of the killings, focalizing the ninja narrative within the context of their personal experiences and involvement with national Indonesian politics. Some of them, such as Kyai Yusuf Hasyim, endow their narrative with memory of past killings or similar tragedies of violence in other places. Others, such as Amien Rais and human rights activists, will be more concerned with how the ninja killings are related to the contemporary political struggle in which they themselves are important players. Evoking memories or present concerns, they all try to play a role in post-Suharto Indonesian politics.

A more complex process of deliberation emerges in the context of local responses to the ninja killings. Not only do people deliberate in the Habermasian sense of having a discursive exchange, they also resort to collective violence to mediate their anxiety about political transformation. This essay has presented the different contexts that perhaps allow local people in East Java villages to engage in violent retaliation to the ninjas.

First, violence becomes necessary when the normal relationship of recognition between the state and its citizens does not work or is severed (Siegel 2000). In such a situation, violence serves as a language that the state deploys to talk to its citizens. Here I elaborate on Siegel's argument by suggesting that it is not only the state which can invest in, or monopolize, such language of violence; the crowds in East Java villages are equally capable of deploying it. I extend Siegel's argument by bringing back politics into the discussions of cultural agency. Political actors as well as crowds in East Java are not simply performing a cultural discourse shaped by the New Order regime. Rather, by engaging in the debate on the ninja killings, either verbally or in violent action, they manifest themselves as active citizens of the nation-state, citizens who want to take part in the exciting debates within the realm of the national public. In this sense, violence does not exist outside the realm of cultural politics, as Daniel (1996) would suggest, but is itself a form of cultural politics.

Second, social anxieties emerge in a specific historical context. They mediate relationships when ambiguity and uncertainty cast doubt on the sense of order that has previously helped to secure those relationships. In the New Order's discourse of nationalism publicly acknowledged by Indonesians and scholars alike, the nation-state appears as an imagined construct, conceptually finished in the 1928 Youth Pledge or in the 1945 Proclamation of Independence. The reformasi movement of 1997–8 is, in a sense, a call for a total and radical correction to that form of nation. However, a more meticulous exploration of the engagement of Indonesians with the nationalist imagination might reveal that the form of the nation remains a contested rather than a finalized product. The belief that the ideal (but imagined) form of the nation has been completed is actually an illustration of the success of New Order cultural politics, a politics of meaning in which alternative nationalist interpretations have been rigorously contained. In post-Suharto Indonesia, anxiety re-emerged, making Indonesians aware of the fact that nationalism and nation remain contested.

Notes

1   The killing of dukun santet had actually been taking place in various places, and for a long time. When I lived in East Java in the 1970s to 1980s, I often heard narratives about mobs killing alleged dukun santet.

2   Banyuwangi, Jember, Situbondo, Bondowoso, and Pasuruan are in the eastern part of East Java Province. Sampang and Pamekasan are on the island of Madura. These towns have been traditional strongholds of NU.

3   The New Order regime treated resistance movements in the same manner as it did criminality; it regarded both political opposition and criminal acts as provoking "social disorder". Criminals and political activists, therefore, were to be "punished" in the same way. Sometimes this involved techniques that were aimed at restricting the freedom of criminals and political activists. It also involved torture in order to elicit confessions (see Rafael, ed., 1999).

4   If the number of political parties can be taken as an indicator for the proliferation of political interests, post-Suharto Indonesia has witnessed a major change in the political climate. Under the New Order regime, only three political parties existed, and within only a few months after the collapse of the Suharto regime, 148 new parties were established.

5   The politics of Islam in Indonesia are complex and cannot be categorized as simply "traditionalist" versus "modernist". The varieties of political practices within the so-called "traditionalist" or "modernist" groups are often overlooked in the discussion of Muslim politics (Hefner 2000).

6   Here Amien Rais was simply making a pragmatic political move. Like Abdurrachman Wahid, he followed a political trend that was growing stronger in the final years of Suharto's rule; his subsequent maneuvers suggest he tried to gain more support from a range of religious and ethnic groups. Interpreted in this way, one cannot take Rais's political comments as representative of the Muhammadiyah organization.

7   A comparison with East Timor might be interesting. An East Timorese friend told me that the Indonesian military believe that East Timorese combatants planted magical amulets under their tattoos. When the military managed to capture an East Timorese guerrilla fighter, his tattoo was "ironed" to expose the amulet, and of course they found nothing. This example suggests that a narrative — in this case the story shared among Indonesian military about the magical power of the East Timorese — powerfully informs the conduct of torturers.

8   Siegel (2000) tells a similar story about the importance of the identity card for members and supporters of the Free Aceh Movement (*Gerakan Aceh Merdeka*): to have an identity card means to participate in the imagined community of Aceh.

9   A KTP denotes various levels of geographical units of its owner's residence, the lowest unit being *Rukun Tetangga* (RT, a neighbourhood unit), the highest *Propinsi* (province).

Remembering and Forgetting War and Revolution[1]

ANTHONY REID

The origins of this essay lie in the year 1995, now so long ago, when the world was obsessed by memories of 50 years earlier. Indonesia (along with Vietnam, Korea, etc) was remembering its dramatic if messy assertion of independence in the wake of the Japanese surrender, while much of the rest of the world was remembering in diverse ways the end of the war itself. 1995 was the last year of something like the "normality" of Suharto's 30-year rule, the only stability Indonesians remember except for the now fading *zaman normal* of Dutch rule. Suharto's "normality" is now emphatically rejected as normative, just as the 40-year "normality" of Netherlands India was rejected 50 years earlier. Nevertheless in both cases the structures and frames of reference of that kind of relative stability have a way of enduring, and already one finds nostalgia for some of its essential features.

I think therefore the reflections of 1995 are curiously of interest in the present crisis. Will Indonesian collective memory be reconstructed for a more democratic era, in ways which commemorate the victories of democracy? Or will it fragment? Or have the educational norms of Suharto's Indonesia taken such root that the past will play little part in contemporary debates?

I was depressed to hear from Indonesian colleagues recently that enrolments in History Departments had declined rather than increased since the democratization of Indonesia, with Bali's rather strong department (14 lecturers) getting only one student in 2001. Some programs may have to close. This is the opposite of what I would have hoped from an era of democratization, when the past needs to be rigorously re-examined and rediscovered. I have never ceased to marvel at the transformation of Thai students in 1973, when a vigorous student movement helped overthrow military rule. Suddenly the proverbial shy Thais in the class

(I was then at Yale) became outspoken and analytical, and a whole new generation of outstanding historians was born — Thongchai, Kasian, and Thanet among them. So the Indonesian case troubles me not just for my profession but for what it may say about the nature of democratization.

Australia

The 50th anniversary of the Japanese attack on Pearl Harbor, celebrated on 8 December 1991, began a period when the Australian media could not get enough of World War II. During the subsequent year not a month went past without some new commemoration, ceremony or reflection on the battles in which Australians had been among those attempting to stem the Japanese tide. The capture of Rabaul, the fall of Singapore, the battle of the Java Sea, the fighting on Ambon, the air raids on Darwin and Broome, the occupation of Timor and Australian guerrilla activity there, the fighting for the Kokoda Trail behind Port Moresby, the Battle of the Coral Sea, and the remarkable Japanese mini-submarine raids on Sydney harbour — all were revisited with lengthy articles in the press, interviews with survivors, and solemn commemorations of those who died.

The then new Prime Minister, Paul Keating, added further excitement by seizing the opportunity to portray himself as a nationalist with his feet firmly planted in Australia and its region, strongly implying that all his older predecessors and rivals were still unsure where their loyalties lay. During the commemorations of the fall of Singapore he attacked Britain for having abandoned Australia to its fate, arousing one of the periodic Anglo-Australian squabbles which delight the London tabloids. A few months later, on the day after Anzac Day (25 April — Australia's national holiday in honour of the Gallipoli landings of 1915), he visited the memorial of the battle for the Kokoda Trail in now independent Papua New Guinea. He spoke movingly about how Kokoda, Timor, Java and Malaya meant that Australians had begun to fight and die for the region in which they lived, no longer for distant imperial ideals defined in Britain. He then, in a gesture much photographed and inflated to epic symbolic proportions, knelt to kiss the Papuan ground. We learned subsequently from one of his advisers that this was not part of the programme but had been his quick response to the dilemma of having four military monuments to honour but only three wreaths to lay, so that he was left standing awkwardly before the fourth until he spontaneously decided to kneel and kiss the ground. There was, however, much media celebration of this apparent symbol of Australia's identification with its northern neighbours, and the recognition it marked of the Australian blood spilt there.

The whole year ending on 15 August 1995, 50th anniversary of the end of the Pacific War, was devoted to an elaborate program of commemorations called "Australia Remembers 1945–95". This was on a scale surpassing any other anniversary I am aware of except the centenaries of European settlement — war and colonization seem to vie with each other as defining moments for Australian identity. Canberra's newspaper had a daily column on the war. It was noted at some of the conferences around the world that this world war appeared to become more central in memory in the 1980s and 1990s, just as it ought to be faded in the consciousness of the now-dominant generation. Why Australia is even more preoccupied than other countries with events for the most part beyond its shores might have to be explained in part by the absence of other unifying symbols in a culture generally skeptical and sardonic about heroic claims. It is also true that since the truly horrifying trauma of the First World War (in which Australia is said to have lost more men per population than any other combatant), Australia has retained some rather unique institutions dedicated to keeping memories of war alive — a Government Department of Veterans' Affairs headed by a junior minister, and a well-funded Australian War Memorial which is one of the most visited places in the country. These institutions control the rituals and symbols of remembrance in negotiation with veterans groups. They thereby ensure a more conservative national iconography than might be the case elsewhere. The only woman honoured in the special set of postage stamps issued, for example, is the widow of the most senior general killed.

There may be another, more political, reason why this war was particularly celebrated under a Labor Government proud of its links with the Curtin Labor Government, which in 1942 had defied Churchill by bringing Australian troops back from the Mediterranean to fight their own war against the Japanese. When Keating expressed the hope in launching "Australia Remembers" that it "will help us recognize how important it is to believe in ourselves", he probably hoped that would define him, rather than his Liberal Party opponents, as heir of a particular kind of practical nationalism which sees Australia for what it is and where it is.

Indonesia

Japan's southward advance was objectively more important for Indonesia than for Australia. Quite apart from the hundreds of thousands of casualties of a three-and-a-half year occupation, it ended an imperial system which had seemed unshakeable; it catapulted the nationalists from the wings to the centre of the political stage; it established the army as the central long-term force in the country; and it made Bahasa Indonesia almost overnight the national language, with incalculable consequences for the culture of Indonesia. Yet the Indonesian public recognition of these events seems very muted in comparison with that of Australia, the Netherlands, and other involved countries.

Since I passed my 1995 about equally between Australia and Indonesia (with shorter periods in Malaysia, Holland, London), I was struck at the huge amount of attention Australia devoted to commemorating every turning point of the Pacific war, and the indifference of Indonesians about doing so even though the war was objectively far more traumatic and decisive for them. In March 1992 I had attended the only Indonesian conference to commemorate 50 years of the end of Dutch rule, on the anniversary of General Ter Poorten's surrender to the Japanese on 9 March 1942. Although this date is arguably the real watershed of modern Indonesian history, it was of strangely little interest to prominent Indonesians. The conference was held in Jakarta under *Lembaga Ilmu Pengetahuan Indonesia* (LIPI, Indonesian Institute of Sciences) sponsorship, though on the initiative of Japanese scholars and using Japanese money. Japanese officialdom became so uneasy about the possible backlash against "celebrating" a Japanese victory that all mention of the significance of the date was totally suppressed, the conference blandly relabelled as about "modern Indonesian history" and the contents focused broadly on the early 1940s. There was very little media interest in either the conference or the anniversary itself.

Is it, as Goenawan Mohamad noted, that "Memories die fast and young in this country"[2] — that there is little sense of connectedness to a past? Certainly there does appear to be little interest from the government or from social organizations to use important anniversaries to re-evaluate the past. So rapid and turbulent have been the processes of change since 1942 that little remains to remind Indonesians of their collective histories. Dates and historical figures were selected and promoted as a means to claim a prominent place in the national myth for a region, ethnic group or city, and less if at all to mourn, to reconcile or to celebrate the past. Many cities in 1995, for example, put up slogans across prominent streets announcing by how much the city predated the country. In Jakarta it was "50 years of my country; 468 years of my city", but this was trumped by a banner in the small Sumatran coastal town of Barus (where French archaeologists were uncovering shards of the 5th–10th centuries CE), "50 years of my country, 5000 years of my city"!

Fifty-year anniversaries are more emotive than 100-year ones because some of the participants are in their last stage of life. Many of those who fought in World War II were in their 70s at the anniversaries. This became the last chance to honour them and their last chance to pass on a vision, articulate a grievance, or lay to rest a ghost. Australians, like Netherlanders, commemorated the war largely because this generation were emotionally involved actors in it. Indonesians were not the primary actors in the events that overwhelmed and transformed their country in 1942, and reflecting on those events does not serve any purpose of those now powerful. Indonesians were also actors in the war, and some of them fought bravely in it. But this active minority is divided between those who fought on the Allied side (few but influential) and those on the Japanese side (historically important, notably in Aceh and the TNI, but awkward once the Japanese were defeated). There is no agreed national point to make about the historically "correct" position, and no institutions or organizations, as far as I know, who identify their interests with these particular traumas.

Indonesians suffered, certainly, and might be expected to remember their dead and their crippled as do even those on the "wrong" or defeated side of the war, notably Japanese or the Germans. They might mourn the destruction of Balikpapan in 1945 (by the Australians) as the Germans do Dresden or the Japanese Hiroshima; they might grieve for much of the intellectual and political elite of West Kalimantan, massacred by the Japanese in 1942, as the Poles remember Katyn. They might remember the famines of 1944–5 as Amsterdam commemorates its winter famine of the same time. They might make some tribute to the hundreds of thousands of *romusha* who suffered and died on the Burma railway and elsewhere, as the Australians honour their few thousand who did so. But although families may quietly remember their dead, and some women's groups have recently begun to take an interest in the "comfort women" issue, the major national institutions are not much interested. The one strong organization which drew political capital from excoriating the memory of the Japanese occupiers and their collaborators, the communist party (PKI), was brutally removed from the debate in 1965–6.[3] These anniversaries therefore pass without public fanfare or tears.

Overlaying private and family memories of the war, and increasingly replacing them in the consciousness of youth, is official history. This has always been closely related to the perceived needs of national identity and unity. Since the first anniversary in 1946, the independence proclamation has been celebrated every year on 17 August, with flags, red-and-white bunting, marches and speeches all serving to emphasize that this was the central birthdate of the nation. In the popular mind the date and its constituent numbers, 17-8-1945, often assume the nature of a cabalistic mantra of mysterious power. In the late Soekarno period official history was explicitly revolutionary, negating the pre-1945 past except as prelude to revolution, and pointing to an elusive messianic future.

Under Suharto's New Order the reconstruction of the past became more purposeful, effective and militarized. As Klaus Schriener has well shown, a cult of heroes, and especially the military dead, was dramatically focused around war cemeteries, monuments and annual rituals (Schreiner 1995, 2002). To the compulsory school curricula for History, and for Pancasila Education, was added in 1985 a further subject, "Education in the History of the National Struggle" (PSPB), on the initiative of the then Minister of Education, military historian Nugroho Notosusanto. In the senior secondary (SMA) syllabus these three subjects between them occupied 32 hours, as against ten for mathematics and 18 for all the sciences. The tenor of the "National Struggle" syllabus, even at Senior Secondary level, can be gauged from the curriculum guide, which lists as its first aim: "That students realize that the Indonesian nation/race (*bangsa*) struggled constantly from the time of the coming of the Dutch colonizers. That there is a realization that this struggle led to the growth of the values of unity and oneness." (cited in Leigh 1991: 18; see also Leigh 1991: 24; Bourchier 1994). In addition all officials and teachers underwent courses "for the realization and implementation of Pancasila" (P4), which also took a strong position on the centrality of the national struggle for independence. The official memory reflected in all these ways was very specific. It nested all local, ethnic, and personal histories within the great purpose of national history; it placed the Indonesian Army and Suharto himself at the centre of that national history; and it subordinated all other dates to those of the revolutionary struggle — especially 17 August 1945 (Leigh 1991: 25–31). The Japanese

Occupation was important as a prelude to that event, but to commemorate its portentous happenings as turning points in their own right would
risk diluting the transcendent quality of 1945, and giving the Japanese
a share in the glory that belongs to Indonesians themselves in asserting
their independence.

As Suharto in his last phase sought to cement his place in Indonesian
history, he was even shifting the spotlight away from 1945. The 50-year
celebrations of Indonesian independence in August 1995, he ensured,
were not devoted to reviving interest in the revolutionary deeds of
Soekarno, Hatta, Sjahrir, Tan Malaka, Nasution, and the *pemuda* (youth)
in the 1940s, but to "bringing out what has been achieved throughout
this half-century"(Suharto speech to DPR, 5 January 1995). Suharto may
have believed that some of his rivals, like Soekarno's daughter Megawati,
the Forum Demokrasi (with its *merdeka* [freedom] slogan), or even the
army which had so busily rewritten the revolution as a TNI-led war of
independence, were more likely to profit from the legacy of 1945 than
himself. His downplaying of 1945 itself may have been a factor in his
snub to the Dutch, who had hoped, in vain, that their queen would
be invited to attend the 17 August 1995 ceremonies in a dramatic
demonstration of healing.

For Suharto, it seemed, this commemoration should focus primarily
on the achievements of his 30 years in power, as the obvious fulfillment
of the 20 years of painful struggle which preceded them. The most well-
publicized official activity was all along these lines. Symptomatic was the
presentation of the book *50 Tahun Indonesia Merdeka* (50 Years of
Independent Indonesia) to Suharto in a solemn ceremony on 12 August.
This coffee-table blockbuster included 50 messages from world leaders;
50 essays by different authors, 50 significant numbers, 50 books about
Indonesia, and so forth (Sutresna 1995).

Judging by those I witnessed in North Sumatra or saw on TV from
Jakarta, the ceremonies everywhere were basically the same as had been
routinized through all preceding 17 August ceremonies of the Suharto
period. Let me describe what happened in Kebanjahe, the Karo Batak
capital in North Sumatra. On the afternoon of the 16th the national
flag was received and raised with smart military style, and military-led
marchers who had revisited some events of the revolution were welcomed
back. Later that evening there was a parade of torchbearers, soldiers, and
then school pupils in vast numbers. Later still, perhaps in a feature not
replicated in less "revolutionary" cities, aging veterans of the revolutionary

struggle were entertained by the *bupati* (district chief). On the 17th itself the key ritual was a highly militarized "ceremony to remember the moment of the proclamation" at 9:45 in the morning. After the flag was very solemnly raised and the 1945 proclamation read, there were re-enactments of guerrilla battles.

These rituals had been choreographed according to an annually repeated score developed by the military since the early years of the New Order. The publications and graphic displays which had to be developed specifically for the 50th anniversary may give a better insight into how local and national official memories interacted. The Karo Bataks of North Sumatra were unusually enthusiastic participants in the revolution (including its destruction of Malay royal claims over them), and remember it as both suffering (especially through the scorched-earth retreat before the second Dutch action in 1948) and liberation (Reid 1979: esp. pp. 255–6; Steedly 1993: 63–6). The largest display in Kebanjahe graphically portrayed on one side these revolutionary events, and on the other the achievements of modernity, in which the military was again prominent, but the Karos' pride in their educational success could not be overlooked (Kipp 1993: 158–60, 181; Reid 1997: 76–7).

In the main square of multi-ethnic Medan a great display board was erected some weeks before 17 August, seemingly integrating instructions from Jakarta with the local memory of some government agencies of North Sumatra. The display was dominated by the contrasting images of angry youth breaking their chains at top left, and a benign Suharto face amid signs of achievement and modernity at top right. In between was a small picture of Soekarno and Hatta proclaiming independence, and the slogan of the commemoration — "To create a feeling of gratitude for independence and to strengthen our Republic's popular roots [*akar kerakyatan*]". The sequence of 18 panels below appeared to have been put together by different agencies, including at least the provincial services of Military History, Information, and Justice. Captions are translated below, with the graphic described in brackets:

1. National Awakening, 1908 [Budi Utomo leaders].
2. One land, race/nation and language, 1928 [a clenched fist symbolising the "youth oath" to this effect]
3. Japanese Occupation [represented by a Japanese soldier]
4. Japan surrenders to the Allies 9 August 1945.

5. [The text of the independence proclamation of 17 August 2605 (the then Japanese equivalent of 1945)]
6. [Insurgent youth armed with sharpened bamboo]
7. [The ailing military commander Sudirman being carried during the 1949 resistance].
8. 27 December 1949: The transfer of Sovereignty.
9. Crush the PKI, and Supersemar [symbols of the 1965–66 transition from Soekarno to Suharto].
10. The 1945 Constitution and "Guidelines of State Policy", GBHN [depicted with the state seal, presumably to represent constitutionality].
11. [Suharto and his wife casting a vote].
12. Prosecutor's Office: The torture of Lt. Sujono at Bandar Betsy, 14 May 1965 [This PKI "provocation" is pictured]. The PKI before the 30th September Movement. Liquor and Narcotics [pictured]. Developing a society conscious of law.
13. Investigation of the captives of the 30th September Movement/PKI [Brig. Gen. Ulung Sitepu, the communist-leaning mayor of Medan in 1964–5, is depicted in court].
14. Corruption, damaging protected forest; stealing fish [these crimes depicted].
15. Justice: information about law [an elite man with megaphone addressing working people, presumably to explain the crimes at left].
16. *Kelompen capir* [more scenes of the spreading of information].
17. National radio and TV.
18. Family Planning [a healthy two-child family].

This progression from the contested turbulence of the past to an orderly society being instructed by paternalistic government marks a moment of official memory in the late Suharto era. The subsequent unraveling of that government may not have transformed official memory as fully as hoped by reform advocates, but it has certainly rediscovered an older pattern of contestation and plural memory. I want now to return to that older pattern to trace the contested ways in which memories of the Pacific war were selected in the turbulent period after 1945.

Western Bitterness

For those who experienced the Japanese Occupation of Netherlands Indies, the dominant immediate perception appeared to have been the breaking of the spell of European superiority through the profound humiliation of defeat. Although this shock was felt everywhere in Southeast Asia, Netherlands Indies constituted an extreme because the European presence had been most pervasive and its humiliation most complete. The Dutch population (240,000 "Europeans" as against fewer than 9,000 Americans in the Philippines, for example) was far greater than that of any other European group in Asia. Yet the Netherlands Indies collapsed almost without a fight, its troops being overrun by better equipped and led Japanese once the naval battle of the Java Sea was decisively lost. The conquest cost the Japanese fewer losses (only 845 men) than they had expected, in only half the time.

The Czech internee and later American historian of Indonesia, Harry Benda, was fond of making the point about this broken spell to his students by instancing the teenage son of his respectful office sweeper, who came and stared at him contemptuously as soon as he had encountered the Japanese and their message.[4] After Benda's death one of those students doubted whether the enchantment of colonial superiority had ever been real. At most, he conceded, the Europeans themselves believed that they had lost this quasi-magical status and their imperial confidence was shattered as a result (McCoy 1980: 8–9). Indonesian memoirs do make the same point, albeit without the sense of surprise that hatreds and resentments against colonialism were at last able to surface (Hanifah 1972: 119; Notosusanto 1975: 5; see also Frederick 1988: 92). As one left-wing nationalist puts it, "The colonial power of the Dutch, so pig-headed and grocer-minded, … was proved to have no firm basis. That power just collapsed at the moment it encountered the Japanese attack" (Kertapati 1957: 14).

For the Dutch and their Allies the bitterness of this humiliation called for revenge. Japanese militarists were naturally equated with the German Nazis who had occupied Holland, the only answer for whom was counterattack, unconditional defeat, and war crimes trials. On any objective moral scale, Japanese atrocities do not compare either in scale or horror with the deliberate extermination of six million Jews and Gypsies. Nevertheless the public, swashbuckling style with which the Japanese went about beheading and beating their captives was particularly repulsive to European sensibilities — especially colonial ones. The post-war rage against the Japanese was no doubt also stimulated by the racist quality of wartime propaganda about little yellow savages, and by the racial discriminations of war itself. As Gavan Daws (1994: 17) reminds us, the war in the Pacific was understood by both sides as the worst of all conflicts — a race war. The war between Germany and the western Allies was fought according to the strangely civilized rules of the Geneva convention, even while millions were slaughtered in battles and bombardments, and the horrors of Auschwitz and Dachau were taking place. For the Japanese military, who trained their own men never to surrender, these European rules were absurd. Disgraced captured soldiers would be treated with all the brutality of war itself. Hence Australians held prisoner by the Japanese died at 12 times the rate of those held by Germans (with the Burma railway alone responsible for 35 per cent of the deaths). The relatively civilized conditions in the POW camps of both sides on the European western front made it possible quite early after 1945 for Anglo-American books and films to feature the "good German" camp guard and portray the whole camp experience as a kind of sport — even though it was already known what utterly different conditions obtained in the Nazi death-camps. The legacy of bitterness carried by western prisoners of the Japanese, on the other hand, is analogous to that which poisoned post-war relations between Germany and Russia, as a result of conditions on the Eastern Front even more appalling than those in the Pacific. About 60 per cent of the Russians captured by the Germans died as a result, as did 45 per cent of the Germans captured by the Russians, whereas only 27 per cent of European prisoners of the Japanese died, and only three per cent of Australians captured by Germans.[5]

This legacy of bitterness, as well as the undoing of the colonial mission itself, ensured that westerners for some time after the war understood the Japanese conquest as a disaster that had to be reversed; a "scourge" (Gerbrandy 1950: 8–9), an anomaly, a dreadful nightmare which had taken Indonesia away from its natural path and into "a series of calamities" (de Graaf 1949: 479). Was it for this reason, or because they sensed nevertheless that an era had ended, that the two major post-war Dutch historians of Indonesia, de Graaf and Vlekke, ended their books with the battle of the Java Sea and ter Poorten's surrender?

For westerners after the war, analysis of the Japanese Occupation became entangled in the debate about the status of the newly proclaimed Indonesian Republic. During the 1940s and early 1950s hostility remained intense to everything the Japanese military represented. The post-war discovery of the fate of Allied prisoners-of-war and Southeast Asian *romusha* prolonged this sentiment, which might otherwise have been expected to subside quickly after the war. Hence those on the Dutch right who wanted to blacken the name of the Republic and oppose any cooperation with it insisted that it was "a dictatorship after the Japanese model" and "simply a Japanese creation".[6] Those seeking recognition and support for the Republic necessarily countered this view by minimizing the debts of Republican leaders to the Japanese period, and differentiating between German-occupied Europe and Japanese-occupied Southeast Asia.

Among the latter, one of the first was the U.S. vice-consul in postwar Jakarta, Charles Wolf, Jr. He argued at length that the duty of "a patriotic nationalist" in Indonesia was much less clear than that of his counterpart in occupied Holland, and that had Soekarno and Hatta not cooperated the Republic would not have had "either the organization or the popular support which it was to need to survive" (Wolf 1948: 9–14). The now classic study of the Indonesian republic by George Kahin was in the same mould but far more substantial and influential. For Kahin too the evil nature of the Japanese regime was taken for granted, though he conceded with some puzzlement that "such a well-balanced person as Hatta" believed that Maeda and his colleagues were sincere in their support for independence (Kahin 1952: 118). He distanced the Republic from the Japanese by giving the role of the anti-Japanese underground a centrality it hardly merited, and explaining the cooperation of Soekarno and others in strategic terms. Like Sjahrir himself, he was then able to attribute all the less savoury aspects of the armed struggle, "the disposition to rely on violence and brutality", to the influence of Japanese propaganda on young and unformed Indonesian minds (Kahin 1952: 107, 130).

In fact more ambivalent views of the Japanese period had begun to surface among close observers of the Indonesian scene far earlier. Many astute Dutch officials, both those who had been in camps (like A.J. Piekaar) and those returning from Holland or Australia, acknowledged the astonishing change in self-respect and national purpose between 1942 and 1945 (Piekaar 1949, van Mook 1950: 144–61). Another to experience these changes at first hand was Harry Benda, then a Czech national and business representative in Java, interned some time after the beginning of the Occupation. After the war his earliest essays already showed his realization of the enormous importance of the Japanese Occupation to

Indonesian political consciousness (Benda 1972 [1950]: 11–6). His more
influential later writing continued to insist that history had been changed
fundamentally by the Occupation. Indeed he suggested that 1942 could
be seen as the break between "history" and the contemporary era, "since
the destruction of the colonial *status quo* directly led to the subsequent,
and still contemporary, era of revolution, liberation, and modern
nationhood" (Benda 1972: 148). As a refugee and self-professed marginal
man, he was also perhaps readier than most to acknowledge that liberal
democracy need not be the "natural" path for Indonesia (Benda 1972)
so that the Japanese interlude could also be seen as part of a process of
returning that country to a trajectory from which Dutch colonialism had
diverted it.

By the 1960s it had become commonplace to argue that the disruption
by the Japanese of established routines, and the mobilization of all groups
and youth in particular, had had a profound and lasting impact on
Indonesia. Elsbree (1953), covering the whole of Southeast Asia, had
already presented a relatively detached picture of the changes which
occurred under the Japanese. Nevertheless it was not until Anderson's
(1966: 13) essay that the dominant assumptions of post-war western
writings about the Occupation were directly confronted:

> The swift Japanese seizure of Southeast Asia was a devastating blow
> to western self-esteem, from which many of us are still far from being
> liberated. The ignominious collapse of the Philippines, the humiliating
> clientship imposed on Vietnam, the fall of Singapore, the surrender at
> Kalidjati, all have conditioned us to seeing the period of Japanese
> domination as a disastrous interregnum, producing a pandora's box of
> political evils which have not ceased to plague 'our' Southeast Asia ever
> since.

On the one hand Anderson argued interestingly for the continuities
between Dutch and Japanese colonial policies. His more helpful contribution, however, was his brilliant delineation of the utterly different
models of political behaviour which flourished under the Japanese from
those under the Dutch. Where Dutch power had been largely based on
a mystique of technical and scientific competence, the Japanese cultivated
a mystique of "spirit" (Japanese *seishin*; Indonesian *semangat*). The melo-
dramatic style of much public ritual under the Japanese, the mobilization

of the population according to functional groups and *aliran*, the legitimacy given to military leadership and to the claims of the nation above the individual, the combination "of traditional and feudal forms, values, and ideas ... with considerable technological progress and formidable military power", all created great resonances in sections of the Indonesian population which had been unimpressed with the Dutch or western model. Doing his fieldwork during the period of Guided Democracy, Anderson was struck (like Benda [1972: 163] before him) at its continuities with the Japanese Occupation:

> the present Rukun Tetangga neighborhood organizations are an obvious revival in weakened form of the Tonarigumi, the Front Nasional strongly recalls the Hokokai, the Gotong-Royong Parliament is clearly a lineal descendent of the Chuo Sangi-in, the indoctrination teams of the Ministry of information both in style and practice bring back memories of the Sendenbu, and in the celebrations of the great national holidays it is not hard to detect traces of the earlier solemnizations of the Emperor's birthday.   (Anderson 1966: 25)

I believe this paper marked a change in the western remembering of the Japanese period, by a generation for whom the antagonisms of the 1940s no longer dominated the discourse. Subsequent scholarship has been more international in spirit, with Japanese as well as Indonesian and Allied sources and participants being consulted. Debates continue about how important the Occupation was, but they are now primarily driven by what is seen to be central in the evolving pattern of independent Indonesia. Some have gone further than Anderson in arguing for the importance of 1942 as a turning point and the centrality of the Japanese Occupation for Indonesia's subsequent development (Kanahele 1967: esp. 242–3; Kurasawa 1987; Reid 1980: 13–26).

The most recent major statement on the subject, by the distinguished historian of the Philippines Theodore Friend (1988; 1986), is novel in being equally distanced from Japanese militarism and Southeast Asian nationalism. His complex and eclectic work is a good demonstration of how far the subject has escaped from Kahin's concern to legitimate the Indonesian republic. He is primarily interested in the psychology of power, and shares his praise and blame, his likes and dislikes, relatively indifferent to which side the actors were on.

Indonesian Ambivalence

When we turn now to Indonesian memories, we must begin by recalling how different was their experience at the time of the Occupation. While westerners were subjected to intense anti-Japanese propaganda for three and a half years, Indonesians heard about the war as it happened chiefly through the medium of Japanese propaganda. The Japanese victories of 1942 were celebrated with annual parades and rallies, and nationalist spokesmen joined Japanese on the rostrums to extol the new age that had dawned with that moment. Initially those sentiments were by no means forced. Japanese solders were greeted with genuine enthusiasm in most parts of Muslim Indonesia, and with active support in Aceh, South Sulawesi, and a number of other places. General Imamura Hitoshi was astonished at the warmth of the welcome given the Japanese on landing in the Banten area, and argued subsequently against his superiors that the severe policies followed elsewhere were inappropriate in Java because of the spirit of cooperation and support displayed by Indonesians there (Imamura 1986: 34–5, 54). Fujiwara (1986: 29) also noted that the cooperation and enthusiasm of Indonesians "far exceeded Japanese expectations" in Sumatra and elsewhere. The Dutch rulers themselves acknowledged that there was little love left for them in Indonesia, and their surrender was speeded by the knowledge that the majority population itself had turned against them.

As has been repeatedly demonstrated in memoirs and local studies, the widespread Indonesian belief that the Japanese had brought a new era of freedom was quickly disappointed. After an initial two months' euphoria, the Japanese dashed all hope of independence and banned all displays in its favour. Those who had most enthusiastically supported the Japanese in the hope of drastic change found themselves denounced by still-powerful Indonesian aristocrat-officials, arrested and marginalized. Although Japanese propaganda proclaimed a new era, and ritually destroyed such symbols as the name Batavia and the statue of its founder, Jan Pieterszoon Coen, it became clear very quickly that the apparatus of colonial rule remained in place. By 1944 the misery to which the Indonesian population became reduced brought many to share the perception of the Dutch that the occupation had been a nightmare, an appalling deviation from the course of Indonesian history.

The extremely rapid developments towards independence during the last eight months of the war again changed the perception of what the occupation represented. Soekarno and others who had gambled on identifying themselves with the Japanese new order appeared once again to be conceivable winners from the wreckage of war. Those millions of young people trained since 1943 in the PETA, Giyugun, Barisan Pelopor, Hizbullah, Seinendan, and other organizations down to school and *Tonarigumi* level could now discern a purpose for what they had been through. If not the birth of Indonesian independence, 1942 now seemed at least the death of the Netherlands Indies, a monster whose post-war resurrection this generation now firmly opposed.

Once Japan surrendered, the manner in which Indonesia should pursue its goal of independence became immediately the central issue. For the radical pemuda, especially those with the best contacts with the Leftist underground network, it was essential that a complete break be made with the Japanese Occupation and its promise of *kemerdekaan hadiah* (independence as a gift). They furiously opposed the idea of Soekarno and Hatta that the Japanese-sponsored preparatory committee should speed up its moves towards independence. But if the members of this committee should not declare independence, who should? Only if the proclamation carried the names made familiar as leaders through Japanese propaganda would it be popularly accepted. The compromise of having Soekarno and Hatta alone sign the proclamation was typical of all the dilemmas of the first year of the revolution — how to appear at the same time to break with the Japanese past symbolically and yet maintain continuity with it organizationally?

The Allied victory and the Western domination of the post-war world made it essential to remove Japanese appearances from the young Republic — a view that the Marxists in any case shared for their own reasons. But the strongest political and military forces within the Republic were those which had been nurtured by the Japanese. This conflict was at the heart of most of the political conflicts within the Republic between 1945 and the Madiun Rebellion of 1948. Sjahrir's *Perjuangan Kita* launched the conflict in the strongest language:

> The revolutionary struggle for democracy began by purifying itself from the stains of Japanese fascism, while shutting out the views of people whose mentality is still influenced by Japanese propaganda and Japanese education .... Every political collaborator with the Japanese fascists ... must be regarded as himself a fascist or as a tool or agent of the Japanese fascists who has already sinned against and betrayed the people's struggle and revolution.[7]

While this sharp attack may have won Sjahrir friends in London and Washington, it probably made more influential enemies in Indonesia, where the Republic rested largely on politicians and soldiers who had risen to prominence under the Japanese. Amir Sjarifuddin, released from a Japanese prison, and the leftists who had served with the underground in Holland, also declared themselves "anti-fascists" whose first priority was to eliminate the heritage in Indonesia left by the Japanese. Even as late as the Madiun affair in September 1948, when the "collaboration" issue had been pushed to the background by new conflicts, Musso's most vicious and constant charge against Soekarno and the "ruling group" was that "At the time of the Japanese occupation they became Quislings, slaves of Japan, romusha-sellers and Heiho propagandists."[8] Although the defensiveness of Soekarno, Subardjo, and others on this issue through most of the Revolutionary period is clear from their memoirs, there was much to be said for their view that the Occupation was an indispensable prelude to independence, in which they had gained experience, stature, and a powerful link with the Indonesian people. "I addressed 50,000 at one meeting," recalled Soekarno afterwards, "100,000 at another. Soekarno's face, not just his name, penetrated the Archipelago. I have the Japanese to thank for that" (Adams 1965: 179). Since the great majority of politicians and administrators had felt obliged to work with the Japanese and many had gained responsibility, confidence and experience in the process, the "anti-fascist" attack on Soekarno did him little harm internally. The counter-charge made against Amir Sjarifuddin, that in forming an underground against the Japanese he had collaborated with the Dutch, was probably much more damaging. It was clear by the end of 1948 that the militant anti-fascists were the losers (Amir Sjarifuddin shot and Sjahrir pensioned), while the Japanese-trained army and Soekarno were the winners.

A striking indication of the debt which some Indonesians felt they owed the Japanese was the treatment of General Imamura after the war, at least as recorded in the undoubtedly self-serving memoirs of Imamura and Soekarno themselves. Soekarno claimed to have saved Imamura from a death sentence at the war-crimes tribunal by threatening van Mook that he would "prove to the world the war crimes that you yourself have committed" if the sentence went ahead. The implausibility of this claim is less important than that Soekarno wanted to make it, and that he continued in the 1960s to be grateful that "This Japanese knight had kicked hell out of the Dutch" (Adams 1965: 245). Imamura's memoirs also mention this incident in more modest terms, arguing that support for what he had done for Indonesia was not limited to Soekarno. He claimed that when he was held in a Batavia prison in 1948, a thousand Indonesian fellow-prisoners joined in singing the Japanese song *Yaeshio* ("The Vastness of the Sea") as a mark of defiance of the Dutch and appreciation of Imamura, who had had the song composed in 1942 in tribute to Indonesian-Japanese friendship (Imamura 1986: 32).

Few went as far as Soekarno in publicly endorsing the direction of the Japanese years, and there were Marxists on the left and westernized liberals on the right who regarded with disgust his condoning of Japanese atrocities at the time and still more in his post-war memoires (Hanifah 1972: 120–8; Malaka 1991: III: 76–8). Yet all who lived through this period understood that it had profoundly changed Indonesia. Adam Malik (1970: 9) was one of the first, in 1947, to write of the effects:

> Because of the extremely heavy and intense oppression by the Japanese Army at the time of its occupation of the Indonesian Archipelago, both in terms of the economic planning they conducted according to a war economy, and because of their forced labor and training system in every field, their influence in changing the mentality and spirit of our nation in four years was enormous; it could be said that in that four years our whole nation underwent a profound spiritual revolution.

Dr Amir, a Sumatran psychiatrist and writer with a Dutch wife and citizenship, who nevertheless joined the Japanese-sponsored movement towards independence and became the only Sumatra-based minister in Soekarno's first cabinet, explained for a Dutch audience after defecting in 1946 that Japanese-inspired propaganda in the year following Prime Minister Koiso's promise of independence, "did more ... for the idea of political unity and urge for independence than ten years of ordinary propaganda before the war".[9] The Marxist Sidik Kertapati (1957: 24) regarded the Japanese as criminal fascists, but he too perceived how much Indonesia had matured as a result:

> The Indonesian people paid dearly for the education and experience they obtained from Japan. For them the Japanese period was a time of cruel plunder, killing, hunger and rape; a dark time when the danger of death was always stalking and threatening, when blood and tears flowed swiftly ...

But for the people of Indonesia it was also a time of transition (*pantjaroba*), like when Gatotkaca went down into the crater of Candradimuka, in order to re-emerge purified and tested in the struggle.

Indonesia and Japan

No Indonesians, not even Soekarno, have denied that the country suffered much from the Japanese Occupation. Foreign Minister Subardjo, himself one of the nationalist leaders with the closest Japanese links, claimed in 1951 that the Occupation had cost the lives of four million romushas, and material damages which were later detailed into a reparations claim of $17.5 billion (Nishihara 1975: 38–9). The Japanese Government of the day of course objected that the figures were absurdly inflated, and that it should not have to pay reparations at all since it was never at war with Indonesia. Some Japanese military spokesmen insisted that Indonesia had been a net gainer from the Occupation, not only in political terms but in taking possession of Japanese equipment and supplies at the surrender. By the time agreement was reached in 1957, at a figure of $400 million in grants (of which $177 million was in cancelling an existing debt), and $400 million in credits, the sufferings of romushas had been completely overtaken by the lobbying of interested parties. The key figures in pushing the negotiations to a conclusion were Subardjo and Adam Malik on the Indonesian side and one of their wartime patrons, Nishijima Shigetada, on the Japanese side, with powerful Japanese industrial interests behind him (Nishihara 1975: 61–76). This Japanese "Indonesia lobby" pushed hard the idea of settling the reparations issue satisfactorily so that economic and political relations would flourish. And flourish they did. In the four years after the signing of the reparations agreement, Japan's exports to Indonesia quadrupled. By 1969 when the payments were complete, Japan had replaced the U.S.A. as Indonesia's largest trading partner. None of these funds were devoted directly, as German reparations were, to the individual victims of the war — the survivors and relatives of romushas and comfort women, and of those murdered on a large scale in Kalimantan and selectively everywhere. In theory the projects were developmental. The bridge over the Musi at Palembang and three major water control projects have indeed been useful.

The most striking beneficiaries of reparations, however, were those who had done very well out of the Japanese Occupation, and particularly those Indonesians who had good Japanese connections from that time. Kickbacks and commissions marked all the projects undertaken. Soekarno's own priorities became increasingly decisive in the selection of prestige projects such as the Hotel Indonesia, three other luxury hotels for which there was then little demand, the 14-storey Sarinah Department store, and the 29-storey Wisma Nusantara office block. On the Japanese side one of the biggest beneficiaries was Kubo Masao, who made contact with Soekarno as a go-between with the gangsters who had been hired to guard him during a visit to Tokyo in 1958. Once again it was wartime associations which had led Soekarno's cronies to propose this gangster arrangement. The following year when Soekarno returned to Tokyo, Kubo introduced him to the beautiful 19-year-old cabaret hostess, Nemoto Naoko. This was a stroke of genius. Nemoto became Soekarno's favourite and soon married him as Ratna Dewi. Kubo landed many of the projects funded under the reparations agreement. There was particular irony in the award to this epitome of Japanese-Indonesian elite cronyism of the contract to build Soekarno's favourite monument to Independence, the massive obelisk in Medan Merdeka known as the National Monument (Nishihara 1975: 80–122).

Japan's contribution to that independence had indeed been critical in far more fundamental ways. Indonesians had been armed and mobilized through the Gyugun/PETA system of military training, the core of the national army. The nationalist elite had been linked to the rural masses through an efficient system of propaganda, state ritual, and youth training. The Japanese system of neighbourhood organization had been firmly implanted throughout Java and Sumatra as the "infrastructure of the social engineering of the masses" (Mangunwijaya 1994: 85). Committees had been assembled to frame a constitution and lay the basis of a secular, unitary Republic as had been the goal of Soekarno.

Let me illustrate the importance of Japanese continuities by returning to my own experience of the 50th anniversay of independence in Kebanjahe, the Karo Batak centre in the North Sumatran highlands. Because the Karo were unusually enthusiastic about the revolution, the Bupati invited a number of the veterans of the struggle (*pejuang*) to his house on the eve of the 17th, including a number of women veterans who had begun to receive their due because of the interest of American anthropologist Mary Steedly in them. After one elderly woman had spoken forcefully about the role of women in revolution, including swearing not to marry until freedom was obtained, the bupati asked if the women could sing a "struggle song" (*lagu perjuangan*). After some initial diffidence they responded rather well, in marked contrast to the men who failed to reciprocate. After much hesitation, however, one of the men began a Japanese song, which was immediately taken up vigorously by both men and women. This success was followed by lively renditions of three more songs either in Japanese or in Indonesian translation of Japanese songs, and most ended with a spirited "banzai".

Important at a symbolic level was the issue of the independence proclamation itself. The radical youth groups had gone to the extent of kidnapping Soekarno and Hatta after the Japanese surrender in order to force them to declare independence in defiance of the Japanese. Yet the older leaders, knowing that they would be the first casualties of any confrontation with the military authorities, insisted on some Japanese guarantees of protection. In the end the Independence Proclamation was negotiated, written and signed at the home of a sympathetic Japanese admiral, Maeda. The Japanese accounts of the event state that three Indonesians (Soekarno, Hatta and Subardjo) sat around Maeda's table with three Japanese, and together they hammered out an acceptable text of the Proclamation. They rejected the demands of the youths assembled in an anteroom for a more radical statement that "administrative organs must be seized by the people from the foreigners who now hold them". Indonesian accounts, on the other hand, either overlook the presence of the Japanese or imply that they were purely passive.[10] In the international atmosphere of the years immediately after the Proclamation, there were powerful diplomatic reasons as well as nationalist ones why any Japanese responsibility for Indonesian independence should be minimized.

There were, however, men in Japan who felt otherwise. Nishijima Shigetada, as a young Indonesian-speaking assistant to Maeda during the build-up to independence had close contacts with the key actors in this drama, and has lived long and influentially in Japan to tell his side of the story. In 1951, after Indonesia's independence was internationally recognized, he was deeply hurt to find that his application to revisit the country was rejected without explanation. He was later told that Soekarno had avoided receiving any Japanese associated with moves towards independence for fear of giving sustenance to the Dutch line that the Republic was a Japanese creation. Nishijima then wrote his first memoir, "The Third Truth" taking issue with already-published texts of Adam

Malik and Hatta which had omitted to mention the support of Maeda, himself, and other Japanese in the Proclamation drama (Reid and Oki 1986: 251). The following year Subardjo visited Japan and renewed his contacts with figures such as Nishijima, paving the way for Nishijima to visit Jakarta in 1953, meet Soekarno again, and begin an active career as Indonesia lobbyist and business go-between. Nevertheless he and his colleagues continued to write in an injured tone about their omission from Indonesian histories, commenting in their 1959 book that "a clarification of this fact now would not soil their national history" (Nishijima *et al.* 1963: 505). This plea was to some extent answered in the years that followed, as Japan became an ever more important factor in Indonesia's economy, Soekarno and his ministers became frequent visitors to Tokyo,[11] and statements became calculated as much for their impact in Japan as in the west. Soekarno's memoirs in 1965 and Subardjo's in 1972 gave much more recognition to the Japanese factor. When Admiral Maeda died in 1977, Nishijima was gratified to receive a telegram from Adam Malik as Vice-president, acknowledging Maeda's "great help in the preparatory stage of our independence" and that "his name will be written in the annals of Indonesia with golden letters" (Reid 1980: 13).

The New Order of President Suharto saw the more passionate memories of the War fade. The most public cooperators died, while their most virulent anti-fascist critics were bloodily swept from the ring in 1965–6. The phenomenon observed in Korea and the Philippines, of women nearing the end of their life finally coming forward to tell their horror stories of being forced into military prostitution, were muted in Indonesia.[12] Suharto stated that Indonesia would make no claims on their behalf, as it would bring shame both upon the nation and the women themselves. Textbook history and Pancasila courses did their best to render the past bland and uncontroversial, and there was plenty of evidence that young people found it (and one fears, still find it) frankly boring.

Yet the controversial legacy of the war would not go away. It was Soekarno (with much help from the Japanese-trained officer corps of the army) who in the late 1950s had established Guided Democracy, returned to the authoritarian 1945 Constitution, and enthroned Pancasila as the unquestioned national ideology. But in his day these elements were imposed on often sceptical Dutch-educated (and to a lesser extent Arabic-educated and Chinese-educated) elites, in an atmosphere of contestation. The passing of the Dutch-educated generation from political and cultural leadership allowed for a seemingly more monolithic hegemony of Japanese-era ideas. In the 1980s the textbooks of the Pancasila (P4) courses began to uphold "integralism" as the supreme Indonesian political principle. Some prominent Indonesian law professors trained in the anti-individualist traditions of Van Vollenhoven and Supomo raised again in the 1980s the idea of the "integralist state" which Professor Supomo, draftsman of the 1945 constitution, had tried to establish in 1945 along the fascist lines of Germany, Italy, and Japan (Bourchier 2001: 118–9; Nasution 1992: 421–3; Simanjuntak 1994; Wahyono 1989).

Nevertheless a democratic critique of this formulation was never silenced. On the contrary critics used the association of these integralist ideas with the Japanese military period to discredit them as fascistic. This strategy was so successful that integralism had to be withdrawn from subsequent textbooks. From the debate developed a more critical view of the 1945 constitution itself in the 1990s, with Buyung Nasution, Marsillam Simandjuntak and Abdurrachman Wahid in the lead. As another of these critics, Jesuit author and architect Mangunwijaya (1994: 86), complained:

> The most influential novelty brought by the Japanese is the entire fabric of social and cultural engineering, with its atmosphere of uniforms, marching, inspection ceremonies, parades, unification of professional organisations, military and paramilitary language, attitude and behaviour, security surveillance, and a whole set of commands and chains of instructions, directed in uni-language formulations with prescribed official interpretations, indoctrinations etc etc., often in a benevolent way and useful, but too often fascistic and communistic in performance and spirit.

As the debate continues, military conservatives and some of their allies in Golkar and PDI-P hold to the "inheritance of 1945" — 1945 constitution, Pancasila, a large military role in government, secularism, centralism, and executive leadership. The reformers in turn increasingly trace the problems they identify in society back to this same package conceived, as they see it, from the fascistic embrace of the Japanese military.

Even if not commemorated in the same ways as elsewhere, the upheaval of World War II remains absolutely central to Indonesia.

Notes

1　The first draft of this paper was delivered to a Conference on "Memory and the Second World War" organized in Amsterdam by the Rijksinstituut voor Oorlogsdocumentatie in April 1995.

2　As quoted by Patrick Walters in *The Weekend Australian* 28–29 Jan. 1995.

3　Pramoedya's sympathetic literary tribute to the Javanese comfort women, apparently abandoned by the defeated Japanese on Buru where he met them 30 years later, is a reminder of the missing voice of the left on these issues in general. Pramoedya Ananta Toer, *Perawan Remaja dalam Cengkraman Militer — Catatan Pulau Buru* (Jakarta, Kepustakaan Populer Gramedia, 2001).

4　Compare the recollection of Bandung just before the invasion: "a hotel servant who left for the comforting surroundings of his village, a shop that no longer filled orders, a cab that did not stop when hailed, a gradually emptying street" (van Mook 1950: 139).

5　I owe this data to an unpublished paper by Hank Nelson (1991); see also Nelson (1993: 19–20).

6　Van Mook to Mountbatten in September 1945, quoted in Wolf (1948: 10). Of course van Mook like many other Dutch statesmen revised this view on greater experience of the Republican movement, and after Sjahrir took over as Prime Minister.

7　*Perjuangan Kita Syahrir* (Bandung, Yayasan "28 Oktober"), p.15. My translation is slightly different from Anderson's (1968) in Sutan Sjahrir, *Our Struggle* (Ithaca: Cornell University Indonesia Project, 1968).

8　My translation of Musso's speech in *Front Nasional* 19: ix.48, quoted in Pinardi (1967: 91).

9　Dr Amir's notes, 14 June 1946, Rijksinstituut voor Oorlogsdocumentatie, I.C. 005964.

10　Japanese accounts derive chiefly from Nishijima Shigetada, whose memoirs are translated in Reid and Oki (Nishijima 1986: 320–4). The most careful Japanese report of the events is in Nishijima Shigetada, Kishi Koichi *et al.* (1963: 502). New data from the Japanese army's viewpoint has recently been brought to light by Vincent Houben (1994). See Hatta (1981: 233–9) and Djojoadisuryo (1972: 103–14) for the key primary Indonesian accounts. The semi-official version written by military historian and Minister of Education Nugroho Notosusanto (1977: 27–9), also apparently present among the youth at Maeda's house, is surprisingly brief.

11　Soekarno made ten visits between 1958 and 1964, always with large entourages (Nishihara 1975: 28).

12　Though *TEMPO* and the Women's magazine *Kartini* published some interviews in 1993 (Hicks 1995: 21–2).

PART THREE

Memory, Knowledge and Reform

DANIEL S. LEV

In Indonesia's post-Suharto "era of reform" since mid-1998, not all that much has happened by way of fundamental reform. Reform groups suggest several reasons for the stall: a recalcitrant or ineffective elite, an army reluctant to retire from political and economic engagement, the lack of well-functioning state institutions of any sort, and outright opposition to basic reforms by well-positioned groups in and out of the state apparatus. Another problem is less evident but fairly significant, however, for it limits reform imaginations by truncating experience. The absence of historical memory — the ability to call up political knowledge and to put it to use in thinking about change — surrounds discussions of reform with a peculiar void. The problem is most evident among younger educated groups most committed to change, but it is evident too in middle-class and middle-aged professional circles, including journalists, intellectuals, and academics, whose understanding of the past is clouded by myths generated long ago to explain Indonesia's rocky post-revolutionary history, and also, in some cases, by the memory of their own early political views.

Political, economic, and other sorts of reform are, or should be, influenced by experience. What works more or less well may be retained, what doesn't is dropped or altered. In the most dramatic of transformations — a social revolution, say — an exploitative aristocratic elite may be crushed and replaced, as in France, Russia, China, and a few other countries. Or, short of utter upheaval, outdated or corrupt institutions may be eliminated or fundamentally made over, subjected to retrievable or altogether new mechanisms of control. Whether reform targets have to do with political leadership, institutional authority, economic policies, social structures, constitutional provisions, or state-society relationships, experience counts.

Experience, however, requires assessment. Its implications are not always obvious. It is subject to variations of interpretation depending on

195

who does the assessing, the interests involved, the approaches used, and the time that has passed. And it depends on the peculiarities of memory, of how people keep in mind and understand and compare sets of experiences, conditions much influenced by how historical knowledge is transmitted, maintained, refined, analysed, challenged, and distorted. The past may be recalled as the good old days or a time of calamity and suffering, as promising or disastrous, a heavenly model or miserable hell. None of it is necessarily accurate, realistic, or sensible. Yet what is forgotten, or how something is remembered, is critically important to evaluating what exists or how it might be changed.

At present in Indonesia, several significant puzzles float around political organization, institutional structures, the constitution, the legal system, political leadership, state-society connections, and much else. Does a presidential system suit Indonesia? Should the 1945 Constitution be amended or replaced? How can the legal system — its courts, prosecution, police, professional advocacy — be reconstituted; and what are the political requirements of an effective legal system? Does Indonesia's own history provide useful answers or even helpful hints?

Few of these questions are dealt with at all, let alone profoundly, in part because a significant block of modern Indonesian history — the parliamentary period from 1950–7 — has either been lost, badly distorted, misremembered, or surrounded by a mythology that renders it inaccessible to those most committed to change.

Not all that much has been written about the parliamentary years either by Indonesian or foreign scholars. The standard study remains Feith's *The Decline of Constitutional Democracy in Indonesia*, published almost 40 years ago (Feith 1962). In 1992 a conference held in Australia began the work of reassessing the early post-revolutionary period by way of a useful contrast with the New Order, but little has been done since to look again at that initial political system (see Bourchier and Legge, eds. 1994, particularly McVey's essay, pp. 3–15). In current discussions of political reform there is seldom any mention of the parliamentary system either by Indonesian or foreign observers. When the subject is raised at all, reactions usually recall the corruption of the period, its political conflicts, regional tensions and rebellion, the self-absorption of political parties, lack of direction, and so on. The constitution of 1950 is almost never mentioned; few admit to having read it.

Yet, it is no stretch of imagination to suggest that the parliamentary system was the most benign political order Indonesia has had since independence. Many of the demands of political reformers now — an effective constitutional order, a reasonably efficient and fair legal system, a responsible and responsive political elite, and a balance of sorts between political authority and social power — were then substantially realized. A few brief comments on those dimensions of the parliamentary order will be useful before addressing the problem of why they are now ignored.

The years immediately following the revolution were filled with enormous difficulties: local rebellions, new groups cast up or liberated by the revolution and demanding political and other kinds of attention, a politically engaged army, lack of trained bureaucratic personnel, limited funds for government programs, growing cold-war pressures from abroad, ethnic tensions, and so on. Even so, the new government worked credibly well until late 1956, when it weakened under pressure from regional dissension and soon, in early 1957, reluctantly gave in to the forces behind its successor regime, Guided Democracy. Working reasonably well meant, for example, that relatively few citizens died as the result of government action or non-action, that policies developed by parliamentary cabinets reflected genuine concerns to deal with social problems, that legislation was seriously debated and well drafted, that public institutions — among them the courts, prosecution, police, and various other agencies — assumed a substantial measure of autonomy and performed with integrity. Moreover, parliamentary governments, while they changed frequently, remained fairly consistent in trying to defuse and resolve issues of ethnic conflict, not least those affecting the ethnic Chinese minority (Feith 1994). During those few years, in addition, governments managed growing cold-war pressures, established Indonesian diplomatic missions, successfully organized the Bandung Conference that launched the Non-Aligned Movement, and held the first national elections in 1955 for Parliament and the Constituent Assembly. Compared with Guided Democracy and the New Order, the parliamentary system achieved an impressive record, by no means flashy or astonishingly effective, obviously, yet one that deserves some respect, even admiration. But that is not how it is remembered now. When the parliamentary period comes up in debates, discussions, or conversations about post-Suharto reform issues, most (not all) participants are essentially dismissive. Young and old both, though for different reasons, are likely to point out immediately, as if in conditioned response, that it was a time of political and social messiness, instability, and corruption. To ask for a comparison of messiness and instability then and now, or all the more so of corruption then with that of the last four decades, is to invite near paralytic surprise, as if the thought had not occurred before. Similarly, to argue that historical evidence suggests that a parliamentary system makes better sense than a presidential system evokes either perplexed silence or the quick reply (from many foreign observers along with well informed Indonesians) that, well, yes, but Indonesia needs strong leadership. Mainly, however, the parliamentary period is a blank page, a time whose example seems to offer little of value to reform minded groups.

Assuming against this grain that the parliamentary order did have significant virtues worth consideration now, what were they and how are they relevant to issues of reform? Several come to mind, beginning with the quality of the political elite, their constitution, a working legal system, and the balance struck between state and social interests. As the argument here is that the parliamentary system worked considerably better than either Guided Democracy or the New Order, some explanation is needed of why it collapsed, for this history too has been subverted.

The parliamentary system worked in good part because Indonesia's political leadership then, by and large, wanted it to work both for their own sake and that of the country. Well educated and long politically engaged in the independence movement, the nationalist commitments of many leaders then were solid, oriented as much or more to post-revolutionary social reconstruction and the creation of an effective state as to personal or partisan advantage. Their political interests were naturally influential, and few of them stood above violating a few public principles for the good of their parties, but their ideological commitments amounted to more than mere grandstanding.

These commitments are best judged in terms of the work undertaken during the six full years of parliamentary government. Parliamentary cabinets developed, funded, and implemented an educational policy that secured Indonesian as a national language and made for an increasingly literate society. Public health policies figured importantly. The Ministry of Justice, with parliamentary support, established a uniform judicial system throughout the archipelago. The several governments encouraged an actively free press, or in any case did not discourage it through intervention. Local rebellions were resolved not by means of military suppression alone but also by political negotiation and compromise that probably reduced death rates. It is worth pondering, again, how few citizens died as the result of government decisions during those early post-revolutionary years compared with post-1960 realities. With hindsight, these were respectable accomplishments, hardly the work of an elite stratum obsessed with its own narrowly conceived interests.

Neither the constitutional foundation which that first generation of political leadership chose to establish, nor the parliamentary process itself, were insignificant achievements. The Provisional Constitution of 1950, an amended version of the federal Constitution of 1949, was one of the most progressive instruments of its time (Supomo 1964; Suradji and Tatanusa 2000).[1] Part V (articles 7 through 34) of the first chapter of the provisional constitution, following formal definitions of territory, language, flag, citizenship and the like, is devoted to fundamental human rights and freedoms, drawn from the Universal Declaration of Human Rights; and Part VI (articles 35 through 43) to basic principles meant to define the political, social, and economic purposes of the independent state. Among these principles were that public authority is based on the will of the people expressed in "periodic and genuine elections"; that government "shall promote social security and social guarantees" including "favourable conditions of labour", prevention of unemployment and provision of pensions; creating prosperity and raising standards of living; preventing monopolistic organizations; cooperative economic organization and state control of essential economic services; protection of the family, the poor, and neglected children; protection of cultural, artistic, and scientific freedom; promotion of the spiritual and physical development of the people, including literacy and public education; and promotion of public hygiene and health. It all seems rather dreamy, overly idealistic, except that much of the parliamentary political elite evidently took these objectives rather seriously, enough so to explain the attention paid education and health, labour policies, and the persistent (though often ineffective) concerns with economic organization reflected in debates during the early 1950s.

The Constitution of 1950 explains more, however. That it was adopted at all, albeit provisionally, is itself an indication that political leaders meant to live by it, and that it made sense to them ideologically and politically. The strong presidential Constitution of 1945 had been set aside within a few months of the proclamation of independence and replaced by a de facto parliamentary system built around resuscitated political parties. Whatever Soekarno's view of the matter in principle, he accepted his position as constitutional president, though a widely respected and active one with much more than merely symbolic authority. For major party leaders, who had little reason to feel all that confident in their own authority at the outset of independence, the parliamentary order offered both legitimacy and political security.

At the same time, the ideological commitments of many party leaders to a variety of democratic-socialist principles, along with a measure of sensible political diffidence, perhaps awe, before the overwhelming complexity of Indonesian society and the difficulty of holding it together while changing it, may have encouraged some recognition that the state ought not to be too overbearing. For this or whatever reason, the parliamentary state was limited by the balance struck between state authority and organized social power. Labour unions, farmers' organizations, the press, and political parties themselves reflected social interests that no government then was willing to risk waving aside.

Under these conditions, the parliamentary system constituted an arena conducive to the flexible political bargaining and compromise essential to dealing with a large, diverse, and uncertain society. Underlying parliamentary institutions, constitutionalism offered political leadership a guarantee not only of legitimacy but continuity and political safety, survival in defeat, so long as the primary constitutional rules held. This last point may help to explain why the formal legal system worked as well as it did during the parliamentary period. But there is undoubtedly more to it. Significantly, in the uneasy political centre consisting of the PNI and Masjumi that produced most Prime Ministers, many of the key players were practicing lawyers. Moreover, the public lawyers who staffed the Supreme Court, prosecution, and top echelons of the bureaucracy were themselves comfortably part of the small national elite. They had no compunctions about exercising their own constitutionally provided authority as they saw fit, without many worries about what their friends in political office happened to think or want. Political leaders sometimes grumbled (and more) about Soeprapto, the Chief Public Prosecutor, or Soekanto, the national police commandant, or occasionally decisions of the Supreme Court or lower courts, but if the constitution was to hold, so too the *rechtsstaat* principle, the *negara hukum* in its Indonesian version, had to hold. It did, despite a hundred difficulties — shortages of graduated lawyers, inadequate budgets, lack of appropriate space and equipment, and in some places a good deal of local puzzlement, even resentment, over unfamiliar legal processes. Courts were respected, judges helped to educate prosecutors and police officers in trial, the Supreme Court began to adapt old law to new circumstances, police arrested suspects, the prosecution indicted them, even if they happened to hold high office, and the courts sentenced or acquitted them on available evidence and legal grounds made quite clear.[2] Members of Parliament and others, including the press, complained about still extant colonial law and the like, but not much about legal institutions.

Parliamentary process itself was reasonably effective, all the more so given profound differences of ideology and interest among the principal parties, pressures from impatient quarters in society, and much uncertainty and differences of policy views about imperative economic and social issues. One measure of parliamentary efficacy is the ability of its diverse parts to negotiate compromises on critical issues, avoiding as much as possible violent alternatives. In both the pre- and post-election (1955) parliament ideological conflict among the parties ran deep, but many of its members had no difficulty crossing such divides outside for cordial chats about family and the old days. The much-respected speaker of the house, Sartono, a senior PNI (Nationalist) figure, set a tone that encouraged cross-party recognition of institutional responsibility. The point should not be exaggerated, for there were distinct limits to political comity, but negotiation was possible within those limits that allowed for some noteworthy legislation — of considerably higher quality than statutes extruded after 1960 — and the avoidance of damaging policy. One example of the latter had to do with the sensitive problem of anti-Chinese pressures from the early 1950s onwards that demanded severely restrictive approaches to citizenship. Years of parliamentary debate and backroom negotiation avoided the worst possibilities and fashioned legislation that was relatively benign and workable.[3] Similarly, the difficult problem of Islamic rebellion in Aceh was dealt with in ways that restrained, confined, and finally ended armed battle in favour of political concessions, by contrast with the brutal repression visited on the province during the last few years.

In short, parliamentary government in post-colonial, post-revolutionary Indonesia was respectably competent. At the time, however, it was also the target of much dissatisfaction. The criticisms were many: of the failure to fashion a successful programme of economic development, of party self-interest, of the failure to replace colonial laws and regulations with "national" law, and above all of corruption and instability, meaning the frequent changes of cabinet as one after another was upset and the party bargaining that followed in efforts to fashion new governments. Corruption and instability require brief comments, because they figure so prominently in the persistent condemnations of the parliamentary system.

There was of course corruption, large and small, though nothing on the scale of post-1960 or, even more so, post-1965 habits. What is surprising, looking back, is not so much the corruption but that its scale was limited and that serious efforts were made to do something about it. As nearly as can be determined, the courts, prosecution, police, and even much of the *pamong-praja* (the regional administration centrally directed by the Ministry of Internal Affairs) were not all that easily suborned. As legal institutions retained both integrity and autonomy, they could and did act against corruption. Trials and convictions even of a few major political players provide persuasive evidence that prosecutors, police officials, and judges exercised their responsibilities as a matter of course.[4] That there was at the time much outspoken criticism of corruption is an indication that it was not yet taken for granted, by contrast with the Guided Democracy and New Order periods when corruption became commonly recognized as a fact of daily life, the subject of a thousand cynical jokes and presuppositions.

Instability is a different, more complex matter. The parliamentary system was unstable, much as the governments of Fourth Republic France and post-war Italy were unstable, what with cabinets frequently falling on votes of no confidence inspired, often enough, as much by ambitions for cabinet appointments as by issues of principle. But this kind of instability, while costly in some respects and likely to provoke much grumbling, dissatisfaction, and contempt, was not the cause of social instability. If anything, in some respects it was itself the consequence of a deeply divided party system that more or less accurately reflected religious, ethnic, and ideological cleavages in Indonesia which, at the same time, parliamentary government tended to cushion by providing a site for debate, along with much name-calling, that was not all that likely to break out in open violence. The party system was regarded as divisive, and the run-up to the elections of 1955 exacerbated religious tensions, but ethnic and religious conflict is socially indigenous and would in any case have to be dealt with. Again, if the parties promoted such tensions, parliamentary process softened them, or anyway directed them away from battlefields. Religious and other ideological tensions did not disappear under Guided Democracy; nor did they do so under the New Order, which simply suppressed them for a time without reducing their explosive potential for violent conflict, as has been evident since 1998. It was this potential that the parliamentary system, in some ways, was able to contain.

None of the discussion thus far has been meant to whitewash the parliamentary order, but only to suggest that it proved safer, less debilitating and less destructive for Indonesia than anything that followed. But not many could possibly have foreseen what did follow, in part because the fall of the parliamentary system was not that well understood at the time and did not become much clearer over the next 40 years or more. This history, too, has been obscured.

The consensus view of why the parliamentary system collapsed is that the elections of 1955, by failing to produce a solid majority government, had left the country dissatisfied; that the government proved unable to deal with regional dissidence; and that many turned to Soekarno for the authoritative leadership Indonesia required. All these propositions are supported by adequate evidence, but they fall short to the extent that they skirt around the critical part played by the army, then led by General Abdul Haris Nasution. From early 1957, when martial law was proclaimed on Nasution's urging in response to the regional crisis, which itself was substantially the result of local military intervention, army leadership had the advantage of political initiative. The army also enjoyed growing American favour as the one force likely to contain or destroy the Communist Party. As the PKI grew more confident after the national elections of 1955 and the regional elections of 1957, moreover, other major and minor parties also began, only a bit more subtly, to hope for assistance from the army against revolutionary ambitions on the left.

It was largely pressure from the army, abetted more or less passively by a civilian political elite that feared for its survival, which was decisive in bringing down the parliamentary system. From early 1957 on the army grew increasingly central to the evolution of Guided Democracy, in which Soekarno became the principal symbol of authority but lacked the political power to go with it. Soekarno could do little more than react to

Nasution's initiatives, trying to contain the raw power of military organization and guns but usually failing (Lev 1966, 1994). The principal innovations of Guided Democracy — functional groups, the Middle Way of the Army (later the *Dwifungsi* or dual-function), and the restoration of the strong presidential Constitution of 1945 — all originated in Nasution's office and reflected precisely the interests and the ideological commitments of a key group of army officers. That these changes carried over comfortably into the New Order with little change is itself ample indication of the extent to which the army determined outcomes during the Guided Democracy years. Fearing a coup, neither political party leadership nor Soekarno could prevent Nasution from remaking Indonesia's political order. But it was Soekarno, not Nasution, who was burdened with responsibility for the dramatic transformation of Indonesian politics after 1958.

By 1959–60 the fundamental characteristics of the parliamentary state were for all intents and purposes gone. The old nationalist elite was out, the parties were rendered powerless except to the extent that they could mobilize on the streets, the elected constituent assembly was prorogued, and parliament itself — whose re-election in 1959 was "postponed" in 1958 by agreement of all major parties except the Communists — was dismissed and then filled with presidential appointees. Citizens were in effect disenfranchised as political and governmental power was concentrated in Jakarta and state-society balances disappeared. In a short time legal institutions were effectively recruited for political purposes, and they and the public bureaucracy generally began their unimpeded slide into corruption and abuse of power.

When after May 1998 demands for fundamental reform sounded loudly across the country, it was nearly impossible for reformers to know just where to begin: how to deal at once with necessary political and economic change, how to identify primary starting points when everything was equally in need of repair, and how to conceive reform strategies with reasonable odds of success. Under the best of circumstances reform was bound to be extraordinarily difficult, because there was so little to build on. No single state institution retained enough integrity or organizational capacity to serve as a base. Available power remained largely vested in those who had most to lose from effective change. But beyond these problems, those most committed to change, including some of the most capable and experienced NGOs, were at a loss for lack of an analytical perspective supported by adequate knowledge of how precisely political and economic conditions had come to this disastrous conclusion. This rather exaggerates the problem, for much was known about the extraordinary corruption and political abuse of the New Order regime, but how these faults were understood was limited by their encapsulation within the New Order period itself, beginning with the massacres of late 1965 and ending, though not quite, with Suharto's resignation in May 1998. Historical origins, conditions, and causes were hopelessly blurred, their relevance uncertain at best. It is not that reform would have been much easier had that history been well known, but rather that without a realistic appreciation of the parliamentary order and why it disappeared, and how Guided Democracy was shaped by the army, it was far more difficult to understand the most critical questions that had to be addressed and to begin to shape sensible strategies of change. Where understanding the progression from parliamentarism to Guided Democracy to the New Order might have made it possible to grasp the institutional and political prerequisites of reform — in part, for example, by calling up models from the 1950s — instead there was a vacuum of knowledge, little or no memory, or a mix of thoughtless cliches and misleading assumptions.

Among young people who matured during the New Order years, received knowledge consists essentially of the regime's rendering of modern Indonesian history, a distorted picture, to put it mildly, but one that has had some influence even on those equipped with memory. An example has to do with periodization, which reasonably should distinguish clearly between the parliamentary, Guided Democracy, and New Order periods by criteria of regime type, leadership, and policies. Instead, the commonly accepted distinction is between only two periods, Old Order and New Order, which conflates the parliamentary and Guided Democracy regimes, implying that both were intimately connected and dominated by Soekarno. (In fact, the parliamentary regime stands alone, while Guided Democracy and the New Order are inextricably intertwined, the latter having grown out of the former and retaining its essential structural features). The more distant parliamentary period is obscured by the more recent and anxiety ridden Guided Democracy years. By implication the parliamentary system then becomes not only unstable but particularly corrupt, full of conflict, led incompetently by selfish parties, roamed freely by Communists, economically primitive, and so on, from which the New Order rescued the nation and brought it stability, prosperity, and development.

Among those who lived through the parliamentary and Guided Democracy times, memory is often flawed, not alone by age. Some who were active politically during the 1950s do regard the parliamentary order as promising — its political elite capable and responsible, legal institutions honest, and so on — but many others oddly share the views of younger generations raised on New Order instruction. Why they do so is subject to no simple answer. For some it is the memory of their own disappointment with and protests against the parliamentary system and the hope they placed in Soekarno, now still a predisposition locked in and resistant to any comparison with succeeding regimes. For others, particularly those who profited in one way or another during the New Order years, the parliamentary system's advantages for the country faded before the New Order's gifts of personal opportunity, wealth, or status.

But another reason why the parliamentary system became frozen in a cloud of epithets is that scholars, intellectuals, and journalists by and large ignored it after the onset first of Guided Democracy and then of the New Order. Nearly all — including foreign observers — focused on whatever happened to be going on in the imperative present, whether that of Guided Democracy or the New Order. This tendency had the effect of encapsulating the New Order period, divorcing it from its genetic sources. (Not only is the 1950s a lost or disappearing decade, as McVey has it, but so for that matter have the five years of Guided Democracy been buried in their own interesting detritus, with almost no research into that dark age).[5] During the 1990s and especially since the fall of Suharto, the early New Order period itself has attracted increasing attention, particularly with respect to its spectacularly brutal start in the massacre of late 1965, but again with little effort to trace and dissect its genesis further back.

Consequently, reform efforts since mid-1998 have been denied, or denied themselves, a significant fund of knowledge essential, or at least useful, to thinking through strategies of political and legal reform. For one example, in the complex matter of constitutional change, relatively few of those engaged have ever read — and some are hardly aware of — the well-drafted and human rights-sensitive Constitution of 1950.[6] For another, rather more telling, much of the thinking about governmental reform takes for granted a presidential system, despite considerable evidence that a strong presidency has hardly proved beneficial for the country. As little is held in mind about the parliamentary experiment, few can assess its advantages for a country as complex as Indonesia; and as knowledge of Indonesia's own experience during the 1950s is scant and memory limited, there is little inclination even to consider the widespread use of parliamentary systems abroad.[7]

Similarly, the parties and party system of the 1950s, problematic as they may have been or are imagined to have been, provide little instruction in evaluating the far more problematic parties now in existence and wondering about how to refashion or replace them. Nor have the parliamentary parliament itself and its legislative products and policy directions served any purpose of comparative example from Indonesia's own experience.

One of Indonesia's most critical problems, the political engagement of the army, has received a good deal of critical attention, but it is striking that many who have engaged in the debates have little knowledge of its origins during the 1950s. Even senior army officers, all of whom still active came into their own under the New Order, are barely familiar with the provenance of their political and ideological bents in General Nasution's measures during the late 1950s and early 1960s. There is little or no (military or civil) memory of how the Indonesian public came to be regarded as unruly, even dangerous, deserving not of respect but firm control, and how this view (rather like that of the colonial administration) transformed citizens themselves into the prime enemy the army lacked from abroad.

Nor, despite the angry attention paid extraordinary corruption and the utter lack of effective legal process, is there much understanding of exactly how and why reasonably useful institutions were degraded, suborned, and subjugated to the political and personal objectives of a political and bureaucratic elite subject to no institutional controls. Even capable young lawyers know little about the parliamentary legal system. Legal history is not taught, judicial decisions of the 1950s are not read, old parliamentary debates attract little interest, and the capable judges and prosecutors of a few decades back are forgotten. Private lawyers, now ten or more times more numerous than 30 years ago and divided among five or six ragged organizations, for the most part have little appreciation of the history of their own profession and even less inclination to try to restore the integrity, skill, and professional commitment that it once represented.[8]

In none of this discussion do I mean to suggest that remembering the parliamentary order or knowing its accomplishments is anywhere near enough to assure Indonesian reform movements a measure of success.

Rather, devoted as many reformers are, lack of that history constricts their effort, denying them access to reasonably clear principles and standards once tried on Indonesian ground. Where memory fails or is subverted, knowledge has to be cultivated. Excavating the parliamentary past is likely to be well worth the trouble.

Notes

[1]   It is not clear who exactly drafted the first document. The 1950 Constitution was discussed in the federal parliament, but no effort was made then to amend the revisions made in the 1949 Constitution, because to do so would have delayed the formal inauguration of the unitary state.

[2]   It is well worth examining the law journal, the *Madjalah Hukum dan Masyarakat* (*Journal of Law and Society*) published from 1947 until 1962 or so, for the quality of judicial decisions, the discussion of them, and articles and essays meant to deal with difficult issues of legal change. No law journal since matches it.

[3]   The 1950s parliament had a number of ethnic Chinese members from several political parties, along with those from the ethnic Chinese organization BAPERKI. The post-1965 Parliament had none, and the earlier legislative approach to minority questions was in practice obliterated.

[4]   One such case was that of Iskaq Tjokrohadisuryo who was convicted but wrote a post-trial defense (Tjokrohadisurjo 1960).

[5]   See Nasution (1992) and Simandjuntak (1994) for two significant exceptions. A few specific studies, particularly of the army, also appeared during the 1990s, but they tend to avoid regime contexts.

[6]   Although the 1950 Constitution has become readily available again in Suradji *et al.*, cited above, as yet there is little indication that many more reformers are aware of its quality. Though several groups insist on a quite new constitution, in and out of Parliament and the People's Consultative Assembly (MPR) the more common inclination is to amend the 1945 Constitution.

[7]   In part this problem has to do with the attraction of the American model among many who have studied in the United States. American political and legal institutions are often too simply and uncritically taken at face value, but in addition little effort is made to analyse their fit in Indonesia or the ease with which they might be transplanted. Other institutional models that may be more useful in Indonesia tend to be ignored, except by those who have relevant experience elsewhere.

[8]   The first (and first rate) major critical study of Indonesia's private legal profession was recently published not by any of the existing professional associations but by the Indonesian Center for the Study of Law and Policy (Pusat Studi Hukum dan Kebijakan Indonesia. PSHK); see PSHK (2001).

Nugroho Notosusanto: The Legacy of a Historian in the Service of an Authoritarian Regime[1]

KATHARINE E. MCGREGOR

A fter the transfer of sovereignty in December 1949, the government of the Republic of Indonesia offered a military education at Breda in the Netherlands to all former members of the *Tentara Pelajar* (Student Army). Fresh from the independence struggle and brimming with enthusiasm for the future of his country, Nugroho Notosusanto was faced with a choice between continuing a career in the military and following in his father's footsteps by pursuing a higher education. On his appointment as Rector of the University of Indonesia in 1982, Nugroho revealed that at the time the offer was made he had indeed wanted to join the military and go to Breda. He reflected, "(m)y father delicately instructed that I follow the second path [that of academia], [and] I have already made an effort to carry out that instruction as best I could, although I have not ignored my first inclination" (Bhakti 1982). Nugroho Notosusanto's thwarted desire to become a soldier provides a key insight into the man most responsible for official New Order history.

While other authors have acknowledged Nugroho to be the most important historian for the New Order regime (Bourchier 1994; Brooks 1995), he has not received extensive attention in scholarship on Indonesia. Every country has official historians and indeed it is not that uncommon for historians to work for the military or for historians to undertake military history projects. However, Nugroho was different in that he devoted himself to producing history for a military dominated regime. He willingly compromised his integrity as a scholar in order to further legitimate the New Order regime and in doing so endured personal isolation and ridicule from other historians. The most puzzling question for those who knew Nugroho, especially fellow historians, was why he made this choice and why he seemed so devoted to the military. The answer to this question lies in Nugroho's life story. As a result of experiences as a member of the Student Army he genuinely believed that the military, which was in his mind a disciplined, determined, and uncompromising force in Indonesia, contained the best possible leaders for the nation. This belief was reinforced by his experience of the Liberal Democracy and Guided Democracy periods.

In addition to examining the influence of Nugroho's life experiences on his character, I will here examine the role he played in shaping official New Order historical discourse. Some of the key history projects of the New Order, and the controversies they sparked, will be addressed. After some further reflection on Nugroho's motivations for producing history for the military, the last part of this essay will reflect on his legacy in the post-Suharto period and how the past is being renegotiated in Indonesia.

Who was Nugroho Notosusanto?

Born on 15 June 1931, in Rembang, central Java with the title *Raden Panji*, meaning prince or descendant of royalty,[2] it appears that Nugroho was a nationalist from a young age. An acquaintance recalls that as a young boy Nugroho "would stand up like a soldier and show his respect" when he heard *Indonesia Raya*, the national anthem, on the radio (Darma 1985). Early in the independence struggle, Nugroho's family moved to Yogyakarta in order for his father, who had trained at the prestigious elite Law School, the Rechtskundige Hogeschool,[3] to take up a position in the justice department in the newly formed government of the Republic of Indonesia.[4] Nugroho joined the independence struggle in 1945 at the age of 14. He served as a member of the Student Army, sometimes referred to as the Seventeenth Brigade of the National Army, which was made up entirely of secondary and university students (Notosusanto 1970: 68–71, 69). Many members of the Student Army originated from youth militias trained in the period of the Japanese Occupation. Although Nugroho was probably too young to have joined these Japanese youth groups he shared with them an acceptance of "authoritarian mentalities with a positive respect for force and emotional anti-Westernism" (Kahin 1952: 107) . These values persisted in Nugroho throughout his life.

The enthusiasm and spirit of the Student Army contributed psychologically to the struggle. The Student Army taught prominent villagers courses with the hope of instilling "a sense of purpose in the people for the success of the *perjuangan*", the struggle (Notosusanto 1973: 121). Nugroho's unit was responsible for guarding Dutch approaches. He notes,

> our patrols were only reconnaissance patrols, they were never combat patrols which was the task of the mobile troops. But sometimes we ran into an enemy patrol or even walked into an ambush where an engagement was unavoidable. Luckily we never lost any men. Some were wounded occasionally. (Notosusanto 1973: 121, 123, translations as provided in text)

The Student Army also participated in intelligence operations, carried messages, laid traps for the Dutch, and occasionally (when they could come by them) carried arms.[5]

Nugroho's experience of the struggle convinced him of the special role to be played by his generation in the newly born nation. In the 1950s, he published in the ex-Student Army publication "Kompas" a letter to a Dutch writer in which he firmly expressed his views on the distinguishing characteristics of his generation.[6] Nugroho wrote,

> Your introduction to me is at the same time an introduction to a still newer generation of Indonesian young people which has already gained its position in the community even though it has not yet completely voiced its ideas. Three or four years ago we were known as the Student Army. That was the name which our society came to give to all the secondary school and university students who freely left their desks for interests greater than personal ones to join in a life-and-death struggle to save our people from drowning in the mud of history.
> (Notosusanto 1970a: 68–9)

Despite Nugroho's admission at a later date that the Student Army rarely engaged in armed combat, immediately after the struggle he emphasized the sacrifices of the Student Army in a spirited fashion.

In this letter Nugroho demonstrates considerable resentment, if not a patronizing attitude, towards civilian leaders of the struggle, particularly those involved in diplomatic negotiations. He notes,

> As a matter of fact, our *bapak*s (fathers) who are now giving themselves to so much theorizing, were trembling in fear and were counselling us

on the need to start negotiations. We had better negotiate and keep on
negotiating, without building up as much support as we could. They
were full of deference to the 'international standard' whereas we were
struggling against mountains of difficulties. And when these mountains
had been dug away, it was easy for them to pat their *pemuda*s (youths)
on the back and give them fulsome praise, which stuck like syrup...
                                        (Notosusanto 1970a: 70)

Nugroho, like many ex-Student Army Members, blamed the lack
of progress in the 1950s on the failures of the older generation and
their abandonment of the *semangat* (spirit) of the struggle (Feith 1962:
463–4). Part of the semangat mentality to which the Student Army, the
army, and many other struggle groups subscribed was an unwillingness
to compromise and a sense that those who negotiated during the struggle
had made unnecessary concessions to the Dutch.

Nugroho's reference to "bapak" is ostensibly directed at nationalist
leaders who he implies were not responsible for the real work of the
struggle. His criticism can also however be read as referring to his own
father, who was a member of the negotiating team for the Republic of
Indonesia at the Round Table Conference of 1949.[7] A possible reason
for this resentment was his father's decision that Nugroho should not
pursue a military career. The most likely reason Nugroho's father dis-
couraged him from joining the military after the struggle related to a
general attitude of wariness towards the military shared by many older
members of the nationalist movement such as Soekarno and Hatta. Both
his father's actions and the anti-military attitude of the nationalist
group, sometimes referred to as the "1930s generation", forged Nugroho's
own theory on the distinctiveness of his own generation.

Nugroho once declared General Sudirman, the first commander of
the Armed Forces, to be his only idol because he displayed sacrifice,
loyalty, and a strong sense of nationalism.[8] Similar to Sudirman, who was
an early advocate of a political role for the military (Penders and
Sundhaussen 1985: 76–7), Nugroho's experience of the independence
struggle convinced him that because the military did not compromise
with the Dutch they were greater patriots, and more capable leaders,
than civilians. Although he obeyed his father's wishes and pursued an
education, Nugroho continued to strongly identify with the military
throughout his life.

Despite his temporary departure from the military world, Nugroho's romantic view of the independence struggle — a dominant theme in literature in the 1950s (Teeuw 1967: 230) — endured in the short stories he wrote afterward. In contrast to the cynicism of some writers, Nugroho represented the struggle as very much worth fighting and dying for. He was drawn to the romanticism of sacrifice for one's nation and his stories were concerned primarily with soldiers' experience of comradeship, loyalty, and masculinity.[9]

After the transfer of sovereignty from the Dutch to Indonesia, Nugroho enrolled in the Faculty of Letters at the University of Indonesia, Jakarta. He became well known as a result of both his short stories and his activities as a student leader. His peers (including Onghokham) and mentor, Priyono, had great hopes for Nugroho to become a future leader.[10]

Nugroho spent nine years as a student in the Faculty of Letters, eventually specializing in history and then taking up a teaching position. He had a short break from the University of Indonesia between 1960–2 when he received a scholarship from the Rockefeller Foundation for a masters program in Historical Method in the School of Oriental and African Studies at London University. When Nugroho returned to Indonesia in 1962, the fervently nationalist "return of Irian Jaya" campaign was under way. The Indonesian Communist Party was gaining strength and competing vigorously with the military for power. Nugroho resumed teaching at the University of Indonesia and was installed as the head of the History Department.

While Nugroho is most closely associated with history making in the New Order period following the attempted coup of 1965, he was first recruited by General Nasution to join the military history project *Sedjarah Singkat Perdjuangan Bersendjata Bangsa Indonesia* (SSPBB, A Short History of the Armed Struggle of the Indonesian Nation) in 1964 (Mokoginta 1964). This publication was largely a response to a planned National Front history publication in which the Madiun Affair, commonly represented as a communist plot, was to be left out (McGregor 2002). One reason Nugroho joined the army history centre was his admiration for Nasution as a successful military leader with a demonstrated interest in history.[11] In the context of late Guided Democracy his decision to join the project possibly also represented a commitment on Nugroho's behalf to challenging the communists, in line with Nasution's intent.

It is difficult, however, to determine the strength of Nugroho's commitment to anti-communism in the Guided Democracy period, and all too easy to project backward the sentiments he displayed in his history projects after 1965. Nugroho had not openly emerged as anti-communist, although he did have several links to anti-communist groups. He had acquaintance with sympathizers and members of the PSI (*Partai Sosialis Indonesia*), the Indonesian Socialist Party, several of whom taught with Nugroho at *Sekolah Staf Komando Angkatan Darat* (Seskoad, Army Staff and Command School) as part of the army's professional training scheme. Despite the label "socialist", members of this party were fittingly described as *kaum sosialis salon* (salon socialists) and were firmly anti-communist (Gie 1983: 45). From his days as short story writer in the 1950s Nugroho also had links with writers including H.B. Jassin, a key signatory to the hastily banned *Manikebu* (*Manifes Kebudayaan*, Cultural Manifesto). In that document, signatories rejected the idea of "Politics is the Commander" espoused by Lekra, the communist affiliated cultural organization, and instead defended the right to freedom of expression (Mohamad n.d.: 2–3, 13). Goenawan Mohamad, another signatory, claims that Nugroho in fact agreed with the banning of *Manikebu* on the grounds that he did not support the kind of freedom of expression advocated in the manifesto, believing that the arts should also be geared towards the project of revolution.[12] What this suggests is that Nugroho was more of a chameleon than many would allow, and was comfortable with the authoritarianism of the Guided Democracy period.

Nonetheless, Nugroho was perhaps cautious about communism because of his religious background. His father, who became Professor of Islamic law at Gadjah Mada University, was known as a pious Muslim and this influence on Nugroho might have fostered wariness, shared by many other Muslims, of the link between Communism and atheism (van der Kroef 1985: 162). His involvement in Nasution's history project no doubt also drew him closer to the anti-communist elements of the army, including to Nasution himself.

From Nasution's perspective, Nugroho's recruitment served to strengthen ties between students of the University of Indonesia and the army. At the time he was appointed to the history project Nugroho was working at the University of Indonesia as both Head of the Department of History and Assistant Rector in charge of student affairs. The campus of the University of Indonesia was dominated by *Himpunan Mahasiswa Indonesia* (HMI), the Muslim students' organization, and to a lesser extent by *Perhimpuan Mahasiswa Katolik Republik Indonesia* (PMKRI), the Catholic students' organization. Both these organizations were anti-communist.[13] Nugroho's position as Assistant Rector in charge of student affairs therefore put him in a position of influence among anti-left forces.

As the left gained support at the national level in 1964–5 (Hauswedell 1973: 112–4, 129–41), tensions heightened on campus. The Muslim student organization HMI came under attack as "counter-revolutionary" (Maxwell 1997). Despite his careful positioning Nugroho, who worked on this HMI-dominated campus, also became a target of leftist resentment. His position became increasingly uncomfortable when in 1965 he became the centre of a scandal for screening "imperialist" American and English films at a fundraising activity for the 15th anniversary of the University of Indonesia held at the state palace (*Harian Rakyat*, 19 February 1965 and 21 February 1965).

Although Nugroho seems to have positioned himself close to anti-communist elements, a student activist of the 1966 generation notes that resentment from leftist groups stemmed perhaps from their inability to convert Nugroho to their views, rather than from his own actions or the sentiments he displayed.[14] At all times, Nugroho is said to have acted with caution and balance.[15]

The completion of Nasution's military history project resulted in the founding of the Armed Forces History Centre. Nasution appointed Nugroho its head and in this capacity that he presided over many official New Order history projects, as we will see below.

Nugroho's Major Historical Projects

(1) Histories of the coup attempt of 1965

In the early hours of the morning on 1 October 1965, six of the most senior army generals and one lieutenant were kidnapped from their homes and murdered by members of the Cakrabirawa presidential guard. Because an attempt had also been made on the life of General Nasution, the position of his aides was considered unsafe. Nugroho and other staff were temporarily relocated from their homes to a private residence in Kemang,[16] and at this point he, as head of the History Centre, was called upon to write the first version of the coup attempt.

Nugroho produced the publication *40 Hari Kegagalan "G-30-S" 1 Oktober-10 November* (The Forty Day Failure of the September 30th Movement October 1 to November 10) shortly after the events themselves.[17] The book, in which the coup attempt was described as a plot of the PKI (Indonesian Communist Party), was a consolidated version of official army propaganda released in the first two months after the coup attempt.[18] It included descriptions of the prologue to the coup attempt, the event itself (complete with photo "documentation" of the retrieval of corpses from the well at Lubang Buaya), and a brief description of the combined efforts of the people and ABRI to crush the uprising.

40 Hari Kegagalan "G-30-S" was perhaps the most important history project Nugroho completed on behalf of the regime. In the days following the coup attempt, there was much confusion as to who was behind it. President Soekarno's refusal to blame the Communist party posed a significant challenge to the military, for the legitimacy of the army take-over rested on the general public's belief that the coup attempt was a plot of the PKI and not an internal military affair. The army had a lot of rebutting to do, particularly given that the coup plotters themselves had declared in their initial broadcast on 1 October that "the 30 September Movement" was an internal military conflict (Anderson and McVey 1966: 134). The army also had to consolidate their version of events in order to provide continuing justification for the mass killing of communists, which they had set in train following the coup.[19] In this way Nugroho's publication made an important contribution towards attributing responsibility for this event to the PKI. The priority awarded to this project was also made clear by the fact that Nugroho and his team of assistants worked day and night to complete the publication (Pusat Sejarah dan Tradisi ABRI 1994: 23).

While Nugroho's role in writing the first version of the coup attempt is well known, his contributions to establishing a new political order on the campus of the University of Indonesia are less recognized. Once the atmosphere of uncertainty after the coup attempt had passed, Nugroho emerged from temporary hiding to play an active role in the transition by using his influence on the campus. In October 1965 the Rector, Brigadier General Sjarief Thayeb, held discussions with student leaders agitating for retribution for the deaths of the murdered generals. These discussions resulted in the formation of the Indonesian University

Student Action Front (*KAMI — Kesatuan Aksi Mahasiswa Indonesia*) (Maxwell 1997: 13–4). At this time Nugroho became the students' military contact and assisted in building and coordinating a student-military alliance. He had two primary contacts prior to and during the student demonstrations. One of these was Soe Hok Gie, Nugroho's own history student with whom he consulted in order to monitor student activities. The other was his wife's uncle Lieutenant General Suwarto (then the Commandant of Seskoad), through whom he ensured the military's support and protection prior to student demonstrations (Gie 1983: 45, 159, 162). The University of Indonesia was a key campus in fielding the KAMI-led student demonstrations of 1966. These demonstrations provided the momentum that forced Soekarno to hand over powers to Suharto in March 1966, and contributed to the subsequent banning of the PKI. It was not obvious that Nugroho facilitated military and university links during this time.[20] The army, under Suharto's leadership, sought to appear loyal to President Soekarno and responsive to the people's will rather than imposing their own agenda. Nugroho was said to be very clever at positioning himself.[21] Behind the scenes, however, Nugroho made a significant contribution to the campaign to oust Soekarno, further evidence of his commitment to a new, military-dominated government.

Apart from the first Indonesian version of the coup attempt, Nugroho was also responsible, together with Ismail Saleh, for the production of an official English version released in 1968 (Notosusanto and Saleh 1968). Prepared with the assistance of Guy Pauker of the Rand Corporation in California, this was a rebuttal of the "Cornell Paper" which put forward the theory that the coup attempt was most likely the result of severe intra-army conflicts. In this way Nugroho contributed to defending the military regime to the outside world.

The central aim of both Nugroho's Indonesian and English versions of the coup attempt of 1965 was to implicate PKI-affiliated institutions such as the leftist youth group *Pemuda Rakyat*, the progressive women's organization *Gerakan Wanita Indonesia* (Gerwani), the labour union *Sentral Orginisasi Buruh Seluruh Indonesia* (SOBSI, Central Organisation of Indonesian Workers) and the farmers' union *Barisan Tani Indonesia* (BTI) in the coup attempt.

In addition to acknowledging Nugroho's hand in producing these written versions of the 1965 events it is also important to note the extent to which his official narrative of the coup attempt was consolidated, embellished, and repeated in school texts, a monument, a museum, and a film. As early as 1967 the army began work on constructing an elaborate monument at the site in Lubang Buaya at which the bodies of the army victims were dumped.[22] Nugroho's version of the coup attempt is detailed in the monument's portrayal of the martyrs of communist betrayal and the defenders of Pancasila,[23] and in the relief beneath Pancasila Sakti Monument.[24] Every year Nugroho's version of the coup attempt was also invoked in official commemorations held at this site and in newspaper and broadcast media coverage.[25]

Despite the mass killings of communists or suspected affiliates which followed the 1965 coup and the banning of communism in 1966, the government continued to circulate this version of the coup attempt as a means of keeping the myth of a communist threat alive. The principal reason for doing so was to provide ongoing justification for the killings, but also to maintain a convenient and potent label for quashing political dissent. Heryanto aptly describes the perpetuation of the threat of communism as an instrument of authoritarianism (Heryanto 1999: 156).

In 1981 the government decided it was necessary to remind Indonesians of the coup attempt especially because of the emergence of a young generation born after 1965 (Sri Suko 1986: 6). Two projects emerged for which Nugroho was responsible, namely a museum and a film about the coup attempt. Museum Monumen Pancasila Sakti, which Nugroho personally curated, includes diorama representations of the prelude to the coup attempt, the actual event and its aftermath, as well as portraits of the heroes and displays of their original blood-stained clothes and personal artifacts. Nugroho's film project "Pengkhianatan Gerakan 30 September" (Treachery of the 30 September Movement) is doubtless the most famous representation of the coup attempt (Sen and Hill 2000: 147–50; Shiraishi 1997: 77–80). Although the film was made by Brigadier General Dwipayana and directed by Arifin C. Noor, the film script was based on Nugroho's historiography and he, as editor, also made final decisions on the film's content.[26] Consistent with Nugroho's written work, the film features detailed accounts of the kidnapping and death of each of the army victims. In contrast to the written accounts, however, both the film and the museum depict acts of torture being performed by PKI members on the generals.[27] The film also shows members of Gerwani performing the "dance of fragrant flowers" at

Lubang Buaya while torturing the generals.[28] Representations of the torture allegedly carried out at Lubang Buaya were also replicated in school texts. A unit of Nugroho's *Pelajaran Sejarah Perjuangan Bangsa* (PSPB) history course for primary school students, for example, included a dramatic script of the events at Lubang Buaya to be used to stage class plays. Students were required to depict "the cruelty at Lubang Buaya" using replica weapons. Dialogue consisted of simplified phrases such as "kill him, kill him", "cut up his flesh", "crush his head", and "cut off his tongue and his hands" (Trisaksono 1985: 40–3).

The regime recycled early propaganda about the torture of the army heroes in later history texts, most likely motivated by their increasing confidence that, because so much time had passed, their version of history would not be challenged, at least from inside Indonesia.[29] These potent representations were designed to incite hatred of communists, for which Nugroho must be held accountable. Representations of the official version of the coup attempt in monuments, museums, film, history books, and in annual commemoration of 1 October, all contributed to the persecution of former leftists and their families (Amnesty International 1997: 102–8; *D&R*, 3 October 1998; *Prisma* 1997: 12–9; Wieringa 1998: xxxii). For ex-political prisoners, the repeated circulation of these images, combined with social restrictions including limitations on job choice and freedom of movement, contributed to prejudice and isolation (Amnesty International 1994: 94).

Due to the central importance of Nugroho's official narrative to the legitimacy of the New Order regime, the government deliberately prevented the circulation of other versions of the coup attempt. The publication *Bayang Bayang PKI* (Shadows of the PKI) (Institut Studi Arus Informasi 1995), was one of the first Indonesian publications to challenge the official version of the 1965 events. The book was quickly banned on the grounds that the facts and representation of historical truth (*fakta dan kebenaran sejarah*) were not acceptable.[30] While repetition of standard versions of the coup attempt sometimes had the effect of creating fascination with alternative versions (Vickers 1998: 781), the continual suppression of alternative accounts, along with the associated stigmatization of communism, meant that there was scant room for the expression of public sympathy for communists and affiliated organizations, the actual targets of post-coup violence.

(2) Nugroho's Pancasila Theory and other episodes of de-Soekarnoization

The most controversial of Nugroho's projects during the New Order period was his theorizing of *Pancasila*.[31] Formulated by Soekarno in June 1945, Pancasila is Indonesia's national philosophy, consisting of five principles: belief in one God, humanitarianism, nationalism, democracy and social justice. In September 1967, very close to the point at which power had passed from Soekarno to Suharto, Nugroho began working on a theory of the origins of Pancasila (Pusat Sejarah dan Tradisi ABRI 1994: 24). The timing of this project is of relevance because of the New Order's attempt to identify itself with defence of the Pancasila at an early point in the regime. Indeed, one of the most central themes of the official version of the coup attempt was that the army, under Suharto's leadership, had "saved" Pancasila by suppressing the coup attempt (Mortimer 1974: 94).

In the 1970s Nugroho began to circulate his theory that Soekarno was only one of three *penggali* (excavators) of Pancasila, and that the real birth date of the ideology was 18 August 1945, the date on which Pancasila was legally confirmed together with the 1945 Constitution.[32] He based his theory on material in a book by Muhammad Yamin which a five-person investigative committee headed by Mohammad Hatta, the first vice president, had found to be incorrect (Abdoelmanap 1997: 77–169).

Nugroho's work on the origins of the Pancasila was perhaps the most blatant case of historical manipulation for the purposes of the then present regime. His theory was clearly designed to disassociate the Pancasila from Soekarno. In the early 1980s his theory prompted a polemic in the mass media and a national seminar entitled "Who really discovered Pancasila?"[33] Criticisms directed at Nugroho's work attacked his distortion of available evidence and his reliance on suspect sources. Some historians branded Nugroho's book a "pamphlet", implying it was not a sufficiently researched or balanced scholarly work. Nugroho responded that if what was meant by the term "pamphlet" was that the material was in accordance with the opinion of the present government, then "that was only a coincidence" (Bujono 1985: 14–5). Nugroho was also accused of attempting to tarnish Soekarno's historical image and to deny his role as the "discoverer" of the political concept Pancasila, which the New Order regime hoped to appropriate.

Despite the controversy over Nugroho's work, his theory remained part of the government's Pancasila indoctrination courses (known as P4, *Penataran Pedoman Penghayatan dan Pengamalan Pancasila*) and continued to be included in Volume Six of the National History Series (Abdoelmanap 1997: 29).[34] The Department of Education also made Nugroho's book on the Pancasila theory compulsory reading for schoolteachers who taught the Pancasila Moral Education course, and as a reference book to accompany the National History Series (Brooks 1995: 72).

Nugroho was also criticized for minimalizing Soekarno's historical contributions in various school texts (Leigh 1991: 30–1). One academic accused him of attempting "to ruin the name of Soekarno as proclaimer of Independence in the eyes of our students", and consequently concluded Nugroho's histories "were not a good example of historical study material and did not educate this generation" (Historical Research Centre, University of Indonesia 1985). Historians also criticized the disparaging representation of political parties and the belittlement of Soekarno's achievements in Nugroho's contribution to the contemporary history volume in *Sejarah Nasional Indonesia*, the Indonesian National History series (Bourchier 1994: 57).

Nugroho was also at the centre of another scandal over *Sejarah Nasional*. As the first comprehensive history series to be written by Indonesians, this was a prestigious project, the result of the collaboration of many well-known and respected historians from the leading campuses in Indonesia. Along with Sartono Kartodirdjo, Dean of History at the Gadjah Mada University and Abdul Rachman Surjomihardjo of *Lembaga Ilmu Pengetahuan Indonesia* (LIPI, The Indonesian Institute of Social Sciences), Nugroho was one of the editors for this project. When the deadline for the project was approaching, some writers had finished their chapters for the volume Nugroho was in charge of and some had not. Nugroho, who has been described as more disciplined than ordinary military personnel, had become accustomed to enforcing deadlines for his history projects at the Armed Forces History Centre. In his capacity as an editor, he instructed his assistant to procure a copy of the manuscript draft of Volume Six on spurious grounds and then immediately published it in its unfinished form.[35] Other members of the project were furious, feeling professionally betrayed,[36] and condemned Nugroho's actions as out of character and almost unbelievable.[37]

(3) Promoting the military's historical image

The Indonesian military claimed its political role in national life on the basis of the non-neutral leadership role the military played in the independence struggle (1945–9). In an important 1966 army seminar in which military doctrine was reformulated, participants proposed that

> The army which has been born in the cauldron of the revolution, has never been a dead instrument of the government concerned exclusively with security matters. The army, as a fighter for freedom, cannot remain neutral toward the course of state policy, the quality of the government and the safety of the state based on Pancasila. The army does not have an exclusively military duty but is concerned with all fields of social life.   (Crouch 1988: 345)

Because of the importance of the national struggle as a means of justifying this dual political and defensive role (*dwifungsi*), the military paid considerable attention to promoting their version of its role in the struggle.

One of the aims of the 1972 Seskoad seminar on the transfer of 1945 values was to promote acceptance of the military's "dual function" by means of history projects.[38] In this seminar the concept of the 1945 values was loosely defined as values consistent with Pancasila and the 1945 constitution. Seminar participants suggested that these were the values for which those of the 1945 generation, who in 1972 included many of the nation's military leaders, had fought (Angkatan Darat 1972: 2). Because the evidence shows specific recommendations for how the transfer should be enacted, I believe that the term "1945 generation" refers particularly to the youth of the independence struggle who fought with arms, and was essentially used as a code for promoting military values and for acceptance of the military's political role (McGregor 2002).

Nugroho was assigned the task at the seminar of making specific suggestions regarding the transfer of values through history. He recommended use of memoirs of revolutionary heroes, curricula within the military and in schools, the media, films, commemoration of heroes and monuments, and museums.[39] After the seminar he implemented many of these ideas through his roles at the military history centre and later as Education Minister. While it could be expected that a military museum would promote martial glory, the diorama scenes in Museum Pusat ABRI Satriamandala, the first museum of the History Centre, virtually deny the existence of a civilian government. Representations in this museum, which concentrate primarily on the period of the independence struggle, rarely mention Soekarno or civilian diplomats (see Pusat Sejarah dan Tradisi ABRI 1994). The museum narrative also emphasizes, as Antlöv has noted, the projection of a path towards increasing national stability after 1965, ending in the ultimate scene of Suharto, son of the military, being appointed to the Presidency (Antlöv 1996: 10).

Beginning in 1974, the Armed Forces History Centre was also included in research and preparation of school history texts and in the design of school history curricula. As noted earlier Nugroho headed the writing team for Volume Six of the national history landmark work, dealing with history from the Japanese period to the transfer of power to Suharto in March 1966. Consistent with the concept of the "transfer of 1945 values" this volume, particularly the section on the Independence struggle, emphasizes the development of the military from spirited youths and military actions such as the crushing of the Madiun rebellion. It also includes a section on defence, security, and *dwifungsi* (Bourchier 1994: 51–3; Kartodirdjo *et al.* 1976: 339–48).

During his assignment as Minister for Education from 1983 until his death in 1985, Nugroho inserted the notion of transfer of values further into the education system by means of the *Pendidikan Sejarah Perjuangan Bangsa* (PSPB, History of the National Struggle) course. This mandatory school curriculum privileged the armed struggle over diplomacy and began with the proclamation of Independence, as one critic noted, "as if Independence Day had fallen from the sky and had no relationship with the pre-proclamation nationalist movement" (Historical Research Centre, University of Indonesia 1985). In an ensuing debate over the starting point for this history curriculum between Nugroho and senior UI scholar Bahaziar Bactiar, the latter argued for inclusion of the emergence of the nationalist movement. Nugroho defended his position, arguing that the only history worth studying was that of the revolution. For Nugroho, Indonesian history commenced at the proclamation of independence (17 August 1945), soon after which he and the Indonesian military entered the Indonesian historical stage.

There is also a sense that Nugroho genuinely believed in the promotion of militaristic values in order to ensure national development.

As Minister for Education and Culture, in a speech titled "Regeneration and Motivation" he noted,

> (s)ince the New Order period began, education has never been a routine activity, rather it has been perceived as the formation of cadres to continue the nation's struggle or cadres for national development and the implementation of Pancasila.   (Notosusanto 1985: 3)

This commentary is consistent with the notion that there should be no distinction between citizens and members of the armed forces in terms of the need for indoctrination into military ways.[40] Nugroho's efforts at promoting military values in school curricula were thus part of a broader New Order pattern of militarization. By means of these and other history projects Nugroho therefore attempted to reinforce the legitimacy of a military dominated authoritarian regime.

Reflections on Loyalty and Motivation

Nugroho's public commentary suggested that he continued to believe whole-heartedly in the New Order, yet it is difficult to discern how much of this was attributable to the value of military loyalty to which he firmly subscribed. In an interview in 1981, he said that among his literary works his favourite short story was *Sungai* (River). In the story, a man experiences a conflict of interest as a father who loves his child and as also a Commander who must save his troops. While crossing a river in close proximity to the enemy, the father drowns his crying child so as not to alert the enemy to the presence of his troops. "This is the effect of big events on ordinary people" he suggested (Notosusanto 1981). Nugroho's preference for this story reflects his own romanticized perception of military loyalty and the lengths to which he would go to defend it despite the personal cost. The example he uses also reflects a certain coldness in Nugroho, which Jassin commented was characteristic of his literary style (Jassin 1967: 7).

When Nugroho did criticize the military he did so guardedly. In a 1970 piece on *dwifungsi* he noted the abandonment within the Indonesian military of what Janowitz termed a typically puritanical attitude of armies in new nations. "Since the period of 'Guided Democracy' dominated by the flamboyant President Sukarno, there is a feeling that too many high ranking officers have abandoned this 'puritanical' attitude" (Notosusanto 1970a: 9 fn. 5). Whilst Nugroho made this and other criticisms in the early years of the New Order,[41] he seems to have resigned himself in later years to merely serving the regime. He was rewarded for his loyalty in his later promotions to Rector of the University of Indonesia and then Minister of Education and Culture.

While Nugroho was Head of the Armed Forces History Centre he remained an employee of the Department of History in the Faculty of Letters at the University of Indonesia. He held these two roles for almost 20 years, but the demands of the two worlds were often incompatible. In 1978 Nugroho told a friend that in the world of the army people have a sense of honour and are not always competing with each other, whereas at university everyone was out for themselves. This reaction was probably based on a sense of rejection from the academic world following some of his controversial projects.[42] Yet while Nugroho felt the military world was more honourable, he was not completely accepted within that world either. A military man in the employment of the Army History Centre based in Bandung once posed a question to historian Sartono Kartodirdjo comparing Nugroho and himself: "Tell me, Sartono, what is worse — a military man who pretends to be an historian or an historian who pretends to be a military man?"[43] Nugroho's life reflected the tension of the frustrated soldier.

Nugroho would have received financial rewards for his work, yet it seems that for him military promotions held more importance as a source of motivation. Nugroho was awarded titular rankings because of his position as head of an ABRI institution directly accountable to the Armed Forces Commander. In 1968 he was appointed Colonel, in 1971, Brigadier General. He considered the award of these ranks as a sign of respect from the leaders of ABRI, indicating their trust in his ability to head an ABRI institution. One acquaintance of Nugroho's recalls him saying that he liked to travel overseas as it enabled him to wear his uniform and insignia.[44] This suggests not only a motivation linked to concerns for status, but also Nugroho's nostalgia for the military career he might have had.

In 1981 Nugroho made a very revealing comment about the confines within which he, as a military historian, was bound in the histories he produced. He noted:

> What used to motivate me to write fiction was its attraction as a way
> to express my feelings ... I cannot use history to express my sympathy
> for the ordinary people in the viciousness of big events that they cannot
> control. Yes, ordinary people who are knocked over by big events. This
> wish I must fulfil through fiction, because history is the macro perspective,
> about big movements and mankind in collectivity ... Large historical
> events produce different emotions, colossal emotions ... History cannot
> capture subtle emotions.   (Notosusanto 1981: 46)

In this passage, and in his short story writing, Nugroho demonstrated
that he understood the effect of large events on ordinary individuals. This
suggests an awareness of his own historical work as necessarily and
exclusively meta-narratives.[45] Yet it is impossible to tell whether Nugroho
extended his sympathy to victims of 1965, or if he was perhaps reflecting
solely on unsung heroes of the independence struggle such as the
Commandant and child in his story *Sungai*.[46]

Nugroho's Legacy in the Post-Suharto period

Although Nugroho died in 1985 many of his legacies, including the
official version of the coup attempt, Pancasila theory, and the museum
projects, survived him. While many of these projects were challenged
during the New Order period, both within and outside Indonesia, the
expansion of freedom of expression accompanying the collapse of the
New Order regime precipitated some of the most direct attacks on these
histories.

The endless repetition and hegemony of Nugroho's version of the
coup attempt ensured that it was the first part of official New Order
history to be challenged. A few days after Suharto's resignation,
Lieutenant-Colonel Latief, a political prisoner convicted of involvement
in the September 30th Movement, revealed that the night before the coup
attempt he had forewarned Suharto that the Generals would be kidnapped,
and that Suharto had chosen not to act until the coup was completed
(*The Australian*, 25 May 1998). This testimony sparked a series of press
articles questioning Suharto's role in the events of 1965.[47] At the same
time, other theories about the September 30th Movement (including CIA
involvement, Soekarno's role in the coup, and occasionally the Cornell
theory, according to which the coup was an internal military affair)
were increasingly aired.[48] Senior historian Taufik Abdullah criticized

Nugroho's version of the coup attempt on the basis that it constituted history for the purposes of exacting revenge (*Kompas*, 1 October 2000).

In an important step towards dismantling the official version of the coup, some aspects of military propaganda — which Nugroho helped cement during the New Order period in his film and museum projects and in the school curriculum — were also openly challenged.[49] Arif Budianto, a member of the autopsy team that investigated the bodies of the seven army heroes, revealed in an interview that he did not find any evidence to suggest that the penises of the victims were cut off or that their eyes had been gouged out.[50] In August 1999 an Indonesian version of Wieringa's thesis, which debunks many of the myths about Gerwani, was also published in Indonesia (Wieringa 1999). Kuntowijoyo noted that the publication of this book shocked many with the revelation that dioramas at national monuments might be based on fabricated history (*Jakarta Post*, 23 August 2000). Although annual screening of the film "Gerakan 30 September" ceased on the first anniversary of the coup attempt following Suharto's resignation, the question of what is to be done with representations of the 1965 events at Monumen Pancasila Sakti has not yet been addressed. Asvi Warman Adam has suggested that multiple versions of 1965 should be presented in future history texts (Asvi Warman Adam, *Kompas*, 24 April 1999).

The "P-4" indoctrination course in which Nugroho's version of the birth of the Pancasila was taught was scrapped early in the *reformasi* era (*Kompas*, 5 June 1998). One of the post-Suharto Education Ministers, Sudarsono, commented on the treatment of leaders in the historical record and how this must be changed. He noted that

> Until now, history books accentuated the roles of powerful persons, not the *hakikat* (truth or essence) of the event and the historical message. Such that when such persons fell from power their historical role also disappeared and was replaced with the heroic stories about the powerholders in the next regime. It is this pattern of writing history that will be changed. The result will be that history will not be rewritten each time the government changes, like in the Soviet Union.
>
> (*Gatra*, 17 October 1998)

As we have seen, Nugroho played a large part in this pattern of history-writing through his efforts at de-Soekarnoization. Sudarsono claimed that the time had come to examine both Soekarno and Suharto's historical roles from a more balanced perspective.

After the resignation of Suharto in May 1998 multiple cases of military abuses of human rights around the country began to be exposed.[51] Intense media and public criticism during this era prompted the military's decision to gradually rescind its political role and adopt military professionalism.[52] Yet the question of how representations of the military's historical role in the Independence struggle and thereafter, which were used to define and defend *dwifungsi*, will be readjusted or dismantled has not yet been addressed in substantial way.

Nugroho's legacy as a historian in service of an authoritarian regime was to turn history into a tool for regime legitimation, an instrument for the perpetuation of authoritarianism. He used history as a means to discredit past leaders, to incite and perpetuate hatred of communists, and to glorify the military. The degree of penetration of these patterns in Indonesian historiography remains to be seen, as scholars attempt to revise history in the post-Suharto era. While school texts are one of the most malleable mediums of popular history and most easily rewritten, significant changes to the school history curricula and national history will require major shifts in thinking. Historians will need to consider revisions to history not just from the perspective of which leaders do or do not appear in the historical record, but which historical forces and players gain a voice in history. This is important because of the contingency of the interpretations of the past on claims for rights in the present, such as the right for the military to play a political role, or the right for families of victims of 1965 violence to ask for a full accounting from the state. Nugroho's choice, as a trained historian, to defend an authoritarian regime — which necessarily meant condemning its enemies — is a blunt reminder of the moral choices historians make in choosing which stories to tell and which to suppress.

Notes

[1]   I would like to thank Irma Nugroho Notosusanto, the staff of the Armed Forces History Centre, Herb Feith, Robert Cribb, Onghokham, Hardoyo, Arief Budiman, and Sartono Kartodirjo, each of whom shared their knowledge with me. Thanks also to Charles Coppel, Helen Pausacker, Henk Maier, William Frederick, Herb Feith, Ros Lethbridge, and Gerry van Klinken for their comments on drafts of this paper and on a related chapter in my thesis (McGregor 2002).

[2]   The term Raden Panji is a term of address somewhere between Raden, "prince" and Raden Mas, "son of nobility". Nugroho is listed as Raden Panji Noegroho

Notosoesanto in Bachtiar (1988: 227). He dropped this title from his name although he continued to think of himself as a person of *priyayi* or upper class Javanese origins. All translations provided of Indonesian texts are the author's except where indicated.

3 This school was part of the reluctant Dutch expansion of education in the Netherlands Indies whereby both law and engineering colleges were opened in 1924 as elite institutions of higher learning (van der Kroef 1953: 230, 234).

4 Irma Nugroho Notosusanto, interview, Jakarta, 11 Feb. 1998.

5 Jai Singh Yadava, discussion with author, Yogyakarta, Feb. 1998.

6 The article dated 15 May 1952 was a response to the letter of Jef Last, who had mistaken Nugroho for another Noegroho with seemingly more moderate views. The difference in spelling between these two versions of Nugroho/Noegroho denotes technically a change in the spelling of Indonesian language introduced by the Republic whereby the Dutch "oe" became "u". People who were born before this change often kept the original spelling of their name, e.g. Sukarno remained "Soekarno". In Nugroho's case he wanted to be identified as an up and coming leader, and a progressive, hence his insistence on Nugroho.

7 Such language to describe one's father is particularly impolite when emanating from a Javanese son.

8 Irma Nugroho Notosusanto, interview, Jakarta, 11 Feb. 1998.

9 Among Nugroho's best-known short stories are "Hujan Kepagian" (Rain in the Morning, 1958), "Tiga Kota" (Three Towns, 1959), "Hijau Tanahku Hijau Bajuku" (Green is My Land, Green are My Clothes), and "Rasa Sayange" (What a Pity, 1961). The style of his short stories was sympathetic and humanistic, reflective of a particular genre of the 1950s (Teeuw 1967: 243–4).

10 Onghokham, interview, Jakarta, 29 Sept. 1997. In the 1950s, a student in the Faculty of Letters could study unattached to a particular discipline. It was only at the end of his time in the faculty that Nugroho chose history as his field.

11 Nugroho praises Nasution's efforts to record history; see Notosusanto (1977: 34).

12 Goenawan Mohamad, interview, Los Angeles, Apr. 2001.

13 Regarding elite students at established universities, such as the University of Indonesia, McVey (1979: 20) notes their "class attitudes and anti-establishment ideals combined among them to produce a virulent anti-communism".

14 Arief Budiman, interview, Melbourne, 28 Apr. 1998.

15 Observations in this paragraph based on discussion with former head of *Consentrasi Gerakan Mahasiswa Indonesia* (CGMI, Indonesian Student Movement Center), Hardoyo, interview, Jakarta, 17 Mar. 1998.

16 Irma Nugroho Notosusanto, interview, Jakarta, 11 Feb. 1998.

17 As with many other official Indonesian publications, Nugroho's name does not appear on the cover of this book, which is listed as an official publication of the Armed Forces History Center. It is, however, clear from the foreword that he was responsible for the publication.

18 The publication was compiled from contemporary newspaper reports and from interviews of the families of the *pahlawan revolusi* (heroes of the revolution), the army victims of the coup attempt. On the initial propaganda surrounding the coup attempt see van Langenberg (1990: 45–62) and Wieringa (1995: 307–21).

[19]   After the crushing of the September 30th Movement up to one million people were killed and many others imprisoned, for membership or affiliation with the PKI (Cribb 1990: 13; Angkatan Darat 1990: 159–67).

[20]   Arief Budiman, interview, 28 Apr. 1998.

[21]   Hardoyo, interview, Jakarta, 17 Mar. 1998.

[22]   General Suharto, in his capacity as Minister of Defence and Commander of the Army, recommended preservation and memorialization of the well from which the bodies were originally hauled at Lubang Buaya in the months following the coup attempt. An official instruction for the commencement of the monument project was issued from the army on 2 December 1965 (*Surat Perintah* 517/12/65) (Soedjono 1975: 351–3).

[23]   See chapter by Klaus Schreiner in this volume.

[24]   Although the relief was designed by Major General Sudjono of *Lembaga Pembinaan Mental dan Tradisi ABRI* (The Institute for ABRI Mental Upgrading and Traditions), it obviously draws on some of Nugroho's themes. The relief begins with a representation of the Madiun Affair (the "prelude" to the 1965 coup attempt), and alludes to the rumour of the existence of a Council of Generals (interview with artist Drs. Saptoto, Yogyakarta, September 1997). The scene in the relief depicting events at Lubang Buaya features the myth of the "dance of fragrant flowers" in which Gerwani women allegedly danced around the well prior to killing the generals (Wieringa 1998: 163–4).

[25]   Throughout the New Order the press were required to reproduce annually the official version of the coup attempt (McGregor 2002 ASR). In 1988 when the daily *Merdeka* suggested that historians were still asking many questions about this event, it was threatened with closure (see *Far Eastern Economic Review*, 20 Oct. 1988).

[26]   The opening credits of the film acknowledge that the screenplay is based on Nugroho Notosusanto's version of the coup attempt. Actor Subaah Asa, who played the role of PKI leader Aidit in the film, told the weekly *D&R* (3 Oct. 1998: 19) that director Arifin C. Noor was forced by Nugroho to change his script. Before screening the film was reviewed by prominent figures in the actual events, e.g. Lieutenant General (now President) Suharto, Colonel Sarwo Edhie, and other senior military figures. [Amaroso Katamsi (actor who played Suharto's role), interview, Jakarta, Feb. 1997.]

[27]   Although they imply torture, neither of the two written publications includes gruesome accounts of mutilation of the generals such as are found in the film and museum displays, as well as in a colossal diorama next to the Lubang Buaya monument added to the complex at a much later date (Pusat Sejarah dan Tradisi ABRI 1997: 26).

[28]   This was just one part of a larger propaganda campaign targeted at members of Gerwani. Other rumours suggested these women sexually fondled and then castrated the army victims prior to their deaths (Wieringa 1998: 163–4).

[29]   At the time Nugroho produced the English version of the coup attempt as a rebuttal to the Cornell Paper he could not, for example, be sure as to which documents the authors of the Cornell paper had in their possession (Anderson 1987: 109–34).

[30]   Similarly, the Indonesian translation of Harold Crouch's book, *The Indonesian Military and Politics*, was banned for mentioning the theory that Suharto might have

been involved in the coup attempt, while Oei Tjoe Tat's memoir was banned on the grounds that it was in error about the G30S-PKI episode and about communism (*Merdeka*, 29 Sept. 1995).

31 Because several authors have covered this topic and the controversies it aroused, the Pancasila project is dealt with briefly here (see Abdoelmanap 1997; Brooks 1995: 61–99; Lee 1982).

32 Nugroho first published *Naskah proklamasi yang Otentik* in 1971. His ideas were elaborated in *Naskah Proklamasi Yang Otentik dan Rumusan Pancasila yang Otentik* (the Authentic Proclamation text and the Formulation of the Authentic Pancasila), Balai Pustaka Jakarta, 1978, and "Mengamankan Pancasila Dasar Negara" in the magazine *Persepsi*; in 1981 his ideas also appeared as a four-part series in *Merdeka*, 8–12 Aug. 1981.

33 Nugroho's work was attacked in a seminar held at Hotel Wisata Karya, Jakarta on 10–14 Nov. 1981; the newspaper polemic was covered in 29 papers of the day (Abdoelmanap 1997: 32; Yayasan Idayu 1981). Note that from 1978 onwards Nugroho's theory was incorporated into mandatory Pancasila courses in schools and government departments throughout the country.

34 See MPR decision Keputusan No II/MPR/1978, 12 Maret 1978

35 Onghokham, interview, Jakarta, 29 Sept. 1997.

36 Herb Feith, interview, Yogyakarta, 9 Sept. 1997.

37 Arief Budiman, interview, Melbourne, 28 Apr. 1998.

38 The purpose of this seminar was ostensibly to check to what extent young officers' values matched those of the "1945 generation" before transferring military leadership to the next generation, and to ensure continuity in the ongoing struggle of national development (Notosusanto 1974: 1).

39 Some more specific suggestions for school curricula were that primary schools should teach national history and struggle songs and civics, that high school curricula include national history and *dwifungsi ABRI*, and that at the university level the 1945 values, defence matters and national strategy should be taught (Dharma Pusaka 45: 48, 65).

40 The transfer of values was not restricted to ABRI circles (Seskoad 1989: 98).

41 "One important obstruction to the smooth transfer of the values of 1945 is in fact that several members of the Generation of 1945 itself have deviated from those values" (Notosusanto 1974: 14).

42 Herb Feith, interview, Yogyakarta, 9 Sept. 1997.

43 Sartono Kartodirdjo, interview, Yogyakarta, Sept. 1997.

44 Robert Cribb, interview, Jakarta, 29 May 1997.

45 They were meta-narratives in the sense that they told singular big-picture versions of the past without considering alternative voices or narratives.

46 Interestingly Nugroho did, however, supervise Soe Hok Gie's thesis at the University of Indonesia on the communist victims of Madiun, which was only published many years after the thesis was produced (Gie 1997).

47 See for example *Adil* (Tabloid Berita Mingguan) 30 Sept.–6 Oct. 1998, and *Tajuk* 17 Sept.–30 Sept. 1998. In Sept. 2000 a seminar on Suharto's role in the coup attempt was held at Jakarta's Center for Strategic and International Studies.

[48] Illustrative articles include *Kompas*, 17 Jan. 2000; *D&R*, 3 Oct. 1998; *D&R*, 10 Oct. 1998; *Gatra*, 9 Oct. 1999; *Forum Keadilan*, 8 Oct. New books included Center for Information Analysis Yogyakarta, *Gerakan 30 September: Antara Fakta dan Rekayasa: Berdasarkan Kesaksian Para Pelaku Sejarah*, Proyek Historiografi, Center for Information Analysis, Yogyakarta, 1999.

[49] Although this propaganda had long been dismissed in the outside world the Indonesian public did not on the whole have access to this knowledge — thus the importance of documenting when and how this information came out.

[50] He did state that there were multiple bullet wounds on the bodies and that the condition of one victim's hand suggested he had been tied up prior to death. "Meluruskan Sejarah Penyiksaan Pahlawan Revolusi", *D&R*, Oct. 1998. A further interview with Dr Budianto also appeared in *Forum Keadilan*, 30 Sept. 2000 as "Tidak Benar Penisnya Dipotong".

[51] For commentary on just a sample of the many reported abuses on Aceh see *Tajuk*, Aug. 1998; on Tanjung Priok see *Gatra*, September 1998; on East Timor see *TEMPO*, 10 Sept. 2000.

[52] In September 1998 the Indonesian military felt compelled to hold a seminar on their role in the 21st century at which a decision was made that the military had no choice but to listen to the people's demands that they "return to the barracks" and rescind their political role; see *Gatra*, 10 Oct. 1998. For discussion of the potentially enormous scope of change in military roles and policy since 1998, see *Indonesia* (2000: 133, 138).

The Battle for History
After Suharto

GERRY VAN KLINKEN[1]

W hen President Habibie announced in late January 1999 that an independence ballot would be held in East Timor, teachers there panicked. The teachers association pleaded with Jakarta to transfer the non-locals among its teachers out, saying they were being constantly harassed. "Their presence is rejected by the bulk of society," the association said. Soon after, money was made available to move thousands [sic] of them out.

A year later, the same thing happened in what is now officially called Papua (formerly Irian Jaya, or West Papua in Western activist terminology). History teachers in remote highland postings in February 2000 found themselves fleeing to the safety of a town after parents threatened them for teaching a version of national history in which Papuans had no role.

Nor was the post-authoritarian revolt against official versions of history confined to Indonesia's "colonial" periphery. In West Kalimantan, a teacher confessed: "To be honest, our students often accuse us of lying to them, for example about the Communist Party and about Supersemar [the way Suharto came to power]. It hurts, but it is an occupational hazard. We're just sticking to what the government has laid down" (*Kompas*, 29 April 2000, "Ketika"). Pressure of this kind — as well as internal criticisms that often preceded public outcry — led Habibie's Education Minister to initiate a review of the school curriculum. As we shall see, the review limped along for a couple of years and was then buried under the weight of institutional inertia.

Ever since nationalism became a key new element in the nation-states of Western Europe in the early 19th century, history has been conscripted by states in order to define a national identity that suits modern demands.

In Indonesia, the historical argument early on became an important weapon in anti-colonial discourse (Reid 1979b). After independence, the precariousness of the state, as most Indonesian elites soon perceived it, lent the "history for nation-building" project a sense of urgency, and raised its stakes.

Nationalism has inclusive, democratizing forms that emphasize the attachment to a set of political ideas and institutions [sometimes, following Kohn (1945: 18–20), called "civic nationalism"], as well as to exclusionary, essentialist forms highlighting myths of origin ("cultural nationalism", or "ethnic nationalism"). The nation-building project in Indonesia has made use of both, but co-opted them for a statist ideology that was asserted in the mass media and especially in the classroom (Leigh 1991; van de Kok *et al.*, 1991). School history lessons, ignoring every other social, cultural or economic dynamic, turned the previous three centuries into one continuous struggle for the Indonesian state against an array of enemies — first the colonial Dutch, then internal enemies such as communists and separatists.

The loss of faith among Indonesian pupils in 1999–2000 signified a revolt against a historical discourse that has been mainstream since the Japanese Occupation. Klooster, in his survey of Indonesian historiography, describes how the Japanese introduced the anti-colonial historiography of Muhammad Yamin and Soekarno into Indonesia's formal schooling during 1942–5 (Klooster 1985). In the 1930s, these two ardent and romantic nationalists had developed a three-stage concept of Indonesian history for use in their struggle. Soekarno (1975 [1931]) called it the *trimurti*:

> What about activating nationalism? How do you bring it to life? There are three steps. First, we show the people that the life they led long ago was a good life; second, we intensify the realization that theirs is a dismal life today; third, we turn their gaze to the bright and shining rays of a future day, and we show them ways to reach that promise-filled hour.

In other words, the PNI [Soekarno's Nationalist Party] aroused and activated in the masses an awareness of their "bounteous past", their "dark ages", and the "promise of a brightly beckoning future" (Soekarno 1975 [1931]: 79).[2]

The first national school history text, written under the Japanese, remained in print for many years. Its author, Sanusi Pane, was a mild-mannered and sophisticated intellectual. He later acknowledged with some regret that his was a history of wars. Other authors followed, equally gifted yet equally unable to extract themselves from the idea that history's main task is to create patriots. Muhammed Ali was Indonesia's major historiographer during the Soekarno period. He, too, held sophisticated, original ideas, wanted to write a history of "ordinary" Indonesians, and rejected Yamin's romanticism about the past. Yet he approved of government intervention in history writing to promote a national mentality. Only one participant in the History Seminar that brought together Indonesian historians for the first time in 1957 argued that history should not be used to promote nationalism.[3]

Official nationalist history took a martial turn under Suharto's New Order not unlike that once promoted by the Japanese. Its mandarin was Nugroho Notosusanto, who directed Pusat Sejarah Abri (the Center of Army History) before becoming Minister of Education and Culture in the early 1980s. Under Nugroho's supervision, the historical establishment churned out one cardboard cutout "national hero" biography after another. Nugroho also directed the writing of the final, sixth volume of the official "National History of Indonesia" (Sejarah Nasional Indonesia, 1975) which dealt with Indonesia's living history, 1945–65. It was largely this volume (or rather the school-texts based on it) that provoked the public's annoyance described above. Its stark anti-communism privileged the military as national saviours at every crucial moment. The sheer anti-intellectualism of this particular, martial view of national history, reinforced by monuments, films, and national commemorations must bear much of the responsibility for the appalling historical ignorance even among liberal arts university students today.[4]

In private, Indonesian historians often squirmed at the manipulations that this monological project required of them. So many biographies (no doubt interesting in their own right) forced into the narrow mould of the "national hero". So many internal conflicts (the seeds of change in any unconscripted history) written out of the record. So much context abandoned to see great men and glorious moments better. Yet when the publication date approached for a new school textbook, they usually complied: the alternative, they told themselves, seemed to be confusion and chaos.[5] Indonesia's leading elder historian, Sartono Kartodirdjo, said in 1997 that he had not changed his mind on the importance of history in the nation-building project since the History Seminar of 40 years earlier. National history was a "symbol of Indonesian national identity", he said, and therefore had to have a high "affective value" for its young consumers (Kartodirdjo 1997).

More to the point, most historians were dependent on the state, in ways that shaped how and when they voiced their dissent. Bintang Prakarsa has shown that protest against what the historian Taufik Abdullah called the "hegemonic knowledge" of the state in the historical area was limited to a few individuals. Mostly western-trained academic historians, they felt out-numbered by the well-endowed and well-connected "state intellectuals" and their equally dependent "educator" colleagues, and thus kept their protest muted (Prakarsa 1994).[6]

Yet all notions — even those of national identity — are fragile. When the press in 1998 exploded some of the key historical myths upon which the nation-building project had been built, and parents began to accuse hapless teachers around the country of teaching "lies", the custodians of national history faced a difficult choice. They could transform their subject into something more popular and less statist, or try to hang on to the old formula. Thus far, they have chosen the latter course. Their indebtedness to state officials, and hence their inability to respond creatively to societal pressures, exacerbated the eroding legitimacy of Indonesian nationalism created by Suharto's militarism.

However, the battle for history after Suharto did not belong to historians alone. Out in the market of ideas, now much less controlled by state censors, were a host of alternative histories, whose persuasive power could determine not merely the future of the nation-building project, but perhaps that of the Indonesian nation itself. "History", in what follows, is not the stuff of specialized academic journals.[7] It is the important stories about the past that, to some extent, have become common property. Everyone can read them in school texts, in newspapers and books, or see them on films and television, and then discuss them. In reality, there is no single Indonesian history, but numerous histories. The processes by which those many histories are reduced to a handful of more or less "accepted" ones within the nation tell us how power, together with resistance to it, shape what is seen as national history.

The Challenge of Alternative National Histories

Under the New Order, ordinary Indonesians had their past served to them from above as a "legacy", merely requiring passive assent. Suharto's New Order history textbooks, like their Stalinist counterparts, were mind-numbingly dull accounts, liberally sprinkled with bad photographs of soldiers and rows of grim men at diplomatic conferences.

After Suharto's resignation in May 1998, a much freer publishing environment saw long suppressed historiographies reemerge and vie for new adherents, similar to the Thai experience as it emerged from military rule. Winichakul (1995) observed several currents of historical discourse emerging in that country after the student anti-military protests of 1973. His four new streams were: a critical reaction to the conventional nationalist school, a Marxist economic history school, a non-racist revision of early history, and a greatly increased interest in local histories. Indonesia has not seen the greatly increased enrollment in university history departments that Thongchai reported, but it has seen a similar proliferation of historical debate in the public arena.

We can identify four historiographical streams in post-New Order Indonesia. The first is (1) the orthodox nationalist stream, which remains dominant even after Suharto, though challenged from within on some details, and increasingly disbelieved without. None of the three others are unprecedented, as we can see from Klooster's survey, but each has emerged with fresh energy.[8] We might call them (2) societal historiographies on the national level, (3) ethno-nationalist historiographies in some sub-national regions, and (4) a renewed interest in (not necessarily political) local histories that can be seen as the local equivalent of item two above.

Studies of historical discourse in other post-authoritarian countries suggest that, even under sustained challenge, myth-making is too useful to be simply abandoned. Much more likely is that the effort is redirected to new ends.[9] In Indonesia, too, authoritarian nationalist historiography is by no means dead. It has abandoned Suharto, but not the central role of the army in more recent national histories, nor the statist ideology that underpins it.

The post-Suharto reaction was initially directed mostly against a version of recent Indonesian history in which, despite Suharto's feigned protests against a "personality cult", his role had been elevated to almost superhuman heights in films, monuments, museums, and annual ceremonies. Two films made at the height of the New Order depicted Lt-Col Suharto's heroic role in a historical episode of Indonesia's war for independence in 1945–9.[10] The city of Yogyakarta had been the revolutionary capital of the Republic of Indonesia, but Dutch troops seized this last key stronghold on Java in December 1948. When republican troops managed to re-enter it on 1 March 1949, albeit briefly, they helped turn the tide of world opinion, and this led to international recognition of Indonesia's independence by the end of 1949. By placing the military, under Suharto, at the centre of this event, Suharto's admirers were implying that he personally had brought the nation to birth. The message was reinforced in two huge Yogyakarta monuments built in the Suharto era — one to commemorate the 1 March 1949 attack, and one to commemorate the return of Yogyakarta to its position as the republican capital four months later.

Suharto also played the central role in the film "Pengkhianatan G30S/PKI" ("The treachery of the 30 September Movement/Indonesian Communist Party").[11] This violent account of the way Suharto decisively took over the reigns of power in the days following the coup attempt on 30 September/1 October 1965 highlighted the "treacherous" role of the Communist Party. Communist women were portrayed as frenzied killers at Lubang Buaya, in Jakarta's air force base, where several generals were murdered. Every 1 October for nearly two decades, this film was all but compulsory viewing. Television broadcast it in prime time. Although school children accustomed to violence on screen increasingly found it slow-moving, whole classes were taken to see it at the local cinema (at their own expense).

Like the 1949 event, the 1965 event was immortalized in massive monuments and graphic museum dioramas — the latter routinely included in school history tours. Every 1 October, President Suharto led a solemn ceremony at Lubang Buaya named "Hari Kesaktian Pancasila" in honour of the "supernatural efficacy" (*kesaktian*) of the Pancasila state ideology. The message of the ceremony was clear: on this day the nation was saved from communism. Nothing was said about the murders of hundreds of thousands of communists and others that followed this event (on Lubang Buaya, see McGregor 2002). Moreover, Armed Forces Day, commemorating the 1945 birth of the military on 5 October, underlined the same message with large military parades. Finally, 11 March 1966 was another sacred date in the New Order's "hegemonic knowledge". On this day each year, newspapers carried "eyewitness accounts" of the decisive manner in which General Suharto restored order by arranging for President Soekarno to sign over most of his powers.

Various challenges to these versions of Indonesian history emerged during the years of the New Order, along with persistent attempts to deal with them by censorship and book banning. Over 2,000 books are estimated to have been banned over the three decades of Suharto's rule (Human Rights Watch 1998). A report on these bans discusses 12 historical titles in the last decade alone. Most dealt with the events of 1965–6, but others took up the regional revolts of 1957–8 and the role of Indonesians of Chinese descent. The attorney general maintained that the banned works "inverted the facts", which could "lead the public astray" and ultimately "disturb public order".

In the New Order's later years, increasingly, hegemonic knowledge was being undermined by new technologies: the uncontrollable internet began to flourish in the mid-1990s and combined with the photocopy machine, it reached large numbers of people. Private television, more attractive than the under-funded state broadcaster, began to test the bounds of censorship. Publishers brought out bannable books very quickly, knowing they could recoup their investment before officials had time to react. Newspapers introduced a skeptical note into the obligatory "eyewitness" accounts printed on the New Order's sacred dates, for example by asking where the original Supersemar document had gone. Among the first to challenge the Suhartoist version of history openly were former state actors whom Suharto had purged for their association with (his predecessor) Soekarno, and although their historical appeals remained focused on statist ideas, the challenge itself was a revelation to the public.

On 1 June 1998, not yet two weeks after Suharto resigned, Soekarno's daughter Megawati Soekarnoputri joined a group of retired military officers, a Soekarno-era foreign minister, and even some serving Foreign Affairs Department officials, to commemorate the day in 1945 on which her father Soekarno had formulated Pancasila (*Kompas*, 2 June 1998, "Peringatan Hari"). Suharto had eliminated the day as part of an anti-Soekarno purge, preferring to link Pancasila with his own intervention on 1 October 1965. (Strangely, President Megawati did not go on to restore 1 June as a national day.)

Next, ex-officers who had been prominent in the Soekarno era teamed up with student demonstrators to challenge Supersemar, the 11 March 1966 letter General Suharto wrung from President Soekarno to obtain his emergency powers. Although the original letter has never been seen in public, New Order spokespeople routinely described it as the regime's genuine legal basis. However, this challenge did not go unanswered. In July 1998, the military faction in parliament told protesters that "straightening out the historical record" should be limited to discovering the missing Supersemar document (*Kompas*, 21 July 1998, "Ketua F-Abri"). In late 1998 the police called in a former Soekarno bodyguard, who had challenged the New Order account of Supersemar on some crucial details. He was indicted for "false testimony" (*Bernas*, 2 February 1999, "Soekardjo Wilardjito").

Reformers had more success with their assault on the Suhartoist version of the 1 March 1949 dawn attack on Yogyakarta. The event lay in the distant past and, more importantly, the official version had deeply offended the then-Sultan of Yogyakarta, Hamengkubuwono IX, who had played an important role in conceptualizing the diplomatic thrust of the attack but had been written out of the story. That sultan had since passed away, but his son (Hamengkubuwono X) had taken over as governor of the Yogyakarta Special District. Hamengkubuwono X had inherited his father's resentment of Suhartos' claims about the 1949 episode, and was an important figure in the "reformasi" politics of 1998 that unseated Suharto.

In September 1998 retired General Nasution, more senior than Suharto in the 1945–9 revolution but sidelined by Suharto in 1966, stated that Suharto never fired a rifle during the Yogyakarta attack, and was in fact sheltering with the Sultan at the time. This was contrary to the claim of "official" history (*Jawa Pos*, 28 September 1998, "Pak Nas"), of course, and by the time the 1 March anniversary came around in 1999, the impact of Nasution's remark had swelled into a storm of contempt. Some old guerrillas who had fought for Suharto tried their best to maintain their commander's prestige, but in the end they moved their commemoration to a secret location for fear of disruption. The New Order version of history had, on this issue, been decisively discredited (*Bernas*, 2 March 1999, "Dialog SO 1"; *Suara Pembaruan*, 28 February 1999, "Setengah abad"; *Bernas*, 1 March 1999, "Pakar"; *Suara Pembaruan*, 1 March 1999, "Mendikbud"; *Bernas*, 2 March 1999, "Sultan HB IX"; *Tajuk*, 4–17 March 1999, "Serangan Oemoem"). By March of the following year, it was possible for state radio RRI to broadcast a panel discussion of the event that completely undermined Suharto's claims (*Kompas*, 1 March

2000, "Soeharto bukan"; *SiaR*, 1 March 2000, "Batara"; Hartono *et al.* 2001). In his stead, the prestige of the Yogyakarta sultanate had risen considerably. On 29 June 2000, the sultan was present at the unveiling of a new (though more modest) monument to commemorate his father's role in the return of Yogyakarta to Republican hands.

The Air Force was another once powerful group aggrieved by the Suharto version of history, especially the events of 1965. Its leadership had sided with Soekarno and with members of PKI-affiliated groups against the army leadership for years. The propaganda film "Pengkhianatan G30S/ PKI" depicted leftist militias training at Halim Air Force base in Jakarta in September 1965. Soon after winning power, Suharto had removed the Air Force from all positions of influence. Late in 1999, to considerable advance publicity, former Air Force Chief-of-Staff Air Marshall Sri Mulyono Herlambang and a group of retired Air Force officers brought out a book to "straighten out the historical record" and clear the Air Force's reputation of its alleged communist stain (Katoppo 1999). The book traced the 1965 event to rivalry between the services, with the army as the bad guy, and not to ideological conflict within society. Former Air Force Chief-of-Staff Omar Dhani, imprisoned in 1965 and not released until 30 years later, kept his lips sealed, but published his 1966 defence speech (Soerojo and Supartono 2001).

Similar accusations that Suharto had sacrificed brothers-in-arms under the cloak of an ideological civil war he himself had helped instigate could be read in books published by an old navy man and a key Soekarnoist soldier. A.M. Hanafi was a former marine, a Soekarno loyalist, and in 1965 the Indonesian ambassador to Cuba (Hanafi 1998). More important was the defence speech of Abdul Latief, an infantry commander in Jakarta in 1965 and a Soekarnoist. He was arrested on 11 October 1965 for his involvement in the kidnapping and murder ten days earlier of six generals whom he and his colleagues had suspected of plotting against Soekarno. He was not sentenced until 1978. After suffering terrible privations, he was finally released on 25 March 1999. His book accused Suharto of complicity in the murder of the generals of which he himself had been accused (Latief 2000).[12]

Largely under pressure of this internal kind by former state actors, interim President Habibie's Education Minister Juwono Sudarsono announced in October 1998 that he had formed a team to review the school history textbooks and produce a more "balanced" curriculum

(*The Australian*, 3 October 1998, "Suharto's Murky Past"). Juwono then said he had ordered changes in five areas: the 1945 birth of Pancasila, the 1 March 1949 Yogyakarta attack, the 1 October 1965 event, the 11 March 1966 Supersemar, and the 1976 "integration" of East Timor into Indonesia (*Jakarta Post*, 30 December 1999, "Education Ministry").

However, rather than a new curriculum, the Education Department on 19 October 1999 issued a guide for teachers — apparently one of several for different school levels — on how to cope with the discrepancy between "official" (*resmi*) and media accounts of history (Dirjen Pendidikan Dasar dan Menengah, 1999).[13] The project was coordinated by the Departmental historian Anhar Gonggong, a protégé of Nugroho Notosusanto and illustrates how little enthusiasm for fundamental change there still was within the political and cultural establishment in the post-Suharto period (*Kompas*, 8 April 2000, "Anhar Gonggong").[14] The reason given for writing the guide was that "uncertainty" would end in "negative consequences for national togetherness ['kebersamaan']." It did not, however, challenge the orthodox nation-building historiography of the New Order, and did no more than faithfully reflect the slight shifts within the power elite after Suharto.

Meanwhile, the military remained powerful enough to suppress other dissident accounts. Soekarno's Foreign Minister Subandrio, imprisoned by Suharto for 30 years, also prepared his memoirs, but his Jakarta publisher backed off from the project and destroyed all 10,000 copies of the print run just before release in late 2000.[15] Other negative reactions to historical revisionism were evident, as in May 2001 a newly formed alliance of anti-communist vigilante groups held a public burning of books they considered "leftist". The alliance, which the press alleged had links with both the Suharto-era state political party Golkar and the army, threatened to raid bookstores on 20 May, National Education Day. In response, big bookstores removed books by Pramoedya Ananta Toer and other titles from their shelves.

In March 2000, President Abdurrachman Wahid took up the demand of a group of former civilian communist prisoners to revoke the ban on communism brought down by the People's Consultative Assembly in 1966 (Stanley 2000; *TEMPO*, 30 August–5 September 1999, "Sulasmi").[16] On 14 March he issued an unofficial yet unprecedented apology on behalf of the Islamic organization Nahdlatul Ulama he once led, for the violence its youth organization committed against communists at that time. The storm of establishment outrage that greeted Wahid's announcements highlighted the failure of *reformasi*. Without the military needing to raise its voice, civilian commentators from all sides of parliamentary politics united to depict Wahid as an "unpredictable", "controversial", and "confusing" figure. In May 2000, all factions in parliament rejected Wahid's proposal to lift the communist ban. Wahid had been isolated and appeared to be the only liberal figure in government.

Hostility to "communism" remained the key conviction of the great majority of state actors. True, President Habibie's Information Minister Yunus Yosfiah cancelled the annual broadcast of the unpopular "Pengkhianatan G30S/ PKI" but a less bloodthirsty anti-communist film was screened in its stead.[17] In 1998 and 1999, President Habibie still led the 1 October *Hari Kesaktian Pancasila* ceremony in honour of the murdered generals, just as Suharto had done since 1966. In 1999, newly elected PDI-P parliamentarians boycotted it, saying it was time to "desacralize" the day, although by the next year all was forgiven (*SiaR*, 1 October 1999, "Anggota").[18] Renamed the "Commemoration of the National Tragedy due to the Betrayal of the Pancasila", the year 2000 ceremony watered down the military emphasis but remained an occasion for anti-communist speeches (*Jakarta Post*, 2 October 2000, "Betrayal"). Clearly, the long-established New Order version of history had been little dented even by the tumultuous resignation of its central figure Suharto.

Societal Historiographies at the National Level

The reactionary official nationalism described in the previous section, part intellectual inertia among opinion-makers still comfortably dependent on the state, part persistent interests of powerful state officials in the post-Suharto period, shows how little had changed within the power elite. However, if it were to succeed in recovering even some of its former dominance, the elite would have to deal with a variety of counter-hegemonic movements whose combined effect was stronger than anything it had ever faced before.

One element of this resistance is an intellectual ennui that parallels the protests of primary school pupils, described above. The deceits of the New Order, remembered amid the multi-dimensional crisis the nation faced in its aftermath, had gone so deep that for some, little remained to inspire the thought that Indonesia as a nation-state remained a worthwhile project. The journalist and historian Parakitri Simbolon (2000) chose to open the thick end-of-millennium volume *1000 Tahun Nusantara* with the following pessimistic reflection:

> During the crisis [of the last two years] it became clear that Indonesia really is a 'make believe' country, a heap of delusions. Of all the ideals that have been paraded for decades and that people have believed in, not one could survive. Even so, this harsh reality was still not strong enough to produce any satisfactory change.

This was a rarely heard view, suggesting the possibility, of which Robert Cribb has written briefly elsewhere (Cribb 2001), of a loss of the will for empire at the centre. Empires often crumble not from the edges in but from the centre out. Emerging Turkish nationalism, Cribb recalled, caused the Ottoman Empire to collapse at the beginning of the 20th century, while at its end resurgent Russian nationalism helped topple the Soviet empire.

Societal or populist historiographies on the national level present themselves as histories of ordinary Indonesians struggling for justice against an oppressive state. Most are leftist, but some are Islamist. While always outvoted within a deeply nationalist establishment, leftist historiography has long been important. Its most significant difference with the nationalist mainstream is that it recognizes the reality of conflict within Indonesian society, and traces it to the greed of the powerful. Its best-known early exponent was Tan Malaka, who rejected the glorious first phase of Soekarno's trimurti (discussed above) because he saw nothing but authoritarianism and feudalism in the distant past (Malaka 1991).

Another variety of leftist commentary on the past was spurred by Sulami, a former secretary-general of the women's organization Gerwani that was banned early in the New Order. Active in women's movements since late colonial times, Sulami was arrested by the military early in 1967, tortured, and only sentenced in 1975. International pressure helped free most political prisoners by 1979, but she was not released until 1984. In April 1999 she and some other ex-political prisoners set up an organization to recover the historical truth about the 1965–6 massacres. One of her associates in this organization published a thick autobiography with the provocative title, *Struggle of a Muslim Communist* (Raid 2001).

A re-emergent leftist historiography goes far beyond the demand for justice for one's own political group. With the New Order's xenophobia seriously eroded, long-ignored investigations of the 1965–6 killings by several foreign authors began to appear in translation, and Indonesian commentators felt free to publish work they researched overseas and to quote foreigners who would once have been described as "anti-Indonesian".[19] The list of books about 1965–6 now runs into the dozens, too many to list here. Many are by long-silenced witnesses, others defend the New Order viewpoint.[20]

Another significant educational effort was the film produced early in 2000 on the 1965 killings by Indonesia's best-known filmmaker, Garin Nugroho. "Puisi tak terkuburkan" (Unburiable poetry) shows a few days in the life of a prison cell in Aceh in 1965, where condemned leftists await execution. It was funded from overseas and only briefly played in the commercial cinemas, but was widely reviewed nonetheless.

A compassionate discourse on the healing importance of remembering the dark 1965–6 tragedy became, for the first time, more regular fare in the better print media. Examples include the chapter on "victims" by feminist Karlina Leksono-Supelli (2000) in a thick end-of-millennium historical volume; a column on "remembering" by political analyst Kusnanto Anggoro; and similar columns by the scholar Budiawan and the short story writer Seno Gumira Ajidarma: all opened up new horizons of civil discourse on what was once the greatest of taboos (Ajidarma 2000; Budiawan 2000; *Jakarta Post*, 7 April 2000, "Uncovering").

TEMPO, the prestigious weekly once banned by the New Order, ran many special supplements detailing historical debate around key national episodes, from the Revolution, through the 1950s regional revolts, to 1965–6. On the left, there are now new books about (or reprinted books by) Semaun, Tan Malaka, and Marco Kartodikromo, all late-colonial communists whose names were never mentioned in public during the New Order.[21] The biggest impact was achieved during the commemorations of the centenary of Soekarno's birth, in June 2001. A flood of at least ten new books, a serialized documentary on Soekarno on private television, and a thick supplement to *Kompas*, the nation's largest daily, attempted to reverse the systematic "de-Soekarno-ization" of the New Order, yet without setting him up as a nationalist icon once more.[22]

That the left has been more active in reoccupying the post-authoritarian historiographical imagination is largely due to the towering talent of Pramoedya Ananta Toer. This man was already an important novelist when Suharto's military arrested him soon after 1 October 1965 for belonging to Lekra, the Institute of People's Culture. Somehow, amidst the privations of his 14 years on the penal island of Buru, he managed to write prodigiously. Most of his writing is historically inspired. All of his Buru works were smuggled out (some remain lost until today) and some were first published overseas. Until the regime collapsed in May 1998, the New Order routinely banned them, though often only after large numbers had been sold. Today his Jakarta publishers are producing reprints of his older work as well as his Buru works.

Pramoedya's historical work should certainly be read as a veiled attack on Suharto's militarism, but it bears broader and more universal themes as well. His first tetralogy, *Bumi Manusia* (This earth of mankind), was a reinterpretation of the origins of Indonesian nationalism. The central character in that early movement (fictionalized as Minke in *Bumi Manusia*) is the journalist Tirto Adhi Soerjo.[23]

The next tetralogy, named after its third title *Arus Balik* (Counter-current), remains partly lost and has not yet been translated into English. Its dramatic stage is not early 20th-century Java but the pre-colonial East Javanese kingdoms of the 13th and 14th centuries AD. These historical novels reinterpret the popular legends of these kingdoms in a determinedly democratic, egalitarian spirit.[24] In his old age Pramoedya has addressed the 1945 revolution, bringing out a two-volume chronicle that apparently aims to re-include long-neglected social forces, including leftists, in the dynamic history of this period, however without engaging in a polemic (Toer *et al.* 1999).

Populist historiography, however, is not confined to the left. There is an Islamist historiography in Indonesia (that is, one in which religion becomes the central ideological motif). I have not included it as a separate category in this discussion because Islamism tends to be contextual — a shade of opinion within larger streams of historiographical debate. Some of it is nationalist, some of it regionalist. Kartosuwiryo was executed in 1962 for having led an Islamic rebellion in West Java for 15 years. In some religious student circles during the New Order he was revered as the model "radical Muslim". In 1999, two biographies of him appeared celebrating him as the "proclamator of the Indonesian Islamic State" (Awwas 1999; Chaidar 1999).

Muslim activists also pushed more insistently than ever before for justice for Muslims who died in several army massacres in the Suharto era. The two key horrors were a bloody confrontation between soldiers and demonstrators in Tanjung Priok, the harbour of Jakarta on 12 September 1984, and an army attack on an Islamic sect in Lampung, southern Sumatra, on 7 February 1989. Their demands met much opposition from within the establishment — once more underlining the tenacity of pro-military views there. Nevertheless, the relative paucity of Islamic historical revisionism in the post-Suharto era is somewhat surprising in view of the new freedoms. Very little among the explosion of pious literature flooding the market today is historically oriented.

Regional Ethno-nationalisms

Post-colonial nation-building in Indonesia has taken place in the context of a variety of ethnic units that each occupied a more or less distinct territory, usually created by the colonial government, more or less in consultation with local elites. After independence in 1945, the nation-building project recognized these units as "ethnic groups" (*suku bangsa*) rather than as "nations" (*bangsa*); they were part of the Indonesian nation on the basis of the national slogan "Unity in Diversity" (*Bhinneka Tunggal Ika*). In the years after Suharto's resignation, ethnic consciousness has grown rapidly in many parts of the country, always informed by long repressed historical memories.

For example, some of the more militant Ambonese on the Protestant side of the Maluku wars of 1999–2000 announced in December 2000 that the separatist *Republik Maluku Selatan* (RMS) movement of 1950 had been a valid declaration of the independence of the "*Alifuru*" people, "based on history that began with the Haria proclamation of 1817".[25] In August 2000 a Greater Minahasa Congress in largely Protestant North Sulawesi declared that the people of "*Tanah Toar Lumimuut*" would demand their "right of self-determination" if Muslim interests succeeded in even slightly compromising the religiously neutral 1945 Indonesian Constitution, for which Minahasans had also fought.[26] The terms Alifuru and Tanah Toar Lumimuut had been rarely heard in Indonesia since independence. Both evoked ethnic identities rooted in place and ancient mythologies.

The Maluku and Minahasa statements were ambit claims made by local leaders to pressure Jakarta. Similar claims were heard in West

Sumatra, Riau, East Kalimantan, Flores, and elsewhere. However, such claims were hardly the expression of separatist movements: arguments about a noble history of autonomy prior to the birth of the Indonesian Republic have become important weapons within Indonesia politics. Two new provinces — Banten and Gorontalo — were created in late 2000 on the basis of such arguments put forward by their respective elites, and others are likely to follow.

The ethno-nationalist historical claims heard in Aceh and Papua, on the contrary, were well-developed and clearly separatist in intent. The enthusiasm with which many Acehnese and Papuans took them up reflects a widespread disappointment with the Indonesian state which they experienced in its most violent and imperialistic mode. The activities of these separatist movements demonstrate again that historical discourse does not stand alone, but is an effect of contemporary politics. However, an ethno-nationalist instrumentalization of the past often contains anti-democratic assumptions that, if they were examined more carefully, would rob it of much of its appeal.

There is one simple reason for the longevity of nationalist historical myth-making: it works. In the early anti-colonial phase, the nationalist myth had the fresh purity of a societal historiography about it, a movement for justice written from below, and it inspired thousands of young revolutionaries in 1945–9. As the Revolution fades from memory, however, and those who profess it most ardently come to be moved less by the need for justice than for survival, they increasingly turn it inward upon backsliders and traitors. Given the fragility of nationalist historiography at the Indonesian level, perhaps the most striking development in post-Suharto historiography is the emergence of ethno-nationalist discourses in various regions.

These discourses differ from the Indonesian model in subject but not in form — they, too, adopt Soekarno's trimurti of a bounteous past, a dark present, and a brightly beckoning future reached through struggle. They, too, are written by dissident elites aspiring to power, this time in the regions, and they, too, are strong on sacred dates, great men, and legal milestones. More research will show who creates these accounts, how they are disseminated, how much variety exists within particular movements, and how much resistance there is to them.

One such ethno-nationalist is Hasan di Tiro, the central figure in the Free Aceh Movement, described as "father of the nation" (*wali negara*), and heir apparent to the position of Sultan. Yet he is a mysterious man who has lived in Sweden in a kind of double exile for decades. He has not been in Aceh since 1979, and some whisper that he left the United States (where his son and estranged wife still live), because of a business conflict. In interviews he likes to bring out an old letter from "my friend" Ed Lansdale, the Cold War CIA operative who won fame and notoriety for his anti-communist techniques in Vietnam and the Philippines (Lintner 1999; Mann 1999).[27] He turned 70 in September 2000.

Hasan di Tiro's political manifesto is contained in "The Price of Freedom", which recounts a two year and five month sojourn as leader of a clandestine movement in the Aceh mountains from late 1976 to early 1979 (Tiro 1984).[28] It grounds key statements about the Acehnese nation and its character in the writings of early 20th-century Dutch authors.

Di Tiro's historical argument for Acehnese national identity consists of two parts. One is that the Dutch fought the "Acehnese nation" (*bangsa Aceh*) but never defeated it. Aceh consequently retains its sovereignty — over against the Netherlands and therefore over against the colonial successor state of Indonesia. The other is that his own family connections with the most prominent figures in the Acehnese war against the Dutch make him the natural inheritor of Aceh's leadership. "The family of the Tengku di Tiro is the holiest family that Acheh has ever recognised," he quotes (Tiro 1984: 4) from a 1925 book by the Dutch colonial author Zentgraaff. A genealogy (Tiro 1984: 140) traces the connections.[29]

On 4 December 1976 the small group accompanying Hasan di Tiro declared Acehnese independence by raising a flag in the forest at Tjokkan Hill, in Pidie district. It was the day in 1911, Hasan di Tiro said, that the Dutch shot dead the last "Head of State", Tengku Tjhik Maat di Tiro ("my uncle") in Alue Bhot (Tiro 1984: 14).

On 10 March 1977 Hasan di Tiro issued a new calendar. It combined sacred Islamic dates with commemorations of great battles in the 1873–1911 war against the Dutch (all of which, he stressed, had been fought by his relatives). The only exception to this central focus on the Aceh war is 27 December, remembered as the day in 1639 when Sultan Iskandar Muda died, whom many Acehnese honour as personifying the ideal model of Acehnese statehood. The calendar does not refer to the 1950s Darul Islam revolt against Indonesia led by the charismatic Daud Beureueh. Di Tiro's was no longer a movement to cut deals with Jakarta, as Daud Beureueh's had been, but genuine separatism.

The self-interest in Hasan di Tiro's declarations is obvious. He had oil interests in the US before he began the guerrilla campaign. He was probably aware earlier than most Acehnese that the recently discovered gas deposits at Arun were very large. But the appeals in his published diary are to romantic notions of history and identity, rather than to economic nationalism.

Amid mounting Indonesian army counter-insurgency operations in the second half of 1978, he began writing a historical play entitled "The drama of Acehnese history 1873–1978". It was later finished by his closest lieutenant, Husaini Hasan (Hasan 1984: 186, 201, 220), and apparently it still circulates in Aceh. On 29 March 1979, telling comrades he was going to buy arms, Hasan di Tiro slipped through the closing Indonesian army noose and out of the country.[30]

Hasan di Tiro's supporters in Stockholm have produced an entire historiography of Acehnese nationalism. It begins with the autonomy of the Islamic Samudra-Pasai kingdom of the 13th and 14th centuries over the Indonesian kingdoms (so depicted in the Indonesian historiography) of Sriwijaya and Majapahit. It then goes on to recount Acehnese resistance against the Portuguese and the far more devious Dutch, and closes by claiming that the (federal) Republic of the United States of Indonesia of 1950, which ended the Indonesian war for independence, did not include Aceh (Sudirman 1999). This historiography originates in Sweden and circulates mainly on the internet, but Hasan di Tiro's argument has also been aired in Aceh's mainstream print media (*Waspada*, 8 January 1999, "Surat Hasan").[31]

Like much other nationalist historiography, these claims do not concern themselves greatly with accuracy. This is a ruthlessly simplistic account whose purpose is purely propagandistic: Aceh in early 1950 was in fact part of the Republic of Indonesia, which was in turn a member of the United States of Indonesia, and Daud Beureueh was the republican-appointed military governor of Aceh, Tanah Langkat, and Tanah Karo.

In August 1999 a small group of Acehnese students occupied the grounds of the Dutch embassy in Jakarta for three days to demand that the Dutch government should withdraw its formal "declaration of war against the sultan of Aceh on 26 March 1873", and hence acknowledge Acehnese sovereignty (*Waspada*, 7 August 1999, "Maklumat"). As an ambit claim it was unlikely to fly, but it was perhaps the first time that some Indonesians had publicly turned the oft-heard argument on its head that Jakarta had spoken for all Indonesians when it signed an agreement to end hostilities with the Netherlands in 1949.

The students were probing a distinct weak spot in the nationalist myth that all resistance to the Dutch had been "Indonesian" and not Acehnese, Javanese, Makassarese or Ambonese. After all, if anti-colonial resistance was the yardstick of legitimacy, as it is in the mythology, who was to say which was the more legitimate — the resistance in the 1870s by an Acehnese sultanate with a long history of international recognition, or the resistance in the 1940s by "Indonesians" with a history of resistance to colonial authority that lacked a military dimension and did not extend to challenging the very notion of the Netherlands Indies as a state? The students did not pursue the argument in quite such ruthless terms, but the backward-looking appeal to the sultanate was characteristic of much post-Suharto legitimation discourse, and not only in Aceh. "The way we fight is to reclaim the triumphs of Acehnese history, from the time of Sultan Iskandar Muda [1607–36]," a one-armed Acehnese fighter told the foreign press, in terms reminiscent of Soekarno's trimurti (England 1999).

At the other end of the country, Papuan independence activists have similarly turned to history as an important tool in their fight.[32] The large Papuan People's Congress held in Jayapura, 29 May–4 June 2000, claimed to be the second in a series begun in 1961. It followed a series of conferences and a book,[33] and its theme was "Let us straighten out the history of West Papua".

Using a phraseology that was quite distinct from the Acehnese, key Papuan spokespersons insisted that Papuan history had been "twisted" — by Indonesia,[34] but also by the Netherlands, the United States, and Australia — since 1961.[35] The mission now was to "straighten out" this twisted history. This idealized concept of history-as-it-should-have-been may not appeal to professional historians, but its proponents clearly felt it had enormous force.

The argument is that Papuans never belonged to the Indonesian nationalist movement, and that Indonesians have been even more colonial towards Papuans than were the Dutch. If Papua had been part of the kingdom of Majapahit at all (through the latter's vassal the Tidore sultanate), it was as a mere tributary to a tributary. Papua had a different, evidently less destructive memory of Dutch colonialism than did Indonesia. Several of Indonesia's key founding fathers such as Hatta had argued in

August 1945 that Papua did not belong to Indonesia, and its negotiators
had agreed with the Dutch in 1949 to exclude Papua from their borders.
The transition after 1962 to Indonesian rule, ratified in the 1969 so-called
Act of Free Choice (*Pepera*), had been a performance whose plot was
written by the world's great powers. Papua's subsequent history under
Indonesian rule had been one of oppression and exploitation.[36]

The key event in Papua's nationalist history as fashioned in recent
years was a flag-raising ceremony on 1 December 1961. On that day the
Dutch had agreed to let a Papuan Morning Star flag fly alongside its
Dutch counterpart, to signify the Dutch intention to begin a decade-long
transition to independence. That event prompted an intensification of
Indonesian campaigning (diplomatic, agitational, and military) to push
the Dutch out, and by May 1962 it was clear that the campaign had
succeeded. By May 1963 Indonesia was in control of what they called
"Irian Barat" and many of the key figures of 1 December 1961 had fled
to Holland. Indonesian soldiers took the flag down on Soekarno's orders
on 1 May 1963.

The 1961 occasion is remembered today as the declaration of Papuan
independence. To be sure, the Dutch decolonization program, of which
Papuan independence was a part, is potentially embarrassing and is thus
rarely mentioned. Flag-raising ceremonies on this day since 1998 have
always been marked with expositions of the Papuan history described
above, by way of political education. "Papua has already been independent
since 1 December 1961. History proves it," claimed the late Theys Eluay
(the self-confessed "Great Papuan Leader"). In a sense which evokes
Christian eschatology (where the Kingdom of God is "among you"
through the birth of Christ but will not be seen in its fullness till he comes
again in glory), the "not yet" had become an "already" in that flag raising
of 1961.

Spokespersons for all-Indonesian nationalism have written counters
to these militant new historiographies. One Indonesian magazine said
Hasan di Tiro was lying when he claimed to have the blue blood of the
heroic anti-Dutch fighter Cik di Tiro in his veins — he was no more than
a peasant's son (*Gamma* 1999, "Hasan Tiro"). Aceh's Indonesian military
commander published a highly selective history of Aceh to bolster his
assertion that the separatist movement GAM was a minority phenomenon
(Syarifudin Tippe 2000). In Papua, the military tried holding their own
seminar series to "straighten out history", but this time from a national

New Order perspective (the perspective Papuans had declared "twisted"). It was important, the presiding colonel said, to stress that, when Indonesia and the Netherlands were at loggerheads over the future of Papua in the early 1960s, there had been Papuans who fought to integrate with Indonesia (Isman 2000; *Kompas*, 11 April 2000, "Sejarah Papua"). Academic Ikrar Nusa Bhakti portrayed the 1961 event as related to Dutch colonialism, and an anonymous publisher underscored the point by republishing the 1961–2 speeches of President Soekarno about the "liberation" of "West Irian" (*Kompas*, 19 June 2000, "Sisi lain").[37] The governor of Papua, Freddy Numberi, adopted a more daring, theological approach. "The God we worship in Jesus Christ is the Lord of history," he said. "We must be open to accept the will of the Lord for this land as it came to expression in the history of the Act of Free Choice, which made Irian Jaya an inseparable part of the unitary state of the Republic of Indonesia" (*Cenderawasih Post*, 12 October 1998, "Tak benar").

Local Histories

An interest in local history characterizes the final category of "history writing" in post-Suharto Indonesia. This is not a new category by any means, but it holds the potential of being more subtly subversive than the ethno-nationalistic historiographies discussed above, precisely because these local histories are not so obviously manipulated by elite interests. Local histories differ from ethno-nationalist ones because they do not explicitly resist the nation-state. Instead, they develop local identities that coexist with the national identity. As a genre, the creation of local history remains largely unexplored.

In his book on Indonesia's historians, Klooster (1985) notes that most of Indonesia's western-trained historians, especially under the New Order, chose to develop a regional specialization. Sartono Kartodirdjo, a historian who was to become as important in the New Order as Muhammed Ali was in the Soekarno era and carried himself with the same personal integrity, set the tone with his 1966 study of the 1888 peasant's revolt in Banten.[38] Local issues have continued to preoccupy the academic discipline in Indonesia.

Much of this genre finds no particular conflict between the local and the national, yet in so (not) doing it helps erode the absolutist claims of the national by resisting its propagandistic simplicity. There is a class of historical novels and biographies that can be read as affirming the realities of local life as much as celebrating local "contributions" to the Indonesian nation.[39]

Cities around the country have taken to celebrating their "birthdays" with considerable fanfare. Exactly how the precise year of birth is calculated is not always clear, but the historical snippets local newspapers carry connect the city with what its inhabitants know about national history. For the sake of nation-building, the New Order in 1971 renamed the South Sulawesi city of Makassar as Ujung Pandang, a name with fewer ethnic associations. When President Habibie gave the city back its original name in October 1999, he was no doubt linking local pride to his own hopes in the upcoming presidential election. Museums devoted to local history and culture often play the same nationally integrating function.[40]

This growing body of local historical scholarship probably connects more closely with people's everyday lives than nationalist myth-making. It does not systematically avoid conflict within society. It interacts dialogically with the local stories kept alive in local cultural expressions. Of course it too is likely to be quarried by political actors — either to the advantage of Jakarta, as with Habibie, or to that of local elites, as with the warlords on both sides of the Maluku wars of 1999–2000. But its humanism and rooted quality may offer some of the same liberating perspective on the local level as the societal historiography of Pramoedya Ananta Toer does on the national. Moreover, the strength of local histories helps inoculate us against fears that the "disintegration" of the Indonesian national state will leave an identity vacuum that can only result in violence. Quite possibly, local histories reflect the (re)emergence of complex and hybrid identities that generally go unacknowledged in the exclusive absolutism of 19th-century nationalist historiography.

Conclusion

The search for freedom is as persistent in Indonesia today as it has ever been. It is a search with a history as broad and diverse as it is profound — far more so than the statist history-for-nation-building genre can ever explain. The greatest disservice to the cause of freedom was committed at the moment its history was captured by men for whom exclusive loyalty to a state was its only permissible expression. That disservice has been committed against generations of Indonesian schoolchildren ever since independence — especially during the militarized New Order. Who can really still believe that nationalism alone, and its attendant historiography of sacred dates, great men, and legal milestones can bring salvation?

History writing, as Pramoedya Ananta Toer has shown, can buttress the desire for freedom in sturdy ways without selling itself into the servitude of today or tomorrow's state elites. Real liberation often flies in the face of nationalism, as the history of Indonesia's own revolution abundantly shows. It is important to underscore the difference between Indonesia's national revolution for independence from the social revolution for a more equal society. The distinction remains important but neglected. The histories of the strivings for a just society — among Papuans, Acehnese, and others within the Indonesian fold — have largely still to be written.

Notes

1   Thanks to Asvi Warman Adam, Ed Aspinall, John Butcher, Lance Castle, Mochtar Pabottingi, Sylvia Tiwon, Michael Vatikiotis, and especially Herb Feith and Richard Tanter, for helpful comments on earlier drafts. An earlier version appeared under the same title in *Critical Asian Studies* 33, 3 (July 2001): 323–50.

2   Bintang Prakarsa (1994: 24) points out that Soekarno's trimurti was incorporated into the second paragraph of the opening of the 1945 Constitution, was then promoted as the "perspectivist" view in the official historiography under Soekarno, and was finally incorporated, renamed "trimatra", into the official historiography under Suharto by Kharis Suhud.

3   Soedjatmoko later edited the interesting volume, *An Introduction to Indonesian Historiography* (Ithaca, NY: Cornell University Press, 1965).

4   On film, see Sen (1994); on monuments and museums, see Schreiner (1997); on Nugroho's work, see McGregor, this volume.

5   A glimpse into this soul-searching among historians can be had in a book of papers by a team set up by the Education Department to weed out historical "errors" in school textbooks; see Lapian (1985) and Leirissa (1985).

6   Taufik Abdullah himself provided the strongest and most consistent criticism. See for example his writings in Abdullah and Surjomihardjo (1985), and in Koentjaraningrat (1975). Taufik used the phrase "hegemonic knowledge" in "Taufik Abdullah: Orba memang murid Snouck Hurgronje yang paling patuh" (*Panji Masyarakat*, 29 Sept. 1999).

7   For example *Sejarah* (Indonesian Academy of Sciences, LIPI), or *Lembaran Sejarah* (Gadjah Mada University).

8   Klooster (1985: 55–9) implicitly distinguishes nationalist, ethnic/ regionalist, Islamist and Marxist history writing. I have not considered Islamist history-writing a separate category, and have added local histories as a new category.

9   For example, post-Soviet Russian school texts replaced communism with an ideology of "Russianness" that highlighted Dostoyevski, no longer the defender of the poor but of "a unique and superior Russian culture that is hostile to Western bourgeois individualism" (see, e.g., Lisovskaya and Vyacheslav 1999: 522–43).

10   "Janur kuning" (Young coconut leaf), directed by Alam Rengga Surawidjaja in 1979 and "Serangan fajar" (Dawn attack), directed by Arifin C. Noor in 1981. See Irwantono 1999.

11   Arifin C. Noor, director, 1981.

12   The introduction was written by Ben Anderson. See Suharto's rebuttal in what may turn out to be his last coherent published interview: *SiaR*, 19–25 Apr. 1999, "Wawancara eksklusif".

13   This is the guide for junior high school only. I have not seen the others.

14   His office's publication record included a history of East Timor that angered so many East Timorese in early 1999 (Lapian and Chaniago 1988).

15   The manuscript circulated in photocopied form before finally being brought out by a small Jakarta publisher (Soebandrio 2001; Adam 2001).

16   The ban is known by the designation Tap No 25/MPRS/1966.

17   The new film was "Bukan sekadar kenangan", directed by Tatiek Maliyati and J. Sihombing, of which little has been heard since then. See also Klaus Schreiner, this volume.

18   It was the day they were sworn in as new MPR members.

19   Translations of foreign works include Crouch (1999) and Wieringa (1999). An Indonesian who published work researched overseas was Sulistiyo (2000); see also Krisnadi (2001). Western publications include: Cribb (1990); Carmel Budiardjo (1997); Robinson (1995); Siregar (1995); McGlynn and Steward (2000).

20   Among the most important are some already mentioned: Institut Studi Arus Informasi (1995); Crouch (1999); Katoppo *et al.* (1999); Hanafi (1998); Hasan (2001); Abdul Latief (2000); Soebandrio (2001); Soerojo and Soeparno (2001); Wieringa (1999).

21   For example, see Kartodikromo (2000), Malaka (1999, 2000), Soewarsono (2000), and a translation of a 1976 biography of Tan Malaka (Poeze 1988).

22   See the review in *Kompas*, 3 June 2001, "Soekarno Bukan". A wonderful 32–page Kompas supplement, written by 27 serious, mostly Indonesian scholars (*Kompas*, 1 June 2001, "Bung Karno") explored Soekarno and his times in a refreshing, non-doctrinaire manner, including his leftism and the G30S event as seen from his experience.

23   Pramoedya Ananta Toer's first tetralogy, *Bumi manusia, Jejak langkah, Anak semua bangsa*, and *Rumah kaca*, were first published in Jakarta in the 1980s but each was soon banned. They were then reissued in the Netherlands and Malaysia. The collapse of the New Order allowed Hasta Mitra in Jakarta to reissue them. *Sang Pemula* (1985) was similarly banned, and reissued elsewhere.

24   Pramoedya Ananta Toer's second tetralogy is *Arok Dedes* (1999), *Mata pusaran* (still lost), *Arus balik* (1995), and his only play: *Mangir* (2000).

25   The Haria proclamation was part of the short-lived Pattimura revolt against the Dutch (*Siwalima*, 5 Jan. 2001, "Waeleruny"; *Siwalima*, 30 Dec. 2000, "Basudara"; *The Straits Times*, 23 June 2000, "Independence").

26   "Deklarasi Kongres Minahasa Raya", 5 Aug. 2000 at Bukit Inspirasi Tomohon
     (gopher://gopher.igc.apc.org:2998/7REG-INDONESIA).
27   For background information on Aceh, especially the 1989–92 episode of violence,
     see Kell (1995) and Robinson (1998).
28   Translated extracts of this were published in March 1999 on the anonymous Indonesian
     internet news service MeunaSAH (<gopher://gopher.igc.apc.org:2998/7REG-
     INDONESIA>).
29   The Zentgraaff quote, we observe incidentally, is an interesting piece of post-coloniality.
     Di Tiro uncritically lifts quotes about Aceh's history and national character traits
     from several such colonial sources. Yet Zentgraaff had in the 1920s a reputation
     among Indonesian nationalists as a white supremacist.
30   On Acehnese oral history that remembers the Dutch wars, see Siapno (1997).
31   ASNLF, Hasan di Tiro's Stockholm-based organization disseminates an electronic
     bulletin called "Sumatra Ku" on the mailing list Keyakinan (<http://groups.yahoo.com/
     group/keyakinan/messages>), from whence it is widely reposted.
32   There is still no good political history of Papua in English; see May (1986), Osborne
     (1985), and Sharp (1994).
33   The Papua Plenary (Musyawarah Besar Masyarakat Papua) held near Jayapura 23–
     26 Feb. 2000 had the theme "Straightening out history"; Papuans in Jakarta held
     a seminar on 24 May 2000 entitled "Reinterpreting the juridical status of Irian Jaya
     from a historical and international legal perspective"; the First Papua Youth Congress
     held in Jayapura 23–27 May 2000 was preoccupied with history. A new book timed
     to coincide with the People's Congress presented a well-researched history of Papuan
     resistance against colonialism from Dutch to Indonesian times: Pigay (2000).
34   The standard account of a history Papuan nationalists would call "twisted" is *Sejarah
     kembalinya Irian Jaya ke pangkuan Republik Indonesia* (Direktorat Organisasi
     Internasional Departemen Luar Negeri 1998).
35   The main Papuan spokesperson for this view was the late Theys Eluay; for example,
     see *Kompas* (31 May 2000, "Kongres").
36   Coherent recent statements of this historical argument include *Kompas* (19 June
     2000, "Mereka"); articles by the Papuan activist in the Netherlands Ottis Simopiaref,
     Suara Mambruk, 10 Feb. 2000, *Manipulasi* and Papua (internet mailing list) 5 June
     2000, *Dasar dasar*; Studi 1999; and Rumbiak 1999. Over against the more purely
     legal arguments of these histories, George Aditjondro (2000b: 5–37), an Indonesian
     sympathizer with Papuan nationalist aspirations, produced a history of great Papuans,
     carefully formulated to accord equal weight to various tribal districts.
37   *Bebaskan Irian Barat: Kumpulan pidato Presiden Soekarno tentang pembebasan
     Irian Barat 17 Agustus 1961–17 Agustus 1962* (Yogyakarta: Ragam Media, 2000).
38   Others with regional specializations are Taufik Abdullah (who wrote on Minangkabau),
     Ibrahim Alfian (Aceh), Edi S. Ekadjati (West Java), A.B. Lapian (maritime history),
     R.Z. Leirissa (Maluku), Onghokham (Madiun), F.A. Sutjipto (Yogyakarta), and
     Soemarsaid Moertono (Java). Only a few did take up national issues: Alfian (Muham-
     madiyah), Abdurrachman Surjomihardjo (nationalism), and Uka Tjandrasasmita
     (archaeology).
39   A good example is Mangunwijaya (1983), a novel on Ambon's history.

Gerry van Klinken

40   For a description of one Javanese town anniversary (Purwokerto) see Quinn (2002); see also Anthony Reid, this volume. On a regional museum in South Sulawesi, see Robinson (1997). On the Makassar renaming see Morrell (2001). See also the 85-part series on Batavia in *The Jakarta Post* 2000–1 (the last [1 Sept. 2001] was Ida Indawati Khouw, "Jakarta a 'city of hell' during occupation").

PART FOUR

Lubang Buaya: Histories of Trauma and Sites of Memory[1]

KLAUS H. SCHREINER

Vielleicht

Erinnern
das ist
vielleicht
die qualvollste Art
des Vergessens
und vielleicht
die freundlichste Art
der Linderung
der Qual
(Erich Fried 1983: 124)[2]

The demise of Suharto's New Order is marked by the emergence of repressed personal and collective memories of the violence that preceded his rise to power. Official historiography, memorialization, commemoration, and rituals served to repress traumatic and violent memory as they simultaneously, and over a sustained period of time, raised sites of memory that served to support Suharto's regime. Individually and collectively, Indonesians are actively creating new interpretations of events and monuments, and are beginning to expose deep trauma that suggests a step towards the dual processes of remembering and forgetting. This chapter focuses on how Indonesia's present can be understood by using the two otherwise independent theoretical frameworks of trauma and memory as presented in the works of S. Freud and P. Nora.[3]

Introduction and Background

In the early morning hours of 1 October 1965 armed soldiers of the infantry abducted six generals and a lieutenant from their Jakarta homes, and killed them during or after the abduction. The bodies were disposed of in a dry well in a banana grove generally known as Lubang Buaya, located close to the airfield Halim Perdanakusuma in South Jakarta. Two days later they were found in a putrefying condition. After army doctors performed autopsies, the generals were solemnly buried on 5 October at the Heroes' Cemetery at Kalibata.[4] A group of young officers belonging to the Presidential Guard under the command of Colonels Untung and Latief claimed responsibility, justifying the events by maintaining that the abducted generals belonged to a "Generals' Council" planning to topple President Soekarno. In the immediate aftermath of the abductions and murders, at least 500,000 Indonesians allegedly or actually associated with the communist movement became victims of an unprecedented mass killing.[5] This chain of events culminated in Soekarno's fall from power and removal from office and the transition to the New Order administration of Major-General Suharto in 1967.

Suharto's administration (1967–98) took seriously the task of producing an official narrative of the events preceding his rise to the Presidency. Histories were (re)written, monuments erected, and ceremonies inaugurated to establish a particular memory and memorializing process that ultimately served to legitimize and stabilize the new regime. These histories, monuments, and ceremonies can be examined critically as sites of memory. They are symbolic, material and functional manifestations of the regime's power to define the collective meanings of events.

While Suharto's regime lasted, the official narrative dominated the discourse, but since May 1998, debate about the events of the 1965-killings and their aftermath has gained unprecedented liveliness and breadth in Indonesia. Memory is being (re)constructed by the many survivors and victims who finally dare to speak out, and the process of memorializing and establishing meaning is as complex today as it was in the immediate aftermath of the events. While growing numbers of victims offer testimony, many New Order insiders justify their roles in the regime publicly by offering counter-narratives in extensive interviews and published memoirs.[6] Still others, like the members of the Indonesian Air Force, endeavour to "straighten out" the historical record and to remove suspicions of communist infiltration that they believe stain their public image.[7] The new and modified ways that sites of memory are being used and produced suggests that the power of Suharto's New Order regime to define events is increasingly dwindling. Gradually, personal and traumatic memories are finding a place for expression in collective Indonesian life. In what follows, I begin with the present, with recent developments in expressions of collective memory that bring issues of repression, trauma, and the construction of collective memory to the fore.

The film "Bukan Sekadar Kenangan" (Not Just a Remembrance) commissioned in 1998 for screening as part of the annual commemorations of Suharto's rise to power reinforces the official narrative of the events described above, but also manifests a fundamental transition in its introduction of personal perspective. This film replaced its predecessor "Pengkhianatan G30S" (The Treason of the 30 September Movement), which was screened annually between 1981 and 1997. From the early days of the regime, however, Suharto organized many other commemorations, rituals, and memorializations of Soekarno's fall and the rise of the New Order. The official narrative is a two-sided coin, one scorning the communist insurrection and the other celebrating the continuity of Indonesian nationalism. In addition to the annual film screenings, I will discuss the memorialization of the Lubang Buaya site in the days immediately following Suharto's appointment as president, as well as the opus of historiography that built the regime's official narrative. I then turn to a discussion of two fields of theory that provide insights to understand the transition that, I argue, the film "Bukan Sekadar Kenangan" represents.

New Political Environments and the Reconstruction of Memory

In 1998, the new film "Bukan Sekadar Kenangan"[8] rendered the story of a young woman whose marriage is unexpectedly cancelled because her father is allegedly supporting a communist group. Searching for the background of the sudden turn of her fate, she discovers that her bridegroom's aunt became mentally disordered because she saw her husband being tortured to death by communists. The plot of this film, commissioned by the Directorate General for Culture of the Ministry for Education and Culture, combines two very sensitive and fundamental issues. In my reading, the first has a more Indonesia-focused scope: the staunch anti-communism of the Suharto-regime and the mass killings of 1965. The second issue is more universal in character and is particularly important for the theoretical development highlighted in this chapter: the problem of silencing traumatic experiences. While still maintaining an anti-communist tone, "Bukan Sekadar Kenangan" presents a refined and personal perspective. It attempts to convey its message by arousing and appealing to the sentiments of the audience. The bridegroom's aunt is depicted in this film as a victim in two regards: she became a widow when the communists killed her husband, and she became mentally ill because she had to witness her husband's torture.

The Department of Education and Culture presumably commissioned the new film to replace the earlier "Pengkhianatan G30S", a National Film Company production whose artistic director was the renowned Arifin C. Noor.[9] Although the new film framed the historical events of 30 September 1965 very differently from Arifin's, it continued to negate the suffering of the New Order's victims in an annual commemoration of Suharto's regime and the "sacred Pancasila". Arifin's film claimed to be a documentary reconstruction of the general's killings, and was incorporated along with newspaper articles into the stimuli for annual public remembering. "Pengkhianatan G30S" was broadcast on "Hari Peringatan Kesaktian Pancasila" (The Day of Sacred Pancasila Remembrance), the anniversary of the generals' killing, by the state-owned television company, and set the tone for annual ceremonies on the following day (Sen 1988:58). The film reached further into the general population than any of the formal rituals, and became an important source of popular knowledge about this historic episode for the younger generation.[10]

Edi Sedyawati, at that time the Director-General for Culture and one of the initiators of the new film, justified the treatment of the historic trauma in the film "Bukan Sekadar Kenangan":

> This film wants to remind the people to be cautious towards communism, because the PKI has twice revolted against the government of the Republic of Indonesia, that is in 1948 and in 1965. The victims were innocent people.[11]

Edi's statement regarding the innocence of victims would hold equally true for the many people murdered for their alleged or actual affiliation with the communist movement. Thus while the film's representation of the issue of repression of traumatic experiences is in itself noteworthy, it virtually denies the memory of many victims.[12]

The new film brings an important element into the official narrative — that of individual, personal trauma. Although this element is presented within a plot of Communist insurrection against the State, its presence marks the beginning of a transitional stage as the New Order began to crumble. As the political environment began to change, repressed memories began to surface, even in the unintended form of a plot in a new, official commemorative film.

Lubang Buaya and Historiography in Indonesia

The following section highlights "sites of memory" and versions of official narratives, created by the New Order regime, that systematically repressed traumatic experiences. The most prominent and reified symbols of the generals' deaths and the mass killings of 1965 are found at Lubang Buaya (Crocodile Hole) in East Jakarta and are tied directly to the New Order regime. The original construction of the site included three main elements: a plaza to hold ceremonies (*lapangan upacara*), an elaborate monument called *Tugu Monumen Pancasila Sakti*[13] (Monument of the Sacred Pancasila), and a simple, traditional Javanese style pavilion (*pendopo*) marking the site of the well itself. A mammoth Garuda (mythological eagle) looms over the monument, and a bas-relief presenting the story of the events leading up to the generals' murders covers its massive pentagonal pedestal. In fact, the five corners of the pedestal symbolize the five principles of the New Order ideology *Pancasila*, and thus even the shape of the monument marks the ideology enshrined at the site (Leclerc 1997). Lubang Buaya, in many ways, embodies the drama of its creation in the details of its construction and as such refers to both the material site itself as well as the traumatic events that spurred its creation.

The material representations of events created at Lubang Buaya by Suharto's New Order regime constrain the meanings and interpretations of events available to those who visit the site. The historian Pierre Nora's (1990) explication of the "sites of memory" is helpful in understanding the social nature of remembrance. For Nora, borrowing the concept of collective memory from the French sociologist Maurice Halbwachs,[14] human beings can remember their history but cannot freely choose the circumstances and conditions of their remembering. In other words, social environments influence and shape an individual's capacity to remember and to recall. On the collective level, memories are constructed within present frames of reference (Halbwachs 1985) such that sites of memory are defined as places and items that possess the capability to store memory and to trigger acts of remembering. The construction of particular, material components that make up the Lubang Buaya site are examples of how the events depicted are linked to the well and to the New Order's Pancasila philosophy, together shaping the way that individual visitors will remember, and give meaning to, the events.

The creation of the site itself was an early exercise of Suharto's power as new President to write the history of the New Order, and as a metaphor of the 1965 regime change, Lubang Buaya clearly embodies traumatic events and political struggle. As soon as the news of the abduction and killing of the generals spread on 1 October, President Soekarno was suspected to have encouraged or even masterminded the plot, which was, after all, undertaken in his name and with the declared goal to protect him from the generals' bid to overthrow him. Immediately, a fierce struggle for the symbolic potency of the generals' death broke out between Soekarno and Suharto's group. Soekarno rebutted suspicions and attempted to prop up his position by claiming the generals to be martyrs of the "Indonesian Revolution" of which he was the "Great Leader", even issuing a decree awarding them the title "Pahlawan Revolusi" (Hero of the Revolution) on the eve of their funeral.[15] President Soekarno's Guided Democracy rhetoric was, however, unconvincing to his enemies within the army, and to the general public. General Suharto, on the other hand, rapidly enlarged and strengthened his power-base within the Armed Forces and the population, and ultimately had Soekarno deposed as president.[16] Immediately and skillfully, the new President Suharto exploited the symbolic power of the murdered generals by commissioning a memorial on the spot where the victims had been found dumped in a well, transforming what was once a simple banana grove into a shrine and symbol of the New Order.[17]

As the details of Lubang Buaya's construction embody the Pancasila ideology of the New Order, so also does the static and motionless form of the monuments reflect the New Order's authoritarian stance.[18] While Soekarno sought to maintain a tense balance between a rising communist movement and the anti-communist military, Suharto's New Order formed as the Cold War intensified and the conflict in Vietnam was evolving, and took a hard line on destroying any remnants of communism. The form of the monument at Lubang Buaya thus embodied the victory of Suharto's New Order over Soekarno's so-called "old order" (orde lama), including this anti-communist element and the authoritarian character of the new regime. At Lubang Buaya, "educational" devices were added to the site over the years by the Center for History and Tradition of the Armed Forces that continued this style: personal belongings, letters, uniforms, and blood-stained clothing of the generals are on display in a special exhibition, and within a replica of the original shelter that stood close to the well, a life-size diorama displays the gory scene of the generals allegedly being tortured and humiliated by communist youth.[19] Another addition is the "Museum of the Communist Treason", with its collection of 32 dioramas about the "treacherous" acts of the communist movement since the *Peristiwa Tiga Daerah* (Three Regions Affair) in 1945.[20] The dioramas in the neighbouring *Museum Pancasila Sakti*, Museum of the Sacred Pancasila, focus on the various episodes directly connected to the events of 1965 (Pusat Sejarah dan Tradisi ABRI, 1994). In each of these exhibitions, the same motionless, *nature morte* presentation of history characterizes the New Order's authoritarian control over how events are depicted and constructed as sites of memory.

Sites of memory, as well as memory's dimensions, are complex. Lubang Buaya as a topographic and symbolic site is but one instance of the memorializing of 1965. A site of memory can be an artifact, a monument or a ritual that incites remembering. Lubang Buaya as a historical event became a symbol of political change as discussed above, but it also triggered the creation of a whole set of manifestations that are by Nora's definition "sites of memory" (see below). A corpus of historiography, and the films and rituals discussed here, each fulfills Nora's definition of the nature and function of sites of memory in that they serve the purpose of conveying and maintaining a certain view and interpretation of the past that is meaningful for the present and the future.

Suharto's administration controlled the content of many Indonesian accounts of the events of 1965 in a fashion similar to its control over the construction of symbolic memorials. A prominent and influential historiographic account of the generals' murder and ensuing mass killings of 1965–6 was published by the Center for the Indonesian Armed Forces' History and Tradition. The publication was compiled by Nugroho

Klaus H. Schreiner

Notosusanto and Ismail Saleh as an expanded version of a preliminary report, published by Nugroho almost immediately after the generals' murders (Notosusanto and Saleh 1968). It portrayed the attempted coup in a manner which could provide the historical basis for the memorialization at Lubang Buaya.[21] The standard textbook of Indonesian history and historiography, *Sejarah Nasional Indonesia* (Departemen Pendidikan dan Kebudayaan, several editions), also presents in its last volume a controversial account of the events. In general, textual representations of 1965 events, like the memorializing monuments, were controlled and censored to produce a single collective memory.

The link between the 1965–6 events and the New Order's anticommunist cause was maintained throughout Suharto's regime. Innumerable articles were customarily published in all newspapers around 30 September each year, each uncritically reinforcing the regime's official version of history and invoking Pancasila as the sole protection against the danger of communism and a communist take-over. As late as 1992, the State Secretariat published a "White Book" on the history of the Indonesian communist movement since its beginnings in the early 1920s. It places the events of 1965 in a comprehensive historical framework of repeated communist "insurrections" against the national cause and interprets them as the most recent attempt to overthrow the national state. The explicit purpose of the publication, as then State Secretary Moerdiono stated in his preface, was to enforce the national assembly's decree of 1966 (TAP MPR) that banned all kinds of communist ideologies in Indonesia (Sekretariat Negara Republik Indonesia 1994 [1992]). Since Suharto's fall from power, this White Book has been withdrawn as a reference book for history textbooks at school and will not be reprinted (Suara Pembaruan 2001).

Foreign observers also began soon after the mass killings to describe and analyse the violence, and put forward alternatives to the Suharto regime's accounts. The most well-known is doubtless the so-called "Cornell Paper" by Benedict Anderson and Ruth McVey, which challenged the official Indonesia version of a communist plot and argued that a power struggle within the armed forces had led to the attempted coup (Anderson and McVey 1971 [1966]). Many other authors have researched the events and the background of this bloody overthrow and offered different and at times conflicting theories (Cribb 1990: 1–44; Sulistiyo 2000). Despite the breadth of alternative political accounts, however, historians, political scientists, and others interested in Indonesian history are only beginning to sense how deeply rooted both collective and individual memories among millions of Indonesians are and to what extent both the repression of memory and the indoctrination by the "New Order" regime did shape historical perceptions.

An important dynamic in the above accounts of monuments and historiography is reflected in the fact that each site has been constructed with an "imperative to remember" (Grütter and Theodor 1999: 4). Clearly, sites of memory are not created only retroactively after a society becomes aware of the threat of losing the memory, as Nora suggests, but in some cases are purposefully constructed by those who possess the power to define collective symbols.[22]

Sites of Memory and Trauma: A Theoretical Synthesis

Through the multi-faceted manifestations described above, the events of 1965–6 came to occupy a central role in the political discourse of the New Order. As Pierre Nora and his colleagues have shown, sites of memory or "lieux de mémoire" provide a present frame of places and symbols by which the past is recalled and remembered. Nora's theory is built from Halbwachs' work on collective memory, which claims that when, how, and in what form recollections of the past emerge is shaped by present circumstances and conditions. "Collective memory" is therefore, according to Halbwachs, "the complete stock of memories, a society of each epoch can reconstruct within its present frame of reference" (Halbwachs 1985: 390).[23]

Nora's contribution to the development of this field has been in the conceptualization of "sites of memory" as the places and items that possess the capability to store memory and to trigger acts of remembering:[24]

> *Lieux de mémoire* are complex things. At once natural and artificial, simple and ambiguous, concrete and abstract, they are *lieux* — places, sites, causes — in three senses: material, symbolic, and functional.
> (Nora 1996:14)[25]

Not only must sites of memory contain meanings constructed with the intention of inciting memory; their meanings also change as people make use of them. Linking history and memory, Nora thus establishes sites of memory as the specific places where historical consciousness is generated. In accord with Nora's explications on the nature and function of sites of memory, we can see that memorialization, historiography, museums, rituals, and films relating to Lubang Buaya as a historical event and as political symbol thus convey and maintain a certain view and interpretation of the past that is meaningful for the present and the future.

The intentional creation of sites of memory raises questions of who has the power to create them, when they are created, what alternative forms they might have taken, and the relationship between what is memorialized and what is not. Here, theories of trauma at the individual level provide a frame that Nora's theory alone does not address. As a site of memory, Lubang Buaya supported for many years the official acceptable version of history. It epitomized the triumph of the military and the foundation of the New Order. It is, however, not only a symbol of power and authoritative interpretation of history but also the negative expression of the trauma surrounding the generals' deaths and the mass killings.

The concept of "trauma" has made its way from medicine through psychiatry and psychoanalysis into history and other humanities. The term originally denoted an organic or physical wound; the connotation of trauma as referring to a person's psychic state after suffering such an injury evolved in studies of the Holocaust in particular, and has been extended to denote the response to terrible events with or without physical harm to the individual. Building on Freud's conceptualization developed in the work *Beyond the Pleasure Principle* (1953–74), Cooper (1986) suggests that psychic trauma is:

> an event that abruptly overwhelms the capability of the ego to provide a minimum sense of security and integrative completeness and that results in an overwhelming fear or helplessness or in a situation where these [states] are imminent. Moreover, it leads to a permanent change of the psychic organisation.

Other essential features of traumatic events are their suddenness and uniqueness. The events of 1965 at Lubang Buaya were unprecedented, and thus could not be incorporated into existing explanations of reality at the individual and collective levels. Connecting, Loewenberg (1998: 128) argued that "the trauma is the theoretical link between individual and group [...]"thereby linking Freud's understanding that history is a "history of traumata" to Halbwachs' notion that individual recollections are shaped by society.

Finally, trauma is simultaneously a continuous and interrupted process. It marks a deep interruption in the life story of any individual and in the history of a society, but at the same time represents the beginning of a new history that is linked to that very event. Caruth (1995: 14) demonstrates this in her examination of Freud's essay "Moses and Monotheism", by showing how "the exodus from Egypt that shapes the meaning of the Jewish past is a departure that is both a radical break and the establishment of a new history." Thus trauma is, on the one hand, the interruption of history; on the other, it is the continuation of the past into the present.

At the individual level, the excessive force and violence of a traumatic experience is a fundamental obstacle in overcoming the psychic injury inflicted by the event. The trauma lives within the person without being expressed or reconciled. This is the paradox of the traumatic situation to which Roth (1998: 168) alludes:

> If the trauma is unforgettable, then it is paradoxically so, because it could not be remembered, not be re-narrated. As soon as it becomes part of the historical consciousness,[26] it may gradually fade away.

Untold trauma remains in the painful latency of memory. There it will develop its disruptive, paralyzing, and debilitating effect.

The strategies to cope with the persistent present of trauma are applicable at both the individual and collective levels. Trauma retold will become (hi)story and therefore treatable, resolvable and thus can be forgotten. Lyotard establishes (as does Assmann) the stabilizing — as well as paralyzing — effects of trauma. He argues that only those items can be forgotten that have somehow been recorded, because these records can be erased. What never has been inscribed, may also never be forgotten, because it is not accessible to forgetfulness. Assmann concludes:

> Monuments are for him [Lyotard] 'representations' and as such they serve as a relief for the memory, thus in truth: as strategies of forgetting. [...] What has been fixed, can also be extinguished; however, something that never acquired the form of a sign, of a rememberable symbol can, according to Lyotard, therefore not be denied or forgotten.
>
> (A. Assmann 1995: 149)[27]

A person remains in the numbness of the trauma, unable to deal with it, unless he or she develops strategies in the form of narration of any

272 Klaus H. Schreiner

verbal or symbolic kind. At the collective level as well, sites of memory are one form of symbolic narration where trauma can be reactivated and thus put to rest.

The activities of the Indonesian Institute for the Study of the 1965–6 Massacres (*Yayasan Penelitian Korban Pembunuhan 1965/66*) are an example of the effort to give memory a proper site and to lay to rest — literally and figuratively — the memories of the dead in an appropriate manner. In March 2001 this association of victims of the Suharto regime planned to conduct a solemn reburial of remains from a mass grave linked to the 1965/6 killings in the district of Wonosobo in Central Java. The trauma in this way could conceivably be transformed into a tangible symbol, creating a new site of memory serving the immediate emotional needs of survivors and relatives, and simultaneously aiming at national reconciliation.[28] The speaking, the telling, the narrating, the acting out, and also the creation of sites and symbols and assigning meaning to them, is a way to re-integrate the suppressed memory into the identity of a person and then consequently put it to rest: in this sense, a "pacified" forgetting (Weinrich 2000: 174). In the case of Indonesia the power of dominant symbols is only gradually waning to allow for the overcoming of this numbness.

Conclusion: Remembering and Forgetting (at) Lubang Buaya

From the preceding discussion it becomes evident that the monument and related installations at Lubang Buaya are indeed a "site of memory", combining both topographical and functional aspects of Nora's concept. The functional (rituals, ceremonies, commemorations, etc.) and topographical (monuments, cemeteries, museums, etc.) expressions emerge, as Nora emphasized, at those times and in such places where a break with the past — either perceived or construed — occurs. They identify those intersections of individual and social life stories that mark discontinuity (Nora, 1996:7). Trauma is a form of break with the past that paradoxically includes traits of continuity and discontinuity at the same time. Thus sites of memory are the visible marks of breaks that are associated with traumatic events.

The monument and its companion installations occupy the very site where the New Order came into existence, the birthplace of Suharto's regime. The violent and traumatic events accompanying its emergence mark the break with Soekarno's Guided Democracy and the preceding period of liberal democracy. In order to avoid a complete severance from the struggle of independence as the legitimizing ideological basis of the Indonesian nation, the new regime redesigned and consecrated Pancasila to maintain this continuity and safeguard the identity of the Indonesian nation.

The monument and the museums at Lubang Buaya turned the site into the centrepiece of a new political universe. As symbolic centre and topographical site of memory, Lubang Buaya became the place to perform newly conceived rituals to maintain and strengthen a newly established authority (Kertzer 1983: 63). From 1967 onwards Suharto and the highest representatives of his New Order annually carried out the ceremonies of the Day of Sacred Pancasila Remembrance (*Hari Peringatan Kesaktian Pancasila*)[29] to commemorate the birth of the New Order. The political myth of the continuation of the revolution after the independence struggle, which served as the ideological basis of Soekarno's rule, was replaced by the myth of the invincibility and the sacredness of Pancasila. The murdered soldiers became the "saints" of the New Order in Indonesia.[30] As I have argued elsewhere (Schreiner 2002) the populist mass rallies and participatory style of Soekarno's political ceremonies faded and was replaced by the formal and exclusive rituals of the 1 October remembrance.

Because Lubang Buaya was erected as a monument and a memorial it is not just a venue that incites remembering, it also expresses an inherent imperative to remember. Therefore the monument *Tugu Tujuh Pahlawan* (Monument of the Seven Heroes) and the surrounding installations originally had a twofold purpose. On the one hand the monument served as a constant reminder of the threat originating from communism, and as a token of Pancasila's strength and invincibility. The meaningfulness of the generals' "sacrifice"[31] did not end, however, with the salvation of Pancasila from the chaos of the old order. They were actually considered to be the progenitors of a successor regime, as the ancestors within the New Order's myth of origin.

On the other hand the monument at Lubang Buaya commemorated — until the fall of the Suharto regime — only the permissible aspects of the past. The negative and repugnant dimensions of mass violence, though always present, were repressed to maintain the New Order. As that regime began to crumble, however, Suharto's modes of repressing memory and trauma became less efficient. Victims of the New Order increasingly speak out to question the official version of 1965 history. A recent feature in *The Jakarta Post* (Fitri 2002) illustrated an emerging debate as to whether the memorial and adjoining museum should be demolished, or rather maintained as testimony to the distorted representation of the past. How necessary such sites may become is evident from ongoing efforts to locate and rebury victims of killings.[32] In many Javanese communities there is common but unspoken knowledge of the location of anonymous mass graves where victims of the killings were hastily interred by their murderers. Efforts to exhume and rebury these remains are an attempt to bring hidden knowledge and hitherto suppressed memory into public consciousness and acknowledgement. The painful memories of the victims deserve a place, spatially and figuratively, where society can take note of and be confronted by them. However, the negative, even violent reactions of some Indonesians illustrate how painful the process of remembering — which is only beginning — can be. Efforts to spur public acknowledgement are still considered by many Indonesian citizens to be a breach of longstanding taboo. Such reburial of remains can create new sites of memory that will counter and interact with the monument at Lubang Buaya and will provide the necessary complement to the act of remembering at Lubang Buaya itself.

In conclusion, an important feature of sites of memory is "to generate new [meanings] along with new and unforeseeable connections" (Nora 1996: 15). Whereas the form and design of these sites may remain unaltered, people will interpret the represented history anew under changing political conditions. In Indonesia at present, memories of a shared history are conflicting with each other. Crystallizing at different places, they will nevertheless contribute to a more complete perception of the past. In a changing political climate and challenged by the newly emerging counter-memory, the monument at Lubang Buaya can function to instigate the task of remembering the past. The traumatic events have to be brought forward, have to be told and narrated. To overcome the alienation from her history and to heal the trauma of the past, Indonesia needs sites of memory to be able to cope with the aftermath of authoritarianism and to pacify haunting recollections.

Notes

1. The ideas presented in this chapter were discussed at various occasions and in various contexts. I gratefully acknowledge comments and criticism of R. Cribb, S. Drews, M. Pabottingi, and G. Robinson. The core of this paper was concluded in May 2002. I am indebted to M. Zurbuchen and J. Winther for their help to prepare the paper for publication.

2. Perhaps. // Remembering / that is / perhaps / the most painful way / of forgetting / and perhaps / the kindest way / of soothing / this ordeal.

3. Influenced by the French School of the Annales, Nora was the rector spiritus and editor of the huge enterprise to register and describe "sites of memory" of the French nation. The project resulted in the seven volumes of "Les Lieux de Mémoire", a collective work involving more than 100 French historians. It is in itself an impressive example of what Nora called "the obsession" to make an inventory of and save in storehouses every item to history. See also Connerton 1989 or the volume *Social Memory*, ed. by James Fentress and Chris Wickham (1992).

4. In New Order terminology these events are usually referred to as *Gerakan Tiga Puluh September* (30th September Movement). The related acronym *Gestapu* alludes to the German acronym *Gestapo* for the Nazi secret police during the Hitler regime. As a counter-move, Soekarno referred to these events usually as *Gestok* (1 October Movement).

5. For a discussion of the estimation of the numbers of victims and their respective sources see Cribb 1990: 1–44.

6. This new body of historical sources still awaits comprehensive assessment and evaluation (see also van Klinken, this volume).

7. See, for example, *Kompas*, 22 November 2002, "PPAU". The effort to publicly refute the allegations of communist infiltration or leftist leanings on the part of the Air Force also speaks to the prevailing anti-communist phobia in the post-Suharto political discourse.

8. *Suara Pembaruan* Daily on-line 30.09.1998: *"Bukan Sekadar Kenangan* pengganti film *Pengkhianatan G30S/PKI"*. The film was directed by Jonggi Sihombing.

9. Many prominent actors were also recruited for the project: Umar Kayam appeared as Soekarno, Amoroso Katamsi as Suharto. See also the interviews with some of the actors and the Arifin's widow in *DëTAK* 1, no. 13 (6–12 Oct. 1998): 13, partly distancing themselves from their role in blaming the prevalent conditions at the time of the film's production, partly justifying their involvement in the project. The interviews were published after the annual screenings of the film had stopped.

10. During a visit to Lubang Buaya in 2000, I discussed the various versions of the events with some university graduates. I noticed that they only knew the official version and considered the alleged Communist origin of the coup as proven historical fact.

11. *Suara Pembaruan* Daily on-line 30 Sept. 1998.

12. Two other famous examples for this attitude are the films "Janur Kuning" (1979) and "Serangan Fajar" (1981), which celebrate Suharto's role in the guerrilla attack on Yogyakarta on 1 Mar. 1949.

13   The monument is also known as the "Monument of the Seven Heroes" (*Tugu Tujuh Pahlawan*).

14   Born in 1877, student of the philosopher Henri Bergson and of Emile Durkheim, one of the progenitors of sociology. He taught sociology in Strasbourg and Paris. Arrested and, deported by the Gestapo in 1944, he died in the concentration camp of Buchenwald in 1945. In 1925 he published his first study on this topic "Les cadres sociaux de la mémoire" (The Social Conditions of Memory). His second major work on collective memory was left behind only in fragments and was posthumously published in 1950 as *La mémoire collective*.

15   Typically, various committees have to cooperate in the lengthy process of selecting, screening, and declaring a "National Hero". However, Soekarno frequently circumvented these regulations. For the production of national heroes in Indonesia, see Schreiner 1997.

16   Suharto forced Soekarno to sign the "Supersemar"-authorization of 11 Mar. 1966, which became the basis for the banning of the PKI. In March 1967 Soekarno was deposed and stripped of all his offices and power; Suharto succeeded him as acting president, to be officially confirmed as president a year later.

17   For contemporary accounts see e.g. *Indonesia Raya*, 2 Oct. 1970 and *Kompas*, 27 Sept. 1970.

18   The New Order's authoritarian stance and the paralysis of political culture under the regime are explored in Sekimoto (1990) and Schreiner (1997).

19   The official autopsy report states that no traces of torture or maltreatment could be found on the corpses of the soldiers; see Anderson (1987) and Cohen (1991).

20   Left-wing nationalists seized local power in the Pekalongan region of Central Java in 1945, shortly after the declaration of independence. On this event, see Lucas (1991).

21   See also McGregor in this volume.

22   Thus the creation of "sites of memory" is not only the result of a democratic movement as Nora suggests, but is prone to become part of a deliberate strategy to dominate the ideological discourse and the memory of a society.

23   Halbwachs as a sociologist was interested in the societal dimension of collective memory and its horizontal network of societies. The art historian Aby Warburg, the second important influential academic in the development of the idea of a "collective memory", was more interested in the ways collective memory is being handed down from generation to generation, i.e. in its vertical dimension (see Warburg 2000). Studying the reflections of the classical Greek and Roman cultures in the pictures, paintings and sculptures of later ages he believed that the persistence of classical antiquity was not merely materialistic, in the sense of preservation of artifacts. Warburg became convinced that it is mainly the result of intellectual appropriation and transference of each. For him, culture — visible and tangible in works of arts, paintings, monuments, and symbols in a broad sense of the word — is an objectification of the experience of human beings. Even after centuries their inherent impulse can be activated to become effectual again. Warburg considered culture as a phenomenon of memory, while Halbwachs saw memory as a product of culture. The former was

interested in culture as particular form of memory activity, the latter looked at culture's shaping impact on memory.

[24] In his conceptual scheme, Nora borrows the term *loci memoriae* from classical mnemotechnique, which associates ideas and thoughts to places, thereby stressing the topographical dimension of memory. He refers to Frances A. Yates (1966).

[25] All places in the literal sense of the word, i.e. topographical and spatial, belong to the first category: battlefields, monuments, buildings, etc. The second group may comprise charters, constitutions, and other concrete items that are figurative "places". The third division refers to distinct and prescribed patterns of behaviour, i.e. rituals, festivals or ceremonies. Nora's extensive introductory chapter "Between Memory and History" (Nora 1984, 1990, 1996) provides the most thorough elaboration of the concept of "sites of memory".

[26] That means that the trauma can be verbalized and expressed, thus becoming part of memory's narrative.

[27] She refers to Jean-François Lyotard's, "Heidegger" and "The Jews", two lectures given in Vienna and Freiburg in 1988 (English translation, University of Minnesota Press, 1990).

[28] Press Release of "Yayasan Penelitian Korban Pembunuhan 1965/1966", in Dec. 2000, circulated by the ASIET News List (see "Press Release", 2000).

[29] "But the truly unique New Order ritual celebration was to be that which is held on 1 October, [...] the 'Day of the Remembering of the Spiritual Power of Pancasila'. It was proposed in 1967 that annually a brief ceremony be held on the parade grounds of Lubang Buaya, [...]" (Purdy 1994: 230).

[30] The performed rituals are very simple. They mainly consist of the recitation of the ideologically most important texts of the New Order: the Pancasila itself, the preamble of the Constitution of 1945, and an "oath of resoluteness to defend the Pancasila. The ritual's design and its liturgical elements remained unchanged until the end of the Suharto era. Though the ceremonial itself appeared to be rather unpretentious, it gained increasing ritual importance, as Purdy notes in her analysis of this memorial observation. Over the years a growing number of government functionaries and high-ranking generals took part in the event. The authorities commanded representatives of an expanding spectrum of societal groups and parties, as well as of scouts', women's, and veterans' associations to participate in the ceremony at Lubang Buaya (Purdy 1984: 239).

[31] Yani and his comrades are the "sacrifice" that had to be made to salvage the very foundation of the state, the Pancasila. They heroically gave their life for the common cause.

[32] "Memory needs a place, a context." (Kenny 1999: 421). According to his conclusion the places of memory are the "interface between individual and collective memory".

Material Witnesses: Photographs and the Making of *Reformasi* Memory[1]

KAREN STRASSLER

When a severe economic crisis hit Indonesia in 1997, students began agitating for lowered prices, an end to corruption, and democratic reforms. As the crisis deepened and the movement gained force in 1998, students took to the streets at universities across Indonesia, braving increasingly severe military and police repression. Their movement coalesced around a single goal: bringing an end to Suharto's 32-year authoritarian regime, the New Order. In mid-May four students were shot to death by military troops on the campus of Trisakti University in Jakarta. The deadly and destructive rioting that ensued was the final blow to Suharto, who announced his resignation on 21 May 1998. Images of student protests throughout that turbulent period gave the term *reformasi* global currency and powerfully shaped public opinion within Indonesia. As the writer Goenawan Mohamad has commented, "Suharto was brought down by the photograph" (Personal communication, 9 July 2001).

In a gesture of his commitment to reform, one of President Habibie's first acts after Suharto stepped down was to relax press controls, releasing a flood of reformasi images into the public domain in the form of television and newspaper pictures, visual chronicles of reformasi, calendars, and exhibitions of journalistic photographs. Book publishing boomed, and hundreds of new tabloids competed for attention, often using sensational photographs as a draw.[2] At bookstores and news magazine stands, tight circles of students thirstily read publications they couldn't afford to buy. Stirring images of students — some joined in defiant protest, some cringing from police blows — were hailed as "witnesses of history" (*saksi sejarah*). In this essay, I look at the "social life" (Appadurai

278

1986) of these reformasi images in the transition period of B.J. Habibie's presidency before the selection in October 1999 of Abdurrachman Wahid as Indonesia's fourth president.[3] I examine how nostalgia, amnesia, and mythic historical narrative worked to shape popular memory of reformasi — particularly among students themselves — even as the project of reformasi remained unfinished.

An intention of this article is to point out some of the ways students' historical agency was contained by the very discourses that framed them as heroes of reformasi. These discursive constraints became particularly visible as reformasi was becoming memory, a process significantly mediated by the circulation and consumption of photographic images. This essay's critical perspective on students in the post-Suharto period is in no way meant to belittle their achievements in pushing forward the reform movement. Many limitations of the student movement might be attributed to the characteristic traits of "youth". Like youth activists in other places and times, Indonesian students' daring and passionate involvement was at times limited by naive idealism, self-absorption, and a failure to reflect critically upon their own historical and social location. Coming of age in an exciting moment, students were as concerned with defining themselves as they were committed to effecting change. But in Indonesia, these predictable characteristics of youth activism were compounded by the elitist exclusions built into the very social category of "student" and the systematic depoliticization of students under the New Order regime.

The student movement did not end with Suharto's resignation, and major student protests occurred sporadically well into 1999. But with Suharto gone, students no longer had a common goal behind which to unite. The epicentre of action was moving increasingly off-campus into new arenas: sectarian conflicts in Ambon, freedom movements in Aceh and East Timor, and political campaigning for the 1999 general election. As politics, not moral outrage, increasingly became the order of the day, many students were reluctant to join the fray.[4] Significantly, students and the general public often framed the student movement as a moral rather than a political movement. Their aversion to the "dirty business" of politics was a product, at least in part, of longstanding New Order efforts to "normalize" (depoliticize) university campuses. An image of youth as idealistic, "pure" actors had long been fostered in New Order narratives identifying "youth struggle" (*perjuangan pemuda*) as the motivating force behind Indonesian history.[5]

Reformasi photo exhibitions became extraordinarily popular among students at precisely the moment that the student movement was splintering and losing direction. In the first part of this essay, I argue that exhibitions of photographs mark a shift towards memorializing reformasi. At photography exhibitions, students responded to reformasi images as tokens of their own personal histories, blurring the lines between journalistic and personal genres of photography. Revisiting these images helped confirm students' sense of their own heroic role as makers of history. But while often empowering, this highly personal engagement in historical process could give way to a narcissistic nostalgia. Increasingly, students turned to photographs of their struggle to bring down Suharto as memorials to their (already past) moment-in-history. The premature foreclosure of the student movement is both in evidence at, and partially produced by, such events as reformasi photo exhibitions that congealed reformasi as memory.

Circulating ideas about the vulnerability of history to manipulation form a crucial context for the celebration of reformasi images as "witnesses of history" at reformasi photo exhibitions. The public display of formerly taboo images showing student demonstrations and military brutality was enthusiastically hailed as a sign of the achievement of reformasi and a new era of transparency. The accumulation of photographic witnesses as historical "proofs", students suggested, would preempt future attempts to distort or erase the history of their movement. Student desire to collect and re-witness images of reformasi also spoke to a utopian ideal of popular participation in an inclusive, public archive, a fantasy that history might no longer be monopolized by the powerful but open to all.

But this faith in photographs as an answer to historical distortion and erasure was itself based on an act of forgetting. In the second part of the essay, I juxtapose the reform-era reception of photographs with the production and display of journalistic and student images in the early New Order, a period of transition whose similarities to the reformasi period often went unremarked. During the New Order, photographic "witnessing" was employed — in photo exhibitions, films, school textbook illustrations, and museum displays — as a device to achieve popular acquiescence to official versions of history, and images of student protest were co-opted into signs of support for the regime. Amnesia about the use of photographic images to fashion New Order versions of historical events perpetuated an unexamined continuity with New Order ideologies and historiographic practices. As students at reformasi exhibitions fetishized the photographic document as the locus of historical truth, they bypassed important questions about the contexts of image production and consumption and about the extent to which images of "their own" struggle might be framed within historical narratives not of their own making.

Indeed, as they were collected and displayed by state institutions, reformasi images were increasingly incorporated into a mythic history of "youth struggle". In the third part of this essay, I examine contemporary state efforts to archive and display reformasi images. In gathering reformasi images, these state institutions claimed their authoritative role as the guardians of national memory. Now firmly situated in national rather than personal memory, reformasi images were incorporated into a dominant nationalist narrative that constructs youth as an ahistorical subject who will rise up in moral outrage at times of crisis only to retreat when a proper political authority has been restored. As students revelled in their heroism captured in these photographs, the fact that reformasi was being conflated with the student movement of 1998 and thus significantly narrowed in its scope tended to escape notice. The wide currency of this heroic nationalist narrative may have contributed to the narrowed sense of possibility for political action and the rapidity with which students consigned their own historical agency to the past.

Student Protest, Gadjah Mada University, March 1998 (photo by R.A.B. Widjanarko).

Students burn Suharto in effigy, Gadjah Mada University, Yogyakarta, 11 March 1998 (photo by Danu Kusworo).

The Photograph as Material Witness

In the popular language surrounding reformasi photographs in Indonesia, the images themselves, as well as their makers, were called "witnesses of history" (*saksi sejarah*), a term that captures both the moral efficacy of photographs and a problematic tendency to treat them as if they were independent from their conditions of production and consumption. Pulled from the daily flow of images whose significance is only momentary and put on display in public exhibitions, journalistic photographs cease to function as "news". They become memorials. Barthes (1981) argued that in the modern age, the photograph had replaced the monument as the ultimate commemorator of the past. Modern society had made "the (mortal) photograph into the general and somehow natural witness of 'what has been'" (Barthes 1981: 93).[6] If Barthes points to the photograph's fit with the temporal experience of modernity, one might also look to questions of scale and authenticity. The miniature size of the photograph, an object that can move fluidly in and out of private and public spheres, also makes it a memorial object suited to a modern notion of history made and authenticated by ordinary people.

It is a commonplace that the photograph is privileged as historical evidence because of its ideological construction as an "objective", mechanical recorder of reality (Tagg 1988). This ideological construction, in turn, is based on the photographic sign's indexicality, the physical connection that appears to efface the gap between an event and its photographic representation (Barthes 1981, among others). But the idea of the photographic witness so prevalent in Indonesia also suggests that the photographic image preserves and embodies the subjective act and moral force of seeing. A witness is an agent who in the act of observing becomes charged with the authority and obligation to bear witness to others. The photographic witness enables an act of seeing, located in a particular time and place, to be extended and collectivized by means of a material trace. In Scott McQuire's phrase, the camera "functions as a space-time machine capable of instantiating a potentially infinite chain of eye-witnesses" (McQuire 1998:133). As a visitor to an exhibition of reformasi images in Yogyakarta noted in a written comment addressed to the photographer, "your witnessing has become our witnessing".

The prevalence of this trope of the photographic witness illuminates some of the complexity of image consumption in Indonesia during the reformasi period. The idea of the photograph as a witness that produces new witnesses among its viewers suggests photography's capacity to gene-rate an interpretive community grounded in a common visual vocabulary and sharing an engaged and moral stance towards historical process. The emphasis on witnessing further resonates with a desire for historical narratives to be anchored in self-authenticating proof, rather than propagandistic claims and obfuscating monuments (Barthes 1981: 87).

However, the idea of the photographic witness also treats the photograph itself as a self-contained agent of history, suggesting that its ability to bear witness is untouched by its conditions of production and the interpretive contexts of its consumption. The absence of the photographer in the photograph — the invisibility of the intentioned agent — allows the photograph to be seen as a condensation of a "look" without problematizing the conditions of that act of seeing.

Consuming Images, Remembering *Reformasi*

The photos are amazing, for memory and as historical proof. (*Foto-Foto hebat, buat kenangan dan bukti sejarah*)

— Kiswanto, from the comment book at the "My Witnessing" exhibition, February 1999

In "Understanding a Photograph", John Berger (1991) put forward a model for a way of reading journalistic photographs that would promote an ethical engagement with history. Responding to critics like Susan Sontag (1977) who argued that photographs foster a distanced relation to the past, Berger (1991: 54) contrasted public images — which he called "dead objects", decontextualized and discontinuous with the spectator's experience — with private, personal images. Personal images, he argued, are not "dead objects" because memory provides a rich and connected context for them, embedding spectator and image in the same historical and social field. In students' responses to reformasi images as tokens of their own histories, there is a powerful sense of agency and engagement, a collective connectedness akin to the kind of "social memory" Berger envisioned might ideally animate otherwise "dead" images of public events. For students, there was no clear divide between the public historical and the personal value of these images. Students' fascination with images of "their own" struggle was not surprising, but its effects were significant. In recycling images from the "glory days" of their struggle, students were increasingly relegating their history-making to a nostalgically recalled past.

Images of reformasi were always in high demand among students. Well before the relaxation of press freedoms, photographs taken by student photographers at demonstrations had circulated informally among students.[7] Often students who saw themselves in other students' photographs would ask for copies, and some student photographers sold their photos to other students as souvenirs. Enterprising student photographers even made holiday greeting cards from reformasi photographs by selling them to their peers on campus. With the new climate of openness under President Habibie, exhibitions of student and press photography could be held in public places, and these were always heavily attended by students. Students from 24 colleges and universities, for example, put on a joint exhibition called "Exhibition of Indonesian Student Photographs: Witnesses of the Action 1998" (*Pameran Foto Mahasiswa Indonesia: Saksi Seputar Aksi 1998*), that travelled from Jakarta to Yogyakarta in December 1998 and then on to other cities.[8] Film footage shot by students was also shown at the exhibition. Thousands crowded in to see it during its four-day stay in Yogyakarta.

The press at this time was also actively promoting its newly invigorated role as archive of public memory, sponsoring exhibitions, and publishing calendars and chronicles of reformasi. In February 1999, a young photo-journalist named Eko Boediantoro at the local Yogyakarta newspaper *Kedaulatan Rakyat* exhibited 80 of his photographs.[9] The title of the exhibition, "My Witnessing" (*Kesaksianku*), emphasized the personal nature of witnessing and, at the same time, conflated the subjective act of witnessing with the photographs themselves.[10] The flyer for the exhibition noted that at the time the photographs were taken, the press was still heavily censored. Many could not be published and so "only entered into (his) private documentation". The idea of formerly secreted truths newly made public was a common trope of the reformasi period, heard often in cases of political figures offering new accounts of controversial historical events. In this case the idea of first-time public exposure served to establish the photo exhibition itself as a sign of the achievement of reformasi.

Two months later, journalists from Yogyakarta and Solo curated an exhibition, called "Presenting Three Orders of Yogyakarta-Solo Photo-journalists" (10–18 April 1999), which contained photographs by both students and journalists. The exhibition displayed photographs from the "three orders" of postcolonial Indonesian history: Soekarno's Old Order, Suharto's New Order, and the Reformasi era. Its advertising again promised that some of these photographs had never before been shown in public. As one organizer of the exhibition told me, by showing "these historical witnessings ... we want to reopen the album of history." The flyer notes the photographers' sense of their historic mission:

> ... in the midst of the stinging smell of tear gas and the sound of guns
> firing, we increasingly became aware that event after event of the recent
> days were part of an historical process that it was important to record.
> We, with students and other members of society, have become witnesses
> who record the historical course of the nation.

An overwhelming proportion of the images were photographs from the
reformasi period. But if the present seemed to dwarf the past, the inclusion
of "historical" photographs in the Three Orders exhibition served, also,
to frame reformasi as (already) an historical period, a present already
anticipating its own closure.

At both the "My Witnessing" and "Three Orders" exhibitions, crowds
pressed into the narrow spaces of the galleries night after night. While
members of the general public — including families with small children
— did come to these exhibitions, by far most of those attending were
university students. Thousands took the time to fill out the comment
books left open on tables, an indication in itself of their enthusiasm and
engagement with the images on display. By inviting people to contribute
their comments, the books made viewing the exhibition a collective project, reinforcing a sense of community forming around the images. Like
the exhibitions themselves, the books, too, are collections of "witnessings"
— signs of a widespread desire to participate, to bear witness, to be part
of history. Full of impressionistic jottings written in the informal tone
and slang-filled language of students, the comment books read like an
intimate, informal dialogue among peers.

Many of the comments in the books stress the importance of the
photographs as "witnesses" (*saksi*) and "authentic evidence" (*bukti otentik*)
of history. "Have these exhibitions often, so that the history of the people
of Indonesia will no longer be monopolized" (*Sering-2 dibikin biar
bangsa Indonesia tidak dimonopoli lagi sejarahnya*), wrote Ko Hue at the
"Three Orders" exhibition. "Witnessing that can't be denied by those in
power" (*Kesaksian yg tak bisa dipungkiri penguasa*), wrote Ato Suprapto.
Others wrote that "photographs don't lie", and, simply, "this is the
truth." Echoing these sentiments, alongside the photographs at the "My
Witnessing" exhibition hung a large framed, handwritten message from
Yogyakarta's Sultan, a prominent figure in the reformasi movement:[11]

> These photographs are witnesses of what happened. They are authentic
> proof (*bukti otentik*) that cannot be denied. Changes have taken place.

Reform. The era has already changed to become the era of reform. Long live Reform.

Hamengkubuwono X. 8 February 1999

That so many people would respond to reformasi photographs as "visual facts" is unsurprising given the global currency of ideologies of photographic truth. But emphasis on the value of "authentic proof" (*bukti otentik*) also indexed a growing popular perception of the New Order as a regime built on historical distortion and the manipulation of evidence. As historical controversies, most notably the case of *Supersemar* (the founding document of the New Order),[12] began to tumble onto newspaper pages day after day in the period following Suharto's resignation, the idea that proper documentation was the key to ensuring an accurate historical record was heard in many domains. And, as student photographers emphasized to me, the photographic image was often held to be inherently less vulnerable to manipulation — more reliable — than written words.[13]

If many students commented on the historical value of the photographs, the pleasure in visiting the exhibitions seemed to be in confirming their own place in that history. Going to the exhibition was, for students, a bit like opening up a personal photo album. Over and over again in the comment books, students expressed satisfaction in seeing their own image, or took the opportunity to assert that their image was included. "Hello 'brother journalist', thanks truly, 'cuz I was photo-ed!" (*Hello "bung wartawan" makasih tenang gue dipoto*) wrote one Wewe, at the "Three Orders" exhibition. Others jokingly expressed disappointment at their exclusion: "Good, but how come there's no picture of me?" (*Bagus, tapi ... kok foto gue nggak ada sih?*), wrote Lya, at the same event. Such comments, though humourous in tone, indicate a desire to be recognized as participants in reformasi through inclusion in this archive of images. Some described personal memories triggered by the photographs, asserting their own acts of witnessing. "Good, makes me remember my motorcycle that was trashed & when I fell off and I was beaten up! Please show these photos to the military" (*Bagus jadi ingat motorku yg rusak & waktu jatuh trus degebukin! tolong photo2nya dipamerin buat bapak2 ABRI*), wrote Sandra at "Three Orders".

Just as students wished to find themselves in the images, so they often expressed a desire to possess them for themselves. "Wanna take home all the photos" (*pingin ngambil semua tuh fotonya*), wrote Fatur, at "Three Orders". "If possible, we want to ask for a photo as a souvenir" (*Kalau boleh mau diminta fotonya buat kenangan*), wrote Wid and Sri, at "My Witnessing".[14] Students also expressed concern for the future safekeeping of this archive of images. "Wow ... really cool ... I ask that no matter what, don't let these be lost, they're all for tomorrow, for our grandchildren. Cool. Thanks" (*Wu ... keren tu ... gue pesen pokoknya jangan nyampe ilang itu semua buat besok anak cucu kite! oke!!! tanks!*), wrote Asep at the "Three Orders" exhibition. "Every photo invites our memories about the times that later can be recounted again to our grandchildren!" (*Setiap foto mengundang ingatan kita akan masa-masa yang nantinya bisa diceritakan kembali pada anak-cucu kami!*), wrote Didik and Anton also at the "Three Orders" exhibition. "The photos are great, save them well for our grandchildren, OK?" (*Foto-fotonya bagus-bagus, disimpen ya buat anak cucu kita!*), wrote "QQ" at "My Witnessing". The repeated use of the idiom "for our grand-children" may be just a cliché, a way of talking about the future. But, in placing the images in an imagined familial context, it also expressed the idea that what was at stake in preserving these images was not only the history of the nation, but students' personal memories as well.

Many comments expressed nostalgia for the sense of purpose and solidarity that had accompanied the reform movement up until Suharto's fall: "Reminds me of when together we became makers of history " (*Jadi inget saat itu bersama-sama kita menjadi pelaku sejarah*), wrote Heni Widi, at the "My Witnessing" exhibition. Others wrote of being "moved", "wanting to cry," "being reminded", and of "nostalgia for the student struggle". If nostalgia for momentous events in which one has participated — not to mention for one's school days — is not unique to Indonesian students, what was perhaps surprising was how quickly it became the dominant mood. The charged and crowded space of the exhibition halls allowed students to experience (once again) the thrill of being part of a collectivity. But dialogues among students were more oriented to revisiting the past than shaping the future. Informal, moderated discussions at photo exhibitions and video screenings were opportunities for photographers to describe their experiences at demonstrations, and for students to add their own stories. These eyewitness accounts were offered, as students often put it, "to complete" the picture provided by the photographer (or videographer).

Despite the lauding of reformasi images as "proof", there were, in fact, numerous complaints among students that the representation of reformasi in the exhibitions did not show the full or "complete" (*lengkap*) reality. In fact, the Sultan (who had celebrated the exhibition as 'authentic proof' of reformasi) actually had a role in crafting the content of the "My Witnessing" exhibition. The Sultan had asked Eko Boediantoro, the photographer, not to show too many pictures of rioting and violence so that if "the public" (*masyarakat*) saw the images they would not "misunderstand" the true meaning of reform.[15] Thus, as the exhibition director explained, images of peaceful student protest predominated.[16] In the comment books, some students complained that the photographs exhibited were not as "harsh" (*keras*) and "daring" (*berani*) as the photographs displayed at exhibitions showing exclusively the work of student photographers. One young woman observed to me that these images were "already ordinary" because they were no different from those in newspapers and did not "show the violence". Student activists complained that it presented too sanitized a vision of reformasi, in particular because it only showed conflicts between the police and the students, "and not a single photo that records the behavior of the army" (Sebayang 1999).[17]

These critiques and the outpourings of student memories at discussions of reformasi photo exhibitions might suggest a resistance to the reduction of the experience of reformasi to its photographic traces, a sense that the image could not, after all, stand alone as a "witness", unattached to narratives and actors. Yet this urge "to complete" the picture seemed often to entail a faith in the *potential* for an adequate documentary record. It was as if one could compile all of the subjective acts of seeing into one publicly affirmed, collective archive of reformasi witnessings. Rarely was the ideal of "completeness" itself in question. The comments of a moderator at a discussion (following a showing of video footage of a demonstration) exemplify this desire for an inclusive public archive — an expanded historical "album":

> This video, this witnessing (because this is a witnessing), is only from one set of eyes. That has to be stressed. There are still many witnessings that have to be witnessed, many students from Gadjah Mada University, from Atmajaya University, from the Indonesian Art Institute ... it will be richer, and the public will know more, if we are open to other witnessings too.

The desire to collect these witnessings was, in part, a healthy reaction against state monopolies on the making of history and skepticism towards the mainstream press's commitment to handling sensitive material. Yet the emphasis on collecting *student* witnessings carried its own exclusivity, implicitly denying that there could be other sites of history making and other agents of reformasi. Despite the critique of the exhibitions' narrow depiction of reformasi, moreover, students rarely questioned the status of the photograph itself as "proof". The celebration of these photographs as "witnesses of history" that would ensure that their acts of heroism would be remembered was, in fact, based on a collective forgetting of the contentious use of photographs — including photographs of and by students — to support the very New Order historical accounts students had learned in school and were now learning to question.

Forgotten Histories

Students' faith that photographic witnesses would tell the truth of their history was predicated on amnesia about the extent to which images of

Textbook illustration, "Tritura" (People's Three Demands) demonstration, January 1966.

student struggle and ideologies of photographic truth had been mobilized during the New Order. In 1965–8 as in 1998–9, photographs played a significant role in generating collective memories of a dramatic political transition. Documentary "evidence" of communist violence was used to cultivate shared sentiments of outrage and terror, while images of "student struggle" provided proof of popular support for the New Order regime.[18] The display of violent images would be an enduring tactic of the New Order in its efforts to instill particular kinds of memories of national history.

Clearly there are significant differences between the photography of 1965–6 and that of the reformasi period, differences that were rightly celebrated in students' enthusiasm for gathering an inclusive archive of photographs of their movement. Limitations on who could photograph and the extent of control over the production and distribution of images were certainly far greater in the early New Order — in part because of the scarcity of photography and other image-making technologies and in part because of extreme conditions of terror. The extent and efficacy of state control over images and information marks a profound difference between the transition period of the mid-1960s and that of the late 1990s. But beyond the obvious contrasts were less recognized similarities in the use of images and the ideologies of photographic truth that underlay them.

Alongside the photographs of reformasi at the "Three Orders" exhibition were a number of photographs taken by journalists in 1965–6. One of these showed a group of women stomping on a communist symbol taped to a tile floor. The photograph documents an event held for women in a town near Klaten, at which they received "information" from an army officer clearly intended to generate group anti-communist sentiment. Organized public events, including photograph exhibitions and film screenings, were important propaganda tools for various groups in the early New Order period.[19] As early as November 1965, there were showings of documentary films put on by the state. In Yogyakarta, a documentary film of the burial of the generals killed in the alleged coup attempt was shown, and the press urged that "this film should be witnessed by every loyal Pancasila-ist" (*Kedaulatan Rakyat*, 27 November 1965, "Film Indonesia").[20] An exhibition in celebration of Independence Day in 1967 sponsored by the military and the government displayed photographs alongside bloody articles of clothing — indexical signs of traitorous violence allegedly perpetrated by the communists. An article paraphrases a speech by a military officer:

> [The exhibition] gave the greatest of stimuli to every visitor by displaying the photos of the Revolutionary Heroes who were killed in a cruel way at Lubang Buaja and the shirt of the late General Yani soaked in blood. From the photos and the shirt it is hoped will come the awareness to always be on the watch (*waspada*) for the remnants of G30S/PKI who it is clear have become our enemies. (*Kedaulatan Rakyat*, 22 August 1967, "Pameran ABRI").[21]

In addition to such explicitly state-sponsored displays of documentary images were exhibitions sponsored by journalist and student groups. One of the early promises of the New Order was the restoration of freedom of the press, a promise that helped secure support for the new regime among many students and intellectuals. But the so-called honeymoon between the press and the government was achieved through the purging of "communists" from the ranks of the PWI (*Perhimpunan Wartawan Indonesia*, the Association of Indonesian Journalists) and by the closing of leftist newspapers (See *Kedaulatan Rakyat*, 16 October 1965, "PWI petjat"; 11 November 1965 "Gestapu"; 11 December 1965, "PWI Jogja"). Nevertheless, photo exhibitions of the early New Order were often hailed as signs of a new climate of openness and political freedom. In 1967, the Yogyakarta newspaper *Kedaulatan Rakyat* sponsored a large exhibition on the press as an institution (*Kedaulatan Rakyat*, 14 August 1967, "Pameran"; 16 August 1967, "Pameran"). Articles about the exhibition describe crowds eagerly filling out comment books in an atmosphere of excitement about a new era of openness and transparency. A visitor's comment reproduced in the newspaper echoes commentaries written at reformasi exhibitions: "The *KR* exhibition ... succeeds in providing to the public historical content that is pure (*murni*), so that the people will not any longer be kept in the dark (*diabui*) by two-faced leaders."[22] Also quoted is a speech by Samawi, the head of *Kedaulatan Rakyat*, labelling Soekarno's dictatorial Guided Democracy a "dark age for the Indonesian press" and proclaiming that "freedom of thought, freedom of speech, and freedom of writing have become the slogans of the people and the Government".[23]

In May of 1966, the anti-communist student group KAMI (*Kesatuan Aksi Mahasiswa Indonesia*, or Indonesian University Students Action

Front), together with the Yogyakarta branch of the PWI, put on an exhibition displaying photographs of their "struggle ... to uphold justice and truth" (*Kedaulatan Rakyat*, 27 May 1966, "Pameran photo").[24] An article about this exhibition ran the headline, "Looking at the Photo Exhibition, Youth Are Spurred on by History" (*Kedaulatan Rakyat*, 30 May 1966, "Melihat"). It reported that the photo exhibition received "great attention from the public, such that the exhibition space was packed," and noted that "the photographs picture the actions of KAPPI (*Kesatuan Aksi Pelajar-Pelajar Indonesia*, Indonesian Students' Action Front)-KAMI to defend truth and justice which began on January 10, 1966 ... all over Indonesia." The polemical nature of the exhibition is indicated by the quotation of a caption placed under a photograph, which reads, "We can't be disbanded, because history is in our camp" (*kami tidak bisa dibubarkan, karena sedjarah sedang singgah ke kemah kami*).[25] The article also quotes a local visitor to the exhibition, described as "riveted looking at a photograph," commenting: "For a long time I have been struck by an image ... the jacket of Rachman Hakim[26] soaked in blood. These photographs truly speak to us so that we know the struggle of KAPPI-KAMI." This sense of historic import and of images that "speak to" viewers, interpellating them as witnesses and generating highly personal and charged reactions, parallels the atmosphere of the photo exhibitions of 1999.

Exhibitions sponsored by student groups appear to have taken place throughout the early years of the New Order.[27] But while photographs of (and sometimes by) anti-communist students and journalists survived to bear witness to history, those by student photographers on the wrong side of the political fence never entered the public archive. Djoko Pekik, today one of Indonesia's most prominent painters, was a student photographer in the early 1960s. But in 1966, when he was arrested, he lost everything — his cameras and his film, along with all of his papers and belongings:

> The police took it all, I was left with a pair of pants and one shirt, for seven years. Everything was taken, all my film and photos, and I had a lot of documentation. My photos of the demonstrations of that time are all lost.

Even had the police left his belongings alone, he added, his own family would probably have destroyed his photographs once he was arrested:

"Then no one was brave enough to save anything. If you had the (communist) newspaper *Harian Rakyat*, or books that smelled of the communist party, or photographs of Gerwani they were all thrown away, burned."[28] The eradication of photographs like Djoko Pekik's helped pave the way for the New Order use of images of "youth" demonstrators. Images of "student struggle" were co-opted into generalized signs of support for the New Order regime, erasing the complexity and internal divisions within the history of student activism.

Most of the photographs from the early months of the New Order displayed at the "Three Orders" exhibition were taken by a veteran *Kedaulatan Rakyat* photojournalist, Moelyono. The "history" of these images offered by the exhibition literature was that they had never before been shown publicly; they had remained within the photographer's "private collection". Once again, their covert survival in private hands seemed to provide a kind of political alibi, as if attesting to their opposi- tional authenticity. Like the display of reformasi images formerly too explosive to show publicly, the emergence of these once suppressed images was an affirmation that reformasi itself had been achieved. (In fact, only a few of the images had not been published at the time they were made). There was another history to which the exhibition literature offered no reference: the actual conditions of the images' production.

Moelyono's photographs helped shape a particular vision of the local eradication of communists during the first months of the New Order. But viewers of the exhibition seemed content to view them as "witnesses of history" divorced from the agency of the person who made them; when Moelyono was invited to speak about his experiences as a photographer during the turbulent period of 1965–6 at a discussion of the "Three Orders" exhibition, oblivious and obviously uninterested students talked so loudly to each other that the moderator asking Moelyono questions finally gave up. Moelyono's own status as a witness was over- looked, and the troubling things he had to say about the manufacture of photographic proof went unattended.

My subsequent interviews with Moelyono indicated the extent to which the production and circulation of his images were carefully con- trolled and strategically used by the military.[29] A photojournalist who began his career in the early 1960s, Moelyono described in great detail his sojourn as a reporter accompanying the military as it searched out, captured, and killed communists in the region of Klaten (about 15 miles from Yogyakarta), a stronghold of communist sympathy. Listening to Moelyono tell of these experiences as we sat in the fading light in the front room of his small home, I was struck by the incongruity of the peaceful setting of our interview with the violent memories he calmly recounted. Moelyono's house is nestled at the end of a narrow alley within the old walls of the *kraton* (Sultan's palace), a quiet neighbourhood of whitewashed houses and graceful pavilions. A slender, agile man in his early 60s, Moelyono is a devotee of traditional Javanese dance and often dances the *halus* ("refined") male roles with a local troupe. A gentle breeze wafted through the open door bringing the smell of frying garlic, shallots and coriander, and the sound of *gamelan* music from a neighbour's radio. His two-year-old granddaughter toddled unsteadily in and out of the room, as he told about how he had become accustomed to the sight of human slaughter: "at first, when I saw the blood flowing I was often afraid, the feeling was like ... what? Yeah, it made me feel sick, but after reporting the events for a while it became normal, because almost every day I saw blood flowing ...."

When it came to coverage of the military's campaign to wipe out communists in late 1965, the press was brought tightly under the control of military commanders.[30] Only certain journalists were "invited" to cover the military campaign to eradicate communists from Klaten at the end of 1965. Because of the alleged danger in the area, the journalists were not allowed to travel unescorted by the military. For three months, Moelyono lived with the army in Klaten, returning to Yogyakarta weekly in order to print his photographs in his darkroom at home and submit those that were to be published to the editorial office at *Kedaulatan Rakyat*. He was driven back and forth to Yogyakarta in a military car and accompanied by a member of the military police, who would wait at his home while he printed his photographs and would review them when they were done. The military command in Yogyakarta often asked for his film in order to print their own copies of the photographs for their archives. Usually his negatives were returned, he recalled, but occasionally they too would be kept.

Moelyono initially told me that there were no restrictions on what he could photograph. But as our conversations progressed it became clear that this was not the case. Sometimes he would be directed to take a particular photograph for publication in the newspaper. An example he mentioned was a photograph of the excavation of a mass grave of 25

Two dead Pemuda Rakyat (People's Youth), Klaten area, 1965 (photo by Moelyono).

people (allegedly) killed by the communists in Klaten, an image clearly intended to legitimize retaliatory violence against communists.[31] Other pictures showing captured communists almost always included a gun-wielding soldier in clear control. Recalling the soldier's pleasure at being photographed thus, Moelyono told me, "the soldier would even take on a pose!" Certain scenes that were too "sadistic" could not be shown: "you were allowed to photograph it, but the photo and the negative would right away be asked for". One could photograph a corpse, but not the act of killing:

> So it was like this, if there was a prominent PKI (Communist Party) figure who was captured, if he was a prominent figure, that is, ... he would be straightaway killed, the killing would be at the river, the river that doesn't have any water ... When Battalion F did the killing it was there, but the killing wasn't allowed to be photographed ... Not allowed, but after they were corpses, then photographing was allowed.

If one did photograph a corpse, the face could not be visible. Pointing out a photograph of two dead members of the People's Youth

(*Pemuda Rakyat*), Moelyono told me that he had witnessed these young men being shot as they tried to escape capture.[32] They had been shot separately, but their bodies were arranged together for the photograph. "Their faces weren't allowed to be shown. I don't know why, I guess it was a military secret." This was one of the photographs displayed at the "Three Orders" exhibition in 1999. Its presentation there as documentary evidence elided the fact that it was a constructed image made through negotiation with military command.

At the exhibition, pre-reformasi historical photographs seemed less compelling to spectators than the reformasi images. Moelyono himself expressed annoyance that the exhibition was so heavily weighted toward the present and that students were so historically myopic: "The things you already know, what's the use? If I've seen the event myself, (and) then I'm asked to look at the photograph, there's no point."[33] Beside the fact that most visitors to the exhibition were more interested in their own historical moment, images like that of the two dead People's Youth members perhaps caused little reaction in part because they are images of violence that manage not to be particularly disturbing. As Moelyono pointed out, the faces of the young men are concealed; without their faces, they are less "recognizable" as human beings, less available for identification in all senses of that word. Their bodies are shown in an almost graceful tangle on the ground as mere objects, signs of death. The closely cropped image seems to cut out all context, making the photograph itself, to borrow Berger's phrase, a "dead object". Except for what look like ropes around the wrist of one of the young men, there is nothing to suggest the circumstances of their killing. The image thus lends itself to incorporation into whatever narrative offered to explain their deaths — whether a story about communist betrayal or a story about New Order violence. In Barthes' terms, the image is all *studium*, all easily-read surface, there is no *punctum*, no unanticipated "prick" to rouse the viewer.[34]

The photograph by Moelyono that drew the most attention at the exhibition was an image that was taken before the eruption of violence in 1965. This is the picture: a group of young people at a mass rally for the Indonesian Communist Party in 1965 on the *alun-alun* (the large square field in front of the Sultan's palace) in Yogyakarta. The orator is outside the frame; one sees only the crowds of seated listeners who appear to be casually enjoying themselves, as if at a big picnic. The

Communist Party rally, Yogyakarta, 1965 (photo by Moelyono).

picture was taken at a distance, the young enthusiasts are small, but
their expressions are clear. In the centre of the photograph is a young
woman, probably a teenager, who has turned her head sideways so that
she happens to face the camera. She is laughing. Her hair is well-combed,
she is dressed stylishly and neatly. Her face is, in a word, lovely. Around
her are other young men and women, similarly conveying the health
and optimism of youth. There is nothing sinister in this photograph,
nothing that would conform to the evil image of communists perpetuated
by the New Order regime, nothing that would suggest the future that
awaits them.

    Many of those who came upon this photograph seemed arrested by
it. I heard some murmur to their companions, "they look so young",
"they're just teenagers", or comment on the girl's beauty. Occasionally
someone would reach up a finger to touch the photograph (the photos
in the exhibition were framed but not behind glass, so the actual surface
of the photograph could be touched) as if they wished to stroke the
girl's face, to make contact.[35] Nor could one look at her face without
wondering what fate had befallen her — even, perhaps, precisely

because she had had the misfortune to appear in this photograph.[36] Sympathy for these innocent youth, so oblivious to their fate, was not particularly radical. The idea that the masses of communist followers "knew nothing" of the maneuvers of elite politicians had become a truism, especially among students. But the strong reaction to the image suggested that it tapped into something deeper, more unexamined, than an accepted position on matters of historical and political debate. Perhaps it was the visual contrast of this young innocent girl with the internalized memory of violent scenes from the state-sponsored film on the "coup" produced in 1985 and obligatorily watched by all school children. How could this sweet girl be reconciled with the scenes of evil and deranged communist women and youth dancing in an orgy of torture at Lubang Buaya?

Or perhaps what troubled people was an unanticipated feeling of recognition. What visitors saw was not just an image that challenged New Order demonization of the Indonesian Communist Party. They saw a reflected image of themselves; they felt, perhaps, a recognition that broke through the "otherness" of the past. The girl is the *punctum* of the image; she draws us in and at the same time takes us beyond the photograph's immediate frame and ostensible documentary message. Her innocent smile is an arresting detail that "pricks" the viewer, not only because it makes one think about her "whole life external to her portrait", but because it triggers a connection that links subject and viewer (Barthes 1981: 57). In the context of the exhibition, dominated by images of the idealistic youth of 1998 she eerily resembled, she breaks through the comfortable deadness of the past. There is no easy way to predict which images have the potential "to destroy the mythic immediacy of the present," but perhaps it is telling that only in unexpectedly "seeing themselves" were students roused to a more provocative engagement with the complex pre-history of their own movement (Susan Buck-Morss 1991: x). The image viscerally, if only momentarily, ruptured the smoothness of a history whose questioning in the moment rarely disturbed the clean membrane between present and past, between "our" history and "theirs".

Archives, Museums, and the Mythic History of Youth Struggle

Amnesia about the history of New Order uses of photographs helped perpetuate a discourse of photographic "witnessing" that elided questions about how the contexts of their production and consumption shape the truths to which photographs attest. Maintaining the "otherness" of the past allowed reformasi-era students to avoid difficult questions about the exclusions built into reformasi images, the narratives into which they might be inserted, and their potential to serve political disenabling rather than empowering ends. If students tended to fixate on their own moment in history, escaping the critical self-reflection that a more profoundly historical perspective might have provoked, those state institutions officially designated guardians of history sought to smooth over the historical specificity of the present, placing it within a teleological narrative that erased historical process and contingency.[37] In displaying reformasi images, state museums incorporated them into a mythic narrative of "youth struggle". Posing as history, this myth helped foster the attitudes of nostalgia and amnesia identified in the previous sections of this paper.

I have suggested that students' desire to attend exhibitions was partly driven by their response to the images as tokens of their own personal pasts, as if the public exhibitions were simultaneously serving as private photograph albums. If students at the photograph exhibitions implored photographers to save "our" photographs for "our grandchildren", through its archival institutions the state asserted its authority to play this preservationist role. In February 2000 a article in *Kedaulatan Rakyat* (15 February 2000, "Foto Reformasi") noted proudly that its journalists' photographs and other reformasi materials were being collected by the local branch of the national archive. The article affirms the discourse of photographs as "authentic proof of history", and figures their archiving as an act of "safekeeping". The documents are "stored neatly and safely", and the National Archive has a "commitment" to ensure that the documents are "guarded" such that there will not be "a historical *link* [original in English] that is lost." The archive stakes its claim as guardian of history from a defensive position for the promise of "safe" storage implicitly responds to widespread public criticism of the manipulation and destruction of state documents in the New Order.[38]

Similarly, Yogyakarta's Benteng Vredeberg Museum, a museum dedicated to the history of the revolution and nationalist "struggle", appealed to the community to turn over any objects of "historical value" from the reformasi period so that they could be properly housed and situated within national history.[39] Museum literature states that it uses photographs to authenticate history and bring students "closer" to historical events. In an internal report on an exhibition about nationalism in 1996, for example, "direct" visual contact with photographs and material artifacts is deemed more effective pedagogically than learning history via words alone:

> Much historical evidence has only been heard or read in history books. Not many of the young generation, in particular students (*siswa*), get to see in a direct way (*secara langsung*) historical evidence like the viola of W.R. Supratman that was used at the time of the Student Oath, or the photograph of General Sudirman inspecting his troops at the Borobudur Temple yard, or medical equipment from the time of the revolution and the like. These historical objects form authentic proof (*bukti otentik*) of the history of the Indonesian national struggle. For without authentic historical evidence, the value of a history will be diminished in terms of its credibility.[40]

Students celebrating reformasi images as "proof" of their struggle were reciting lessons well-taught by state pedagogical institutions, then, even as they expressed new awareness of the dangers of historical manipulation.

Moving out of private hands and into public spaces, photographs of reformasi became material for collective remembering of reformasi. But as they became part of the recognized historical record, they also become available for cooptation into official historical narratives. In state museums and agencies, these photographs were incorporated into a nationalist narrative of "youth struggle", according to which students would rise up in moral indignation, bring about a change in government, and then disappear again out of the fray of politics when a proper authority had been recognized. Museum exhibitions displaying reformasi images subsumed the student movement within this narrative celebrating youth as the heroic vanguard of nationalist struggles, transforming a moment of rupture and a period of instability into the reassuring continuity and inevitability of a mythic narrative.

On 4 November 1999, the Benteng Vredeberg Museum held its annual exhibition commemorating the "Youth Pledge" of 1928 (*Sumpah Pemuda*), a key event in which young nationalists from a variety of regions and groups affirmed the basic principles of the Indonesian nation: one people, one land, one language. A newspaper announcement describes it as an "exhibition of documentation of the milestones of the youth struggle from the period 1908–1998", and urges the heads of schools to "invite their students to witness it" (*Kedaulatan Rakyat*, 4 November 1999, "Pameran dokumentasi"). (When I visited the exhibition on several occasions, groups of school children were the only other visitors.) This exhibition consisted almost entirely of photographs, alongside artifacts like cooking utensils, clothing, swords, typewriters, and furniture that had some connection to particular historical events or figures.

Captions next to the photographs depicting key events of nationalist history recited the familiar narrative of "youth struggle". Included at the end of this exhibition were three significant images. First, an image of the *Malari* student demonstrations in 1974, the first major convulsions of anti-New Order student protest.[41] Next, an image of Sultan Hamengkubuwono X addressing the crowd during the massive peaceful march in Yogyakarta of 20 May 1998, and third, an image of students occupying the People's Consultative Assembly building in Jakarta on 21 May 1998. The inclusion of the Malari image was striking because it would not have been shown during Suharto's rule; its very presence was a sign of reformasi.[42] At the same time, the image helped establish continuity between the student demonstrations of 1966 (also shown in the exhibition) and the student movement of 1998. The final two images tacked the reform movement onto this preexisting narrative. The image of the Sultan reassured viewers that there was a proper authority in control and reinforced a local story that Yogyakarta's "peaceful" reformasi was contingent on the Sultan's authority. The student uprising was figured as an appeal to authorities to listen, not a seizure of power. Similarly, the final image of the students triumphantly occupying the People's Consultative Assembly building implied that this climax of the student movement was also its appropriate end; by gaining entry to the People's Consultative Assembly building they had gained the ear of the established political centre.

When I asked a staff member, Suryanto Pamuji, about the exhibition, he recounted to me (in the language and tone he might have used to speak to the groups of schoolchildren he guides through the museum) the familiar story of "youth" in Indonesian history. His telling incorporated the reform movement almost seamlessly into this well-rehearsed script. He began by asserting that "the youth have a role that is very important in determining the course of the national struggle." Next he traced the key moments in nationalist history from Budi Oetomo in 1908,[43] to the Youth Pledge of 1928, to the declaration of Independence on 17 August 1945, to the Revolution. He then recounted the New Order project of "giving substance to freedom" (*mengisi kemerdekaan*) through development as the next phase of youth struggle. But, he said,

> In that development there were also shortcomings ... right? So therefore the youth also straighten out those shortcomings. Like what happened recently with total reform from the youth and the students, who asked for there to be total reform. Because they considered the government wasn't straight, wasn't right. So with the youth united and helped by the students and helped by the other members of society, finally there was total reform, with demonstrations, because demonstrations are part of democracy ... are they not? Finally it all took place smoothly (*Akhirnya semua terlaksana dengan baik*).[44]

His narrative epitomizes the containing effect of this mythic story of youth struggle. A narrative of nationalist progress that begins in 1908 concludes reasonably with the reform movement of 1998, which is depicted as a "straightening out", a correction of "shortcomings", rather than a radical break of any kind. The only hint of hesitation lies in his rhetorical questions ("right?"; "are they not?") that seek my agreement.

It is notable, however, that in his telling Suryanto Pamuji chose to skip entirely over the student demonstrations of 1966, even though these were visually incorporated into this narrative in the exhibition. He presumably skipped over them in dialogue with me because the entire period of transition to the New Order had become profoundly controversial, such that previously accepted versions of that historical moment were no longer comfortable. To include the 1966 demonstrations in support of the New Order in this narrative of continuity may have seemed contradictory, given that the 1998 student actions were agitating for its demise. Prior to reformasi, the 1966 demonstrations were featured prominently in school texts and museum displays. An internal report on a similar exhibition in 1995, "Portrait of Indonesian Youth in History from 1908–1966", concluded with the student demonstrations of 1966, identifying students as the initiators of the New Order.[45] The report notes that even though the particular challenges faced by youth at various points in time are different, youth possesses a "characteristic dynamic spirit" and "are always visible at the vanguard of every historical event and always emerge in front full of creativity and initiative". Historical contingency and specificity are replaced with a teleological narrative and an essential and monolithic actor: Indonesian youth.

The archiving of reformasi photographs by state institutions frames them within nationalist history (rather than the personal history of students), and the museum exhibitions use these images to support a mythic narrative that constructs "youth" as an ahistorical subject, severing their ties to particular social and political contexts. Signs of student struggle, in line with the narrative scripts of nationalist history, come to stand for a broader historical process that was far more messy, unpredictable and incomplete in its resolution. The broad effects of this narrative, with its elitist emphasis on "pure" youth sacrifice, explain in part why the deaths of four university students in May 1998 evoked so much public mourning in comparison with the more than 1,200 people killed, and the numerous Chinese-Indonesian women raped, during the rioting that followed. Students can be mourned because we already know they are heroes; the deaths of rioters in burning malls and the suffering of rape victims have no place in this narrative, remaining senseless and publicly unmourned. Photographs of students united in protest displayed

Outdoor Exhibition, Yogyakarta, April 1999 (photo by Karen Strassler).

at public exhibitions and in museums helped to repress more disturbing fissures in Indonesian society, and within the student movement, that were becoming particularly visible at precisely the moment that the public was eagerly consuming them.

Conclusion: Signs of Protest

This essay has traced discourses and practices surrounding reformasi images in order to examine how nostalgia, amnesia, and mythic history are giving shape to memories of reformasi, especially among students. I argued that students responded to exhibited reformasi images simultaneously as historical "evidence" and as records of their own personal histories. Their highly personal stake in the historical events of 1998–99, I suggested, was both a measure of students' empowering sense of historical agency and an indication of some of the limitations of their participation in reformasi as an ongoing and socially broad movement. By spring 1999, many students seemed to be more interested in luxuriating in nostalgia for the heroic history of their own struggle than in participating in efforts to reform Indonesian politics and society that were taking place, increasingly, off campus. I also argued that the celebration of reformasi images as "witnesses" and "proof" was in part a product of productive debates underway about the manipulation of history during the New Order. Yet this faith in photographic truth was itself based on collective amnesia about the use of photographic "evidence" to shore up state-controlled historical narratives. Despite important differences between 1965–7 and 1998–9 in terms of the degree of control over the production and circulation of images, the forgotten history of Moelyono's photographs and of student exhibitions in the 1960s suggests a failure among students to grapple in a profound way with the historical (and visual) construction of their own movement. Finally, I argued that reformasi images collected and displayed in state historical institutions were coopted into a dominant New Order narrative of "youth struggle". This narrative works to contain students as historical actors by constructing them as a unified, ahistorical subject, isolated from other significant and potentially allied groups in society.

My argument is not that photographs inherently support nostalgia, amnesia, and mythic historical narratives, although I have shown their participation in this process. If there is a general statement to be made about photography, it is that photographic efficacy has no predetermined effects. Rather, I have hoped to draw out in this analysis of photographic "witnesses of history" their utter dependence on context, their ability to tell different stories and to generate distinctive relationships to historical process. As objects of memory and as historical evidence, photographs of reformasi also remind us of how impossible it is to sustain a romantic notion of popular memory as an oppositional reservoir of alternative historical truths untainted by the ideological effects of official history. Photographs move in complex ways in and out of personal and national realms of significance, simultaneously challenging and supporting received historical narratives and ideologies of historical evidence.

In closing, I want to turn briefly to an effort to use reformasi images as "witnesses of history" that might escape the containing gestures of state historiography and nostalgic recollection. In April 1999, students in Yogyakarta held what they called an "Outdoor Exhibition". In the glaring mid-day heat, students marched through the city carrying blown-up photographs of the student movement taken by students. The photographs, which showed the brutal repression of student protests, were offered as signs of what organizers called, "the New Order culture of violence" (*budaya kekerasan Orba*). Their banners urged people to remember a series of violent events in the distant past and the ongoing present: "Remember: Aceh, Ambon, Tanjung Priok." "Remember, 1965, Malari, East Timor." As they marched, they chanted "Our History is Full of Tears." Using the inclusive form of "our" (*kita*), they sought to connect these images of their own specific history to a broader, shared history of violence.

The students concluded their march at a site that had become a symbol of manipulated state versions of national history, the monument to the revolutionary "General Attack" (*Serangan Umum*) of 1949. Suharto had buttressed his revolutionary credentials by claiming to have initiated and led the famous attack. Before heading back to campus the students unfurled rolled photocopies of the photographs they carried and pasted them to the monument gates, thus marking the gates of official history with images of the student movement intended to expose an entire New Order (military) history of violence. The outdoor exhibition aimed to create a public space — neither the elite spaces of campus and exhibition hall nor the state-controlled spaces of museums and archives — where "history" could circulate and be witnessed. As motorists wearily tolerated the delay and passers-by peered casually at the images, it was difficult to feel that this demonstration was having much impact. Still, the effort itself seemed significant, if not for its immediate effects then for its potential as a moment in which students actualized a broader vision of their own historical agency. I conclude, then, with this small token of possibility: that reformasi images might do more than isolate students within their own mythic history, serving to extend their witnessing to other witnesses, their history to other histories.

Notes

1   Acknowledgements: Thanks are due to Ilana Feldman, Nancy Florida, Carina Frantz, Pamila Gupta, Rachel Heiman, Webb Keane, Laura Kunreuther, Mani Limbert, Brian Mooney, and Geoffrey Robinson for insightful readings of earlier drafts.

2   For example, Yogyakarta's local newspaper *Kedaulatan Rakyat* (1998) published a *Book of Reform Documents* that it advertised as a book "for students and the public who support Reform." A review calls it "a factual portrait of the historical journey of reform of the Indonesian nation. A book that can become a source of authentic data (*data otentik*) for today's generation and the future." There were even reformasi photo contests sponsored by newspapers and other groups (*Bernas*, 21 Apr. 1999).

3   From November 1998 until May 2000 I was living in Yogyakarta, conducting fieldwork for a dissertation on popular photography in urban Java.

4   I speak here primarily of the thousands of students who participated in the demonstrations of 1998 but who were not necessarily activists or student leaders.

5   On relations between the student movement and the military, see Aspinall (1995). Campus "normalization" followed a crackdown on student activism in 1978. For comments on students and reformasi specifically, see Siegel (1998), where he also describes the mythology surrounding "youth" and the elitism of the student movement of 1998 with its profoundly middle class orientation.

6   There is a venerable tradition in various scholarly fields of rejecting photographs as a "replacement" of "true" or authentic memory. I begin from a premise that all remembering is necessarily material, and that the reliance on technologies of memory is not a characteristic of the modern period alone. What is significant, then, is not the fact that people rely on objects to consolidate and recall memories, but the specific qualities and meanings attributed to those objects.

7   While beyond the scope of this essay, it is important to note that many students took part in photographing student demonstrations against the Suharto regime; see Strassler (2003).

8   Numerous exhibitions of reformasi images took place during this period. Two of the most significant were the "09:02:45: Reformasi and Democracy" exhibition at the Antara Gallery in Jakarta in June–July 1998 and, in December 1998, "*Dari Lengser Sampai Semanggi*", sponsored by the newly formed Association of Indonesian Photo Journalists (*Pewarta Foto Indonesia*, PFI) (also at the Antara Gallery).

9   The exhibition was held from 9–14 Feb. 1999. See articles from *Kedaulatan Rakyat*, 5 Feb. 1999, "Kesaksianku"; 11 Feb. 1999, "Pameran"; 14 Feb. 1999, "Fotografi".

10   The suffix *-ku* on the word for "witnessing" is a first person possessive used in informal settings and conversation among intimates.

11   The Sultan was at the time both the Governor of the province of Yogyakarta and the traditional ruler of the region. He was credited with supporting the students, and his charisma and authority were often cited as the reason that protests in Yogyakarta did not degenerate into rioting as they did in the nearby city of Solo.

12   *Supersemar (Surat Perintah Sebelas Maret* — Letter of Instruction of the Eleventh of March) was the founding document of the New Order regime, in which Soekarno signed over authority to Suharto. The original was "lost" and the document presented by the government was of questionable authenticity. (See also G. van Klinken, this volume.) The destruction of records has been a constant theme in reformasi efforts to "straighten out" (*meluruskan*) various historical controversies. For example, materials (i.e. hospital records) that might reveal how many people were actually killed in the Tanjung Priok massacre of Muslim protesters in 1984 in Jakarta, were destroyed. "*Sebagaian dokumen kasus Priok dimusnahkan*", *Kompas*, 8 May 2000.

13   One student commented that he and his friend took photographs because "we have a principle: not all of the news that is written is true." Interview, Fatchul Mu'in, 4 Dec. 1998, Yogyakarta. Another told me, "photographs will always be more like facts, (more able to) prove history: 'the event was really like that'". Interview, Patmawitana, 11 Feb. 1999, Yogyakarta.

14   Some of these comments are joking critiques of the sale of reformasi images for exorbitant prices: "Won't ya give them out for free?" wrote one. Although selling photographs was not a primary goal of the exhibitions and few photographs actually were sold, they were available for purchase for anywhere from $100 to $500 — prohibitively expensive for all but the very wealthiest Indonesians.

15   Interview with Eko Boediantoro, 12 Feb. 1999, Yogyakarta.

16   The Sultan was quoted in a newspaper article about the exhibition saying: "Actually, reform action is not rioting action. These are different and have to be differentiated" (*Kedaulatan Rakyat*, 9 Feb. 1999, "Foto Aksi").

17   Another comment in the "impression" book read: "Congratulations! But where are the ruthless 'green uniforms'?" (*Selamat, tapi mana 'wereng hijau' yang buas?*) — Irfan Afandi, "My Witnessing". Another wrote: "Not sadistic enough! Where are the really horrible ones? Like when I was beaten by six intel (intelligence agents)?" (*Kurang sadis! Sing ngeri-ngeri endi? Koyo pas aku dibut intel 6*) — Keliek, "My Witnessing".

18   An American anthropologist who was in Yogyakarta in 1967 recalls attending a photo exhibition that showed images of dead communist party members and other gruesome scenes of violence (Margot Lyon, personal communication, Yogyakarta, 11 Apr. 2000).

19   The newspaper *Kedaulatan Rakyat* in November and December 1965 articles frequently mentions activities of the "Commando Team for Mental Operations of the Yogyakarta Region" (*Team Kommando Operasi Mental DIJ*), including "information" sessions targeting those considered "at risk" for sympathy with the communists. For a detailed

discussion of anti-communist media and propaganda campaigns in Bali, and nationwide, see Robinson (1995: chapter 11).

20 Pancasila is the official state ideology.

21 Images of the exhumation and descriptions of the murdered officers' allegedly mutilated and tortured bodies were important rhetorical weapons in whipping up mass hysteria and hatred of the communists. Lubang Buaya was the well where the bodies were discarded, and General Yani was one of the murdered officers. G30S/PKI ("The Movement of 30 September/Communist Party of Indonesia") is the acronym by which the coup attempt allegedly orchestrated by the Communists became known. See *Kedaulatan Rakyat*, 18 Aug. 1967, "Pameran ABRI".

22 *Kedaulatan Rakyat*, 16 Aug. 1967.

23 Sri Paku Alam (ruler of Yogyakarta's lesser royal palace) also gave a speech calling on the press to "serve the people". *Kedaulatan Rakyat*, 16 Aug. 1967, "1958–1965, masa suram bagi pers Indonesia".

24 The headline for this article, "KAMI's photography exhibition is not a Show (English in original): Documentation from the Results of their Struggle", emphasizes that this was not "entertainment" (they use the English word "show", perhaps to emphasize a foreign and somewhat corrupt activity) but rather the more sober-sounding "documentation".

25 This statement of refusal to be disbanded may be a reference to Soekarno's ineffectual attempt to disband KAMI in Feb. 1966.

26 Rachman Hakim was a student killed in demonstrations against Soekarno on 24 Feb. 1966.

27 An exhibition of photographs of "Lobang Buaja" sponsored by KAPPI in Medan, Sumatra was held on the one-year anniversary of the alleged communist coup. The exhibition was "an effort to increase the awareness (mental) of the people of Medan in particular towards the cruelty of G30S" (*Kedaulatan Rakyat*, 30 Sept. 1966, "Pameran foto2"). An exhibition in Yogyakarta of photographs and political caricatures was held in June 1967. According to an article about the exhibition, there were 200 photographs exhibited taken by members of KAMI. Images at this exhibition showed, among other events, the "first action of KAMI in Yogyakarta on 7 March 1966" and a parade honouring the fallen student heroes Arief Rachman Hakim and Zubaidah (*Kedaulatan Rakyat*, 26 June 1967, "Pameran foto"). A similar exhibition was held a year later (*Kedaulatan Rakyat*, 24 May 1968, "Pahlawan2"). If members of KAMI were taking and exhibiting photographs, one wonders who supplied cameras, film and money for exhibitions; at the time, the cost of camera ownership and access to supplies was prohibitive, as professional and studio photographers recall.

28 Interview with Djoko Pekik, 21 Feb. 2000, Bantul. Djoko Pekik was imprisoned in 1966 by the New Order for 7 years without trial for being associated with the communist affiliated Institute of People's Culture (*Lembaga Kebudayaan Rakyat, Lekra*).

29 I conducted two formal taped interviews in addition to a number of more informal conversations with Moelyono over a one-year period. Material for the following section is taken primarily from two interviews conducted in Yogyakarta on 5 May 1999 and 6 Apr. 2000.

30 According to Moelyono, even before the events of 30 Sept. 1965, the army had cultivated a close relationship with reporters. In 1964, a special unit of "war journalists" (*Corps Wartawan Perang, CWP*) was formed in Yogyakarta under Colonel Katamso and was called upon for coverage of all army-related events. Although the CWP was disbanded following Katamso's death in 1965, as a former member, Moelyono was chosen to report on the capturing of communists in Klaten in 1965–6 (Interview, 5 May 1999).

31 He may be referring to a photograph that appeared in November of 1965 with the caption, "Eighteen victims of G-30-S dug up in order to be buried properly" attributed to "M/KR" (*Kedaulatan Rakyat*, 16 Nov. 1965).

32 "Shot while trying to escape capture" was a common euphemism for the murder of political prisoners in 1965 as well as during the "Petrus" killings of "criminals" in the early 1980s.

33 Interview with Moelyono, Yogyakarta, 5 May 1999.

34 The studium is the overt message, while the punctum is a "prick" or a "wound", a rupture of the surface message of the image, an accidental detail that "occurs in the field of the photographed thing like a supplement that is at once inevitable and delightful"; Barthes (1981: 47).

35 This physical contact with the photographic surface could also take violent form. At the same exhibition, a close-up photograph of Suharto praying on Idul Fitri 1999 was marked with the pens of visitors who wrote insults and derogatory epithets across his face. Both forms of contact with the image illustrate Benjamin's (1968: 223) famous statement that "everyday the urge grows stronger to get hold of the object at very close range by way of its likeness, its reproduction".

36 When I asked Moelyono about this photograph he told me he actually knew the young woman. She was a neighbor of his, and at the time the photograph was taken was still in junior high school, a member of a student group (IPPI, *Ikatan Pemuda Pelajar Indonesia*) that was "under PKI". He said that "everyone in that family was PKI" and that they were all captured and sent to prison "for years, maybe ten years, they were finally let go around 1975–76" (Interview, Yogyakarta, 6 Apr. 2000).

37 While one should always be wary about treating the state as a monolithic actor, the institutions I discuss in this section were closely supervised and controlled by their counterparts at the "centre" in Jakarta.

38 The "poor image" of the state archives, noted in a newspaper article, was attributed to its "bad quality" administration, lack of funds, and poorly trained personnel (*Kedaulatan Rakyat*, 30 Jan. 2000, "Citra Arsip").

39 The museum, originally a Dutch fort and later a prison, was founded in 1987 as a project of the Department of Education and Culture. In 1998 museum head Drs. Budiharja wrote to his superiors at the Department of Education and Culture that "Museum Benteng Yogyakarta, as one of the organizations given the task of gathering, caring for, studying, and communicating historical materials to the public, hopes that prominent figures (*tokoh*), fighters, leaders of organizations/agencies and the public will give documents, posters, photographs and reformasi banners (*spanduk*) that are still left over and that form authentic evidence of the

unfolding of an event in the historical course of the Indonesian state, in order to become material in the collection of the history of the national struggle" (*"Laporan Survai Pangadaan Koleksi Tahun Anggaran 1998/9"*).

40 *"Laporan Pameran: Dokumentasi Lintasan Sejarah Pergerakan Nasional sampai dengan Orde Baru"*, 14–18 Oct. 1996. The report on this exhibition notes the pedagogical value of "authentic proof" (*bukti otentik*) and "historical evidence" (*bukti-bukti sejarah*) in order to make students and the next generation "value and respect the service of the heroes".

41 *Malari* is an acronym of *"Malapateka Januari"* or "January Disaster", the name given to student demonstrations and riots that greeted the visit of Japan's Prime Minister Tanaka to Indonesia in 1974, which were intended to critique New Order foreign investment policies and perceived elite control of the economy.

42 A staff member of the museum told me that the image of the Malari riots could not previously have been displayed. In the delicate way of cautious bureaucrats, he said that they had had to be "very selective" about what they showed during the New Order (Interview with Suryanto Pamuji, 11 Nov. 1999, Yogyakarta).

43 Budi Oetomo (a proto-nationalist organization founded in 1908) has an enshrined place in nationalist narratives as the origin of the nationalist movement.

44 Interview with Suryanto Pamuji, 11 Nov. 1999, Yogyakarta.

45 From the *"Laporan Pameran"*, for the exhibition held 31 Oct. to 4 Nov. 1995 at Benteng Vredeberg Museum.

Monument, Document and Mass Grave: The Politics of Representing Violence in Bali

DEGUNG SANTIKARMA

Tracing the line of the shore, he crossed over several small rivers, jumping over some, fording others by plunging into the swift current.[1] His steps were heavy, as if it was wearying to slog so slowly over the wet sand. But Pak Nyoman stopped only briefly to wipe his sweat, heading straight for his destination, careful, determined, heart pounding. As he arrived, his face filled with lines of sadness and anger. He stood upright, then threw himself suddenly to the ground. Face down on the dirt, he whispered: "Oh my friends, if it ever becomes possible, I will bring you up from the belly of the earth!"

At first glance, the landscape surrounding him appears abandoned, traceless, covered with wild grasses, and mounds of dirt. It's a quiet place, far from the traffic and crowds, with only the pounding of the waves to break the silence. Nearby stands an old temple, its outer courtyard graced by a *wantilan* pavilion surrounded by coconut palms, a lovely vantage point from which to gaze down at the ocean's edge. Isolated and still, this place is thought eerie by local residents, who avoid coming near it. But should a tourist happen upon it, they would likely think it bore a striking resemblance to the paintings and postcards of idyllic Balinese beauty that are sold in the island's art shops and markets.

For Pak Nyoman, however, this place is far from vacant. Rather than an empty field, it is a field of terror, saturated with memory. It stands as silent witness to a night in late 1965 when Balinese were hauled one by one off trucks and made to stand on the ground. The edge of this land, behind a stand of brush, is where Pak Nyoman hid after fleeing in fear. He heard shots exploding and watched as a squad of Balinese paramilitaries wielding swords herded their victims, hands behind their

312

backs, thumbs tied, to line up before four wide holes that men of the village had been forced to prepare beforehand. By Pak Nyoman's count, around 220 people met their end on this field, under the executioners' deadly command.

With his simple, modest manner, Pak Nyoman doesn't look like someone who was once swept up in the surging storm of national politics. But this humble appearance hides bitter experience. Barely on the threshold of adulthood, he found himself imprisoned without trial, having lost friends, a brother and several other relatives in the violence. Even after his release, he spent over 30 years detained by the designation of "unclean environment" (*tidak bersih lingkungan*), the New Order's terminology for those considered to have links to communism. Pak Nyoman's suffering as a former political prisoner "is like that of a dog with rotten, gaping wounds, kicked and driven away by society", he says. As one marked with the stamp of "communist", he lived mute — not in the silence of protest where the taped mouth can be unmuzzled, nor in the isolation of the artist whose soliloquies are sent off to a waiting audience — but as a permanent condition where memory is exiled from language. "To whom could I speak of this? Where could I bear witness?" he asks — with no one to offer him an answer.

Near another beach, around 20 kilometres to the south, dozens of foreign tourists stand transfixed, their heads bowed in sadness before a small *pelinggih* shrine crafted from young bamboo stalks just sprouting their first leaves. Undisturbed by the rush of passing traffic, they embrace each other with emotion. Some of them huddle together, whispering and shaking their heads over the small offerings, flower bouquets and baby clothes that have been hung from the metal fence surrounding the wreckage. They pore over letters of condolence, written by the friends and loved ones of the victims, that have been taped to the barricade. "Ground zero" has become an arena opening onto memory: memories of the 202 children, spouses, lovers, siblings and friends who were buried in the ruins, burned by the raging fire, pulverized in the horrific explosion of the bomb. And it is not only the victims' families who are bound by the collective memory that has emerged from the rubble of the Sari Club. The traffic that passes back and forth along the main road bordering the ruins moves slowly. Drivers pause to take a brief look, and bus passengers jostle to hang their heads from the windows, eager to become momentary witnesses to human brutality.

Two fields of terror, each of which claimed more than 200 human lives. One has become a centre of public attention, to the point that there are now debates raging over how best to commemorate it with a monument. The other has become a document that is forbidden to be read, like the "leftist books" locked up in the backs of libraries during the New Order — documents that even the powerful did not dare to understand before banning. One has entered the circuits of global media, making major news all over the world. The other lies hidden, without publicity, with neither gravestone nor ceremony to mark it. One has produced witnesses who pile into the courtroom to make public their memories. The other has witnesses who are silenced, and perpetrators who are not only free but have been called heroes. One has become a site of pilgrimage, a mandatory stop on the Bali tourist itinerary. The other has been erased from the historical map, visited only by one man who dares to remain loyal to the memory of comrades and their cruel deaths.

During the months that followed the October 2002 bombing of the Sari Club, Balinese demonstrated that they are not reluctant to speak about violence. For the explosion affected far more than its immediate targets; its repercussions could be seen in the dejected face of the street trader, the dull eyes of the art shop sales clerk, the sad smile of the artisan, and the lengthy lines of the unemployed. The violence of the bombing became a major topic of conversation in every coffee stall and hamlet meeting hall across the "Island of the Gods". Details of the bombing were made available not only to the international media but to local media as well, to the extent that many Balinese reported feeling "terrorized" by repeated television broadcasts of graphic footage of the victims' corpses. For several weeks after the explosion, Balinese — young and old alike — were inundated with images of what E. Valentine Daniel (1996) has called a "pornography of violence": hundreds of tourists burnt and blistered, their dismembered naked bodies filling the television screen. Yet the violence of 1965, during which as many as 100,000 Balinese — 500 times the number of Sari Club victims — were killed by means no less brutal, still cannot be spoken of in the public domain. What kind of politics of representing violence is at work in Bali?

Image and Memory

A response to this question is not quite as simple as acknowledging that violence has the potential to damage Bali's reputation as an "island of peace", negatively impacting the smooth flow of tourist capital. Tourists are, in fact, often prime consumers of certain sorts of Balinese violence, that which can be decontaminated of the germs of contemporary politics. Stories of ruthless kings, of widows burned with their husbands on cremation pyres, of trance ceremonies where people stab themselves with mythical *keris* daggers, and of magical battles between sorcerers, have all become standard material for tour guides and guidebooks. The original pillar of Balinese tourism itself, the Bali Hotel in Denpasar, was in fact built on the blood-stained land of the 1906 *puputan* massacre, in which hundreds of Balinese marched into Dutch cannon fire. But violence cannot simply be offered for consumption as raw blood. It must be made to take discursive form, its material reality packaged in watertight symbols that can be set sail on the currents of assumptions about Bali. It must be detached from the concerns of the present, made historic, exotic or extraordinary — and thus unthreatening.

Within a few weeks of the Bali bombing, government officials, investors, and local cultural observers became aware that what they confronted were not only the problems of caring for the wounded, holding ceremonies for the deceased or tracking down the perpetrators, but a challenge of representation. In his report on the Kuta tragedy presented as a welcome address to an ASEAN conference in December 2002, the Governor of Bali began with the statement that what had happened in Kuta was "the worst tragedy" that had ever been experienced on the island. He continued: "Bali has not changed. The beach is still there. The culture is still there. Friendliness of the people is not disappearing. What has been loosed [sic] is the image. Since tourism depends significantly on the image, recovery of the image is the first step to recover tourism in Bali. And the recovery of tourism is the key of the recovery of the development of Bali" (Governor of Bali 2002).

The project of "restoring Bali's image" — a project supported by the state, the tourism industry, the local media, and a host of new NGOs born in the wake of the bombings — began by excavating layers of cultural stereotypes, selectively accumulating certain images that had been created to meet the needs of different eras, and combining them into a synthetic archaeology of power fit for public display. The first of these strata was the image created by the colonial regime that extolled Balinese peasants (as opposed to the Balinese aristocracy) for their authentic proto-democracy, as seen in the concept of the "village republic" that regarded local institutions such as the *banjar* (hamlet) as an egalitarian space in which all opinions are valued and conflicts are muted in the name of social harmony. On top of this were cemented the constructions of late colonial anthropologists such as Margaret Mead and Gregory Bateson, who identified a refined and repressed "Balinese character", a homeostatic "steady state" Balinese culture, and a Balinese temperament and historical consciousness lacking in climax (see Bateson 1970; Bateson and Mead 1942). These archaic and naïve views of culture were preserved by the new image-making alliance of the state and tourism capital to reinforce the notion that contemporary Bali remains isolated from modern social upheavals. Political matters such as demonstrations, party congresses, presidential instructions and decrees, leadership transitions and cabinet mutations become the affairs of "important people" in the center of power who have no relevance for Bali as a "cultural region". The history of the 1940s, 1950s and 1960s, when many Balinese were deeply involved in party politics and debates over issues like modernity, feudalism, land distribution, gender and international capitalism, were swept aside with the broom of "tradition".[2] Bali's retreat from the national arena into a postmodern nostalgia for a museum-worthy past was encouraged not only by Balinese and their foreign guests, but by middle class Jakarta culture enthusiasts who need Bali to provide them with a kind of "fantasy island" offering respite from the stress and turmoil that have spread through other regions of Indonesia. The lines of demarcation erected around Bali after the bombing have taken the form not only of security officers at ports and the airport, but also of a symbolic boundary that isolates Bali as a "faraway realm", free from the effects of encounter with historical complexity or conflict. Bali could be victimized by violence, but its essence remains stable. Bali had become a terrorist target, but terror itself was alien to Balinese.

   This symbolic operation was further supported by the fact that the perpetrators of the bombing were identified as Javanese Muslim "outsiders", not Balinese. This information was offered as proof to both the world and the Balinese themselves that the romanticization of Bali was not just lovelorn praise but rather a claim that had been tested and found valid. The foreign media reproduced this narrative of inherent Balinese peacefulness, not necessarily because they believed wholeheartedly in the machine of Bali tourism promotion but because it also served their own representational needs. Bali as an innocent victim, as a Hindu minority island afloat in the midst of a majority Muslim archipelago, drew sympathy and affection from those in the West who found in Bali a mirror for their own grief and anxiety.

But the image is a slippery creature, one quite difficult to control. To "guard the image" (*menjaga image*), as Balinese have been exhorted to do, it is not enough simply to issue rosy press releases or to assemble a corps of public relations specialists. Global information flows are not neutral channels but currents of contestation, and such verbal offensive can be easily parried by sources considered more authoritative, such as *The New York Times, The Sydney Morning Herald* or CNN. An image that diverges too blatantly from reality only serves to discredit the image and its creators. The correspondence between Bali as image and Bali as place, people, and practices risked being unhinged by Balinese themselves.

The image of Bali as an isle of peace, invulnerable to its own history of violence, is not, in fact, new. Since the 1970s it has become essential not only as an export commodity that can be traded for tourist dollars, but as an important item of domestic consumption. The concept of "cultural tourism", which promoted not only Bali's natural beauty but the Balinese themselves as a tourist attraction, required the production of both cultural spectacle and appropriate Balinese subjectivities. Government agencies charged with promoting tourism as the key to developing Bali have recognized the power of tourism to not only attract foreign exchange but to work as a call to self-control for Balinese, who are exhorted not to protest or strike, not to hack apart bodies during cremation ceremonies to make them burn faster nor to rip at the corpses of arrogant men before cremating them, not to bare their breasts nor to wear see-through *kebaya* blouses, not to use the rivers as toilets nor to keep pigs too close to the home, not to wear one's ritual headdress sloppily tied nor to eat too much shrimp paste if one is a tour guide, not to push in line at the supermarket nor to call public attention to everyday acts of violence within families or communities — all because a fickle tourist audience might be watching.[3]

The Kuta bombings placed Bali even more squarely under the global spotlight. After the explosion, Balinese were made aware by the government and the local media that they were being watched, tested, and inspected by this foreign gaze. The presence of the international press functioned not only to transmit images elsewhere but as a surveillance camera — or, following Foucault, a panopticon — that by monitoring Balinese movements reinforced a sense that the Balinese were on stage and the performance was entitled "Peace". The inter-ethnic tensions that in fact did follow the bombing, with Balinese *pecalang* militias carrying out "sweeping" raids (see Santikarma 2003), checking identity cards of non-Balinese residents and exacting payment from Indonesian immigrants who wished to remain on the island, were rarely mentioned in the local media or acknowledged by Balinese cultural observers in their conversations with journalists, except as theoretical references to Bali's problem of "population" (*kependudukan*). The bombing produced conflict, but it also produced a tacit agreement that this must be hidden under the mattress so that Balinese could sleep peacefully, dreaming of the jingle of tourist coin. On the one hand, the Kuta explosion certainly sent shrapnel that punctured the tires on the wheels of Bali's economy; on the other, the Sari Club tragedy only served to strengthen a sense of Balinese identity as defined in opposition to "outsiders".

Yet if the Kuta bombing, in all its horror, has been able not only to find a place in the discursive arena but to be transformed into proof of the truth of Bali's image, why cannot the Balinese image accommodate Pak Nyoman's memories, or the bones turning to dust under a seemingly vacant field? Why is it so impossible to imagine a monument that would remind us of the violence that took place in the midnight darkness of 1965, away from the cameras and microphones? "1965" as an image has indeed been memorialized by the state, which created the Lubang Buaya Monument and the "documentary" film "Pengkhianatan G30S PKI" (Treachery of the 30th September Movement of the Indonesian Communist Party), both of which aim to present citizens with an official version of history. But a mass grave is a document that is far more dangerous. If this document were to be read, if the bones were allowed the opportunity to speak, what we would hear is that images and reality disarticulate. In contrast to the Bali bombing, which has reinforced a belief in the inherent peacefulness of the Balinese, the violence of 1965 deconstructs the Balinese image. The people of Bali are not just artists, but also murderers. The people of Bali are not only dancers, but also perpetrators. The people of Bali are not just storytellers, but also supporters, through both acts and silences, of violence in their own homes and communities. Mass graves reveal that the image of Bali, as formulated in the government tourism mantra of the *sapta pesona* or "seven enchantments" that Balinese must embody for tourists — friendliness, safety, beauty, orderliness, cleanliness, tradition and memorableness — is a strategic attempt to cultivate Balinese subjectivities that can be both sold and controlled.

Monuments and Memory

How then can we ensure that violence, with all its complexities and challenges, is not simply erased from our history? Andreas Huyssen, a philosopher from Germany — a country that for half a century has struggled with its own horrific memories — writes that "the more monuments there are, the more the past becomes invisible, the easier it is to forget: redemption, thus, through forgetting" (Huyssen 1999). A monument may intend to remind us, but a monument can also wipe away the blood of victims with aestheticism, with grandeur, satisfying us to the point that we no longer need to ask, that we forget what actually lies beneath the monument's base. Faced with a monument, we may become the *kebo mebalih gong* of the Balinese proverb, the "buffalo watching the performance" who, entranced by spectacle, is rendered speechless.

In Bali there are in fact quite a few monuments that were erected by the New Order regime, including those to commemorate the Puputan Badung, the Independence Struggle of the Balinese People, the Jagaraga Battle, the Puputan Klungkung, and the Puputan Margarana. As Margaret Wiener notes, these memorials were created as part of the project of nation-building, giving motivating form to the force of the postcolonial developmentalist agenda (Wiener 1999). If in Bali a statue is believed to be able to embody living energy *(taksu)*, the New Order brought its monuments to life through political slogans: "Come, let us successfully develop Bali with the spirit of *puputan*!" (*Mari kita membangun dengan semangat puputan!*) By building monuments, the New Order created representations of the past that suited its own concerns. Bali's history of colonial violence was transformed into a spur to extract free labour, exploiting the tradition of "mutual aid" (*gotong royong*) to clean up the island's gutters, latrines, cemeteries, irrigation channels, and houseyards, and to encourage Balinese participation in competitions to tidy, beautify, and love one's village.

Despite their orientation toward a political present, monuments can still, of course, serve as aids to memory. However, the learning process they engender may not be very deep. The Lubang Buaya monument, certainly, does not promote reflection on a human capacity for violence but rather advertises a narrative of how memories can be erased by a regime with the power to create history. Lubang Buaya in no way encourages the humbling experience of gaining insight from the mistakes of the past; rather, it offers the reverse: the glorification of a monolithic truth. Such monuments celebrate history, but as something which, once manipulated into form, becomes fixed and rigid, unable to be dislodged by either questioning or experience. While counter-readings are always possible, the tight weave of official historical narrative can be extremely difficult to unravel.

We might ask, therefore, what we might expect of a monument to the Kuta tragedy. Can a monument to the bombings bring Balinese toward a better understanding of the inter-religious issues facing Indonesia, for instance, how fundamentalist religious movements can emerge and whether Islamic fundamentalism should be countered with Hindu fundamentalism? Can it teach us why tourism is regarded as a symbol of global neo-imperialism or hedonism by certain hardline groups and what grain of truth — despite our repugnance at the way in which it is expressed — can be found in these claims? Can it answer questions now being raised in the international media, including whether the Bali bombing and incidents like it around the world are related to a grand narrative of the "clash of civilizations", as so many have assumed? And can it tell us whether it is possible — or whether it has ever been possible — for the Balinese to remain uninvolved in the world around them? Or would a monument to the bombings follow the model of so many other monuments, stressing shape, composition, and the fixedness of history as expressed through concrete, iron frameworks, copper, gold, and bronze?

In Balinese philosophy, to immortalize violence in the form of a monument challenges the logic of the cosmos. In Bali, death is considered a release, a departure that leaves no material trace. The flames and mantras of cremation (*ngaben*) are believed to provide a return to the five elements from which all life arises: the *panca mahabhuta* of earth, water, fire, air, and space. This philosophy can be seen at work in the preparations for cremation: in the construction of the tiered cremation tower, the animal-shaped sarcophagus, and the ritual offerings in all their color and complex detail. Preparation for a cremation can involve hundreds of people and many months of labour, yet the process of obliterating these creations may take only a few minutes. Death flows as part of the cycle of life — *utpetti, stiti,* and *pralina,* or creation, preservation, and destruction. The souls of the dead return in human incarnations to improve the *karma* of their earlier lives — history as an endless series of progressions and returns, not as solid structure or as permanent absence which calls for monumental presence to effect memory.

Yet this does not mean that a Balinese approach to death and violence is free from worldly concerns, trapped within static tradition. A striking feature of much of the international media coverage of the Kuta bombings was the intensity of its focus on the "ritual" nature of the Balinese response. The *Pemarisudha* ceremony, organized by the Regional Government of Bali, the Parisadha Hindu Dharma Indonesia (the official state-supported Hindu organization for Indonesia), and the village (*desa adat*) government of Kuta and carried out *en masse,* was witnessed by tens of thousands of TV viewers around the world. But this ritual was not simply a grassroots effort, a peaceful religious response by Balinese believers to the trauma of mass violence, but also a state attempt to define and manage violence. This ritual — never before held in Bali — mobilized Balinese to channel their emotions in spiritual rather than political directions. It attempted to standardize responses to violence by organizing community participation in the ritual down to the level of every household on the island. And by framing the ritual as one specifically for a natural disaster, it erased human agency from violence. Yet this state project did not go unchallenged. Many residents of Kuta claimed to see ghostly apparitions and hear strange voices by the bombsite even after the ceremony, testifying to its possible ineffectiveness. Other Balinese argued that different rituals should have been performed, the most popular alternative being that for victims of war. And still others, those who had lost family members in 1965, asked quietly among themselves why such large-scale rituals were being performed for murdered tourists when Balinese themselves who had been killed in 1965 received no such acknowledgement.

The involvement of the state in organizing a ritual response to the Kuta tragedy can be compared with the fate of victims of the 1965 violence, many of whom lie under the earth of mass graves without ever being touched by the holy water of high priests, or accompanied by processions of offering bearers, gamelan players, and the boisterous shouts of those carrying the corpses. The victims of the Kuta bombing were not only provided with grand public death rituals, but with the attentions of the international community, including the involvement of Interpol, forensic experts, international medical teams, and local and international voluntary organizations vying to provide assistance. For those slaughtered in the violence of 1965, even the mention of their names is still seen as subversive. The families of those who died in 1965 were compelled to carry out cremations in the absence of bodies, in secret and in fear. No one dared to sound the *banjar* drums as a public signal of a death in the community, and finding a high priest to officiate was next to impossible. Yet the real issues still at stake for the families of victims of 1965 and for survivors like Pak Nyoman have been not the scale of ceremony or the building of monuments in order to remember, but rather how to regain human dignity in their communities.

Perhaps we do not even need sophisticated social theory to understand the relationship between monuments, violence, and memory. Beli Mudra, a handicrafts vendor who owns a shop near the ruins of the Sari Club, knows that no monument can contain our memory, fragmented and enveloped in the everyday as it is. "At most it will just be government officials who visit", he replied when asked if he agreed with the plan to build a monument in Kuta. In Beli Mudra's opinion, it would be better to leave the bombing site as it is now, open to everyone who passes, free to those who would witness and read the scraps of memory that have been placed there. "People can remember while buying handicrafts or cold drinks", he says.

If Beli Mudra is right, remembering violence does not require an elaborate tomb, a guarded gravesite or a lavish ceremony, much less a monument. What is needed is a space to speak and communicate freely and without fear, and a language that can encompass both those who would speak and those who would listen for wisdom. What is needed is a way to live together — or at least to survive side by side — with what can never be forgotten, with losses that can never be restored.

Notes

1.   This essay is a translated and revised version of an article originally published in *Kompas* ("Politik Representasi Kekerasan di Bali", 1 Aug. 2003). It is based on over two years of collaborative field research into the cultural and political aftermath of 1965 in Bali, with Leslie Dwyer, funded by a MacArthur Foundation Research and Writing grant and a grant from the H.F. Guggenheim Foundation.

2.   See Robinson (1995) for a similar critique and a discussion of 20th-century Balinese political history.

3.   See Santikarma (2002) for a tongue-in-cheek overview of the self-presentation expected of official tourist guides in Bali.

Dealing with the Past: Reflections on South Africa, East Timor and Indonesia

PAUL VAN ZYL

I n the past decade a growing number of countries have experienced fundamental change from repressive and authoritarian rule to democratic governance. As a result new leaders have had to confront the inescapable issue of how to deal with a legacy of human rights abuse. Fortunately there now exists a growing body of literature and an expanding pool of experience to guide those seeking to learn from past endeavours. Indeed, "transitional justice" has now emerged as a recognized field of study and is attracting great interest from a plethora of sources including academic institutions, international organizations, governments, human rights organizations, and multilateral institutions. Policy-makers and advocates in transitional societies are now able to study the successes and failures of past experiments in crafting solutions best suited to local conditions.

This paper will reflect on transitional justice initiatives in three countries — South Africa, Indonesia, and East Timor — in order to show how the global exchange of ideas has been both productive and potentially damaging in the formulation of strategies to deal with past abuse.[1] This paper makes two core assertions. First, the globalization of knowledge in this field — the accelerated sharing of experience, information, and analysis between transitional societies — is enormously beneficial, *providing* models used successfully in one country are not uncritically replicated elsewhere without due regard to differences in local circumstances and conditions. Second, if strategies to deal with the past are to maximize their chances of success they must be both holistic and comprehensive and cannot focus too narrowly on any specific strategy or initiative.

Transitional Justice — Preliminary Observations

Over the past decade human rights organizations have been at the forefront of an increasingly successful campaign to end impunity in the aftermath of mass atrocity. Whereas successor regimes previously had great latitude in determining their response to a legacy of human rights abuse, a potent combination of international law and activism has placed current governments under an obligation to take meaningful steps to address the past. The most vocal call made by human rights organizations has been to end *de facto* or *de jure* amnesties by prosecuting those responsible for gross violation of human rights. This campaign has yielded impressive results, including:

- The arrest of General Pinochet in London and the subsequent finding by the House of Lords that neither the Chilean amnesty law nor *head of state immunity* apply to international crimes;
- The invalidation of amnesty laws in several countries including Chile, Peru, and Argentina, by either domestic or international courts;
- The establishment of the International Criminal Tribunals for the former Yugoslavia and Rwanda as well as the Special Court in Sierra Leone with jurisdiction over genocide, war crimes, and crimes against humanity;
- The establishment of the International Criminal Court in June 2002 and the increased acceptance of universal jurisdiction as a basis for prosecuting for international human rights crimes;
- The arrest and prosecution of former Yugoslav President Slobodan Milosevic for several international crimes.

These important victories in the effort to end impunity should not lead to complacency. The prevailing consensus that international crimes should not go unpunished is still fragile and subject to contestation. For this reason it is important that human rights organizations continue to campaign energetically for the prosecution of those responsible for heinous crimes. However, it is crucial that placing emphasis on the undisputed importance of prosecutions does not cause other strategies to deal with past to be relegated to secondary importance. This is because prosecutions are extremely time-consuming and resource-intensive exercises. In transitional societies where tens or even hundreds of thousands of victims have suffered gross violations of human rights it is only ever possible to convict a miniscule percentage of the total number of perpetrators. The statistics regarding current or proposed prosecutorial initiatives are both instructive and depressing:

- As of 4 January 2002, 26 accused have been convicted of international crimes[2] before the International Criminal Tribunal for the former Yugoslavia (ICTY). This amounts to just over three convictions per year for each of the tribunal's eight years of operation. By the end of 2001 the tribunal had cost $471 million. The ICTY employs over 1100 staff members (ICTY, 4 January 2002).
- As of 1 January 2003, fewer than 10 accused have been convicted and exhausted their appeals before the International Criminal Tribunal for Rwanda (ICTR). This amounts to approximately one conviction per year for each of the tribunal's years of operation. The ICTR annual budget for the year 2000 was approximately $80 million. The ICTR employs over 800 staff members (ICTR 2001).
- The Special Court for Sierra Leone will probably prosecute no more than 25–30 persons responsible for gross violations of human rights during that country's civil war. The United Nations initially estimated that this institution would cost $114 million over three years. This figure was then reduced to $57 million due to lack of contributions by UN member states (Amnesty International, 28 January 2002)[3] but actual expenditures over a three-year perod are likely to be in excess of this figure[4].
- In South Africa the trial of one hit-squad leader lasted over 18 months. Over 100 witnesses testified during the trial, many of whom had been placed in expensive witness-protection programs outside the country. The trial cost the state over $800,000 and required the services of dozens of skilled detectives and several experienced prosecutors (van Zyl 1999).
- In Germany after World War II, the authorities embarked on an extensive program of domestic prosecutions. Notwithstanding the fact that these prosecutions occurred in extremely favourable circumstances — the Allies had secured a total victory; the prosecution had unfettered access to the accused and territory in which the crimes were committed; the physical evidence was overwhelming;

and hundreds of reliable witnesses were willing and able to testify — fewer than 7,000 convictions resulted from nearly 86,000 prosecutions. Many of those convicted received lenient sentences and served relatively small periods of time in prison (Rosenberg 1996).

These statistics suggest that criminal justice systems are designed for societies in which the violation of law is the exception and not the rule. When violations of the law become the rule and not the exception (as is the case in most societies which experience widespread and systematic violations of human rights) then it is probable that the overwhelming majority of perpetrators will escape conviction. It is important to accept from the outset that punishment of perpetrators will always be a limited endeavour.

Nevertheless, those prosecutions that do occur often send powerful signals to perpetrators, victims, and society as a whole, and it would be a mistake to undermine the impact of trials by analysing them solely in statistical terms. The Nuremberg and Eichman trials targeted only a small percentage of the total number of perpetrators culpable for the Holocaust, but they set an important precedent and their symbolic value cannot be quantified. But precisely because political, financial, and institutional constraints are likely to significantly limit the total number of trials, additional approaches to dealing with the past should always be considered. Depending on the context, these approaches — which should complement, rather than serve as a substitute to prosecutions — could include the establishment of truth commissions or other initiatives to document human rights abuse, the development of reparation programs, the formulation of institutional and legal reforms, and the promotion of reconciliation. A holistic strategy to deal with the past should involve a careful consideration of all these initiatives while recognizing that each may not be appropriate in every setting. In the following section I will offer a brief account of transitional justice strategies adopted or proposed in South Africa, Indonesia, and East Timor.

The South African Model: Too Successful?[5]

The mechanisms adopted in South Africa for dealing with a legacy of human rights abuse illustrate the fact that the approach taken is strongly determined by the balance of power between the old regime and the liberation movement. The South African liberation movements did not succeed in removing the Apartheid government from office by military means. In fact, throughout the negotiation process, which resulted in South Africa's first democratic elections, the former government retained control over a formidable military and police force. If the former government had wished to dig in its heels and retain power at all costs, it would have done so for a prolonged period of time. However, the balance of power in South Africa did not exclusively favour the former government.

By the late 1980s and the early 1990s, liberation movements commanded the support of the overwhelming majority of South African citizens, as hundreds of thousands of supporters mobilized to defy the government. This mobilization, though costly and disruptive, was unlikely to overthrow the government, as security forces could largely contain it. Nonetheless, the liberation movements gained the support of the majority of the international community that had called for democracy in South Africa. As a result, the country was subjected to a concerted campaign of international isolation consisting of economic sanctions as well as athletic, academic, scientific, and cultural boycotts. This isolation had tremendously detrimental effects on all aspects of South African life and placed the former government under considerable pressure to change its policies.

By the late 1980s, the major parties to the South African conflict realized that matters had reached an impasse that only negotiations could resolve. The government understood that it could no longer ignore or repress the massive domestic resistance to its rule, nor could it indefinitely defy world opinion or weather international isolation. The liberation movements recognized that even if they continued their military campaign against the former government, they were unlikely to win. Furthermore, the two sides realized that if a lasting and viable solution to the South African conflict were to be achieved, both would have to be accommodated in the new order.

The agreement to grant amnesty to those who committed gross violations of human rights must be understood in this context. The former government and its security forces never would have allowed the transition to a democratic order had its members, supporters or operatives been exposed to arrest, prosecution, and imprisonment. The issue of amnesty bedeviled the constitutional negotiations until the last possible moment, such that the final draft of the interim Constitution was completed without agreement on whether an amnesty provision should be included. In fact, amnesty became the final obstacle to transition to democracy: only a few months before the scheduled elections, generals in command of the South African security forces delivered a veiled warning to the ANC that they would not support or safeguard the electoral process if it led to the establishment of a government that intended to prosecute and imprison their members.

The ANC faced a massive dilemma. Without an amnesty agreement, the negotiations would collapse, leading to violence and a return to the politics of confrontation. The ANC also concluded that hostility and opposition from the security forces would have made it impossible to hold successful elections. Dullah Omar, a key ANC negotiator and then the Minister of Justice, stated publicly, that "without an amnesty agreement there would have been no elections." The amnesty agreement occurred so late in the process that it had to be added onto the end of the interim Constitution in the form of a "Postamble". It stated that:

> ... gross violations of human rights, the transgression of humanitarian principles in violent conflicts and the legacy of hatred, fear, guilt and revenge ... can now be addressed on the basis that there is a need for understanding but not vengeance, a need for reparation but not for retaliation ... In order to advance such reconciliation and reconstruction, amnesty shall be granted ...

The Postamble constituted a legally binding promise made at the negotiating table by those expected to win South Africa's first democratic election to grant amnesty to those who had committed political crimes.

The establishment of the TRC is best understood as an attempt to restore moral equilibrium to the amnesty process. The Promotion of National Unity and Reconciliation Act (TRC Act) established a 17–member commission with the following objectives: establishing the causes, nature and extent of gross violations of human rights that occurred between 1 March 1960 and 10 May 1994; establishing the identity of victims and affording them an opportunity to testify about their suffering; recommending reparation and rehabilitation policies; granting amnesty to perpetrators who confessed; recommending measures to prevent future human rights violations; and writing a report to publicize the work and findings of the TRC.

The TRC consisted of three committees: the Committee on Human Rights Violations (HRV Committee), the Committee on Amnesty (Amnesty Committee), and the Committee on Reparation and Rehabilitation (R&R Committee). The TRC also had its own investigative unit and witness protection program.

The HRV Committee's primary function was to gather information from victims in order to establish as complete a picture as possible of past human rights abuse. The Amnesty Committee's task was to consider amnesty applications. To qualify for amnesty a perpetrator must have made full disclosure regarding a political crime as defined in the TRC Act. Only specific categories of person could apply for amnesty, for example members of political organizations, liberation movements, and members of state security forces. The person's motive as well as the nature and context of the crimes were also considered. A person who acted for personal gain was generally ineligible for amnesty as well as someone who committed a crime motivated by personal malice, ill will or spite. The Amnesty Committee held public hearing for all applications regarding serious crimes. If amnesty was granted, a person's criminal record was expunged but his/her name and the relevant crime were published in the official government record.

The R&R Committee members were mostly medical doctors and mental health care professionals. Victims could apply for reparation and the R&R Committee considered these applications in formulating reparation policy that it recommended to the government. The TRC's Investigative Unit consisted of 60 local and 12 international investigators. The Investigative Unit carried out investigations, subpoenaed and questioned people who appeared before the TRC, and had authority to seize or retain any evidence or objects relevant to the investigation. The TRC Act also provided for the establishment of a limited Witness Protection Program. Over 150 witnesses joined the program.

Several features of the TRC's amnesty process are worth emphasizing. First, the amnesty agreement can only be defended because it was indispensable to the transition to democracy.[6] Second, the amnesty process was uniquely structured because it forced perpetrators to publicly disclose their crimes, which subjected them to a measure of public shame and social ostracism. The amnesty process also had a cut-off date, after which perpetrators who did not come forward were liable to prosecution. Third, the amnesty process only worked because a sufficient number of perpetrators feared that if they failed to come forward and disclose their crimes, they would be prosecuted. Although South Africa's criminal justice system was biased and dysfunctional, it constituted a sufficient threat to cause perpetrators to believe that their best interests were served by disclosure rather than silence.

It is useful also to note several criticisms of the TRC process, because an analysis of its flaws and failures has helped policymakers and NGOs elsewhere attempt to avoid making similar mistakes. First, although every victim of a crime for which amnesty was granted automatically *qualified* for reparation, it was not guaranteed that they would *actually* receive any reparation. Therefore a victim whose right to sue a perpetrator for damages was extinguished as a result of an amnesty would not necessarily receive reparation as a *quid pro quo*. Second, although perpetrators who did not apply for amnesty are liable to prosecution, the government has shown no real inclination to investigate and prosecute those who chose to remain silent. By failing to act, the government has granted *de facto* amnesty to perpetrators who spurned the opportunity to come clean about their crimes. Third, although the amnesty process constitutes a significant improvement over any other amnesty — particularly because victims can participate in the process and the truth is revealed regarding serious crimes — perpetrators who receive amnesty pay no price for their crimes, other than shame or ostracism. Once a political decision was made to allow perpetrators to escape criminal liability it would have been preferable to require them to contribute toward reparation payments or perform community service in areas in which victims live. The complete elimination of punishment (even in the form of community service) for serious crime runs the risk of promoting impunity and should therefore be resisted in almost all circumstances.

Indonesia: Benefiting from Experience or Rote Learning?[7]

Gross violations of human rights were endemic during the New Order period in Indonesia (1965–98). Although their modality and intensity have varied, they have almost always been committed with complete impunity. The examples are too numerous to cite more than a few prominent instances: in the aftermath of the 1965 coup, up to a million people were slaughtered and a similar number were imprisoned, mostly without trial; thousands of alleged petty criminals were killed, execution-style, during the so-called *Petrus* campaign of 1983–5; over 1,000 people died and scores of women of Chinese descent were raped in riots in May 1998; an estimated 200,000 people died as a result of the occupation of East Timor from 1975 onwards; and approximately 1,000 East Timorese were murdered, hundreds were raped, and vast portions of East Timor were torched and looted following the Popular Consultation in August 1999.

Indonesia continues to be haunted by its history, and the repression and exploitation of the past is threatening its very existence today. It is perhaps for this reason that influential figures in the country's first post-Suharto government, including former-President Abdurrachman Wahid, called for the establishment of a Truth and Reconciliation Commission or *Komisi Kebenaran dan Rekonsiliasi* (KKR). A draft bill establishing the KKR was submitted to the Indonesian parliament (DPR) in the first half of 2001. After an inexplicable delay the bill was re-submitted in January 2002 but again little progress was made in bringing the legislation to a vote. The legislation was presented for the third time on 28 April 2003 but controversies surrounding its provisions regarding compensation for victims of human rights abuse delayed its enactment (*Jakarta Post*, 10 July 2003).

The primary purpose of the KKR will be to "uncover the truth and facilitate reconciliation" and in order to do so it will establish four sub-commissions to (1) establish the truth concerning past human rights abuse, (2) consider amnesties, (3) facilitate reparation and rehabilitation, and (4) cooperate with foreign countries. The commission is granted fairly extensive investigative powers to facilitate its efforts to uncover the truth regarding human rights abuse and is able to both grant reparation itself and make recommendations to the President in this regard. However, the most difficult and controversial of the KKR's duties will be the granting of amnesty.

Under the Indonesian constitution the President is allocated sole power to grant amnesties. It is proposed that the KKR will consider amnesty applications from perpetrators confessing their crimes and make recommendations to the President as to whether amnesty should be granted. The criteria according to which amnesty recommendations are to be made are not stipulated in the legislation and will be determined by the KKR itself. Once the KKR has received an application that case may not be heard in court, and conversely once a court has ruled on a matter it may not be referred to the KKR.

It is obvious that the design and structure of the proposed KKR has been deeply influenced by the South African TRC. The KKR has similar powers and sub-committees, and its amnesty and reparation processes are closely modelled on the TRC. Two important differences are worth noting: the TRC's amnesty committee made binding decisions and its reparation committee could only make recommendations to the government regarding assistance to victims, whereas the KKR's amnesty committee is only empowered to make recommendations to the President, while its reparation committee can actually award reparation. Nevertheless the KKR, as it is currently proposed, closely resembles the South African TRC with a few relatively minor changes necessitated by Indonesian law or circumstances. There are several reasons to doubt that this wholesale adoption of the South African model will work in the Indonesian context.

First, it is not self-evident that the decision to grant amnesty in Indonesia is either wise or desirable. In principle amnesties should be avoided wherever possible because they undermine the rule of law, raise doubts regarding equal treatment, promote cynicism and disillusionment among victims and citizens, weaken deterrence, and embolden perpetrators. Although Indonesia's military continues to wield enormous power and retains the ability to subvert democratic rule, it has not explicitly demanded an amnesty as a pre-condition to the holding of democratic elections or the preservation of democratic rule. No convincing rationale for amnesty has been articulated and no persuasive argument regarding the danger of failing to do so; absent such justification, amnesty should be avoided.

Second, the Indonesian criminal justice system is too corrupt and weak to constitute a sufficient threat to cause perpetrators to apply for amnesty. Transparency International has ranked Indonesia 119 out of 123 countries in its 2000 Corruption Perception Index. There is ample evidence to suggest that officials in the criminal justice system regularly accept bribes that affect the outcome of cases. Furthermore, during the New Order the judiciary was stripped of its independence and it is now difficult to receive an impartial hearing, particularly regarding political cases (*Human Rights Watch*, 25 January 2002). The trials of persons allegedly responsible for horrendous crimes committed at the time of East Timor's independence ballot provide a telling insight into the nature of Indonesia's justice system. The Indonesian Ad Hoc Human Rights Tribunal indicted 18 individuals and only five persons have thus far been convicted receiving sentences ranging from three to ten years (Cohen 2003: 1). The trials have been criticized on several fronts including:

- The lack of politicial will to genuinely pursue prosecutions.
- The failure of the prosecution to produce sufficient inculpatory evidence, despite its ready availability.
- The failure of the prosecution to produce a coherent and credible account of the violence in East Timor, including a failure to identify and prosecute those most responsible (Cohen 2003: 3–4).

Perhaps the incident which best illustrates the fraudulent nature of the trials is the call for the acquittal of Gen. Adam Damiri *made by the prosecution* when it seemed possible that the judges who had been hearing the case might find him guilty (Cohen 2003: 2).

In a context where the judicial system is unwilling and unable to prosecute those responsible for human rights crimes, and the government is either indifferent or actively supportive of this state of affairs, it is highly unlikely that most perpetrators will feel sufficiently at risk to cause them to disclose their crimes before the KKR. Why reveal your crimes with no guarantee of receiving amnesty if you consider the likelihood of prosecution to be extremely low or nonexistent? Why risk public shame and social ostracism if there is a very strong chance that silence will lead to no adverse consequences? The truth-for-amnesty formula that worked in South Africa is unlikely to succeed in Indonesia.

Third, the only instance in which a perpetrator is likely to apply for amnesty is in those rare cases in which a successful prosecution seems possible. In such circumstances a confession is unlikely to yield large quantities of new information because a prosecutor with a strong case should already possess a substantial amount of evidence. This approach to amnesty will have the doubly undesirable effect of revealing no new truths and subverting those few cases where convictions seem attainable.

In summary, the South African approach to amnesty, as applied to Indonesia, will succeed in obtaining neither truth nor justice and could quite possibly undermine the few *bona fide* initiatives in this regard.

East Timor: an Important Advance

East Timor has now held democratic elections and achieved full independence, but there is still an obvious need to address its historical legacy of human rights abuse and the more recent violence and destruction of 1999. The presence of thousands of East Timorese in West Timor combined with sporadic attacks by persons suspected of being affiliated with either militias or the TNI, presents an ongoing humanitarian and security problem. While the majority of these refugees are not implicated in the recent violence and wish to return home,[8] it is likely that many bear some direct responsibility for various crimes. A Serious Crimes Unit (SCU) has been established to prosecute the *relatively* small number of persons responsible for serious crimes such as murder and rape (*UNTAET*, 6 June 2000). As of 28 July 2003, the SCU had filed 63 indictments before specially constituted panels of judges termed the Special Panels for Serious Crimes in East Timor. Of those indicted 216 remain at large within Indonesia and 32 have been convicted. Although the Serious Crimes Unit has indicted several top military officers, it is considered highly unlikely in the current context that they will be extradited by Indonesia to stand trial.

It is important not to develop a policy which focuses solely on those most culpable for human rights abuse. It is not possible or practical to prosecute and imprison the thousands of perpetrators responsible for less serious crimes such as looting or minor assaults. If these perpetrators return to their communities without a process of reintegration and some form of accounting for their actions, it is possible that further conflict and destabilization could arise as victims or community members resort to private acts of revenge.[9]

It is for this reason that the authorities in East Timor have established a Commission for Truth, Reception, and Reconciliation.[10] This Commission has focused its activities in three areas of work: truth-seeking, recommendations to Government, and community reconciliation. The Commission attempts to establish as complete a picture as possible of human rights violations in East Timor that occured between 25 April 1974 and 25 October 1999. Through a process of public hearings and statement-taking it allows victims and perpetrators to describe and acknowledge past human rights abuse. The Commission will produce a final report that sets out its findings and make recommendations to the government on measures to promote reconciliation and human rights.

The Commission seeks to promote community-level reconciliation and reintegration by facilitating the use of traditional dispute resolution measures to deal with less-serious crimes. The Serious Crimes Panels retain exclusive jurisdiction to prosecute those responsible for the most serious crimes, such as murder, rape, or organizing the violence in 1999. Other persons, generally those responsible for less-serious crimes such as looting or minor assaults, are to be referred to a commission-mediated process which requires them to admit to and apologize for their crimes and agree to perform community service. For example, a person responsible for burning down a local school could agree to work for a few months on reconstructing local buildings. These "community reconciliation agreements" are brokered at a local level by the Commission and community leaders,[11] and involve mediation between the perpetrator, victims, and the community.

After these agreements are brokered, they are formalized as an order of court, thus acknowledging the importance of courts in dealing with criminal acts and allowing for enforcement of agreements in the event that a person defaults on his or her commitments. The court and the commission work within guidelines which would forbid any agreement or procedure that would violate basic human rights standards, while permitting variations between different forms of traditional dispute resolution as practiced in various districts and villages. Once a person fulfills all of his or her community service obligations, his or her criminal and civil liability is extinguished.

In order to help establish a historical record of violations, the commission is examining broad questions of historical accountability, with the goal of clarifying events, practices, and patterns of abuse that took place from Indonesia's occupation of East Timor until United Nations-led troops put an end to the violence in October 1999. It does this in part by taking testimony from victims of past abuse, thus formally acknowledging their suffering. To promote reconciliation and ensure the support of all parties, the commission will consider abuses committed by all parties[12] during the period under review. In its final report, the commission will recommend a set of reforms to prevent a recurrence of human rights abuse, and might propose either material or symbolic reparations for victims.

There are a number of advantages to the approach being implemented in East Timor. First, it allows for a principled and pragmatic allocation of the resources available to East Timor's criminal justice system, allowing the prosecution and judiciary to concentrate their limited human and financial resources on those perpetrators responsible for the most serious crimes. Second, by undertaking community service, people who participated in past violence are personally able help to rebuild what was destroyed, and communities are able to witness wrongdoers apologizing and contributing to their villages in form of community service. This will help to advance reconciliation and reduce feelings of resentment. Third, the community reconciliation process is shaped by, and draws upon, the existing traditional practices of dispute resolution in East Timor. Great care has been taken to ensure that these traditional practices are not adopted without a close scrutiny of their processes and outcomes. It is dangerous and patronizing to defer entirely to practices merely because they are termed traditional. (This issue is discussed in greater detail below.) Fourth, perpetrators of less serious crimes are offered an incentive to return by allowing them to participate in community reconciliation processes, which carefully balances the demand for some measure of accountability with the necessity of facilitating the return of refugees to their communities from West Timor or elsewhere in East Timor. Finally, the importance of the justice system and the rule of law is affirmed by endeavouring to prosecute those responsible for the most serious crimes and empowering the courts to approve and enforce "community reconciliation agreements".

Reflections

There are a number of interesting lessons to be learned from this brief survey of transitional justice models in three significantly different contexts. It is clear that the South African model has significantly influenced the approaches adopted in Indonesia and East Timor. Unfortunately, by uncritically replicating a model successfully deployed elsewhere, Indonesians risk hampering the pursuit of truth and justice in a country desperately in need of both. In East Timor policy-makers have drawn on the strengths of the South African model but sought to avoid its flaws and weaknesses. In South Africa those responsible for killings, disappearances, and torture have qualified for amnesty, whereas the

model adopted in East Timor responds more directly to the requirements of international law and the demands of victims by insisting on
prosecution for the most serious crimes. Furthermore, perpetrators who
are granted amnesty in South Africa are immune from criminal and civil
prosecution and are not directly obligated to make amends to those
whose rights they have violated. In East Timor the notion of "restorative
justice" is given greater expression through a procedure that requires
perpetrators to attempt to *restore* victims' rights through a combination
of confessions, apologies, and community service commensurate with the
harm inflicted. There is of course no guarantee that what is offered by
this formula will satisfy even victims of "lesser crimes", because no
necessary correlation exists between the most creative transitional justice
solution that East Timor can deliver and what victims may feel they are
entitled to. It is important therefore that East Timor's leaders and
commissioners not explicitly or implicitly require victims to "forgive" or
"reconcile" until they freely choose to do so.

The Timorese approach to learning from past experience is obviously
preferable to that being pursued in Indonesia, and policy-makers elsewhere should seek to evaluate, refine and adapt other models rather than
regard them as a blueprint for national initiatives.

All three approaches represent important attempts to move beyond
"prosecutorial romanticism": the notion that "retributive justice" is a
sufficient response to past abuse. The punishment of perpetrators is
crucial to dealing with the past, but it will always be insufficient response
to mass atrocity, and any successful attempt to deal with the past must
seek to explore other strategies to make victims whole and to prevent a
recurrence of past abuse. By endorsing more holistic strategies, each
model may provide useful guidance to others grappling with similar
dilemmas.

The model adopted in East Timor raises intriguing questions about
the relationship between reparation and development. The requirement
that perpetrators directly make amends through some form of community
service engages a previously destructive sector of society in the development and reconstruction of communities. The interface between this
activity and traditional development initiatives, such as the construction
of schools, clinics or other forms of infrastructure, will require careful
and creative thought. Many post-conflict development initiatives fail to
incorporate the key protagonists in the process of reconstruction, and

this inadvertent marginalization may sow the seeds for a recurrence of conflict. The incorporation of perpetrators into development initiatives is not always necessary or desirable, but in certain circumstances it warrants further consideration.

In each context, the relationship between prosecutorial and non-prosecutorial initiatives has been structured (with varying degrees of success) based on different priorities, possibilities, and strategic assumptions. In South Africa, the perceived imperative of securing a peaceful transition resulted in a truth commission and a conditional truth-for-amnesty arrangement, which trumped prosecutions by allowing perpetrators to confess their crimes until a stipulated cut-off date. The structuring of this inter-relationship proved a sophisticated and rather effective response to the nature of the South African transition, given the *relative* strength of its criminal justice institutions. In Indonesia, partly because of the absence of political will to achieve accountability and partly because of an inappropriate adoption of the South African approach to transitional justice, policy-makers risk structuring a relationship between the proposed truth commission and the criminal justice system that undermines both institutions. In East Timor, the division of competence between the courts and the commission is clear in theory and is based upon a sensible allocation of responsibilities. Unfortunately the vast majority of perpetrators who bear the greatest responsibility for the crimes committed in East Timor both before and during 1999 are currently in Indonesia. It is highly unlikely that the Indonesian government and military under President Megawati Soekarnoputri will permit their extradition to East Timor or undertake *bona fide* trials themselves. The result is highly unsatisfactory: unless there is a radical change of policy within Indonesia as a result of either internal or external pressure those with the greatest culpability will escape justice, while lesser perpetrators in East Timor are either punished before its courts or required to perform community service by its Commission. This inverted allocation of accountability cannot be remedied by changes *within* East Timor's legal system. It illustrates how transitional justice policies are all influenced to a greater or lesser extent by international forces beyond the direct control of national jurisdictions. While national actors should take these forces into account, the international community should also accept its responsibility to ensure maximum accountability for past crimes.

The dilemmas faced and solutions proposed in structuring the appropriate relationship between courts and commissions in South Africa, East Timor, and Indonesia are relevant to over a dozen countries facing similar issues. Lessons learned will quickly be applied in many countries, such as Chile, Sierra Leone, Peru, Burma, Bosnia-Herzegovina, the former Yugoslavia, and Rwanda.

Finally, dealing with the past requires resolving difficult questions in law and public policy, but it also necessitates a fine appreciation of local tradition and culture. All three models under consideration involve an element of disclosure and confession by perpetrators, with a concomitant expectation of forgiveness and/or amnesty by victims and state institutions. Both South Africa and East Timor are predominantly Christian countries with strong religious institutions and relatively devout populations. Reconciliation and forgiveness form a central part of Christian theology and political discourse in South Africa[13] and East Timor[14], and there is therefore at least some cultural and religious receptivity to the approaches that have been adopted or proposed.[15] Furthermore, the African notion of *ubuntu* — the belief that people derive their humanity through communities and their connection with others — and the East Timorese traditional dispute resolution process that is part of local customary law *(adat),* have created a receptivity to notions of apology, forgiveness, and the acceptance and reintegration of certain types of wrongdoers.

It remains an open question whether the confession/forgiveness paradigm enjoys the same level of support in Indonesian society and culture. Asking this question does not imply that it is possible or desirable to discern a monolithic Indonesian "culture" or "character", but rather that an analysis of culture and tradition matters when formulating strategies to deal with the past. Central to this analysis should be a healthy dose of skepticism regarding the very notions of "culture" and "tradition" themselves. The identification of relevant traditional practices in formulating transitional justice policy should not lead to an automatic endorsement thereof because of well-meaning, but misplaced, concerns about cultural imperialism or undue foreign influence. There is no inherent virtue in tradition. Practices that discriminate against women or deny any semblance of due process because of a feudal deference to authority should be resisted. Likewise, powerful internal and external actors may use or distort traditional processes to conceal or justify unequal and unfair social relations. It is vital to recognize that traditional processes can be coercive and disempowering.

Traditional processes can play a significant role in transitional justice strategies to the extent that they arise from consultation and thereby signify local legitimacy and acceptance. They should only be accepted, however, after a clear-eyed appreciation of whose interests they serve and their origins, genesis, and fairness. In East Timor, where elements of traditional practice have been incorporated into the community reconciliation process, each agreement brokered between a victim and a perpetrator is subject to judicial scrutiny to ensure compliance with human rights standards. Hopefully this will help strike the appropriate balance between the value of local tradition and the need to promote rights and fairness.

South Africa, Indonesia, and East Timor continue to grapple with the legacy of human rights abuse. South Africa was deeply influenced by the experiences of Chile, Argentina, Poland, and Czechoslovakia. East Timor and Indonesia have in turn drawn from the South African experience. Contemporary policymakers have the distinct advantage of being able to reflect on the successes and failures of initiatives adopted elsewhere, provided they craft local solutions based on national conditions and experiences.

Notes

1   I am grateful to M. Kelli Muddell, whose meticulous assistance has been invaluable.
2   Many of these convictions are still subject to appeal.
3   Reservations have been expressed by human rights organizations that the reduction in budget will compromise the efficiency of the court.
4   Conversations with staff at the Court indicate that the budget for its second year of operations is likely to be in excess of $30 million. A three-year budget projection is therefore more likely to be in the range of $75–$80 million.
5   This section draws directly from an earlier article of mine; see van Zyl (1999).
6   Several leading African National Congress negotiators have stated that the Apartheid security forces would not have permitted a peaceful and stable transition to democracy without a promise of amnesty for political crimes. These negotiators recognized that an insistence on preserving the right to prosecute would likely have plunged the country into a grave conflict resulting in significant loss of life and serious economic consequences. They chose to prioritize democratization, and although this entailed compromising on accountability, it was probably a wise decision under the circumstances.

7   In the sections on Indonesia and East Timor I draw directly upon unpublished memoranda written by my colleague Priscilla Hayner and myself. I am grateful to her for her insight on these matters.

8   Figures based on conversations with United Nations Transitional Administration in East Timor (UNTAET) staff including UNHCHR Senior Protection Officer in Dili, East Timor on 26 Oct. 2001; on file with author.

9   Although only a small percentage of returnees have been subjected to violence, International Civil Police (CIVPOL) and United Nations High Commissioner for Refugees (UNHCR) have recorded a significant number of incidents in which those returning from West Timor have been targeted.

10   Commissao Acolhimento, Verdade e Reconciliacao de Timor Leste (CAVR).

11   The community leaders participating in the community reconciliation process will be largely drawn from traditional elders who have presided over the traditional justice process.

12   Although Truth Commissions have generally focused on violations of human rights perpetrated by state actors, or on behalf of state actors, they have also examined rights violations carried out by liberation movements and other non-state actors. In the East Timor context this means that the Commission will be entitled to investigate violations by the Indonesian security forces and those acting on their behalf such as militia groups, as well as forces resisting them such as Falintil, which is the military wing of the Fretilin (The Revolutionary Front for an Independent East Timor), and other non-state actors such as UDT (Timorese Democratic Union).

13   See for example African Christianity (1985). The speeches and public comments of leaders such as Nelson Mandela and Archbishop Desmond Tutu are replete with exhortations to reconcile and forgive.

14   Influential East Timorese leaders such as Xanana Gusmao and Jose Ramos-Horta regularly stress the need for reconciliation and reintegration in building a new state and society.

15   In making this assertion I am aware of the grave dangers in making general claims about the cultural content of various religions and the extent to which these have been accepted by large numbers of people. It is dangerous to make a universal claim that adherents to any given religion are more predisposed to "forgiveness" (or for that matter "revenge") than others. Here I make a more modest claim: that the brands of Christianity accepted by most Catholic East Timorese and black South Africans have tended to place value on forgiveness and reconciliation, and while this value has not been universally accepted, it has provided support for institutions that are reliant, to some extent, on these values.

Bibliography

Abdoelmanap, Soerowo. *Republik Indonesia Menggugat*. Jakarta: Pustaka Grafiksi, 1997.

Abdullah, Taufik. "Orba memang murid Snouck Hurgronje yang paling patuh", *Panji Masyarakat*, 29 Sept. 1999.

_____. "Yang Terlupakan, Yang Terpinggirkan", *TEMPO*, 22 Feb. 1999.

Abdullah, Taufik and Abdurrachman Surjomihardjo, ed. *Ilmu sejarah dan historiografi: Arah dan perspektif*. Jakarta: Gramedia, 1985.

Adam, Asvi Warman. "Kesaksian seorang kepala intelijen", *TEMPO*, 4 Feb. 2001.

Adams, Cindy. *Sukarno. An Autobiography*. Indianapolis: Bobbs-Merrill, 1965.

Aditjondro, George. "Ninjas, manggalas, monuments, and Mossad manuals: an anthropology of state terror", in *Death Squad: the Anthropology of State Terror*, ed. Jeffrey A. Sluka. Philadelphia: University of Pennsylvania Press, 2000a, pp. 158–88.

_____. *Bintang Kejora di tengah kegelapan malam: Penggelapan nasionalisme orang Irian dalam historiografi Indonesia*, ed. George Junus Aditjondro and Cahaya Bintang Kejora. Jakarta: Cidesindo, 2000b.

African Christianity. *The Kairos Document*. African Christianity, Bethel College and Seminary, 1985.

Aidit, Sobron. *Kisah intel dan sebuan warung*. Jakarta: Garba Budaya, 2000.

Ajidarma, Seno Gumira. "Indonesia sebagai pasien Jung: Sejarah tak terkuburkan", *Kompas*, 6 May 2000.

Amnesty International. *Power and Impunity: Human Rights Under the New Order*. London: Amnesty International, 1994.

_____. *The Consultative Group on Indonesia (CGI): A Briefing for Government Members and Donor Agencies*. London: Amnesty International, 2000.

_____. *Annual Report 2001: Indonesia*. London: Amnesty International, 2001.

_____. *Establishing a Special Court for Sierra Leone*. London: Amnesty International, 2002.

Amnesty International Indonesia. *Indonesia: An Amnesty International Report*. London: Amnesty International, Indonesia, 1997.

Anderson, Benedict. "Japan: 'The Light of Asia'", in *Southeast Asia in World War II: Four Essays*, ed. Josef Silverstein. New Haven: Yale University Southeast Asian Studies, 1966, pp. 13–50.

———. "Petrus Dadi Ratu", *Indonesia* 70 (2000): 1–7.

———. "Am I PKI or Non-PKI?" *Indonesia* 40 (1985).

———. "How did the generals die?" *Indonesia* 43 (1987): 109–34.

———. "Scholarship on Indonesia and Raison D'Etat: Personal Experience", *Indonesia* 62 (1996): 1–18.

———, ed. *Violence and the State in Suharto's Indonesia*. Ithaca: Cornell University Southeast Asia Program, 2001.

Anderson, Benedict and Ruth McVey. *A Preliminary Analysis of the October 1, 1965 Coup in Indonesia*. Ithaca, NY: Cornell University, 1971 [1966].

Anggoro, Kusnanto. "Uncovering the cemeteries of truth", *Jakarta Post*, 7 Apr. 2000.

Angkatan Darat. *Dharma Pusaka 45, Hasil Seminar TNI-AD Ke iii Tanggal 13– 18 Maret 1972*. Departemen Pertahanaan-Keamanan Markas Besar Tentara Nasional Indonesian, 1972.

———. *Seri Monumen Sejarah TNI Angkatan Darat*. Jakarta: Dinas Sejarah TNI Angkatan Darat, 1977.

———. "Crushing the G30S/PKI Central Java", in *The Indonesian Killings of 1965–1966: Studies from Java and Bali*, ed. Robert Cribb. Clayton: Centre of Southeast Asian Studies, Monash University, 1990, pp. 159–67.

Antlöv, Hans. "The Revolusi Represented — Contemporary Indonesian Images of 1945", *Indonesia Circle* 68 (1996): 1–21.

Appadurai, Arjun. *The Social Life of Things*. Cambridge: Cambridge University Press, 1986.

———. "Dead Certainty: Ethnic Violence in the Era of Globalization", *Public Culture* 10, 2 (1998): 225–47.

Asian Survey. "The Legacy of Violence in Indonesia", *Asian Survey* XLII, 4 (2002).

ASIET. "Press Release: Yayasan Penelitian Korban Pembunuhan 1965/1966". *News List*, 2000.

Aspinall, Edward. "Students in the military: Regime friction and civilian dissent in the late Suharto period", *Indonesia* 59 (1995): 21–44.

The Australian. "Suharto's murky past written into history", *The Australian*, 3 Oct. 1998.

Assmann, Aleida. "Funktionsgedächtnis und Speichergedächtnis — Zwei Modi der Erinnerung", in *Generation und Gedächtnis. Erinnerung und kollektive Identitäten*, ed. M. Dabag K. Platt. Opladen: Leske & Budrich, 1995, pp. 169–85.

Assmann, Jan. "Kollektives und kulturelles Gedächtnis. Zur Phänomenologie und Funktion von Gegenerinnerung", in *Orte der Erinnerung: Denkmal, Gedenkstätte, Museum*, ed. Th. H. Grütter Ulrich Borsdorf. Frankfurt: Campus, 1999, pp. 13–32.

Awwas, Irfan S. *Menelusuri perjelanan jihad SM Kartosuwiryo: Proklamator Negara Islam Indonesia*. Yogyakarta: Wihdah Press, 1999.

Bachtiar, Harsja W. *Siapa Dia?: Perwira tinggi Tentara Nasional Indonesia Angkatan Darat (TNI AD)*. Jakarta: Djambatan, 1988.

Barenboim, Daniel. "Germans, Jews, and Music", *New York Review of Books*, 29 Mar. 2001.

Barthes, Roland. *Camera Lucida*. Translated by Richard Howard. New York: Hill and Wang, 1981.

Basis. "100 Tahun Bung Karno", *Basis*, Mar.–Apr. 2001.

Basri. "Qahhar: Saya Akan Kembali pada Tahun 2000", *Fajar*, 28 Mar. 2000.

———. "Lawan Komunisme Tujuh Jin Dikerahkan", *Fajar*, 29 Mar. 2000.

———. "Qahhar Yang Sulit Dipahami", *Fajar*, 30 Mar. 2000.

———. "Makam Qahhar Belum Ditemukan", *Fajar*, 1 Apr. 2000.

Bateson, Gregory and Margaret Mead, eds. *Balinese Character: A Photographic Analysis*. New York: New York Academy of Sciences, 1942.

Bateson, Gregory. "Bali: The Value System of a Steady State", in *Traditional Balinese Culture*, ed. Jane Belo. New York: Columbia University Press, 1970, pp. 384–402.

Becker, A.L. "The Figure a sentence makes: an interpretation of a classical Malay sentence", in *Syntax and Semantics*, ed. Talmy Givon. New York: Academic Press, 1979, pp. 243–60.

———. *Beyond Translation — Essays toward a Modern Philology*. Ann Arbor: University of Michigan Press, 1995.

Benda, Harry J. "The structure of Southeast Asian History: Some Preliminary Observations", in *Continuity and Change in Southeast Asia*. New Haven: Yale University Southeast Asian Studies, 1972, pp. 121–53.

———. "Indonesia", in *Continuity and Change in Southeast Asia*. New Haven: Yale University Southeast Asian Studies, 1972, pp. 1–22.

———. "Review of Herbert Feith's 'The Decline of Constitutional Democracy in Indonesia'", in *Continuity and Change in Southeast Asia*. New Haven: Yale University Southeast Asian Studies, 1972 [1964], pp. 162–9.

Benjamin, Walter. *Illuminations*. Translated by Harry Zohn. Edited and with an introduction by Hannah Arendt. New York: Schocken Books, 1968.

Benveniste, Emile. *Problemes de Linguistique Générale*. Paris: Gallimard, 1966.

Berger, John. *About Looking*. New York: Vintage International, 1991.

Bernas. "Lomba foto reformasi di DPD AMPI", *Bernas*,1999.

———. "Pakar dan pelaku bongkar SO 1 Maret siang ini", *Bernas*, 1 Mar. 1999.

———. "Dialog SO 1 Maret bingungkan guru dan taruna", *Bernas*, 2 Mar. 1999.

———. "Soekardjo Wilardjito: Saya korban Supersemar", *Bernas*, 2 Feb. 1999.

———. "Lomba foto reformasi di DPD AMPI", *Bernas*, 21 Apr. 1999.

_____. "Sultan HB IX: Soeharto berani terima tantangan saya", *Bernas*, 2 Mar. 1999.

Bhakti, Ikrar Nusa. "Prof Dr Nugroho Notosusanto Rektor UI yang Sejarahwan", *Mutiara*, 3–16 Mar. 1982.

Blackburn, Kevin, and David Lim. "The Japanese war memorials of Singapore", *South East Asia Research* 7, 3 (1999): 321–40.

Bourchier, David. "The 1950s in New Order Ideology and Politics", in *Democracy and Politics in Indonesia: 1950s and 1990s*, ed. David Bourchier and John Legge. Clayton, Victoria: Centre for Southeast Asian Studies, Monash University, 1994, pp. 50–62.

_____. "Conservative Political Ideology in Indonesia: A Fourth Wave?" in *Indonesia Today: Challenges of History*, ed. Grayson Lloyd and Shannon Smith. Singapore: Institute of Southeast Asian Studies, 2001, pp. 112–25.

Bourchier, David, and John Legge, eds. *Democracy in Indonesia: 1950s and 1990s*, Monash Papers on Southeast Asia. Clayton: Centre for Southeast Asian Studies, Monash University, 1994.

Brenner, Bruce C. Campbell and Arthur D. Brenner, eds. *Death Squads in Global Perspective: Murder with Deniability*. New York: St. Martin's Press, 2000.

Brooks, Karen. "The rustle of ghosts: Bung Karno in the New Order", *Indonesia* 60 (1995): 61–100.

Buck-Morss, Susan. *The Dialectics of Seeing: Walter Benjamin and the Arcades Project*. Cambridge, MA: MIT Press, 1991.

Budiardjo, Carmel. *Bertahan hidup di Gulag Indonesia*. Kuala Lumpur: Wirakarya, 1997.

Budiawan. "Menyingkirkan beban masa lalu", *Kompas*, 3 May 2000.

Budiman, Irfan. "Menggugat Kesewenangan Para Dewa", *Teater*, 2000.

Bujono, Bambang. "Perginya Seorang Bapak Asuh", *TEMPO* (8 June 1985): 14–5.

Bukit Inspirasi Tomohon. *Deklarasi Kongres Minahasa Raya*. Bukit Inspirasi Tomohon, 2000.

Caruth, Cathy, ed. *Trauma: Explorations in Memory*. Baltimore: Johns Hopkins University Press, 1995.

Caruth, Cathy. *Unclaimed Experience: Trauma, Narrative, and History*. Baltimore: Johns Hopkins University Press, 1996.

Cavalli, Alessandro. "Gedächtnis und Identität. Wie das Gedächtnis nach katastrophalen Ereignissen rekonstruiert wird", in *Historische Sinnbildung: Problemstellungen, Zeitkonzepte, Wahrnehmungshorizonte, Darstellungsstrategien*, ed. K.E. Müller and J. Rüsen. Reinbek: Rowohlt, 1997, pp. 455–70.

Cenderawasih Post. "Tak benar gubernur perintah oposan ditahan", *Cenderawasih Post*, 12 Oct. 1998.

Chaidar, Al. *Pemikiran politik Proklamator Negara Islam Indonesia SM Kartosuwirjo*. Jakarta: Darul Falah, 1999.

Cohen, Margot. "The Red Menace is Preserved and Well in Java", *Asian Wall Street Journal*, 20/21 Dec. 1991.

Cohen, David. *Report on the Trials before the Ad-Hoc Human Rights Tribunal in Jakarta.* Jakarta, 2003.

Columbia University School of International and Public Affairs. *Seeking International Justice*, Special Issue, *Journal of International Affairs* 52(2) (1999).

Comrie, Bernard. *Tense.* Cambridge: Cambridge University Press, 1985.

Connerton, Paul. *How Societies Remember.* Cambridge: Cambridge University Press, 1989.

Cooper, J. "Toward a limited definition of trauma", in *The Reconstruction of Trauma: Its Significance in Clinical Work*, ed. A. Rothenstein. Madison: Illinois University Press, 1986.

Couperus, L. *Old People and the Things that Pass.* New York: Dodd Mead and Company, 1920 [1906].

Cribb, Robert, ed. *The Indonesian Killings of 1965–1966: Studies from Java and Bali.* Vol. 21, Monash Papers on Southeast Asia. Clayton, Victoria: Centre of Southeast Asian Studies, Monash University, 1990.

_____. "Additional data on counter-revolutionary cruelty in Indonesia, especially East Java", in *The Indonesian Killings 1965–1966: Studies from Java and Bali*, ed. Robert Cribb. Clayton: Centre of Southeast Asian Studies, Monash University, 1990.

_____. *Historical Dictionary of Indonesia.* Metuchen, N.J. and London: The Scarecrow Press, 1992.

_____. "Problems in the Historiography of the Killings in Indonesia", in *The Indonesian Killings 1965–1966*, ed. Robert Cribb. Clayton, Victoria: Centre of Southeast Asian Studies, Monash University, 1997.

_____. "From Petrus to Ninja: death squads in Indonesia", in *Death Squads in Global Perspective: Murder with Deniability*, ed. Bruce B. Campbell and Arthur D. Brenner. New York: St. Martin's Press, 2000, pp. 181–202.

_____. "Independence for Java? New national projects for an old empire", *in Indonesia today: Challenges of history*, ed. Grayson Lloyd and Shannon Smith. Singapore: Institute of Southeast Asian Studies, 2001, pp. 298–307.

Crouch, Harold. *The Army and Politics in Indonesia.* 2nd ed. Ithaca: Cornell University Press, 1988.

_____. *Militer dan politik di Indonesia.* Jakarta: Sinar Harapan, 1999.

Daniel, E. Valentine. *Charred Lullabies: Chapters in an Anthropography of Violence.* Princeton: Princeton University Press, 1996.

Darma, Budi. "Pengalaman Pribadi dengan Nugroho Notosusanto", *Horison*, Sept. 1985.

Das, Veena, Arthur Kleinman, Mamphela Ramphele and Pam Reynolds, eds. *Violence and Subjectivity.* Berkeley: University of California Press, 2000.

348

Bibliography

Das, Veena. "Crisis and Representation: Rumor and the Circulation of Hate", in *Disturbing Remains: Memory, History, and Crisis in the Twentieth Century*, ed. Michael S. Roth and Charles G. Salas. Los Angeles: The Getty Research Institute, 2001, pp. 37–62.

Daws, Gavan. *Prisoners of the Japanese: POWs of World War II in the Pacific*. New York: William Morrow, 1994.

Detik.com. "Guru-guru sejarah di Papua terancam", *Detik.com*, 24 Feb. 2000.

Direktorat Organisasi Internasional Departemen Luar Negeri. *Sejarah kembalinya Irian Jaya ke pangkuan Republik Indonesia*. Jakarta: Direktorat Organisasi Internasional Departemen Luar Negari, 1998.

Dirjen Pendidikan Dasar dan Menengah. *Pedoman bahan ajar sejarah bagi guru sekolah lanjutan tingkat pertama (SLTP/MTs): Kurikulum 1994, Suplemen GBPP mata pelajaran ilmu pengetahuan social*. Jakarta: Depdiknas, 1999.

Djajengminardo, Wisnu. *Kesaksian: Memoir seorang kelana angkasa*. Bandung: Angkasa, 1997.

Djojoadisuryo, Ahmad Subardjo. *Lahirnya Republik Indonesia*. Jakarta: P.T. Kinta, 1972.

Djunaidi, Mahbub H. *Dari Hari ke Hari*. Jakarta: Pustaka Jaya, 1975.

Drexler, Elizabeth. "Struggling with History, Histories of Struggle: Aceh in (Re)forming Indonesia". Conference Paper, History and Memory in Indonesia, University of California, Los Angeles, 2001.

Dwyer, Leslie, and Degung Santikarma. "Speaking from the Shadows: Politics of Remembering 1965 in Bali" (unpublished manuscript).

Echols, John M. and Hassan Shadily. *An English-Indonesian Dictionary*. Ithaca and New York: Cornell University Press, 1975.

Elsbree, Willard H. *Japan's Role in Southeast Asian Nationalist Movements*. Cambridge, MA: Harvard University Press, 1953.

England, Vaudine. "The past is still present in Aceh", *South China Morning Post*, 24 Nov. 1999.

Farid, Hilmar. "Masalah Pelurusan Sejarah". Conference Paper, Jakarta, 2002.

Fasbach, Drs. "Abdul Qahhar Mudzakkar: Idealis Islam revolusioner (1), (2), (3)", *Harian Tegas*, Week IV May; Week I, Week II, June 2000.

Feith, Herbert. *The Decline of Constitutional Democracy in Indonesia*. Ithaca: Cornell University Press, 1962.

_____. "Constitutional Democracy: how well did it function?" in *Democracy in Indonesia: 1950s and 1990s*, ed. Daniel Bourchier and John Legge. Clayton, Victoria: Centre for Southeast Asian Studies, Monash University, 1994, pp. 16–25.

Fentress, James and Chris Wickham, eds. *Social Memory*. Oxford and Cambridge: Blackwell, 1992.

Fitri, Emmy. "Jakarta museum gives 'official' history lesson", *The Jakarta Post*, 10 Mar. 2002.

Fleischman, Suzanne. *Tense and Narrativity — From Medieval Performance to Modern Fiction*. Austin: University of Texas Press, 1990.

Forum Kedialan. "Ini Perbuatan Orang Komunis", No. 15/VII, 2 Nov. 1998, pp. 32–6.

Foulcher, Keith. *Social Commitment in Literature and the Arts: the Indonesian Institute of People's Culture 1950–1965*. Clayton: Centre of Southeast Asian Studies, Monash University, 1986.

Frederick, William J. *Visions and Heat*. Athens, Ohio: Ohio University Press, 1988.

Fried, Erich. *Es ist was es ist: Liebesgedichte, Angstgedichte, Zorngedichte*. Berlin: Wagenbach, 1983.

Friedlander, Saul. "Trauma and Transference", in *Memory, History, and the Extermination of the Jews of Europe*. Bloomington: Indiana University Press, 1993, pp. 116–37.

Friend, Theodore. *Indonesian Destinies*. Cambridge: The Belknap Press of Harvard University Press, 2003.

———. "Introduction: Hellcraft, Nostalgia and Error", in *The Kenpeitai in Java and Sumatra*, by the National Federation of Kenpeitai Veterans Association. Translated by Barbara Gifford Shimer and Guy Hobbs. Ithaca: Cornell Modern Indonesia Project, 1986, pp. 1–10.

———. *The Blue-Eyed Enemy: Japan against the West in Java and Luzon, 1942–1945*. Princeton, NJ: Princeton University Press, 1988.

Fujiwara, Iwaichi. "Fifth-column Work in Sumatra", in *The Japanese Experience in Indonesia: Selected Memoirs of 1942–1945*, ed. Anthony Reid and Akira Oki. Athens, Ohio: Ohio University, Centre for International Studies; Centre for Southeast Asian Studies, 1986, pp. 9–30.

Gamma. "Hasan Tiro pembual besar: Tanjong Bungong sok feudal", *Gamma*, 18 Aug. 1999.

Garfinkel, H. *Studies in Ethnomethodology*. Englewood Cliffs, NJ: Prentice Hall, 1967.

Geertz, C. *The Interpretation of Cultures*. New York: Basic Books, 1973.

Geertz, Clifford. *Local Knowledge: Further Essays in Interpretive Anthropology*. New York: Basic Books, 1983.

———. *Available Light: Anthropological Reflections on Philosophical Topics*. Princeton: Princeton University Press, 2000.

———. "Soekarno Daze", *Latitudes* 8 (Sept. 2001): 10–5.

Gerbrandy, P.S. *Southeast Asia under Japanese Occupation*. London: Hutchinson, 1950.

Gie, Soe Hok. *Catatan Seorang Demonstran*. Jakarta: LP3ES, 1983.

_____. "Orang Orang di Persimpangan Kiri Jalan: kisah pemberontakan Madiun, September 1948", Yogyakarta, Indonesia: Yayasan Bentang Budaya, 1997.

Goffman, Erving. *Frame Analysis: An Essay of Organization of Experience*. New York: Harper and Row, 1974.

Gonggong, A. *Abdul Qahhar Mudzakkar: Dari Patriot hingga Pemberontak*. Jakarta: Grasindo (Gramedia Widyasarana Indonesia), 1992.

_____. "Jusuf Punya Tanggungjawab Historis [Jusuf has a historical responsibility, An Interview]", *Sabili* (Jan. 2001): 85.

Gourevitch, Philip. *We wish to inform you that tomorrow we will be killed with our families*. New York: Farrar, Straus and Giroux, 1998.

Governor of Bali. *The Kuta Tragedy and the Present-Day Bali*. A report presented at the ASEAN + 3 NTO meeting, 11–12 Dec. 2002.

Graaf, H.J. de. *De Geschiedenis van Indonesie*. The Hague, 1949.

Große-Kracht, Klaus. "Gedächtnis und Geschichte. Maurice Halbwachs — Pierre Nora", *Geschichte in Wissenschaft und Unterricht* 47, 1 (1996): 21–31.

Grütter, Ulrich Borsdorf and Heinrich Theodor. "Einleitung", in *Orte der Erinnerung: Denkmal, Gedenkstätte, Museum*. Frankfurt: Campus, 1999, pp. 1–10.

Halbwachs, Maurice. *Das Gedächtnis und seine sozialen Bedingungen*. Frankfurt: Suhrkamp, 1985.

Hamburger, Kaethe. *Die Logik der Dichtung*. Stuttgart: Klett, 2 stark veraenderte Auflage, 1968.

Hanafi, AM. *AM Hanafi menggugat kudeta Jenderal Soeharto: Dari Gestapu ke Supersemar*. Lille: Edition Montblanc, 1998.

Hanifah, Abu. *Tales of a Revolution*. Sydney: Angus & Robertson, 1972.

Harsono, Ganis. *Recollections of an Indonesian diplomat in the Sukarno era*. St. Lucia: University of Queensland Press, 1977.

Hartman, Geoffrey H., ed. *Holocaust Remembrance: The Shapes of Memory*. Cambridge: Basil Blackwell, 1994.

Hartono, A. Budi, Tataq Chidmad and Sri Endang Sumiyati. *Pelurusan sejarah Serangan Oemoem 1 Maret, 1949*. Yogyakarta: Media Presindo, 2001.

Harvey, B. S. "Tradition, Islam, and Rebellion: South Sulawesi 1950–1965". PhD Dissertation, Cornell University, 1974.

Hasan, Aswar. "Kontroversi Kematian Abdul Qahhar Mudzakkar", *Fajar* (17 Feb. 2001).

Hatta, Mohammad. *Mohammad Hatta, Indonesian Patriot. Memoirs*. Singapore: Gunung Agung, 1981.

Hauswedell, Peter Christian. "Sukarno: Radical or Conservative? Indonesian Politics 1964–5", *Indonesia* 15 (1973): 109–43.

Hayner, Priscilla. *Unspeakable Truths: Confronting State Terror and Atrocity*. New York and London: Routledge, 2001.

Hefner, Robert W. *Civil Islam: Muslims and Democratization in Indonesia.* Princeton: Princeton University Press, 2000.

Heider, Karl G. *National Culture on Screen.* Honolulu: University of Hawaii Press, 1991.

Hersri. "Art and Entertainment in the New Order's Jails", trans. Keith Foulcher, *Indonesia* 50 (1985): 1–20.

Heryanto, Ariel. "Where Communism Never Dies: Violence, Trauma and Narration in the Last Cold War Capitalist Authoritarian State", *International Journal of Cultural Studies* 2, 2 (1999): 147–77.

———. "Remembering and Dismembering Indonesia", *Latitudes* 1 (Feb. 2001): 10–5.

Herzfeld, Michael. *Cultural Intimacy: Social Poetics in the Nation-State.* New York: Routledge, 1997.

Hicks, George. *The Comfort Women.* New York: W.W. Norton & Co, 1995.

Historical Research Centre University of Indonesia. *Kesimpulan Seminar Sejarah Nasional Untag: PSPB Produk Nugroho Almarhum Jatuhkan Nama Soekarno Hatta.* Historical Research Centre, University of Indonesia, 1985.

Ho Tai, Hue-Tam, ed. *The Country of Memory: Remaking the Past in Late Socialist Vietnam.* Berkeley and Los Angeles: University of California Press, 2001.

Honna, Jun. "Military Ideology in Response to Democratic Pressure during the late Suharto era: political and institutional contexts", *Indonesia* 67(1999): 77–126.

Hoskins, Janet. *Headhunting and the Social Imagination in Southeast Asia.* Stanford: Stanford University Press, 1996.

Houben, Vincent. "Nakamura Hiroshi's Account of the Indonesian Independence Proclamation". Paper presented at the 13th Conference of the International Association of Historians of Asia, Tokyo, 1994.

Human Rights Watch. *Academic Freedom in Indonesia: Dismantling Soeharto-era barriers.* New York: Human Rights Watch, 1998.

———. *Indonesia: Abdurrahman Wahid's Human Rights Legacy.* New York: Human Rights Watch, 2001.

Huyssen, Andreas. "Monumental Seduction", in *Acts of Memory: Cultural Recall in the Present*, ed. Mieke Bali, Jonathan Crewe and Leo Spitzer. Hanover: University Press of New England, 1999, pp. 191–207.

Imamura, Hitoshi. "Java in 1942", in *The Japanese Experience in Indonesia: Selected Memoires of 1942–1945.* Athens, Ohio: Ohio University Monographs in International Studies, 1986, pp. 31–78.

Indonesia. "Initial Statement of Lieutenant Colonel Untung, Statements of the September 30th Movement", *Indonesia* 1 (1966): 134–5.

———. "Changes in Civil-Military Relations Since the Fall of Suharto", *Indonesia* 70 (2000): 125–38.

Indonesian Center for the Study of Law and Policy (PSHK). *Advokat Indonesia Mencari Legitimasi: Studi tentang Tanggung Jawab Profesi Hukum di Indonesia*. Jakarta: Indonesian Center for the Study of Law and Policy (PSHK), 2001.

Institut Studi Arus Informasi. *Bayang Bayang PKI*. Jakarta: Institut Studi Arus Informasi, 1995.

International Herald Tribune. "The 'Rape of Nanking' Swirls Again in Japan", *International Herald Tribune*, 20–21 May 2000.

————. "Croatians Taking a Closer Look at 1991 Killing of Serbs in Conflict", *International Herald Tribune*, 22–23 Jan. 2000.

Isman, Hayono. "Papua: Demokrasi, keadilan dan kemanusiaan", *Suara Pembaruan*, 16 June 2000.

Irwantono, Budi. *Film, ideologi dan militer: Hegemoni militer dalam sinema Indonesia, Analisa semiotik terhadap 'Enam djam di Jogja', 'Janur kuning' dan 'Serangan fajar'*. Yogyakarta: Media Pressindo, 1999.

Jackson, K. D. *Traditional Authority, Islam, and Rebellion: A Study of Indonesian Political Behavior*. Berkeley: University of California Press, 1980.

Jakarta Post. "Education ministry introduces major changes", *Jakarta Post*, 30 Dec. 1999.

————. "Uncovering the cemeteries of truth", *Jakarta Post*, 7 Apr. 2000.

————. "Betrayal of Pancasila tragedy commemorated", *Jakarta Post*, 2 Oct. 2000.

————. "House off on holiday, leaving a plethora of outstanding bills", *Jakarta Post*, 10 July 2000.

————. "May Monument won't wipe away grief, pains of riot victims", *Jakarta Post* (19 May 2004).

Janowitz, Morris. *The Military and the Political Development of the New Nations: an essay in comparative analysis*. Chicago: University of Chicago Press, 1964.

Jassin, H. B. *Kesusastraan Indonesia Modern Dalam Kritik dan Esei*. Vol. 4. Djakarta: Gunung Agung, 1967.

Jawa Pos. "Pak Nas ragukan kepahlawanan Soeharto: 'Inisiatif Serangan Umum dari Sri Sultan HB IX'", *Jawa Pos*, 28 Sept. 1998.

————. "Guru se-Timtim minta segera ditarik", *Jawa Pos*, 1 Mar. 1999.

Kahin, George. *Nationalism and Revolution in Indonesia*. Ithaca: Cornell University Press, 1952.

Kanahele, G. S. "The Japanese Occupation of Indonesia: Prelude to Independence". PhD Dissertation, Cornell University, 1967.

Kartodirdjo, Sartono, Marwati Djoened Poesponegoro and Nugroho Notosusanto, eds. *Sejarah Nasional Indonesia*. 2nd ed. Jakarta: Departemen Pendidikan dan Kebudayaan, 1976.

Kartodirdjo, Sartono. "Ideologi kebangsaan dan pendidikan sejarah, 1996", in *Subtema Perkembangan teori dan metodologi, dan orientasi pendidikan sejarah*, ed. Sixth Kongres Nasional Sejarah. Jakarta: Depdikbud, 1997, pp. 118–34.

Katoppo, Aristides. *Menyingkap kabut Halim 1965*. Jakarta: Sinar Harapan, 1999.

Kedaulatan Rakyat. "PWI petjat anggauta-anggautanja yang korannja dilarang terbit", *Kedaulatan Rakyat*, 16 Oct. 1965.

————. "Djapen Klaten mulai bergerak: memberi penerangan di daerah konsolidasi", *Kedaulatan Rakyat*, 5 Nov. 1965.

————. "'Gestapu' gagal Kup LKBN 'Antara'", *Kedaulatan Rakyat*, 11 Nov. 1965.

————. "Film Indonesia membangun dan pemakaman djenazah pahlawan Revolusi diputar di Jogja", *Kedaulatan Rakyat*, 27 Nov. 1965.

————. "PWI Jogja lagi memetjat sementara 4 anggautanja", *Kedaulatan Rakyat*, 11 Dec. 1965.

————. "Team penerangan Pantja Tunggal di kemantren-kemantren", *Kedaulatan Rakyat*, 11 Dec. 1965.

————. "'Gestapu' gagal Kup LKBN 'Antara'", *Kedaulatan Rakyat*, 11 Nov. 1965.

————. "Pendjelasan tentang perang urat saraf", *Kedaulatan Rakyat*, 14 Dec. 1965.

————. "Pameran photo KAMI bukan show: dokumentasi dari perdjuangannja", *Kedaulatan Rakyat*, 27 May 1966.

————. "Melihat pameran foto: pemuda2 berpatju dengan sedjarah", *Kedaulatan Rakyat*, 30 May 1966.

————. "Pameran foto2 Lobang Buaja", *Kedaulatan Rakyat*, 30 Sept. 1966.

————. "Pameran foto dan karikatur laskar arma", *Kedaulatan Rakyat*, 26 June 1967.

————. "Pameran ABRI dan Pembangunan dibuka: dipamerkan badju Djenderal Yani jang berlumuran darah", *Kedaulatan Rakyat*, 8 Aug. 1967.

————. "Pameran pers Kedaulatan Rakyat dibuka besok djam 17:00", *Kedaulatan Rakyat*, 14 Aug. 1967.

————. "1958–1965, masa suram bagi pers Indonesia", *Kedaulatan Rakyat*, 16 Aug. 1967.

————. "Pameran pers terbesar jang pertama diselenggarakan oleh Kedaulatan Rakyat", *Kedaulatan Rakyat*, 16 Aug. 1967.

————. "Pameran ABRI dan pembangunan ditutup", *Kedaulatan Rakyat*, 22 Aug. 1967.

————. "Pahlawan2 Ampera di Sonobudojo", *Kedaulatan Rakyat*, 24 May 1968.

_____. *Buku Dokumen Reformasi: Lengser Keprabon*. Jakarta: PT Grafika Wangsa Bhakti, 1998.

_____. "Pameran Foto 'Kesaksianku' Eko Boediantoro: Media refleksi mengakhiri kekerasaan", *Kedaulatan Rakyat*, 5 Feb. 1999.

_____. "Foto Aksi Reformasi merupakan bukti otentik", *Kedaulatan Rakyat*, 9 Feb. 1999.

_____. "Pameran Foto 'Kesaksianku' Eko Boediantoro, meski pahit realitas perlu ditampilkan", *Kedaulatan Rakyat*, 11 Feb. 1999.

_____. "Fotografi jurnalistik diuntungkan situasi", *Kedaulatan Rakyat*, 14 Feb. 1999.

_____. "Amien Dukung Pameran Foto 'Kesaksianku'", *Kedaulatan Rakyat*, 4 April 1999.

_____. "Pameran dokumentasi perjuangan muda", *Kedaulatan Rakyat*, 4 Nov. 1999.

_____. "Citra Arsip masih rendah", *Kedaulatan Rakyat*, 30 Jan. 2000.

_____. "Foto Reformasi yang dimuat KR melengkapi koleksi Arsip Nasional", *Kedaulatan Rakyat*, 15 Feb. 2000.

Kell, Tim. *The roots of Acehnese rebellion 1989–1992*. Ithaca: Cornell Modern Indonesia Project, 1995.

Kenny, Michael G. "A Place for Memory: The Interface between Individual and Collective History", *Comparative Studies in History and Society* 41, 3 (1999): 420–37.

Kertapati, Sidik. *Sekitar Proklamasi 17 Agustus 1945*. 3rd ed. Jakarta: Pembaruan, 1957.

Kertzer, David I. "The Role of Ritual in Political Change", in *Culture and Political Change*, ed. M. J. Aronoff. New Brunswick: Transaction Books, 1983, pp. 53–73.

Khalid, Idham. "KH. Syamsuri dan Fenomena Dakwah", *Fajar*, 8 July 2000.

Khouw, Ida Indawati. "Jakarta a "city of hell" during occupation", *The Jakarta Post*, 1 Sept. 2001.

Kipp, Rita. *Dissociated Identities: Ethnicity, Religion and Class in an Indonesian Society*. Ann Arbor: University of Michigan Press, 1993.

Kittler, Friedrich. *Gramophone, Film, Typewriter*. Translated by Geoffrey Winthrop-Young and Michael Wutz. Stanford: Stanford University Press, 1999.

Klooster, H. A. J. *Indonesiers schrijven hun geschiedenis, De ontwikkeling van de Indonesische geschiedsbeoefening in theorie en praktijk, 1900–1985*. Leiden: Foris, 1985.

Koentjaraningrat. *The social sciences in Indonesia*. Jakarta: Indonesian Institute of Social Sciences, 1975.

Kohn, Hans. *The idea of nationalism, A study in its origin and background.* New York: Macmillan, 1945.

Kommer, Toen H. *Tjerita Nji Paina, satoe anak gadis jang amat satia, satoe tjerita amat indahnja, jang belon bebrapa lama soedah terdjadi di Djawa Wetan.* Batavia: A. Veit & Co., 1900.

Kompas. "Ketua F-Abri soal Supersemar: Saatnya saksi sejarah buka suara", *Kompas,* 21 July 1998.

―――. "Peringatan Hari Kelahiran Pancasila 1 Juni 1998: Megawati-Hentikan menghujat Soeharto", *Kompas,* 2 June 1998.

―――. "Guru berdemonstrasi, mendesak pindah dari Timtim: Rp 50 milyar untuk pindahkan guru", *Kompas,* 9 Mar. 1999.

―――. "Soeharto bukan penggagas Serangan Oemoem 1 Maret 1949", *Kompas,* 1 Mar. 2000.

―――. "Anhar Gonggong: Suplemen pelajaran sejarah tak dikte guru dan murid", *Kompas,* 8 Apr. 2000.

―――. "Ketika sejarah membingungkan guru", *Kompas,* 29 Apr. 2000.

―――. "Sebagian dokumen kasus Priok dimusnahkan", *Kompas,* 8 May 2000.

―――. "Kongres Rakyat Papua: PNG dukung perjuangan damai", *Kompas,* 31 May 2000.

―――. "Mereka ingin luruskan sejarah Papua", *Kompas,*19 June 2000.

―――. "Sejarah Papua harus disosialisasikan", *Kompas,* 19 June 2000.

―――. "Sisi Lain sebuah kenyataan sejarah", *Kompas,* 19 June 2000.

―――. "PPAU Upayakan Rehabilitasi Bung Karno dan 899 Warga AURI", *Kompas,* 22 Nov. 2000.

―――. "Bung Karno 100 tahun (1901–2001)", *Kompas,* 1 June 2001.

―――. "Soekarno Bukan 'Solidarity Maker'", *Kompas,* 3 June 2001.

Krisnadi, I.G. *Tahanan Politik Pulau Buru 1969–1979.* Jakarta: LP3ES, 2001.

Krog, Antjie. *Country of My Skull: Guilt, Sorrow, and the Limits of Forgiveness in the New South Africa.* Johannesburg: Random House, 1998.

Kurasawa, Aiko. "Mobilization and Control: a study of social change in rural Java, 1942–1945". PhD Dissertation, Cornell University, 1987.

Lapian, A.B. and R.Z. Leirissa. *Pemikiran tentang penjernihan sejarah,* ed. Anhar Gonggong. Jakarta: Direktorat Sejarah dan Nilai Tradisional, Proyek Pembinaan Kesadaran dan Penjernihan Sejarah, 1985.

Lapian, A.B. and J.R. Chaniago. *Timor Timur dalam gerak pembangunan.* Jakarta: Depdikbud, 1988.

Latief, Abdul. *Pleidoi Kolonel A Latief: Soeharto terlibat G30S.* Jakarta: Institut Studi Arus Informasi (ISAI), 2000.

Lavine, Steven and Ivan Karp. "Introduction: Museums and Multiculturalism", in *Exhibiting Cultures: The Poetics of Museum Display.* Washington and London: Smithsonian Institution Press, 1991, pp. 1–10.

Leclerc, Jacques. "Girls, Girls, Girls and Crocodiles", in *Outward Appearances: Dressing State and Society in Indonesia*, ed. Henk Schulte Nordholt. Leiden: KITLV Press, 1997, pp. 291–305.

Lee, Oey Hong. *The Sukarno controversies of 1980/81*. Clayton: Centre of Southeast Asian Studies, Monash University, 1982.

Leigh, Barbara. "Making the Indonesian State: the Role of School Texts", *Review of Indonesian and Malaysian Affairs* 25, 1 (1991): 17–43.

Leksono-Supelli, Karlina. "Kisah dialektika kaum korban", in *Seribu tahun Nusantara*, ed. J.B. Kristanto. Jakarta: Kompas, 2000, pp. 34–54.

Lev, Daniel S. *The Transition to Guided Democracy*. Cornell Modern Indonesia Project. Ithaca: Cornell University Press, 1966.

_____. "On the Fall of the Parliamentary System", in *Democracy in Indonesia: 1950s and 1990s*, ed. Daniel Bourchier and John Legge. Clayton, Victoria: Centre for Southeast Asian Studies, Monash University, 1994, pp. 39–42.

Lewis, Steven. "After Rwanda, the World Doesn't Look the Same", *International Herald Tribune*, 10 July 2000.

Lim, Pui Huen P. and Diana Wong, eds. *War and Memory in Indonesia and Singapore*. Singapore: Institute of Southeast Asian Studies, 2000.

Lintner, Bertil. "Giving no quarter: Guerrilla leader runs separatist campaign from Stockholm flat", *Far Eastern Economic Review*, 29 July 1999: 19.

Lisovskaya, Elena and Vyacheslav Karpov. "New ideologies in postcommunist Russian textbooks", *Comparative Education Review* 43, 4 (1999): 522.

Liu, Xin. "Time, Narrative and History: Twentieth-Century China". Paper presented at the Millenium Regional Conference: We Asians: Between Past and Future, Singapore, 21–23 Feb. 2000.

Loewenberg, Peter. "Psychoanalytische Ich-Psychologie, Objektbeziehungstheorie und ihre Anwendbarkeit in der Geschichtswissenschaft", in *Die dunkle Spur der Vergangenheit: Psychoanalytische Zugänge zum Geschichtsbewußtsein*, ed. Jörn Rüsen and Jürgen Straub. Frankfurt: Suhrkamp Erinnerung, Geschichte, Identität, 1998, pp. 101–30.

Lucas, Anton. *One Soul, One Struggle: Region and Revolution in Indonesia*. Sydney: Allen & Unwin, 1991.

Lukacs, Gyorgy. *Theorie des Romans – ein geschithilosophischer Versuch ueber die Formen der grossen Epik*. Neuwied: Luchterhand, 2. verm. Auflage, 1963.

Maier, Hendrik M. J. "Flying a Kite: The Crimes of Pramoedya Ananta Toer", in *Figures of Criminality in Indonesia, the Philippines, and Colonial Vietnam*, ed. Vicente L. Rafael. Ithaca: Cornell Southeast Asia Program, 1999, pp. 231–58.

Malaka, Tan. *From Jail to Jail*, trans. Helen Jarvis. Vol. III. Athens, Ohio: Ohio University Monographs in International Studies, 1991.

_____. *Madilog*. Jakarta: Teplok, 1999.

_____. *Aksi massa*. Jakarta: Teplok, 2000.

Malik, Adam. *Riwajat dan Perdjuangan sekitar Proklamasi Kemerdekaan Indonesia, tjet. 5*. Jakarta, 1970.

Malley, Michael. "The Seventh Development Cabinet: Loyal to a fault?" *Indonesia* 65 (1998): 155–78.

Mangunwijaya, Y.B. *Ikan-ikan hiu, Ido, Homa*. Jakarta: Sinar Harapan, 1983.

_____. "The Indonesia Raya Dream and its Impact on the Concept of Democracy", in *Democracy in Indonesia: 1950s and 1990s*, ed. David Bouchier and John Legge. Clayton, Victoria: Centre for Southeast Asian Studies, Monash University, 1994, pp. 79–87.

Mann, Simon. "Aceh's unswerving prince plots revolution from afar", *Sydney Morning Herald*, 23 Nov. 1999.

Mansyur, A. "Beliau Sudah Mengubah Kehidupannya (He [Qahhar] has changed his lifes), An Interview by Adnan", *Sabili* (Jan. 2001): 84.

Marcoes, Lies. "Theological Debates over Female Leadership: A Feminist History", unpublished conference paper. History and Memory in Contemporary Indonesia, 6–7 Apr. 2001, Center for Southeast Asian Studies, University of California, Los Angeles.

Maxwell, John. "Soe Hok-Gie: A Biography of a Young Intellectual". PhD Dissertation, The Australian National University, 1997.

May, R.J., ed. *Between Two Nations: The Indonesia-Papua New Guinea Border and West Papua Nationalism*. Bathurst, Australia: Robert Brown, 1986.

McCoy, Alfred, ed. *Southeast Asian under Japanese Occupation*. New Haven: Yale Southeast Asia Studies, 1980.

McGlynn, John and Frank Steward, eds. *Silenced Voices: New Writing from Indonesia*. Honolulu: University of Hawaii Press, 2000.

McGregor, Katharine E. "Commemoration of 1 October, Hari Kesaktian Pancasila: A Post Mortem Analysis?" *Asian Studies Review*, 2002.

_____. "Claiming History: Military Representations of the Indonesian Past in Museums, Monuments and other Sources of Official History from Guided Democracy to the New Order". PhD Dissertation, University of Melbourne, 2002.

McQuire, Scott. *Visions of Modernity: Representation, Memory, Time and Space in the Age of the Camera*. London: Sage Publications, 1998.

McVey, Ruth. "The Enchantment of the Revolution: History and Action in an Indonesian Communist Text", in *Perceptions of the Past in Southeast Asia*, ed. Anthony Reid and David Marr. Kuala Lumpur: Heinemann Educational Books, 1979, pp. 340–58.

_____. "The Case of the Disappearing Decade", in *Democracy in Indonesia: 1950s and 1990s*, ed. David Bouchier and John Legge. Clayton, Victoria: Centre for Southeast Asian Studies, Monash University, 1994, pp. 3–15.

Media Indonesia. *TVRI tidak lagi tayangkan film G-30-S/PKI*. Media Indonesia, 1998.

Merleau-Ponty, Maurice. *Phenomenology of Perception*, trans. Colin Smith. London: Routledge & Kegan Paul, 1958.

Minow, Martha. *Between Vengeance and Forgiveness: Facing History after Genocide and Mass Violence*. Boston: Beacon Press, 1998.

Moghalu, Kingsley Chiedu. "Press Briefing by the ICTR Spokesman". International Criminal Tribunal for Rwanda, United Nations, 2001.

Mohamad, Goenawan. *The Cultural Manifesto Affair: Literature and Politics in Indonesia in the 1960s, A Signatory's View*. Clayton: Monash University, Centre for Southeast Asian Studies Working Papers, no. 45, n.d.

_____. "On Being Indonesian", *Latitudes* 6 (July 2001): 18–21.

Mokoginta, A. J. *Sedjarah Singkat Perdjuangan Bersendjata Bangsa Indonesia*. Jakarta: Kelompok Kerdja Staf Angkatan Bersendjata, 1964.

Morrell, Elizabeth. "Strengthening the local in national reform: A cultural approach to political change", *Journal of Southeast Asian Studies* 32, 3 (2001): 437–49.

Morris-Suzuki, Tessa. "Historical revisionism in Japan", *Inter-Asia Cultural Studies* 2, 2 (2001): 297–306.

Mortimer, Rex. *Indonesian Communism under Sukarno: Ideology and Politics, 1959–1965*. Ithaca: Cornell University Press, 1974.

Mrazek, Jan. "Javanese Wayang Kulit in the Times of Comedy, Parts 1 and 2", *Indonesia* 69 (2000): 107–72.

_____. *Puppet Theater in Contemporary Indonesia: New Approaches to Performance Events*. Michigan Papers on South and Southeast Asia. Vol. 50. Ann Arbor: Center for South and Southeast Asian Studies, University of Michigan, 2002.

Mudzakkar, A. Q. *Konsepsi Negara Demokrasi Indonesia*. Makassar: Hasanuddin, 1380 H [1960].

_____. *Revolusi Ketatanegaraan Indonesia Menuju Persaudaraan Manusia*. Makassar: Hasanuddin, 1381 H [1961].

_____. *Tjatatan Bathin Seorang Pedjoang Revolusioner*. 3 vols. Singapore: Qalam Press, 1382 H [1962].

_____. ""Surat pada Soekarno" (A Letter Addressed to Soekarno)", *Sabili* (Jan. 2001): 80.

Murphy, Oren. ""Unburiable poetry" digs up little on '65 coup attempt", *Jakarta Post*, 26 Mar. 2000.

Nasution, Adnan Buyung. "The Aspiration for Constitutional Government in Indonesia: A Social-Legal Study of the Indonesian Konstituante 1956–1959". PhD Dissertation, University of Utrecht, 1992.

Neier, Aryeh. *War Crimes: Brutality, Genocide, Terror and the Struggle for Justice*. New York: Times Books, 1998.

Nelson, Hank. "The History of the Construction of the Burma-Thailand Railway". Unpublished paper (1991).

———. "Measuring the railway: from individual lives to national history", in *The Burma-Thailand Railway: memory and history*, ed. Gavan McCormack and Hank Nelson. Sydney: Allen & Unwin, 1993, pp. 10–26.

New York Review of Books. "Paying Back the West", *New York Review of Books*, 23 Sept. 1999.

New York Times. "In El Salvador, the Slain Finally Rest in Peace", *New York Times*, 11 Dec. 2000.

———. "Poland Faces an Ugly Truth, and Doesn't Blink", *New York Times*, 8 Apr. 2001.

———. "As Its Past is Exhumed, Russia Turns Away", *New York Times*, 20 Oct. 2002.

———. "Spaniards at Last Confront the Ghost of Franco", *New York Times*, 11 Nov. 2002.

———. "Belgium Confronts its Heart of Darkness", *New York Times*, 21 Sept. 2002.

———. "Coming to Grips with the Unthinkable in Tulsa", *New York Times*, 16 Mar. 2003.

———. "Mexico Digs at Last for Truth About 1986 Massacre", *New York Times*, 7 Feb. 2003.

———. "Now the Dirtiest of Wars Won't Be Forgotten", *New York Times*, 18 June 2003.

Nishihara, Masashi. *The Japanese and Sukarno's Indonesia: Tokyo-Jakarta Relations, 1951–1966*. Honolulu: University Press of Hawaii, 1975.

Nishijima, Shigetada. "The Nationalists in Java, 1944–1945", in *The Japanese experience in Indonesia: Selected memoires of 1942–1945*. Athens, Ohio: Ohio University Monographs in International Studies, 1986, pp. 217–50.

Nishijima, Shigetada, Kishi Koichi *et al.*, eds. *Japanese Military Administration in Indonesia*. Washington: U.S. Department of Commerce Joint Publications Research Service, 1963.

Nora, Pierre. *Les Lieux de Mémoire*. Paris: Gallimard, 1984.

———. "Between Memory and History: Les Lieux de Mémoire", *Representations* 26 (1989): 7–24.

———. *Zwischen Geschichte und Gedächtnis*. Berlin: Wagenbach, 1990.

———. "General Introduction: Between Memory and History", in *Realms of Memory: Rethinking the French Past*, ed. L.D. Kritzman. New York: Columbia University Press, 1996, pp. 1–20.

Notosusanto, Nugroho. *The Dual Function of the Indonesian Armed Forces Especially Since 1966.* Djakarta: Department of Defence and Security, Armed Forces History, 1970a.

———. "A New Generation (1952)", in *Indonesian Political Thinking 1945–1965*, ed. Herbert Feith and Lance Castles. Ithaca: Cornell University Press, 1970b, pp. 68–71.

———. "Some Effects of the Guerrilla (1948–1949) on Armed Forces and Society", in *The National Struggle and the Armed Forces in Indonesia.* Jakarta: Department of Defence and Security, Centre for Armed Forces History, 1994, pp. 109–28.

———. *The Transfer of Values in the Indonesian Armed Forces.* Jakarta: Department of Defence and Security, Armed Forces History, 1974.

———. *The National Struggle and the Armed Forces in Indonesia.* Jakarta: Department of Defence and Security, Armed Forces History, 1975a.

———. *The Japanese Occupation and Indonesian Independence.* Jakarta: Department of Defence and Security, Armed Forces History, 1975b.

———. *Sejarah Nasional Indonesia.* Vol. VI. Jakarta: Balai Pustaka, 1977.

———. *Naskah Proklamasi Yang Otentik dan Rumusan Pancasila Yang Otentik.* Jakarta: Balai Pustaka, 1978.

———. "Saya Ingin Mengungkap Simpati Terhadap Manusia Kecil", *Optimis*, 24 Dec. 1981.

———. *Tujuhbelas Tahun — Aksi Tritura Hakekat dan Hikmahnya.* Universitas Indonesia, Seri Komunikasi, Jakarta, 1983.

———. "Regenerasi dan Motivasi". Speech for Hari Pendidikan Nasional Professor, Departemen Pendidikan dan Kebudayaan, Jakarta, 2 May 1985.

Notosusanto, Nugroho and Ismail Saleh. *The Coup Attempt of the 'September 30 Movement' in Indonesia.* Jakarta: P.T. Pembimbing Masa, 1965.

Osborne, Robin. *Indonesia's secret war: The guerrilla struggle in Irian Jaya.* Sydney: Allen & Unwin, 1985.

Panitia Museum Sedjarah Tugu Nasional. *Laporan Lengkap Lukisan Sedjarah Visuil Museum Sedjarah Tugu Nasional: Laporan Umum.* Djakarta: Panitia Museum Sedjarah Tugu Nasional, 1964.

Panji Masyarakat. "Taufik Abdullah: Orba memang murid Snouck Hurgronje yang paling patuh", *Panji Masyarakat*, 29 Sept. 1999.

Papua. "Dasar dasar perjuangan kemerdekaan Papua Barat", *Papua*, 5 June 2000.

Partai Nasionalis Indonesia (PNI). *Rasa Keadilan Berbitjara: Pembelaan Mr. Iskaq Tjokrohadisurjo.* Jakarta: DPPNI, 1960.

Pasadjo, Iskandar. "KH Syamsuri Madjid, Kahar Muzakkar atau Bukan", *Fajar*, 8 July 2000.

Pauker, Ewa T. "Ganefo 1: Sports and Politics in Djakarta", *Asian Survey* V, 4 (1965): 171–85.

Paz, Octavio. *Convergences — Essays on Art and Literature*, trans. Helen Lane. San Diego: Harvest/HBJ, 1990.

Pelinka, Anton. "Tabus in der Politik: zur politischen Funktion von Tabus und Enttabuisierung", in *Tabu und Geschichte: zur Kultur des kollektiven Erinnerns*, ed. P. Bettelheim and R. Streibel. Vienna: Pincus, 1994, pp. 21–8.

Peluso, Nancy Lee. "Weapons of the Wild: Strategic Deployment of Violence and Wildness in Borneo Rainforests of Indonesia", in *In Search of the Rainforest*, ed. Candace Slater. Durham, NC: Duke University Press, 2003.

Pemberton, John. *On the Subject of Java*. Ithaca: Cornell University Press, 1994.

Penders, C.L.M., and Ulf Sundhaussen. *Abdul Haris Nasution: A Political Biography*. St. Lucia, London and New York: University of Queensland Press, 1985.

Peperzak, Adriaan T., Simon Critchley, and Robert Bernasconi. *Emmanuel Levinas: Basic Philosophical Writings*. Bloomington: Indiana University Press, 1996.

Perhimpunan Keluarga Besar Pelajar Islam Indonesia. *Membuka Lipatan Sejarah: Meguak Fakta Gerakan PKI*. Edited by Perhimpunan Keluarga Besar Pelajar Islam Indonesia. Jakarta: Cidesindo, 1999.

Piekaar, A.J. *Atjèh en de oorlog met Japan*. The Hague: Van Hoeve, 1949.

Pigay, Decki Natalis. *Evolusi nasionalisme dan sejarah konflik politik di Papua*. Jakarta: Sinar Harapan, 2000.

Pinardi. *Peristiwa Coup Berdarah PKI di Madiun*. Jakarta: Inkopak-Hazera, 1967.

Poeze, Harry A. *Tan Malaka: Pergulatan menuju republik*. Jakarta: Grafiti, 1988.

Pos Kupang. "NTT siap terima PNS dari Timtim", *Pos Kupang*, 2 Feb. 1999.

Prajogo. *Tugu Nasional, Laporan Pembangunan 1961–1978*. Jakarta: Pelaksana Pembina Tugu Nasional, 1978.

Prakarsa, Y. Bintang. "Penguasa Orde Baru dan sejarah pada 1980an: Pembicaraan dalam beberapa makalah Seminar Sejarah Nasional III-V". S1/ BA thesis, Gadjah Mada University, 1994.

Proyek Historiografi. *Gerakan 30 September: Antara Fakta dan Rekayasa: Berdasarkan Kesaksian Para Pelaku Sejarah*. Yogyakarta: Proyek Historiografi, Center for Information Analysis Yogyakarta, 1999.

Purdey, Jemma. "Problematizing the Place of Victims in Reformasi Indonesia: A Contested Truth about the May 1998 Violence", *Asian Survey* XLII, 4 (2002): 605–22.

Purdy, Susan Selden. "Legitimation of Power and Authority in a Pluralistic State: Pancasila and Civil Religion". PhD Dissertation, Columbia University, 1984.

Purwadi, Budiawan. "Breaking the Immortalized Past: Anti-Communist Discourse and Reconciliatory Politics in Post-Suharto Indonesia". PhD Dissertation, National University of Singapore, 2003.

Pusat Sejarah Angkatan Bersendjata. *40 Kegagalan G-30-S 1 October–10 November*. Jakarta: Pusat Sejarah Angkatan Bersendjata, 1965.

Pusat Sejarah dan Tradisi ABRI. *Mengenal Museum ABRI Satriamandala, Markas Besar Angkatan Bersendajata R.I.* Jakarta: Pusat Sejarah dan Tradisi ABRI, 1994.

_____. *Buku Panduan Monumen Pancasila Sakti Lubang Buaya Jakarta.* Jakarta: Pusat Sejarah dan Tradisi ABRI, 1994/7.

_____. *Sepuluh Tahun Pusat Sejarah ABRI.* Jakarta: Pusat Sejarah dan Tradisi ABRI, 1974.

Quinn, George. "The role of a Javanese burial ground in local government", in *The Potent Dead: Ancestors, Saints, and Heroes in Contemporary Indonesia*, ed. Anthony Reid and Henri Chambert-Loir. Crows Nest, New South Wales: Allen & Unwin, 2002, pp. 173–82.

Rafael, Vicente, ed. *Figures of Criminality in Indonesia, the Philippines, and Colonial Vietnam.* Ithaca: Southeast Asia Program Publications, Cornell University, 1999.

Ragam Media. *Bebaskan Irian Barat: Kumpulan pidato Presiden Soekarno tentang pembebasan Irian Barat 17 Agustus 1961–17 Agustus.* Yogyakarta: Ragam Media, 2000.

Raid, Hasan. *Pergulatan Muslim Komunis: Otobiografi Hasan Raid.* Yogyakarta: LKPSM/Syarikat, 2001.

Reid, Anthony. *The Blood of the People: Revolution and the End of Traditional Rule in Northern Sumatra.* Kuala Lumpur: Oxford University Press, 1979a.

_____. "The nationalist quest for an Indonesian past", in *Perceptions of the past in Southeast Asia*, ed. Anthony Reid and David Marr. Singapore: Heinemann, 1979b, pp. 281–98.

_____. "Indonesia: From Briefcase to Samurai Sword", in *Southeast Asia under Japanese Occupation*, ed. A.W. McCoy. New Haven: Yale University, Southeast Asia Studies, 1980, pp. 16–32.

_____. "Inside out: The colonial displacement of Sumatra's population", in *Paper Landscapes: Exploration in the Environmental History of Indonesia*, ed. Peter Boomgaard, Freek Columbijn and David Henley. Leiden: KITLV Press, 1997, pp. 61–89.

Ricoeur, Paul. *Time and Narrative.* Vol. I. Chicago: University of Chicago Press, 1984.

Ridyasmara, Rizki. "Kabut di Seputar Qahhar Mudzakkar", *Sabili* (Jan. 2001): 72–7.

_____. "Patriot Zonder Kubur", *Sabili* (Jan. 2001): 78–9.

Robinson, Geoffrey. *The Dark Side of Paradise: Political Violence in Bali.* Ithaca: Cornell University Press, 1995.

_____. "Rawan is as Rawan does: The Origins of Disorder in New Order Aceh", *Indonesia* 66 (1998): 127–56.

Robinson, Kathryn. "History, houses and regional identities", *The Australian Journal of Anthropology* 8, 1 (1997): 71–88.

Rochijat, Pipit. "Am I PKI or Non-PKI?" *Indonesia* 40 (1985): 37–56.

Roht-Arriaza, Naomi, ed. *Impunity and Human Rights in International Law and Practice*. New York: Oxford University Press, 1995.

Rolph-Trouillot, Michel. *Silencing the Past*. Boston: Beacon Press, 1995.

Roosa, John, Ayu Ratih, and Hilmar Farid, eds., *Tahun yang Tak Pernah Berakhir: Memahami Pengalaman Korban 65*. Jakarta: Lembaga Studi dan Advokasi Masyarakat, 2004.

Rosenberg, Tina. *The Haunted Land: Facing Europe's Ghosts After Communism*. New York: Vintage Books, 1996.

Roth, Michael S. "Trauma, Repräsentation und historisches Bewußtsein", in *Die dunkle Spur der Vergangenheit: Psychoanalytische Zugänge zum Geschichtsbewußtsein*, ed. Jörn Rüsen and Jürgen Straub. Frankfurt: Suhrkamp, 1998, pp. 153–73.

Roth, Michael S. and Charles G. Salas, eds. *Disturbing Remains: Memory, History, and Crisis in the Twentieth Century*. Los Angeles: The Getty Research Institute, 2001.

Rudas, Stephan. "Stichworte zur Sozialpsychologie der Tabus", in *Tabu und Geschichte: zur Kultur des kollektiven Erinnerns*, ed. P. Bettelheim and R. Streibel. Vienna: Pincus, 1994, pp. 17–20.

Rumbiak, Jacob. "Solusi damai masalah hak-hak kemerdekaan Papua Barat". Conference Paper, Sophia University, Tokyo, July 1999.

Ryter, Loren. "Youth, Gangs, and the State in Indonesia". PhD Dissertation, University of Washington, 2002.

Sahid, M. "Akting Syamsuri sebagai Qahhar; Kejanggalan Akting Syamsuri", *Suara Hidayatullah* (Jan. 2001): 56–7.

Santikarma, Degung. "The Guide License", *Latitudes* 13 (Feb. 2002): 8–9.

_____. "The Model Militia: A New Security Force in Bali is Cloaked in Tradition", *Inside Indonesia*, 2003.

_____. "Politik Representasi Kekerasan di Bali", *Kompas*, 1 Aug 2003.

Sasongko, Haryo H.D. and Melani Budianta, eds. *Menembus Tirai Asap: Kesaksian Tahanan Politik 1965*. Jakarta: Amanah-Lontar, 2003.

Schreiner, Klaus. *Politische Heldenkulte in Indonesien. Tradition und moderne Praxis*. Berlin: Reimer, 1995.

_____. "The Making of National Heroes: Guided Democracy to New Order", in *Outward Appearance: Dressing State and Society in Indonesia*, ed. Henk Schulte Nordholt. Leiden: KITLV Press, 1997, pp. 259–90.

_____. "History in the Showcase: The Representation of National History in Indonesian Museums", in *Nationalism and Cultural Revival in Southeast Asia: Perspectives from the Centre and the Region*, ed. J. Sri Kuhnt-Saptodewo, V. Grabowski and M. Großheim. Wiesbaden: Harrassowitz, 1997, pp. 99–118.

364   *Bibliography*

_____. "'National Ancestors': The ritual construction of nationhood", in *The Potent Dead: Ancestors, Saints and Heroes in Contemporary Indonesia*, ed. Henri Chambert-Loir and Anthony Reid. Sydney: Allen & Unwin, 2002, pp. 183–204.

Sears, Laurie J. *Shadows of Empire: Colonial Discourse and Javanese Tales.* Durham and London: Duke University Press, 1996.

Sebald, W.G. *Austerlitz.* New York: Random House, 2001.

_____. "The Air War and Literature", in *On the Natural History of Destruction.* New York: Random House, 2003.

Sebayang, Heri. "Meski pahit realitas perlu ditampilkan", *Kedaulatan Rakyat*, 11 Feb. 1999.

Sekimoto, Teruo. "State Ritual and the Village: an Indonesian Case Study", in *Reading Southeast Asia*, ed. A. Kahin. Ithaca: Southeast Asia Program, Cornell University, 1990, pp. 57–74.

Sekretariat Negara Republik Indonesia. *Gerakan 30 September: Pemberontakan Partai Komunis Indonesia, Latar Belakang, Aksi, dan Penumpasannya.* Jakarta: Sekretariat Negara Republik Indonesia, 1994 [1992].

Sen, Krishna. "Filming 'History' Under the New Order", in *Histories and Stories: Cinema in New Order Indonesia*, ed. Krishna Sen. Clayton: Monash University, 1988, pp. 49–50.

_____. *Indonesian Cinema.* London: Zed, 1994.

Sen, Krishna and David Hill. *Media, Culture and Politics in Indonesia.* Melbourne: Oxford University Press, 2000.

Seskoad. *Karya Juang Seskoad 1951–1989.* Bandung: Seskoad, 1989.

Setiawan, Hersri. "Sekitar G30S (Sebuah Renungan Pribadi)", unpublished paper presented at the "Forum Diskusi Sejarah Bangsa", Leuven, Belgium, 2000.

Sharp, Nonie. *The Morning Star in Irian Barat.* Melbourne: Kibble Books, 1994.

Shiraishi, Saya. *Young Heroes: the Indonesian Family in Politics.* Ithaca: Cornell University Press, 1997.

Siapno, Jacqueline Aquino. "The politics of gender, Islam and nation-state in Aceh, Indonesia: A historical analysis of power, cooptation and resistance". PhD Dissertation, University of California, 1997.

SiaR. "Anggota legislatif PDI Perjuangan tolak hadiri upacara di Lubang Buaya", *SiaR*, 1 Oct. 1999.

_____. "Wawancara eksklusif dengan Soeharto", *SiaR*, 19–25 April 1999.

_____. "Batara: Fakta baru Serangan Oemoem 1 Maret 1949 (4 parts)", *SiaR*, 2000.

Siegel, James T. "Early thoughts on the violence of May 13 and 14, 1998 in Jakarta", *Indonesia* 66 (1998a): 75–108.

_____. *A New Criminal Type in Jakarta: Counter-Revolution Today.* Durham: Duke University Press, 1998b.

———. *The Rope of God.* 2nd ed. Ann Arbor: University of Michigan Press, 2000.

Simanjuntak, Marsillam. *Pandangan Negara Integralistik: Sumber, Unsur dan Riwayatnya dalam Persiapan UUD 1945.* Jakarta: Grafiti, 1994.

Simbolon, Parakitri T. "Indonesia memasuki milenium ketiga", in *Seribu tahun Nusantara*, ed. J. B. Kristanto. Jakarta: Kompas, 2000, pp. 2–16.

Simopiaref, Ottis. "Manipulasi sejarah dan pencaplokan Papua Barat", *Suara Mambruk 2* (10 February 2000a): 12.

———. "Dasar dasar perjuangan kemerdekaan Papua Barat", *Papua* (internet mailing list), 5 June 2000b.

Siregar, MR. *Tragedi manusia dan kemanusiaan: Kasus Indonesia, sebuah holokaus yang diterima sesudah Perang Dunia Kedua.* 2nd ed. London: Tapol, 1995.

———. *Naiknya para jenderal.* Medan: Sumatra Human Rights Watch Network, 2000.

Sjahrir, Sutan. *Our Struggle*, trans. Benedict Anderson. Ithaca: Modern Indonesia Project, Cornell University, 1968.

Sluka, Jeffrey A., ed. *Death Squad: the Anthropology of State Terror.* Philadelphia: University of Pennsylvania Press, 2000.

Sneddon, James Neil. *Indonesian Reference Grammar.* London: Allen & Unwin, 1997.

Soebandrio, H. *Kesaksianku tentang G-30-S.* Jakarta: Forum Pendukung Reformasi Total, 2001.

Soedjatmoko. *An Introduction to Indonesian Historiography.* Ithaca: Cornell University Press, 1965.

Soedjono. *Monumen Pancasila Sakti.* Jakarta, 1975.

Soekarno. *Indonesia Accuses!* trans. and ed. Roger K. Paget. New York: Oxford University Press, 1975.

Soerojo, Benedicta and G.M.V. Supartono. *Tuhan, pergunakanlah hati, pikiran dan tanganku: Pledoi Omar Dani.* Jakarta: Institut Studi Arus Informasi (ISAI), 2001.

Soewarsono. *Berbareng bergerak: Sepenggal riwayat dan pemikiran Semaoen.* Yogyakarta: LKiS, 2000.

Sontag, Susan. *On Photography.* New York: Anchor Books, Doubleday, 1977.

———. *Regarding the Pain of Others.* New York: Farrar, Straus and Giroux, 2003.

Spivak, Gayatri Chakravorty. "Mahasweta Devi: Draupadi", in *In Other Worlds: Essays in Cultural Politics.* New York: Routledge, 1988, pp. 179–98.

Sri Suko. *Sekilas Tentang Monumen Pancasila Sakti Lubang Buaya.* Jakarta: Senakatha: Media Komunikasi dan Informasi Sejarah, 1986.

Stanley. "Opening that dark page", *Inside Indonesia* (July–Sept. 2000): 6–7.

Steedly, Mary A. *Hanging without a Rope: Narrative Experience in Colonial and Postcolonial Karoland*. Princeton: Princeton University Press, 1993.

Stenus, Hj. Corry Van. "Sudah Terjadi Fitnah (Slander has taken place), An Interview", *Suara Hidayatullah* (Jan. 2001): 54–5.

_____. "Ia telah Menemui Panglima Tertingginya (He has Already Met his Supreme Commandor), An Interview by Adnan", *Sabili* (Jan. 2001): 81–3.

Stoler, Ann. *Race and the Education of Desire*. Durham: Duke University Press, 1995.

Stoler, Ann and Karen Strassler. "Castings for the Colonial: Memory Work in 'New Order' Java", *Comparative Studies in Society and History* 42, 1 (2000): 4–48.

Straub, Jörn Rüsen and Jürgen, ed. *Die dunkle Spur der Vergangenheit: Psychoanalytische Zugänge zum Geschichtsbewußtsein*. Vol. 2, Erinnerung, Geschichte, Identität. Frankfurt: Suhrkamp, 1998.

Strassler, Karen. *Refracted visions: popular photography and the Indonesian culture of documentation in postcolonial Java*. PhD Thesis, University of Michigan, 2003.

Suara Pembaruan. "Setengah abad 'Serangan Oemoem' 1 Maret: Legenda Soeharto, masih ada misteri", *Suara Pembaruan*, 28 Feb. 1999.

_____. "Mendikbud instruksikan sejarawan luruskan 'Serangan Umum 1 Maret'", *Suara Pembaruan*, 1 Mar. 1999.

_____. "Papua: Demokrasi, keadilan dan kemanusiaan", *Suara Pembaruan*, 16 June 2000.

_____. "Pemerintah tak lagi terbitkan Buku Putih, G30S/PKI", *Suara Pembaruan*, 10 Feb. 2001.

Sudirman, Ahmad. *Kesultanan Aceh, RI, NII-Aceh dan NLFA*. Stockholm, 1999.

Sukanta, Putu Oka. *Merajut harkat*. Yogyakarta: Pustaka Pelajar, 1999.

Sulistiyo, Hermawan. *Palu Arit di Ladang Tebu: Sejarah pembantaian massal yang terlupakan (1965–1966)*. Jakarta: KPG (Kepustakaan Populer Gramedia), 2000.

Sundhaussen, Ulf. *The Road to Power: The Indonesian Military in Politics 1945–1967*. Oxford, UK: Oxford University Press, 1971.

Supomo. *The Provisional Constitution of the Republic of Indonesia*, trans. Garth N. Jones. Ithaca: Cornell Southeast Asia Program, 1964.

Suradji, Pularjono and Tim Redaksi Tatanusa, eds. *Undang-Undang Dasar Negara Republik Indonesia*. Jakarta: PT Tatanusa, 2000.

Sutresna, Nana, ed. *Indonesia: The First 50 Years 1945–1995*. Jakarta: Archipelago Press, 1995.

Syamdani. *Kontroversi sejarah di Indonesia*. Jakarta: Grasindo, 2001.

Syamsuri, K.H. "Contohlah Kehidupan Nabi Muhammad, a speech in Masjid al-Markaz al-Islami, Makassar", *Fajar*, 16 June 2000.

Tabloid Star. "Wawancara eksklusif dengan Pak Harto", *Tabloid Star*, 19–25 Apr. 1999, pp. 12–9.

Tagg, John. *The Burden of Representation*. Amherst: University of Massachusetts Press, 1988.

Tajuk. "Serangan Oemoem 1 Maret 1949: Soeharto cuma pelaksana lapangan". *Tajuk*, 4–17 March 1999.

Tambiah, Stanley J. *Leveling Crowds: Ethnonationalist Conflicts and Collective Violence in South Asia*. Berkeley: University of California Press, 1987.

Teeuw, A. *Modern Indonesian Literature*. The Hague: Martinus Nijhoff, 1967.

TEMPO. "Apa dan Siapa Sejumlah Orang Indonesia 1981–1982". Jakarta: Grafiti Pers, 1982.

———. "Investigasi", *TEMPO*, 6–12 Oct. 1998.

———. "Pemerkosaan, Cerita, Fakta", *TEMPO*, 6–12 Oct. 1998.

———. "Wawancara Sri Mulyono Herlambang: 'AURI dikambinghitamkan'", *TEMPO*, 23–29 Aug. 1999.

———. "Wawancara Pramoedya Ananta Toer: Yang tidak setuju, ya minggir saja", *TEMPO*, 4–10 May 1999.

———. "Saya punya obsesi membongkar pembunuhan G30S", *TEMPO*, 30 Aug.–5 Sept. 1999.

———. "Bung Karno Berbisik Kembali", *TEMPO*, special issue, 4–10 June 2001.

Thayer, L. *Communication and Communication Systems in Organization, Management, and Interpersonal Relations*. Homewood, Ill: Richard Irwing, Inc., 1968.

———. *On Communication: Essays in Understanding*. Norwood, New Jersey: Ablex Publication Co., 1987.

The Straits Times. "Independence calls grow in strife-torn islands", *The Straits Times*, 23 June 2000.

Tihami, M. A. *Darul Islam di Masserengpulu: Studi tentang Perubahan Sosial dan Keagamaan di Malua, Enrekang, Sulawesi Selatan*. Makassar: Pusat Latihan Penelitian Ilmu-Ilmu Sosial, Hasanuddin University, 1984.

Tim Studi. *Papua merdeka: Latar belakang, akar masalah, persepsi aktor dan peluang solusi*. Forum Kerja LSM Irian Jaya, 1999.

Tippe, Syarifudin. *Aceh di persimpangan jalan*. Jakarta: Cidesindo, 2000.

Tiro, Tengku Hasan di. *The price of freedom: The unfinished diary of Tengku Hasan di Tiro*. Markham, Ontario: The Open Press, 1984.

Tisna, Anak Agung Pandji. *Sukreni Gadis Bali*. 6th ed. Jakarta: Balai Pustaka, 1978.

———. *The Rape of Sukreni*, trans. George Quinn. Jakarta: Lontar, 1999.

Tjokrohadisuryo, Iskaq. *Rasa Keadilan Berbitjara: Pembelaan Mr. Iskaq Tjokrohadisurjo*. Jakarta: DP. PNI, 1960.

Toer, Pramoedya Ananta. *Bumi manusia*. Jakarta: Hasta Mitra, 1980.

———. *Anak semua bangsa*. Jakarta: Hasta Mitra, 1982.

———. *Jejak langkah*. Jakarta: Hasta Mitra, 1985.

———. *Sang Pemula*. Jakarta: Hasta Mitra, 1985.

———. *Rumah kaca*. Jakarta: Hasta Mitra, 1988.

———. *Nyanyi sunyi seorang bisu*. Jakarta: Lentera, 1995.

———. *Arus balik*. Jakarta: Hasta Mitra, 1995.

———. *The Mute's Soliloquy: A Memoir*, trans. Willem Samuels. New York: Hyperion, 1999.

———. *Arok Dedes*. Jakarta: Hasta Mitra, 1999.

———. *Mangir*. Jakarta: Kepustakaan Populer Gramedia, 2000.

———. *Perawan Remaja dalam Cengkraman Militer — Catatan Pulau Buru*. Jakarta: Kepustakaan Populer Gramedia, 2001.

———. *Mata pusaran*. Jakarta: Hasta Mitra.

Toer, Pramoedya Ananta, Koesalah Soebagyo Toer, and Ediati Kamil. *Kronik revolusi Indonesia*. 2 vols. Jakarta: Gramedia, 1999.

Trisaksono, Poedhyarto. *Sosiodrama Pelengkap PSPB untuk Sekolah Dasar, Jilid 4, untuk kelas VI*. Jakarta: Tiga Serangkai, 1985.

Tsing, Anna Lowenhaupt. *In the realm of the diamond queen : marginality in an out-of-the-way place*. Princeton: Princeton University Press, 1993.

Unfried, Berthold. "Gedächtnis und Geschichte. Pierre Nora und die 'lieux de mémoire'", *Österreichische Zeitschrift für Geschichtswissenschaft* 4, 2 (1991): 79–98.

United Nations. "Press Briefing by the ICTR Spokesman, Kingsley Chiedu Moghalu". International Criminal Tribunal for Rwanda, United Nations, 2001.

———. "Fact Sheet on the ICTY Proceedings". International Criminal Tribunal for Yugoslavia, United Nations, 2002.

United Nations Transitional Administration in East Timor (UNTAET). "UNTAET/REG/2000/15". United Nations Transitional Administration in East Timor (UNTAET), 2000.

van de Kok, Jean, Robert Cribb, and M. Heins. "1965 and all that: History and the politics of the New Order", *Review of Indonesian and Malaysian Affairs* 25, 2 (1991): 84–93.

van der Kroef, Justus Maria. "Dutch Colonial Policy in Indonesia, 1900–1941". PhD Dissertation, Columbia University, 1953.

———. *The Communist Party of Indonesia: its History, Program and Tactics*. Vancouver: University of British Columbia, 1985.

van Dijk, C. *Rebellion under the Banner of Islam: The Darul Islam in Indonesia*. The Hague: Martinus Nijhoff, 1981.

van Klinken, Gerry. "Big states and little independence movements", *Bulletin of Concerned Asian Scholars* 32, 1–2 (2000): 91–6.

van Langenberg, Michael. "Gestapu and State Power in Indonesia", in *The Indonesian Killings of 1965–1966: Studies from Java and Bali*, ed. Robert Cribb. Clayton, Victoria: Centre of Southeast Asian Studies, Monash University, 1990, pp. 45–61.

van Maanen, J. *Tales of the Field of Writing Ethnography*. Chicago: University of Chicago Press, 1988.

van Mook, H.J. *The Stakes of Democracy in South-East Asia*. London: Allen & Unwin, 1950.

van Zyl, Paul. "Dilemmas of Transitional Justice: The Case of South Africa's Truth and Reconciliation Commission", *Journal of International Affairs* 52 (1999): 647–67.

Vickers, Adrian. "Reopening Old Wounds: Bali and the Indonesian Killings — A Review Article", *The Journal of Asian Studies* 57, 3 (1998): 774–85.

Wahyono, Padmo. "Hak dan Kewajiban Asasi Berdasarkan Cara Pandang Integralistik Indonesia", *Forum Keadilan* 9 (1989).

Walker, Kenneth. "The History of South Africa: A Twice-Told Tale", *Carnegie Reporter* 2, 4 (Spring 2004).

Warburg, Aby. *Der Bilderatlas Mnemosyne*, ed. Martin Warnke in cooperation with Claudia Brink. Berlin: Academic-Verlag, 2000.

Weinrich, Harald. *Tempus — Besprochene und erzaehlte Welt*. Stuttgart: Kohlhammer, 1964.

_____. *Lethe — Kunst und Kritik des Vergessen*. 3rd ed. München: Beck, 2000.

Weschler, Lawrence. *A Miracle, A Universe: Settling Accounts with Torturers*. Chicago: University of Chicago Press, 1990.

White, Hayden. *The Content of the Form: Narrative Discourse and Historical Representation*. Baltimore: Johns Hopkins University Press, 1987.

Wiener, Margaret. "Making Local History in New Order Bali: Public Culture and the Politics of the Past", in *Staying Local in the Global Village: Bali in the Twentieth Century*, ed. Linda Connor and Raechelle Rubinstein. Honolulu: University of Hawaii Press, 1999, pp. 51–89.

Wieringa, Saskia. "The Politicization of Gender Relations in Indonesia: The Indonesian Women's Movement and Gerwani Until the New Order State". PhD Dissertation, Amsterdam University, 1995.

_____. "Sexual Metaphors in the Change from Soekarno's Old Order to Soeharto's New Order in Indonesia", *Review of Indonesian and Malaysian Affairs* 32, 2 (1998): 150–66.

_____. *Penghancuran gerakan perempuan di Indonesia*. Jakarta: Garba Budaya & Kalyanamitra, 1999.

Winichakul, Thongchai. "The Changing Landscape of the Past: new histories in Thailand since 1973", *Journal of Southeast Asian Studies* 26, 1 (1995): 99–120.

Wolf, Charles. *The Indonesian Story*. New York: J. Day Co., 1948.

Wolff, Tobias. "War and Memory", *New York Times*, 28 Apr. 2001.

Wong, Diana. "Memory Suppression and Memory Production: The Japanese Occupation of Singapore", in *Perilous Memories: The Asia-Pacific Wars*, ed. Takashi Fujitani, Geoffrey M. White and Lisa Yoneyama. Durham and London: Duke University Press, 2001, pp. 218–38.

Wyschogrod, Edith. *An Ethics of Remembering: History, Heterology, and the Nameless Others*. Chicago: University of Chicago Press, 1998.

Xpos. "TNI-AU meluruskan sejarah, Wiranto marah", *Xpos*, 18–24 Apr. 1999.

Yates, Frances A. *The Art of Memory*. London: Routledge and Paul, 1966.

Yayasan Idayu. *Sekitar Tanggal dan Penggalinya: Guntingan Pers dan Bibliografi Tentang Pancasila*. Jakarta: Yayasan Idayu, 1981.

Yoneyama, Lisa. "For Transformative Knowledge and Postnationalist Public Spheres: The Smithsonian Enola Gay Controversy", in *Perilous Memories: The Asia-Pacific Wars*, ed. Takashi Fujitani, Geoffrey M. White and Lisa Yoneyama. Durham and London: Duke University Press, 2001, pp. 323–46.

Zurbuchen, Mary S. "History, Memory, and the '1965 Incident' in Indonesia", *Asian Survey* XLII, 4 (2002): 564–81.

Index

371